*The Dialogic Emergence of Culture*

# THE
# *Dialogic Emergence*
## OF
# *Culture*

EDITED BY

*Dennis Tedlock and Bruce Mannheim*

UNIVERSITY OF ILLINOIS PRESS
*Urbana and Chicago*

© 1995 by the Board of Trustees of the University of Illinois
Manufactured in the United States of America
1  2  3  4  5  C  P  5  4  3  2  1

*This book is printed on acid-free paper.*

Library of Congress Cataloging-in-Publication Data

The dialogic emergence of culture / edited by Dennis Tedlock and Bruce
  Mannheim.
       p.     cm.
    Includes bibliographical references and index.
    ISBN 0-252-02146-0 (acid-free paper). — ISBN 0-252-06443-7 (pbk.
  : acid-free paper)
    1. Communication in anthropology.    2. Communication in folklore.
  3. Communication and culture.    4. Dialogue analysis.    I. Tedlock,
  Dennis, 1939-    .   II. Mannheim, Bruce.
  GN13.D53 1995
  302.2 — dc20                                              94-37386
                                                               CIP

# Contents

# Introduction

## BRUCE MANNHEIM AND DENNIS TEDLOCK

While Roman Jakobson was writing his reflections on Ferdinand de Saussure, near the end of his life, his thoughts turned to a Russian peasant he had met sixty years earlier. The man was a storyteller, practiced in the art of reshaping traditional tales in a personal, original way. He was utterly "incapable of telling these tales in a monologic fashion" (Jakobson 1990a: 94), and he explained himself to Jakobson this way: "Is it possible to tell stories for no reason at all? No, I come to the inn, we chat, and someone says, 'God does not exist!' So I retort, 'You're lying, you dog, how can it be that there is no God?' And I tell him a story about that. Now another adds, 'It's true, God does exist.' And so I tell him: 'Now you're the one who's lying. Where did you see God?' And I tell them another story, against the existence of God. I'm telling stories only for the sake of contradiction." As Jakobson observes, "for this type of storyteller, the listeners' replies . . . are a basic element of his tales, often even an indispensable element" (ibid.: 94). The idea that folktales could be told monologically, in repeated form from telling to telling, is a fantasy as far as Jakobson is concerned, a projection of otherness that betrays its origins in a world of written literature and individualist social philosophy.[1]

Jakobson argues further that dialogue is a more fundamental form of speech than monologue, directly challenging the Saussurian focus on the individual actor as the source of *parole* or speech. This is a position he had taken long before, going so far as to declare that monologue is a social pathology (Jakobson 1953: 13).[2] One of the consequences of this view is that *langue* or language, as a shared system, becomes an emergent property of dialogues rather than being granted ontological priority over all speech. Dialogues no longer consist of monologues added together, but are the very scene of production for shared language structures that may later be bent to the purposes of a monologue. The speaker of a monologue expects no answer, but must nevertheless take a position in a larger linguistic world that is already constituted, through countless prior interactions, of social relationships among first, second, and third persons.

The relationship between cultural systems and cultural practices is commonly constructed on the same model as Saussure's language and speech, with particular cultural expressions originating from individual actors. Here, we would argue instead that cultures are continuously produced, reproduced, and revised in dialogues among their members. Cultural events are not the sum of the actions of their individual participants, each of whom imperfectly expresses a pre-existent pattern, but are the scenes where shared culture emerges from interaction. Once culture is seen as arising from a dialogical ground, then ethnography itself is revealed as an emergent cultural (or intercultural) phenomenon, produced, reproduced, and revised in dialogues between field-workers and natives. The process of its production is of the same general kind as the process by which ethnic others produce the cultures that are the objects of ethnographic study.

The phenomenological critique of social science recognized the importance of dialogue in fieldwork, locating conversations between researchers and natives on the level ground of "intersubjectivity." There was still a place for the higher ground of objectivity, or the process of "objectivation," but that was supposed to wait for the return from the field. Left out of account was the fact that the production of objects by means of discourse is already under way among the natives before any field-worker gets there, together with the fact that the production of objects within the disciplines of returned field-workers is itself played out on a dialogical, intersubjective ground.

Interpretive anthropology, which found its original justification in the phenomenological argument, continued to construct the relationship between field discourse and disciplinary discourse as a hierarchy. The natives were cast in the roles of producers of texts, whether literal or metaphorical, while the interpretation of these texts was reserved for the writers of ethnography. The literal conversations that took place in the field were submerged beneath metaphorical conversations between interpreters and already-produced texts. The results of these metaphorical conversations were then reported to readers, who were often left without access to the texts.

The dialogical critique of anthropology radicalizes the phenomenological critique, refusing to privilege disciplinary discourse and instead locating it on the same dialogical ground as other kinds of discourse. Even as the voice of objectification or interpretation narrows itself toward an authoritative monologue, it bespeaks, in the mind of an alert reader, the suppression of a multiplicity of other voices, whether they be those of natives, those of the writer in an earlier role as field-worker, or those of alternative interpretations or rival interpreters, among them native interpreters. But the point is not that the writings of returned field-workers should consist solely of "native texts" and transcripts of interviews. Rather, we would argue that the voices of these texts and transcripts should remain in play rather than being pushed into a silenced past. The disciplinary voice still has its place within a multivocal discourse, but this voice now becomes provisional right on its face rather than pretending to finality. The reader, instead of being left with the suspicion that there might be another interpretation, can begin to make that interpretation.

The critique of representations has played a conservative role with respect to the dialogical project, insisting on the impossibility of re-presenting later what was originally present in the field. Evocation of the past is supposed to replace direct quotation, which has the effect of leaving ethnographers as free as ever to replace native words, or words that were exchanged between themselves and the natives, with a discourse that belongs to their own present as writers of disciplinary discourse. Behind such a stance is an unexamined notion that the parties to a face-to-face dialogue, whether they be natives or field-workers, are entirely present to one another, forgoing all temptation to represent or reinterpret anything that has already been said or done, or has yet to be said or done, outside the occasion of their ongoing conversation.

In this volume, it is our purpose and that of our contributors to further the dialogical critique of anthropology, and to explore the practice of an anthropology that actively acknowledges the dialogical nature of its own production. In the pages of this book are dialogues among natives, dialogues between field-workers and natives, and dialogues among returned field-workers. Here, too, is abundant evidence for the dialogical nature of language itself, which requires speakers to locate themselves within a social world and permits even a single individual, speaking without interruption, to enact a multitude of contrasting voices. The shared worlds that emerge from dialogues are in a continuous state of creation and re-creation, negotiation and renegotiation. Whatever claims may be made for the ontological priority of thought over action, or of a culture over its particular historical enactments, it is only in a world that has already been constituted through dialogue that an anthropologist can study the cultures, and indeed the languages, of others.

When the notion that language and culture are irreducibly dialogical in nature is brought together with the notion that culture is an emergent phenomenon, ultimately beyond the control of individuals, they appear as two faces of the same proposition. But they grow out of distinct traditions in recent anthropology and critical theory, the first stressing the heterogeneity of culture and the discursive nature of its constitution, and the second stressing the social and institutional embeddedness of action. From the first standpoint, all culture is "reconceived as inventive process or creolized 'interculture'" (Clifford 1988: 15). From the second, cultural and linguistic forms are exercises in power and the contestation of power.

## DIALOGUE AND DIALOGIC

The root sense of dialogue is that of talk *(logos)* that goes across or back and forth *(dia-)*, and in contemporary English its readiest reference is to a conversation between two or more persons. At a *formal* level, the word carries a sense of the economics of verbal exchange, as when it refers to an "exchange of ideas." But it has also come to be used in other senses: functional, ethical/political, and ontological.[3]

In *functional* usage, a text or a social interaction is treated as a social field across which multiple voices and multiple cultural logics contend with each other. In literary criticism, where the term is used more frequently in the functional sense than it is in other disciplines, the conflict of voices in the text is said to create multiple perspectives that undermine the authority of the narrator and author. A text may be a dialogue in the formal sense but not the functional, or vice versa. The Russian critic Mikhail Bakhtin (1984: 108–12) argued, for example, that the Socratic dialogue fulfilled the formal sense of dialogue but not the functional.[4] He proposed to distinguish *anacretic* dialogues, which are formally but not functionally dialogical, from *syncretic* dialogues, which are functionally dialogical regardless of their form. The distinction is a useful one. The Peruvian military regimes of the 1970s regularly held what they called *diálogos* with peasants and workers, in which a military officer would deliver exhortations to an assembled group of peasants or workers, and the worker-peasant leaders would praise the political approach of the military government. In Bakhtin's terms, these would be *anacretic* dialogues.

The functional use of dialogue lends itself to a third, *ethical/political* sense of the word. In the ethical sense, the ability of a text or social interaction to sustain multiple voices is counterposed to the relative authoritarianism of closed texts. Bakhtin himself was well aware of the ethical dimension (Clark and Holquist 1984: 269ff.), which surely played a role in his rejection of the Futurist poetry and Formalist poetics of "the self-sufficient word." In recent years "dialogic" has taken on strong ethical tones in the evaluation of literary works and of ethnographic texts (D. Tedlock 1979; Dwyer 1982, chap. 12; Clifford 1988, chap. 1).

Finally, both the functional and ethical/political senses of "dialogue" contain within them the seeds of a strikingly original way of seeing the relationship between structure and action, which Bakhtin's translators have called "translinguistics" (Kristeva 1980: 36; Todorov 1984: 24) and Susan Stewart (1983) has called "anti-linguistics."[5] It has become customary in the social sciences to conceive of action (practice, talk, performance, or *parole*) as a simple precipitate of structure (social institution, intent, competence, or *langue*). In contrast, Bakhtin insists that "each word tastes of the context and contexts in which it has lived its socially charged life" (1981: 293), recognizing that every plan, scenario, and conception is always already situated in a social, political, and historical moment. To put this in familiar philosophical terms, every word in language is already a token before it is a type (see Becker in chapter 9, this volume). The traditional relationship between structure and action, in which action is treated as a reflection of a prior mental structure, is rejected in favor of one in which structure emerges through situated action. Words or texts are socially situated and appropriated by, not created by, individuals. At no point in this process is the individual regarded as autonomous or the guarantor of the integrity (authority, consistency, coherence) of the text. It is especially in this last, ontological sense that the recent concern with dialogue has the potential of reshaping the social sciences.

Within anthropology, the dialogic turn offers a way to undo some of the damage that has been done since the study of culture and society was separated from the study of language. There was a time when the same anthropologists who worked at producing ethnographies also worked on text collections, but that came to an end when American cultural anthropology was diverted from its course by British social anthropology, which tended to treat the utterances of natives as falsehoods and illusions concealing truths that could be revealed only by anthropologists.[6] The collection of texts fell to other field-workers whose concerns were narrowly linguistic and who increasingly pursued their careers in academic departments separate from anthropology.

For a twenty-year period beginning in the mid-1940s, the separation between the linguistic and social faces of ethnography increased. Anthropologists came to concentrate increasingly on instrumental aspects of language, culture, and society, trivializing linguistic aspects of culture as "expressive." The turn away from language was extended by a change in the center of gravity of North American anthropology from the Americanist tradition of recovering the Native American past to a more globally conceived imperial anthropology, concentrated especially in the newly emerging spheres of U.S. economic interest in the Pacific and Latin America. The newer work was more likely to concern matters of direct economic and political interest than the older Boasian cultural philology. Meanwhile, linguistic anthropologists tended to identify themselves more closely with the emerging, increasingly technical field of formal linguistics. This entailed a shift of attention away from the text-based ethnographic philology of the Boasians to a preoccupation with grammar abstracted from social action.

Cultural anthropologists, who often saw language only as a means to a specialized end (Mead 1939), shied away from the growing formalization of linguistic findings. They increasingly came to view language in folk terms, reducing it to "talk about" other, more fundamental social and cultural processes. Language was seen as highly structured, accessible to conscious articulation, intellectualized, and representational. Nonlinguistic social and cultural forms were conversely seen as more loosely structured, highly situational, nonconscious, practical, and more densely symbolic. This polarity formed the basis of philosopher Susanne Langer's (1941) distinction between "discursive" (linguistic) and "presentational" (cultural) forms. Although language was a primary vehicle of cultural transmission and social reproduction in the earlier, Boasian framework, in the postwar period it came to be regarded as a secondary representation of independently figured social and cultural forms.[7]

Sociolinguistics, particularly under the rubric of the "ethnography of speaking" (Hymes 1974), has gone a long way toward reestablishing a working relationship between the sciences of language and of culture. But much of this work has been done in the spirit of moving into a previously unoccupied territory, that of the socially situated speech event, as if it had been overlooked by some historical accident and could be explored simply by combining the methods of social anthropology and linguistics. Anthropologists who enter this territory may bring back a renewed sense of language as the primary vehicle for the transmission of culture, while linguists may attempt to codify language use in much the same way they have codified language form. As they continue their respective researches, the particular ground on which they now find themselves meeting face-to-face is the vastly rich one of discourse analysis, and that is where it is becoming clear that despite their apparent differences, they share a common heritage. As Johannes Fabian (1979: 19) would argue the point, they tend to subordinate action, which takes place in "real time and history," to synchronic structure. The locus of this structure remains the individual, and the usual focus of analysis and comparison is the utterances of individual (but purportedly typical) performers whose audiences are reduced to a marginal role. Perhaps the most interesting result of such research is the discovery that when an attempt is made to describe all the structures that would be necessary to account for the audible features of even a small corpus of oral narratives, it is necessary to allow for a higher degree of variability than would be tolerated in a description of syntax, and even to allow room for structures that do not "stack" with syntax (Woodbury

1987). Such findings may pose an annoying problem for linguistics as presently practiced, but a dialogical reshaping of linguistics would allow for the ongoing emergence of diverse structures in socially and historically situated action rather than hoping to trace everything back to a single and self-consistent starting point.

The irony of the lateness of the development of sociolinguistics, and the still greater lateness of the dialogical opening, is that even when language is actualized as a discourse spoken to no one in particular, it already has first and second persons embedded in it, implicitly present even when only the third person is used for the moment. In addition to persons, there are other deictic elements that locate the speaker with respect to a world that already has persons or things in it: in front or behind, left or right, above or below, near or far, visible or invisible. No one can speak or write language, as we now know it, without already being situated in this world.[8] Thus, even when language is understood as a syntactical system that exists outside or prior to its actualizations in speech, it is ready-made for situated dialogues. The elements of this readiness have played useful roles in the synchronic description of syntax, but when we think of them dialogically they are obvious traces of the history of language use.[9] Indeed, the traces of dialogical interaction so permeate the structure of language that they are present even when people talk to themselves. Roman Jakobson, echoing his compatriots Voloshinov and Vygotsky, argued that there is no such thing as individual speech without dialogue. Even "non-exteriorized, non-uttered, so-called inner speech, . . . is only an elliptic and allusive substitute for the more explicit, enunciated speech. Furthermore, dialogue underlies even inner speech" (Jakobson 1953: 15).

Any call for the investigation and description of situated acts of dialogue is subject, as we mentioned earlier, to the critique of representations. Stephen Tyler (1987) has argued that the call is motivated by a longing for a return to an original presence, a return that is bound to be frustrated by the fact that any representation alters what is represented. But this critique seems to be founded, in turn, upon the notion that face-to-face dialogues are themselves instances of pure presence. Here we may argue, after the manner of Bakhtin, that any and all present discourse is already replete with echoes, allusions, paraphrases, and outright quotations of prior discourse. Direct quotation is a linguistic universal, and indeed it is widely preferred, in speaking if not always in writing, to indirect discourse (see Tannen, this volume, chapter 7); on the other hand, the culturally specific form that reported speech takes is both imbued with the culture's linguistic ideology and a central location within which culture, ideology, and social relations are reproduced (see Silverstein [1977], Urban [1984], Rumsey [1990], and Lucy [1994]). We might even say that one of the things language does best is to enable its speakers, in the very moment they are present to one another, to breach that presence.

From within a dialogically constructed world, it seems impossible to hypothesize, or at least to make intelligible or believable, a moment when an individual ancestral human became the first person ever to use language. Individual children may speak for the first time in their lives, but when they do so they begin their entry into a world where countless things have already been said, a world that is always already in process. The first words ever spoken anywhere on earth (if we insist on trying to imagine them) would hardly be worthy of the name "language" unless they were addressed to someone, and unless that someone had the capacity to reply. It happens that performers in many of the societies studied by anthropologists tell creation myths — or, better, emergence myths — in which language does indeed make its first appearance in a dialogue, whether among gods in the plural, or between gods and people, or among people (D. Tedlock 1983: 269–71, 338). When these myths are taken into account, it becomes apparent that linguistics as presently constituted, in locating language structure within the individual speaker, is squarely aligned with the dominant creation mythology — and, at a more abstract level, the metaphysics — of the Greco-Christian world. Jacques Derrida (1976: part 1) missed this point when, in his critique of metaphysics, he focused on the difference between voice and writing while passing over the difference between a singular voice and a dialogue among plural voices.

But a dialogical ethnography cannot content itself with the celebration of a multiplicity of voices, no matter how diverse their social origins. One of the key challenges is to reformulate the problem of the location of culture within a social ontology in which neither individuals nor collectivities are basic units. Thus reformulated, the task becomes one of identifying the social conditions of the emergence of linguistic and cultural forms, of their distribution among speakers, and of subjectivity itself as an embodied constellation of voices (see Hill, this volume, chapter 4).

## CULTURE AND EMERGENCE

To propose that language and culture are dialogical to their core is to relocate them in the interstices between people (as Geertz 1966: 5–6 suggested in a different context), to see language and culture as emergent qualities of action, "as the result of thousands of life-changing dialogues that call into play the affective and corporeal energies of the participants in the history of their times" (Attinasi and Friedrich, this volume, chapter 1). This is the ontological sense of dialogue, discussed earlier. It does not require that linguistic and cultural patterns and social relations be generated anew with every interaction. Rather, every interaction takes place within specific social, institutional, and historical coordinates, all of which color the interaction at the same time as they are reshaped, to greater or lesser extent, by that interaction.[10]

Anthropology and linguistics have been most successful in showing how cultural forms are constrained cognitively and socially, but have fallen short in understanding how particular forms and interpretations are embodied in action. Even the simplest conversation is constructed jointly by its participants, including bystanders and eavesdroppers, who signal acquiescence to their positions in the emerging interaction by such subtle cues as bodily position and rhythmic synchronization.[11] The meanings of each participant's contribution to the event are continually reevaluated by each of the participants as the interaction proceeds; the "meaning" of an action cannot be reduced to the intention or desire of a single actor (see Gumperz 1982). "Language," writes Bakhtin (1981: 293), ". . . lies on the borderline between oneself and the other." In this sense, language has an emergent quality, at one and the same time produced by speakers and estranged from them. The idea of "emergence" is central to understanding how culture and language acquire regularities through the interaction of individuals without being reducible to them (Schieffelin 1985: 722).

The principle of emergence has been most clearly enunciated by biologists, who try to understand how life forms have emergent organizational properties that cannot be predicted from their constituent parts.[12] In the words of Ernst Mayr, "When two entities are combined at a new level of integration, not all the properties of the new entity are necessarily a logical or predictable consequence of the components" (1988: 34; see 1982: 63–64). This definition stresses two conditions: first, that the new level of organization have its own principles of patterning that cannot be reduced to its component principles; and second, that the new level of organization include some degree of contingency.[13] The circulatory system meets the first criterion, in that its organization as a system cannot be predicted from the structure of the individual cells. Ecosystems meet both criteria, although their status as emergent systems is a matter of contention among ecologists. A conversation also meets both criteria, in that the organization of interaction follows regularities that cannot be predicted from the behavior of any of its participants—indeed, the opposite is more likely to be true—and it is subject to all manner of contingency. Edward Schieffelin proposes that Kaluli (Papua New Guinea) ritual séances be understood in these terms. The spirit medium engages and provokes the audience, using a variable combination of ambiguities, dramaturgical devices, and song "to force out dramatic and emotional as much as cognitive significance" (Schieffelin 1985: 721). The beliefs that inform people's understandings of these rituals are also variable, around a common core. A given séance is not the enactment of a fixed set of beliefs; rather, beliefs are contingent on actual performances.

For anthropologists, emergence poses two crucial problems: first, how to recognize that cultural forms have their own principles of organization without resorting to a crude essentialism, in which cultures are treated as fixed and unchanging forms shared by populations; and second, how to construct an account of the relationships between form and meaning, event and interpretation, which does justice to the contingencies around which regularities take shape.

The first problem, which we will call the "location" problem, has been a persistent question in anthropological and linguistic theory. For nineteenth-century social philosophers such as Herbert Spencer, the problem of "emergence" can be seen in the attempt to understand how cultural forms seemed to follow historical principles separate from inorganic and organic matter, and why it was that even though culture was the product of individuals, it seemed to acquire an objective character and loom over them, confronting its creators with something that existed before they did and would continue to exist after. Spencer proposed that culture constituted a separate, emergent level of reality beyond the inorganic and organic, a level that he chose to call the "supra-organic" (1880; 1893: 12–17).

In the United States at the turn of the century, treating culture as emergent took on a political urgency as part of the Boasian repudiation of eugenics and other forms of racism. The cachet of Boasian cultural and linguistic anthropology was in identifying forms of patterning specific to language and culture (and to *a* language and *a* culture), irreducible to physiology (see, for example, Boas 1889). Boasian ethnography centered around work with an individual (or a few individuals) as representatives of a cultural collectivity (see Behar, this volume, chapter 5), and so it is not surprising that the "location" of culture—in social collectivities or in individuals—was to become a major issue for them.[14] Kroeber's celebrated reformulation of Spencer emphasized the social (though not collective) nature of cultural phenomena. Wrote Kroeber (1917: 193), "Civilization, as such, only begins where the individual ends." Kroeber's rhetorical opposition between the individual/mental and the social/cultural entangled the argument over emergence in a social metaphysic that opposes individual and culture. Sapir's (1917: 442) rejoinder, that "it is always the individual that really thinks and acts and dreams and revolts," states the problem squarely as one of locating cultural patterning in the individual or in social aggregates. Sapir was firm in placing a qualitative point of emergence at the divide between the organic and the psychic, not between the organic and the supra- (or "super-") organic.

Sapir's side of the argument won the day. Boas himself rejected Kroeber's conception of culture as "hardly necessary" and a "mystic entity" (1928: 235; see Benedict 1934: 231 and Sapir 1949a: 516).[15] Kroeber finally conceded that "culture exists only in persons in the sense that it resides, has its locus in them" (1948: 408). Ironically, while Kroeber joined the Boasian consensus that culture was located in individuals, Sapir moved toward the position that culture was immanent in social practices and appropriated by individuals.

Sapir proposed a theory of "structuration," as Giddens (1979: 69–73) has called it, dividing the sources of cultural and linguistic patterning between social practices ("interpersonal relationships") and individuals who are endowed with "unconscious control of very complicated configurations."[16] Though acquired through "enormously varied psychological predispositions and types of conditioning which characterize different types of personalities, these patterns in their completed form differ only infinitesimally from individual to individual" (Sapir 1949c: 555).[17] For Sapir, the patterns inherent in language and culture, though self-stabilizing, converged on the individual personality as the central point of reference (Sapir 1949b: 597n.1).

Despite an embedded antinomy between the individual and the social collectivity, the Boasians fell short of identifying culture with the collectivity, as their German contemporaries (such as Bachofen) did. Sapir's turn toward an interactional theory of culture, which was the only real hope for escaping the confines of the antinomy, was lost with his death in 1939.

As American cultural anthropology took on its modern institutional form after World War II, the idea of culture was reinscribed in a new form. The social sciences of the postwar era were wrapped up in a debate about whether individuals or social collectivities were the ultimate unit of analysis (see Watkins 1952; Lukes 1968; Levine 1987). "Methodological holists" argued that the behavior of individuals could be traced in part to the social collectivities of which they were members, and that significant generalizations could be made about the nature, organization, and behavior of the collectivities. "Methodological individualists" argued, on the other hand, that ideas like "group behavior," "society," and "culture" were fictions. At most, these terms referred to the psychological states and behaviors of aggregates of individuals.[18]

Although the individualism/holism debate was constructed within a larger set of philosophical and methodological questions, it was also saturated with two related political discourses of the cold war period. Methodological individualism staked a moral and political claim to the primacy of the individual over any social and political collectivities, and aligned itself explicitly with cold war politics, which increasingly was cast in terms of a moral crusade against the collectivism of the "socialist" states of the period. Paradoxically, methodological holism gained appeal within the same political contexts. Western states, especially the United States and Britain, emphasized the unity of their societies against the divisive polarizations of class, race, and ethnicity. They did so by inscribing these societies with a kind of "mechanical solidarity," a sameness in which individuals became equivalent in their diversity but were always measured against a normative, average person—for example, a white, male, English-speaking person.

Both political alignments of the methodological individualism debate crept into postwar anthropological ideas of culture. Cultures came to be seen as discrete units—the normative, ideational, and expressive sides of societies, in one formulation of the time. In addition, culture came to be opposed to "the individual," meaning a generic member of the "culture-bearing" society as a unit of behavior, as an agent of innovation, or as a psychological unit. Thus, the debate between methodological individualism and methodological holism could also play itself out in anthropology. Although a consensus view of culture was to collapse in the 1960s, in society as well as in anthropology, even today anthropological debates over words like "culture" often fall back on a consensus model (see Clifford 1988: 273). So pervasive is the distinction between individuals and transcendent social wholes that a typified, consensus view of society reappears in the margins of the life histories of individuals. In such works the social side requires the intervention of the ethnographer, while the individual side is represented as if it were transparent (see Behar, this volume, chapter 5). Life histories of women, Behar observes, are doubly supplementary, at once providing an individual view of a society that has been characterized holistically from a male perspective, and providing female counterparts to previously collected male life histories.

The shift to a dialogical approach to language does not mean the end of any interest in the individual speaker, but it does mean that any given speaker at any given moment is immediately an actor within a social and cultural world that is always in process (see Daniel 1984: 42–47). Taking account of this in publication is no mere matter of adding statements about "context" to a collection of native texts or a native life history. All too often, such statements take the form of typifications, broadly describing a world that was already completely there when some native began speaking and remains there, completely unchanged, when the speaking ends. In dialogical terms, the social and cultural world is not something independent from a historical instance of native discourse, but is made and remade precisely in such instances. As Behar suggests, we must now engage native speakers in their active, "world-making" roles.

## EMERGENCE AND PERFORMANCE

In constructing Kaluli ritual as an emergent phenomenon, Schieffelin was guided by the ethnography of performance, one of several related frameworks that have relocated culture in social practices.[19] Ethnographers of performance argue that verbal meaning does not arise solely from texts, conceived narrowly. Rather, it is an emergent property of performance, conceived as a fully engaged social event and constructed jointly through the actions of all participants in the event.[20] The notion of "participant" is fourfold. First, participation roles are created in verbal performances through such formal linguistic devices as deictics and evaluative comments. Second, a verbal performance requires a particular type of participant structure to succeed as a certain kind of social event. Third, participants are socially positioned actors, embodying vectors of power and authority that are repositioned during the performance. And fourth, participants are always specific individuals with specific histories of interaction with the other participants in the performance. Each of these four aspects contributes to the interpretation of the event by the participants, with no guarantee that all participants will understand the event in the same way. These conditions hold as much for verbal performances in which an ethnographer is present as for any other (see D. Tedlock 1990). Thus, a narrative told to an ethnographer is a joint construction of the ethnographer and the storyteller. Conversely, the relationship between ethnographer and subject is constructed partly through the performance event, and is subject to the same irreducible contingencies as any other performance (Behar, this volume, chapter 5; DeBernardi, this volume, chapter 6). In this respect, ethnography is, as we suggested at the outset, a form of "culture making" (a phrase used by Daniel and Ortner among others) like any other.

Although ethnographers of performance tend to emphasize the indeterminacy and irreducible contingency of events, participants engage in an elaborate interactional play through which the range of interpretations is constrained. This includes bodily positioning, adjustments of gaze, shifts in rhythmic synchrony, asides, and other subtle moves, all of which are continuously tracked by and responded to by the other participants in the event. McDermott and Tylbor (this volume, chapter 8) argue that all social events require the tacit collusion of the participants, who implicitly agree that they are interpreting the events within the same general framework. This interactional collusion is not socially neutral; rather, it involves a carefully crafted set of social repositionings in which dominance hierarchies emerge with the collusion (though not necessarily the consent) of the dominated. Such processes are carefully calibrated to the institutional contexts within which the interactions take place, forming, as McDermott and Tylbor put the matter, "a well-orchestrated lie that offers a world con- versationalists do not have to produce but can pretend to live by" (p. 145). They illustrate their point with a reading group in a public school in New York City in which Rosa, a seven-year-old girl, is judged a failure (that is, a nonreader) by her cohort and teacher. Overtly, the purpose of the read- ing class is to teach all the students to read, as the teacher acknowledges. Tacitly, educational institutions sort the students into a hierarchy of gra- dations of success and failure. Rosa's collusion in her own failure is aligned with the unspoken, tacit purpose of the interaction.

For ethnographers who are interested in representing the voices of their subjects, the problem of collusion has disturbing implications. Whose voices are to be represented? The institutional self-representation that as- serts its interest in educating all the students? The teacher's embodiment of the institutional voice? Rosa's, as she asserts that she wants to take her turn at reading? The other students, as they deride Rosa's ability to read? Any single participant is, indeed, positioned socially, but no single voice can be understood except in the context of all the others, against the back- ground of the emergent social reality that both reflects and shapes their interaction.

If ethnography is a form of culture making like any other, then eth- nographers are caught in the same kinds of subtle collusions with their interlocutors as take place in nonethnographic settings. A key difference is that ethnographers will not understand many of the routinized inter- actional cues used by their interlocutors, who themselves will have similar problems. Many interactions take on the rough, asynchronous character of failed encounters within a single culture. Another difference is that ethnographic interactions have shallower, less fine-grained histories. The "interculture" that emerges through ethnography does not pass through as dense a thicket of interactions as other cultural forms.

Ethnographic collusion takes many guises. Ethnographers' words, like any others, are at least half someone else's, including their interlocutors'. Behar (this volume, chapter 5) shapes the context within which her *co- madre* Esperanza recounts her life as a step toward transforming Espe- ranza's life narrative into a book. But Esperanza has already narratized her life, to her children and neighbors, and articulates her discussions with Behar as a kind of confession in which her life will be carried across the border to the United States. For Esperanza, storytelling transmits a bur- den, and Behar unwittingly plays into Esperanza's script and comes to bear the burden that was Esperanza's. Similarly, Jean DeBernardi (this volume, chapter 6), who sought to do a structuralist analysis of Malaysian Chi- nese temple possessions, found that she was "written into scripts not of my own making," as the spirit mediums demanded that she too "drink the water." "You cannot return," they told her, "you are ours" (DeBernardi 1985: 158). She is not permitted to indulge in the ethnographic gaze. Allan Burns (this volume, chapter 3), who was deliberate in shaping his north Florida ethnography to the needs and wishes of his interlocutors, becomes a vehicle through which the story of Lynch Hammock acquires canonical form. In each of these cases, the ethnographer has been drafted into a native hermeneutic that was already at work before the field-worker got there.

It would be a mistake to focus a dialogical anthropology solely on the two-sided interaction between ethnographers and interlocutors, each as an embodiment of a social position. To do so would be to mistake the part for the whole, to claim that the ethnographer's work is constituted by the borders of a preexisting geography of nation-states, rather than being a subspecies of broader processes of social interaction that are constitutive of social knowledge. The location of Behar's conversation with Esperanza is not the U.S.-Mexican border alone, nor an imaginary projection of their respective states as constitutive of Behar and Esperanza as subjects, but the concrete interaction between them that encapsulates these social sites as it draws meaning from them. Ethnography, then, is a peculiar kind of dialogue and a peculiar zone of emergence, at once constitutive of and constituted by radical cultural difference (see Daniel 1984: chap. 1; Rosaldo 1989: 162–65; Bhabha 1994: 33–34).[21]

Ethnographers at one and the same time observe culture and make culture. Consistent with this realization is the suggestion, made by feminists and others, that in matters of race, culture, class, and gender, the beliefs and behaviors of the researcher must be inscribed within the same historical moment, or on the same critical plane, as the beliefs and behaviors of the persons under study (Harding 1987: 9; Rose 1990: 10). The dialogical turn promises, as Attinasi and Friedrich put it (this volume, p. 38), "an ethnography with as much wisdom as structure, and composed not only of codes and messages but of human dialogue in a richer and more significant complexity."

## THE INTERPRETATION OF DIALOGUE

Bakhtin calls attention to a dialogical process, or "dialogism," that manifests at every scale of language use (Bakhtin 1981: 326–30, 426; Kristeva 1980: 68–72). At the broadest level, whenever we speak or write, and whether or not we do so in direct response to another speaker or writer, our discourse occurs in the context of previous (or alternative) utterances or texts and is in dialogue with them, whether explicitly or implicitly.

When we bring these other discourses inside the time or space of our own, whether directly or indirectly, the result is what Kristeva has given the name "intertextuality" (ibid.: 15, 36–38). Some of the intertexts we place within the text of our own discourse may even come from languages or linguistic registers other than our own, producing an effect Bakhtin calls "heteroglossia" (Todorov 1984: 56). Or we may juxtapose passages that belong to differing genres or types of speech, producing "heterology" (ibid.: 56–59).[22] When we quote, speaking or writing in the voices of other individuals, our discourse possesses "heterophony" (ibid.: 56). If we speak or write in the manner of those other voices rather than quoting them directly, adopting what is often called the "free indirect style" in the context of prose fiction, we produce a "hybrid construction" (ibid.: 73) or "double voicing" (Bakhtin 1981: 324–30).

There is dialogism even at the level of the individual words, since a given word exists in an environment of other words that could have been used with reference to the same object (ibid.: 276), words that may come to the mind of our hearer or reader. Conversely, the same word may call up differing objects, producing a small-scale version of double voicing. Bakhtin's examples of this involve the ironic or parodic importation of a word from one genre or speech type into another (ibid.: 305–8), but figurative usage and sound play offer other possibilities. When a word is linked to an object metaphorically, it keeps its connection with its literal object, saying two things at once.

In general Bakhtin follows, as Kristeva puts it, "a logic of analogy and nonexclusive opposition, opposed to monological levels of causality and identifying determination" (1980: 72). In other words, his dialectic tends to be one of complementarity rather than of polar opposition. But Bakhtin entangles himself in something of a paradox when he opposes complementarity and polarity. Dialogism, despite the heterogeneity (and indeed heterodoxy) it would seem to generate in every kind and at every level of discourse, ends up on one side, his side, of a polarity. He champions dialogue over monologue, the heterophony of the novel over the monophony of verse, the parodic over the canonic, and "the flowering of a multiplicity of unmerged consciousnesses" over "monist idealism" (as quoted in Todorov 1984: 104). The explanation for this paradox might be sought in the oppressive political context in which Bakhtin worked, but his deeper condition was that of anyone who confronts, from within the West, the Western metaphysic.

For Bakhtin, the epitome of multivoiced discourse is the novel, and he sets up the Homeric epic, which he deems monophonic, as both its opposite and its historical predecessor (1981: 4–40). Meanwhile (and unlike Jakobson) he completely overlooks the ordinary folktale, which is more widespread (and probably older) than the epic. Skilled oral narrators can and do engage in code switching, which is to say heteroglossia, not only in large urban societies but in small tribal ones as well. As for heterology, storytellers who are not limited to the singing of verse may represent the characters in their stories as conversing, playing word games, using slang, making speeches, praying, chanting, or singing, all of these in appropriate (or markedly inappropriate) social situations. When it comes to heterophony, skilled oral narrators (or at least those who are not limited to the singing of verse) are fully capable of producing as great a density of contrasting voices as any novelist, and indeed these voices are among their principal means for characterizing the actors in their stories (for examples in this volume, see Isbell, Behar, and Mannheim).[23] As a story unfolds they change their pacing, pausing often in one passage and rushing on in another. By means of intonational contours, they can give truncated phrases and even isolated words the finality of complete sentences, or give complete (and declarative) sentences an air of doubt and indecision. In their amplitude they can cover the full range from a shout to a whisper, and execute crescendos and decrescendos, both suddenly and slowly. All the while they produce complex voice qualities that reveal — or, in this case, represent — horror, anger, sorrow, neutrality, confidence, determination, pleasant surprise, and joy. Their moments of dysfluency include representations of the dysfluencies of the characters: mutters, hesitations, speech defects, foreign accents. A novelist must describe these myriad details and shadings of voice in words or else (where feasible) resort to unusual spelling or punctuation, whereas an oral storyteller can speak them directly. Indeed, as Hill demonstrates (this volume, chapter 4), a single speaker can produce as many as twenty distinguishable voices within the space of a seventeen-minute narrative.

The imaginal world that is constructed by the diversification and detailing of voicing, in combination with movements among stratified syntactical and lexical registers, is a social one, complete with contrasting roles based on sex, age, kinship, acquired statuses, and even the very ethnic differences that are supposed to be the special province of the ethnographer.[24] Some of these social differences may be revealed solely by represented voices, rather than being made explicit by the narrator. At a smaller scale are vocal characteristics that identify a particular person rather than a category of persons, and at a still finer scale are changes of voice that signal changes in the emotional state of the "same" character. Aspects of voicing, at whatever level, may spread from quotations into the surrounding discourse, as when a narrator describes the actions of a character in a way that echoes the identifying voice of that character, thus producing the oral counterpart of free indirect style in written fiction.

Other changes of voicing may occur in the discourse that surrounds quotations, which is to say the passages for which the speaker takes responsibility, as when Hill (this volume, chapter 4) finds a narrator sounding neutral at one moment, personally involved at another, or judgmental at yet another. Some of what is said may be in the nature of an *interpretation* of the story being told rather than moving the action forward (D. Tedlock 1983: 51, 169–76, 293), most obviously in the kind of remark that goes under the name of an "aside." Like contemporary philosophical hermeneutics, this kind of interpretation is directed at the elucidation of the world projected by the text and not at the discovery of the intentions of the originators of the text (see Ricoeur 1976: 36–37). Highly formal discourse delivered in public ritual contexts may lack clear-cut hermeneutical moves away from the text proper, but other occasions, such as the transmission of that text to future performers, may be quite open to talk *about* the text. At the smallest scale, when discourse takes the form of semantically constructed parallel verse, each line that moves the topic forward is immediately followed by one or more other lines that are, in effect, brief interpretations of what was just said. In discourse in general, there is an implicit dialogic of alternative or additional words and phrases that could have been used but were not; in parallel discourse, even this small-scale aspect of the dialogical process becomes manifest.

The existence of a hermeneutics that is already at work before the field-worker gets there, whether it is enunciated within native texts or takes shape in native talk about texts, has important consequences for interpretive social science as presently constituted. The phenomenological "intersubjectivity" that has served as the model for the field encounter between self and other immerses the ethnographer in native subjectivity, with the ascendance into objectivity corresponding to the move out of the field and back home. Meanwhile, the self-objectifying, self-interpreting moves of the natives pass unnoticed, though they are in fact essential to productive ethnography.[25] Such moves may be routinely incorporated, without attribution, in the objectifying discourse of the writers of ethnographies, who thus reserve the intellectual domain to themselves. Also concealed behind such discourse is what Attinasi and Friedrich (this volume, chapter 1) call the "dialogical breakthrough," in which a point of turbulence or cathexis in a field exchange produces a "split-second realignment" in the thinking of the field-worker and results in a major change of direction in research.

The present relationship between text and interpretation may be traceable, in part, to the original biblical context of hermeneutics, whose practitioners were concerned with texts whose writers were situated at a vast temporal and spatial distance from themselves. But even in biblical hermeneutics, as practiced to this day in the Christian West, there has been a notable bracketing off of the vast Talmudic (which is to say native) discourse that surrounds the first five books of the Hebrew Bible and brings them into an interpretive, intertextual dialogue. The typological interpretation of those books transforms them into prophetic allegories of Christian texts, much as some kinds of anthropological interpretation have the effect of transforming native texts into allegories of canonical anthropological accounts of social or mental structures and processes.

Whatever the sources of hermeneutical hegemony in the social sciences, there are interpreters of the literature of the historical period in which they themselves live who prefer the closed corpus of a deceased author. In the case of authors who have ventured into the discourse of self-objectification, critics often adopt the same position as ethnographers who set aside native discourse of this kind, invoking the author's subjectivity and claiming objectivity for themselves. Anthropologists have long read the cultures of their contemporaries as if they were dealing with texts from a time other than their own, a point amply demonstrated by Fabian (1983). Some have even made overt moves to close a particular corpus, reserving authentic (as opposed to acculturated) authorship to a dying generation beyond the reach of anthropologists who might come later. Meanwhile, the members of a society are capable of talking across such boundaries, producing, as the three women recorded by Isbell do (this volume, chapter 2), a discourse whose intertextuality spans the differences between generations, between rural and urban life, and between vastly different languages such as Quechua and Spanish, moving through the remembered past and constructing, in the present, a possible future.

Ironically, at the very moment the dialogical ground is extended to the point where field-workers and natives stand in close proximity to one another, even in matters of interpretation, a political objection arises. It is argued that a dialogical representation of the field encounter is likely to create an illusory leveling effect, disguising or glossing over the context of power relationships within which all field dialogues must take place and leading to a celebration of the natives' subjectivity (Handler 1985).[26] Behind this sort of objection there seems to be a new and unexpected form of hermeneutical hegemony. The implicit assumption is that where power relationships are concerned the natives are unwitting participants, while the discussion of the realities of those relationships belongs solely to the objective domain of the social scientist. It is as if politics never appeared within the field dialogues themselves, but could become evident only when investigators described the contexts of those dialogues from somewhere above and beyond them.

To blame dialogue itself for glossing over power relationships is to stand it on its head. When ethnographers and their interlocutors decide that certain discussions should not be published or that the identities of local places and participants should be disguised, this is not because dialogue obscures politics but because the parties to a dialogue discussed politics in ways that made them fear oppression (see D. Tedlock, this volume, chapter 10). In the native world, and in our own as well, conversations that possess not only the form but also the function of dialogue are not the vehicle of suppression by authoritarian elites but are rather the universal object of suppression. Meanwhile the speakers and writers of all languages, which remain dialogical in their very nature, will always find ways, as Bakhtin did under the regime of Stalin, to keep differences in play. For Paulo Freire (1989), to speak plainly about the powers of dialogue and its role in politics meant doing so in exile from his native Brazil.

It is no coincidence that women and ethnic others have figured prominently among the authors of ethnographies that are rich in dialogue, from the beginning right down to the present day (see B. Tedlock 1991). Among the earliest book-length works of this kind were *Spider Woman* by Gladys Reichard (1934) and *Mules and Men* by Zora Neale Hurston (1935). Not only did these works precede the often-cited "conversational" book by Marcel Griaule (1948) but Reichard and Hurston used direct quotation, whereas Griaule glossed over nearly everything said by himself and his interlocutors with indirect discourse. Women in the West, like ethnic others, have found themselves on the outside of a European male subtradition that rests on the myth of a unified self, the kind of self that makes a unified and subordinate object out of plural others (see Callaway 1992). When this unifying project is carried through to its end, it requires that the discourse of those plural others either be reduced to the terms of a European object language or else marginalized or silenced. It is not that there is something essentially male about a reductive and authoritative monologue or essentially female about an expansive multivocality—after all, multivocality abounds even in the texts male field-workers have collected from male others. Rather, the suppression of multivocality may be laid at the door of a particular construction of language and truth that finds its purest expression in the omniscient third-person discourse of a solitary male, whether divine or human. Dialogue, and indeed the fullness of language itself, belong to an irreducibly social world where people ask questions.

## NOTES

In the introduction and the volume, we have benefited from comments by Laura Ahearn, Ruth Behar, Susan A. Gelman, James Herron, Janise Hurtig, Janet McIntosh, Kathleen Stewart, Barbara Tedlock, and Harriet Whitehead. We thank Donna Serwinowski for her excellent editorial assistance throughout the preparation of this volume.

1. Bogatyrëv and Jakobson (1929) propose instead that oral literatures are stabilized through the process of circulation. It is the community of listeners who select the most intelligible and socially useful stories from an open, ever-changing corpus of variant stories and choose to reproduce them. Although this was not Bogatyrëv and Jakobson's point, the process of selection-through-circulation guarantees (through the "intelligibility" criterion) that oral performances refer to other oral performances, forming interlocking networks of intertextual reference.

2. To set the chronology of these papers correctly, the posthumous (1990a) article that we quote at the beginning of this essay was written in draft for oral delivery in 1942; the monologue-as-pathology remark was made at a conference in 1952; and a well-known paper in which some of the linguistic details of this position were sketched was distributed in mimeographed form in 1957 (see Jakobson 1990b).

Jakobson derived his ideas from work carried out in the 1920s by the Russian linguists Lev Jakubinskij, Lev Ščerba, and V. N. Voloshinov. Although Jakobson was one of several who introduced Voloshinov and Bakhtin to the West (Voloshinov was cited in several key works by Jakobson, and Jakobson encouraged the American publication of Voloshinov's *Marxism and the Philosophy of Language*), Bakhtin does not appear as a major light in Jakobson's intellectual constellation, we believe for two main reasons: (1) Although Jakobson is careful to acknowledge his intellectual predecessors, such as Ščerba, he tended to be far more critical of his own and the following generation, and to cite them less (in order not to cite them negatively); (2) Bakhtin and his circle developed many of their ideas in polemic with the Russian formalists, among whom Jakobson was a key figure. The similarity of Jakobson's views with those of Voloshinov and Bakhtin might reflect the influence of the latter (which he at least partially acknowledges), together with the mutual influence that often comes out of intellectual debate. There is also the possibility of the common influence of a third party (Ščerba, for instance).

3. For a parallel discussion with special reference to Bakhtin, see Morson and Emerson (1990).

4. For studies on Bakhtin and his impact on critical theory, see Ivanov (1970), Clark and Holquist (1984), Titunik (1984), Holquist (1990), Morson and Emerson (1990), Danow (1991), Emerson (1992), and the collections edited by Morson (1986), Hirschkop and Shepherd (1989), Morson and Emerson (1989), and Thomson (1990). Of special interest to anthropologists are Abrahams (1989), Babcock (1982), Bauman (1986), Briggs and Bauman (1992), Hill (1986), Irvine (1990), Karp (1987), Lavie (1990), Layne (1990), Limón (1990), Page (1988), Shotter (1992), Stallybrass and White (1986), Trawick (1988), Weiss (1990), and Wertsch (1985, 1991).

5. We would not wish to claim that these are the *only* seeds of the reversal of

the traditional priority of structure over action. Similar moves can be found in the work of Edward Sapir, Peircian semiotic, performance folkloristics, Geertz's more programmatic writings, and ethnomethodology.

6. It is interesting to note, in this connection, that Edward Sapir was succeeded, in the role of the central theoretician in the University of Chicago anthropology department, by none other than A. R. Radcliffe-Brown. One of the symptoms of the intellectual shift was that Radcliffe-Brown successfully convinced the University of Chicago Press to drop its plan to publish Haile's collection of Navajo ritual texts with a sharp attack on the American practice of text collection (Darnell 1990: 138–40).

7. Boas (1911: 63, 67–73) himself distinguished between nonconscious, tacit forms of patterning, or as he called them, "primary formations," and conscious "secondary ethnological phenomena." "Primary ethnological phenomena" included nonconscious forms of cultural and linguistic patterning, which were often subject to "secondary rationalization" by members of the culture in the course of explaining the significance of cultural and linguistic forms to the ethnographer. For Boas, language — as a cognized, tacit system of obligatory grammatical and lexical classifications — was the exemplary "primary ethnological phenomenon" (ibid.: 67ff.). Boas did not deny the distinction between knowledge acquired through experience and "knowledge about"; indeed, the point of his discussion of "primary" and "secondary ethnological phenomena" was to distinguish the two rigorously. But — inserting Langer's terminology into Boas's point anachronistically — Boas insisted that language had presentational as well as discursive aspects. For an extended discussion of this point, see Mannheim (n.d.).

8. On deictics as primary coordinates of language and culture, see Benveniste (1971: 194–204, 217–30), Jakobson (1990b), Luong (1988), Morel and Danon-Boileau (1992), Mühlhäusler and Harré (1990), Silverstein (1976), and Urban (1989). See Hanks (1990) for an extended study of the role of deixis and linguistic spatialization in shaping social relations and semantic reference.

9. See, for example, Brown and Gilman's (1960) well-known study of the sociology of the European honorific "you" and Errington's (1988) account of the history of Javanese deictics.

10. In addition, every interaction is saturated with multiple histories: the history of the interaction as it plays itself out over time; the histories of the cultural and linguistic forms begin used; the personal histories of the participants, including previous interactions; the normative assumptions made by the participants on the basis of their personal histories; the institutional matrices within which the interaction takes place, each saturated with its histories in turn; and so forth. These are a critical source of the dialogical, multiaccentual nature of talk and other social action (see Lavie 1990; Steedly 1993). Because they intersect only in concrete actions (rather than as abstract principles) they are essentially invisible in an anthropology or a linguistics that is limited to the study of abstract codes (see Abu-Lughod 1991; Becker 1995: introduction).

11. There is a strong tradition of studying these issues that crosscuts sociology and anthropology. See, among others, Scheflen (1973), Goffman (1974, 1981), Sacks,

Schegloff, and Jefferson (1974), C. Goodwin (1980, 1981), M. H. Goodwin (1980), Key (1980), Moerman and Nomura (1990), and McDermott and Tylbor (this volume, chapter 8). On rhythmic synchrony, see Condon (1980), Erickson (1980), Kempton (1980), and Kitamura (1990).

12. Key philosophical works on emergence include Pepper (1926), Meehl and Sellars (1956), and Margolis (1986). Recognizing that emergent phenomena have their own principles of organization does not deny that lower-level principles also might be useful to describing them; it only claims that there are principles of organization that do not follow causally from lower-level principles. See Fodor (1974) for a useful distinction between "type reductionism," in which an apparently emergent phenomenon can be redescribed entirely using simpler principles, and "token reductionism," in which it cannot. The idea of emergence is only useful in the latter case.

13. According to Michael Krausz (1981: 143), the painter Kandinsky became a nonfigurative painter after accidentally leaving a figurative painting upside-down and seeing only the abstract arrangements of lines, shapes, and colors. The abstract form, in other words, had emergent principles of patterning that were obvious to Kandinsky only by chance.

14. For a classic, polemical history of this debate, see White (1947).

15. But Benedict (1934: 16) also described culture as "the ideas and standards [people] have in common," and Sapir (1921: 233) defined it as "what a society thinks and does."

16. There are major differences in emphasis between Sapir's embryonic project and Giddens's framework. Giddens (1976: 121) emphasizes the duality of structure as "both constituted by human agency . . . and, at the same time, the very medium of this constitution." Sapir, in contrast, offered the beginnings of a person-centered, psychological account of appropriation of structures, emphasizing especially the second half of Giddens's dyad.

17. See Hymes (1970), Silverstein (1986: 72–74), Handler (1986: 147–50), and Hill (1988: 23–25) for discussion of Sapir's evolving views of the relationship between individual and culture.

18. Methodological individualists were committed to a larger program for reducing the human sciences to more "basic" sciences: social phenomena to individual behavioral and psychological dispositions, mind states to brain states, brain processes to biochemical processes, and "special sciences" such as biology to the master science of quantum physics. For a recent attempt to reformulate the problem of culture in methodological individualist terms, see Sperber (1991).

19. These frameworks, related and partly overlapping, include the recent work by sociologists Giddens, Bourdieu, and Touraine; anthropologists Ortner and Sahlins; and the older American tradition of symbolic interactionism (for example Garfinkel, Goffman, and Sacks, a tradition that is represented here in the essays by Tannen, chapter 7, and by McDermott and Tylbor, chapter 8). Ortner (1989: 11–12) writes that "any form of human action or interaction would be an instance of 'practice' insofar as the analyst recognized it as reverberating with features of asymmetry, inequality, domination, and the like in its particular historical

and cultural setting." She sees an emphasis on social domination as the critical feature distinguishing more recent theories of practice from the older symbolic interactionist tradition. Although some forms of symbolic interactionism were infatuated with their descriptive technology and blind to social domination, works by Willis (1981), Atkinson (1984), Duranti (1994), and McDermott and Tylbor (this volume, chapter 8) show ways in which microinteractional subtleties are the very stuff of politics.

20. See, for example, Abrahams (1968), Basso (1985: 1–10; 1986), Bauman (1977: 37–45; 1986), Briggs (1988), Darnell (1974), Fabian (1990), Feld (1982), Kuipers (1990), D. Tedlock (1983: 16–17), and Toelken and Scott (1981). The ethnography of performance partly builds out of a trenchant critique of the idea that cultural forms, such as narrative texts and rituals, normally have invariant or canonical shapes. Ethnographers of performance have argued that the assumption of canonicity is rooted in the ethnographer's tradition of alphabetic literacy. For ethnographers of performance, culture is more like jazz than like books. When Charles Mingus and his band first performed "Scenes in the City," the performance took shape between the band members, the rhythms of the instruments both leading and following the rhythm of the accompanying narrative. In turn, the narrative took shape around a local, New York African American style of speaking. Once inscribed, first in the form of a live performance and then in the form of a recording of the performance, "Scenes in the City" could be quoted ("covered") by Branford Marsalis. Although the Marsalis performance was a quotation of the Mingus, it too had emergent qualities (distinct from those of the original performance); among other things, the point of reference of the narrative changed. For the earlier performance the narrative evoked a local speech style; for the later performance, it evoked the earlier performance, following the original word-for-word, but differently nuanced.

21. See also Dirks, Eley, and Ortner, who argue that it is the interstitial and dialogical nature of field research that creates a "space for ethnography in a critically self-conscious anthropology" (1994: 39).

22. In biology this term refers to a lack of correspondence in structure or arrangement between body parts. For a discussion of genre within a Bakhtinian framework, see Briggs and Bauman (1992).

23. See also Sapir (1915), Hymes (1981: 65–76), and D. Tedlock (1983: 12–13, 59–60, 245; 1991).

24. Andersen (1990) observes that even preschool children are sensitive to the different linguistic devices associated with different social roles. See also Ervin-Tripp (1973).

25. Understanding the process of entextualization—the ways by which stretches of talk are extracted from their interactional settings—in the native or ethnographic context (Bauman and Briggs 1990: 73; Kuipers 1990: 4) is thus critical to a dialogical reconstruction of anthropological hermeneutics.

26. A similar objection was raised by Joan W. Scott at a lecture given by one of the present authors.

REFERENCES CITED

Abrahams, Roger D. 1968. "Introductory Remarks to a Rhetorical Theory of Folklore." *Journal of American Folklore* 81:143–58.

———. 1989. "Bakhtin, the Critics, and Folklore." *Journal of American Folklore* 102:202–6.

Abu-Lughod, Lila. 1991. "Writing against Culture." In *Recapturing Anthropology: Working in the Present*, edited by Richard Fox, pp. 137–62. Santa Fe: School of American Research Press.

Andersen, Elaine S. 1990. *Speaking with Style: The Sociolinguistic Skills of Children*. London: Routledge.

Atkinson, J. Maxwell. 1984. *Our Masters' Voices, The Language and Body Language of Politics*. London: Metheun.

Babcock, Barbara A. 1982. "Ritual Undress and the Comedy of Self and Other: Bandelier's *The Delight Makers*." In *A Crack in the Mirror: Reflexive Perspectives in Anthropology*, edited by Jay Ruby, pp. 187–203. Philadelphia: University of Pennsylvania Press.

Bakhtin, M. M. 1981. *The Dialogic Imagination*. Translated by C. Emerson and M. Holquist. Austin: University of Texas Press.

———. 1984. *Problems of Dostoevsky's Poetics*. Edited and translated by C. Emerson. Minneapolis: University of Minnesota Press.

Basso, Ellen B. 1985. *A Musical View of the Universe*. Philadelphia: University of Pennsylvania Press.

Bauman, Richard. 1977. *Verbal Art as Performance*. Rowley, Mass.: Newbury House.

———. 1986. *Story, Performance, and Event, Contextual Studies of Oral Narrative*. Cambridge: University Press.

Bauman, Richard, and Charles L. Briggs. 1990. "Poetics and Performance as Critical Perspectives on Language and Social Life." *Annual Review of Anthropology* 19:59–88.

Becker, A. L. 1995. *Beyond Translation: Essays toward a Modern Philology*. Ann Arbor: University of Michigan Press.

Benedict, Ruth. 1934. *Patterns of Culture*. New York: New American Library.

Benveniste, Émile. 1971. *Problems in General Linguistics*. Coral Gables: University of Miami Press.

Bhabha, Homi K. 1994. *The Location of Culture*. London: Routledge.

Boas, Franz. 1889. "On Alternating Sounds." *American Anthropologist* 2:47–53.

———. 1911. "Introduction." In *Handbook of American Indian Languages*, vol. 1, pp. 1–83. Washington, D.C.: Bureau of American Ethnology.

———. 1928. *Anthropology and Modern Life*. New York: Norton.

Bogatyrëv, Pëtr, and Roman Jakobson. 1929. "Folklore as a Special Form of Creativity." In *The Prague School: Selected Writings, 1929–1946*, edited by P. Steiner, pp. 32–46. Austin: University of Texas Press.

Briggs, Charles L. 1988. *Competence in Performance: The Creativity of Tradition in Mexicano Verbal Art*. Philadelphia: University of Pennsylvania Press.

———. 1992. "Since I Am a Woman, I Will Chastise My Relatives: Gender, Re-

ported Speech and the (Re)production of Social Relations in Warao Ritual
Wailing." *American Ethnologist* 19:336–61.

Briggs, Charles L., and Richard Bauman. 1992. "Genre, Intertextuality, and Social
Power." *Journal of Linguistic Anthropology* 2:131–72.

Brown, Roger, and Alfred Gilman. 1960. "The Pronouns of Power and Solidarity."
In *Style in Language,* edited by Thomas A. Sebeok, pp. 253–76. Cambridge,
Mass.: MIT Press.

Bruner, Edward M., and Phyllis Gorfain. 1984. "Dialogic Narration and the Paradoxes of Masada." In *Text, Play, and Story: The Construction and Reconstruction
of Self and Society,* edited by Edward M. Bruner, pp. 56–79. Washington, D.C.:
American Ethnological Society.

Callaway, H. 1992. "Ethnography and Experience: Gender Implications in Fieldwork and Texts." In *Anthropology and Autobiography,* edited by J. Okely and
H. Callaway, ASA Monographs 29:29–49. London: Routledge.

Clark, Katarina, and Michael Holquist. 1984. *Mikhail Bakhtin.* Cambridge, Mass.:
Harvard University Press.

Clifford, James. 1988. *The Predicament of Culture: Twentieth-Century Ethnography,
Literature, and Art.* Cambridge, Mass.: Harvard University Press.

Condon, William S. 1980. "The Relation of Interactional Synchrony to Cognitive and Emotional Processes." In *The Relationship of Verbal and Nonverbal
Communication,* edited by Mary Ritchie Key, pp. 49–65. The Hague: Mouton.

Daniel, E. Valentine. 1984. *Fluid Signs: Being a Person the Tamil Way.* Berkeley and
Los Angeles: University of California Press.

Danow, David K. 1991. *The Thought of Mikhail Bakhtin: From Word to Culture.*
London: Macmillan.

Darnell, Regna. 1974. "Correlates of Cree Narrative Performance." In *Explorations
in the Ethnography of Speaking,* edited by Richard Bauman and Joel Sherzer, pp.
315–36. Cambridge: Cambridge University Press.

———. 1990. "Franz Boas, Edward Sapir, and the Americanist Text Tradition."
*Historiographia Linguistica* 17:129–44.

DeBernardi, Jean E. 1985. "Seng Ma." In *Reflections: The Anthropological Muse,*
edited by J. Ian Prattis, p. 158. Washington, D.C.: American Anthropological
Association.

Derrida, Jacques. 1976. *Of Grammatology.* Translated by Gayatri Chakravorty
Spivak. Baltimore: Johns Hopkins University Press.

Dirks, Nicholas B., Geoff Eley, and Sherry B. Ortner, eds. 1994. Introduction
to *Culture/Power/History: A Reader in Contemporary Social Theory,* pp. 3–45.
Princeton: Princeton University Press.

Duranti, Alessandro. 1994. *From Grammar to Politics.* Berkeley and Los Angeles:
University of California Press.

Dwyer, Kevin. 1982. *Moroccan Dialogues: Anthropology in Question.* Baltimore:
Johns Hopkins University Press.

Emerson, Caryl. 1992. "The Russians Reclaim Bakhtin." *Comparative Literature*
44:415–24.

Erickson, Frederick. 1980. "Timing and Context in Everyday Discourse: Implications for the Study of Referential and Social Meaning." *Southwest Educational Development Laboratory Sociolinguistic Working Paper 67*. Austin: Southwest Educational Development Lab.

Errington, J. Joseph. 1988. *Structure and Style in Javanese: A Semiotic View of Linguistic Etiquette*. Philadelphia: University of Pennsylvania Press.

Ervin-Tripp, Susan M. 1973. "Children's Sociolinguistic Competence and Dialect Diversity." In *Language Acquisition and Communicative Choice: Essays by Susan M. Ervin-Tripp*, edited by Anwar S. Dil, pp. 262–301. Stanford: Stanford University Press.

Fabian, Johannes. 1979. "Rule and Process: Thoughts on Ethnography as Communication." *Philosophy of the Social Sciences* 9:1–26.

———. 1983. *Time and the Other: How Anthropology Makes Its Object*. New York: Columbia University Press.

———. 1990. *Power and Performance: Ethnographic Explorations through Proverbial Wisdom and Theater in Shaba, Zaire*. Madison: University of Wisconsin Press.

Feld, Steven. 1982. *Sound and Sentiment*. Philadelphia: University of Pennsylvania Press.

Fodor, Jerry A. 1974. "Special Sciences, or The Disunity of Science as a Working Hypothesis." *Synthese* 28:77–115.

Freire, Paulo. 1989. *Pedagogy of the Oppressed*. Translated by Myra Bergman Ramos. New York: Continuum.

Geertz, Clifford. 1966. "Religion as a Cultural System." In *Anthropological Approaches to the Study of Religion*, edited by Michael Banton, pp. 1–46. London: Tavistock.

Giddens, Anthony. 1976. *New Rules of Sociological Method: A Positive Critique of Interpretative Sociologies*. New York: Basic Books.

———. 1979. *Central Problems in Social Theory: Action, Structure, and Contradiction in Social Analysis*. Berkeley: University of California Press.

Goffman, Erving. 1974. *Frame Analysis: An Essay on the Organization of Experience*. New York: Harper and Row.

———. 1981. *Forms of Talk*. Philadelphia: University of Pennsylvania Press.

Goodwin, Charles. 1980. "Restarts, Pauses, and the Achievement of a State of Mutual Gaze at Turn-Beginning." *Sociological Inquiry* 50:272–302.

———. 1981. *Conversational Organization: Interaction between Speakers and Hearers*. New York: Academic Press.

Goodwin, Marjorie Harness. 1980. "Processes of Mutual Monitoring Implicated in the Production of Description Sequences." *Sociological Inquiry* 50:303–17.

Griaule, Marcel. 1948. *Dieu d'eau: Entretiens avec Ogotemmêli*. Paris: Éditions du Chêne.

Gumperz, John. 1982. *Discourse Strategies*. Cambridge: Cambridge University Press.

Handler, Richard. 1985. "On Dialogue and Destructive Analysis: Problems in Narrating Nationalism and Ethnicity." *Journal of Anthropological Research* 41:171–82.

———. 1986. "Vigorous Male and Aspiring Female." In *Malinowski, Rivers, Benedict, and Others: Essays on Culture and Personality,* edited by George W. Stocking, pp. 126–55. Madison: University of Wisconsin Press.

Hanks, William F. 1990. *Referential Practices: Language and Lived Space among the Maya.* Chicago: University of Chicago Press.

Harding, S. 1987. *Feminism and Methodology: Social Science Issues.* Bloomington: Indiana University Press.

Hill, Jane H. 1986. "The Refiguration of the Anthropology of Language." *Cultural Anthropology* 1:89–102.

———. 1988. "Language, Genuine and Spurious?" In *The Ethnography of Communication: The Legacy of Sapir, Essays in Honor of Harry Hoijer,* edited by Paul V. Kroskrity, pp. 9–53. Los Angeles: Department of Anthropology, University of California, Los Angeles.

Hirschkop, Ken, and David Shepherd, eds. 1989. *Bakhtin and Cultural Theory.* Manchester: Manchester University Press.

Holquist, Michael. 1990. *Dialogism: Bakhtin and His World.* London: Routledge.

Hurston, Zora Neale. 1935. *Mules and Men.* Philadelphia: J. B. Lippincott.

Hymes, Dell H. 1970. "Linguistic Method in Ethnography." In *Method and Theory in Linguistics,* edited by Paul Garvin, pp. 249–325. The Hague: Mouton.

———. 1974. *Foundations in Sociolinguistics: An Ethnographic Approach.* Philadelphia: University of Pennsylvania Press.

———. 1981. *"In Vain I Tried to Tell You": Essays in Native American Ethnopoetics.* Philadelphia: University of Pennsylvania Press.

Irvine, Judith T. 1990. "Registering Affect: Heteroglossia in the Linguistic Expression of Emotion." In *Language and the Politics of Emotion,* edited by Catherine A. Lutz and Lila Abu-Lughod, pp. 126–61. Cambridge: Cambridge University Press.

Ivanov, V. V. 1970. "The Significance of M. M. Bakhtin's Ideas on Sign, Utterance, and Dialogue for Modern Semiotics." In *Semiotics and Structuralism, Readings from the Soviet Union,* edited by Henryk Baran, pp. 310–67. White Plains, N.Y.: International Arts and Sciences Press.

Jakobson, Roman. 1953. "Discussion in Claude Lévi-Strauss, Roman Jakobson, Carl F. Voegelin and Thomas A. Sebeok," Results of the Conference of Anthropologists and Linguists. *International Journal of American Linguistics Memoir* 8:11–21.

———. 1990a. "Langue and Parole: Code and Message." In *On Language,* edited by Linda R. Waugh and Monique Monville-Burston, pp. 80–109. Cambridge, Mass.: Harvard University Press.

———. 1990b. "Shifters, Verbal Categories, and the Russian Verb." In *On Language,* edited by Linda R. Waugh and Monique Monville-Burston, pp. 386–92. Cambridge, Mass.: Harvard University Press.

Karp, Ivan. 1987. "Laughter at Marriage: Subversion in Performance." In *Transformations of African Marriage,* edited by David Parkin and David Nyamwaya, pp. 137–55. Manchester: Manchester University Press.

Kempton, Willet. 1980. "The Rhythmic Basis of Interactional Micro-Synchrony."

In *The Relationship of Verbal and Nonverbal Communication,* edited by Mary Ritchie Key, pp. 67–76. The Hague: Mouton.

Key, Mary Ritchie, ed. 1980. *The Relationship of Verbal and Nonverbal Communication.* The Hague: Mouton.

Kitamura, Koji. 1990. "Interactional Synchrony: A Fundamental Condition for Communication." In *Culture Embodied,* edited by Michael Moerman and Masaichi Nomura, pp. 123–41. Osaka: National Museum of Ethnology.

Krausz, Michael. 1981. "Creating and Becoming." In *The Concept of Creativity in Science and Art,* edited by Denis Dutton and Michael Krausz, pp. 187–200. The Hague: M. Nijhoff.

Kristeva, Julia. 1980. *Desire in Language: A Semiotic Approach to Language and Art.* New York: Columbia University Press.

Kroeber, Alfred L. 1917. "The Superorganic." *American Anthropologist* 19:163–213.

———. 1948. "White's View of Culture." *American Anthropologist* 50:405–15.

Kuipers, Joel. 1990. *Power and Performance: The Creation of Textual Authority in Weyewa Ritual Speech.* Philadelphia: University of Pennsylvania Press.

Langer, Susanne K. 1941. *Philosophy in a New Key.* Cambridge, Mass.: Harvard University Press.

Lavie, Smadar. 1990. *The Poetics of Military Occupation: Mzeina Allegories of Bedouin Identity under Israeli and Egyptian Rule.* Berkeley and Los Angeles: University of California Press.

Layne, Linda L. 1989. "The Dialogics of Tribal Self-Representation in Jordan." *American Ethnologist* 16:24–39.

Levine, Andrew. 1987. "Marxism and Methodological Individualism." *New Left Review* 162:67–84.

Limón, José E. 1989. "Carne, Carnales, and the Carnivalesque: Bakhtinian Bathos, Disorder, and Narratives Discourses." *American Ethnologist* 16:471–86.

Lucy, John A., ed. 1993. *Reflexive Language: Reported Speech and Metapragmatics.* Cambridge: Cambridge University Press.

Lukes, Steven. 1968. "Methodological Individualism Reconsidered." *British Journal of Sociology* 19:119–29.

Luong, Hy Van. 1988. "Discursive Practices and Power Structure: Person-Referring Forms and Sociopolitical Struggles in Colonial Vietnam." *American Ethnologist* 15:239–53.

Mannheim, Bruce. n.d. "Discursive and Presentational Form in Language." Forthcoming in *Through an Andean Kaleidoscope,* edited by Billie Jean Richerson-Isbell.

Margolis, Joseph. 1986. "Emergence." *Philosophical Forum* 17:271–95.

Mayr, Ernst. 1982. *The Growth of Biological Thought: Diversity, Evolution, and Inheritance.* Cambridge, Mass.: Harvard University Press.

———. 1988. *Toward a New Philosophy of Biology: Observations of an Evolutionist.* Cambridge, Mass.: Harvard University Press.

Mead, Margaret. 1939. "Native Languages as Field-Work Tools." *American Anthropologist* 41:189–205.

Meehl, P. E., and Wilfrid Sellars. 1956. "The Concept of Emergence." In *The Foun-*

*dations of Science and the Concepts of Psychology and Psychoanalysis*, edited by Herbert Feigl and Michael Scriven, pp. 239–52. Minnesota Studies in the Philosophy of Science, 1. Minneapolis: University of Minnesota Press.

Moerman, Michael, and Masaichi Nomura, eds. 1990. *Culture Embodied.* Senri Ethnological Studies, 27. Osaka: National Museum of Ethnology.

Morel, Mary-Annick, and Laurent Danon-Boileau, eds. 1992. *La deixis.* Paris: Presses Universitaires de France.

Morson, Gary Saul, ed. 1986. *Bakhtin, Essays and Dialogues on His Work.* Chicago: University of Chicago Press.

Morson, Gary Saul, and Caryl Emerson. 1990. *Mikhail Bakhtin: Creation of a Prosaics.* Stanford: Stanford University Press.

———, eds. 1989. *Rethinking Bakhtin: Extensions and Challenges.* Evanston: Northwestern University Press.

Mühlhäusler, Peter, and Rom Harré, with Anthony Holiday and Michael Freyne. 1990. *Pronouns and People: The Linguistic Construction of Social and Personal Identity.* Oxford: Blackwell.

Ortner, Sherry B. 1989. *High Religion: A Cultural and Political History of Sherpa Buddhism.* Princeton: Princeton University Press.

Page, Hélan E. 1988. "Dialogic Principles of Interactive Learning in the Ethnographic Relationship." *Journal of Anthropological Research* 44:163–81.

Pepper, Stephen C. 1926. "Emergence." *Journal of Philosophy* 23:241–45.

Reichard, Gladys A. 1934. *Spider Woman: A Story of Navajo Weavers and Chanters.* New York: Macmillan.

Ricoeur, Paul. 1976. *Interpretation Theory: Discourse and the Surplus of Meaning.* Fort Worth: Texas Christian University Press.

Rosaldo, Renato. 1989. *Culture and Truth: The Remaking of Social Analysis.* Boston: Beacon Press.

Rose, Dan. 1990. "Living the Ethnographic Life." *Qualitative Research Methods,* vol. 23. Newbury Park: Sage.

Rumsey, Alan. 1990. "Wording, Meaning, and Linguistic Ideology." *American Anthropologist* 92:346–61.

Sacks, Harvey, E. Schegloff, and G. Jefferson. 1974. "A Simplest Systematics for the Organization of Turn-Taking for Conversation." *Language* 50:696–736.

Sapir, Edward. 1915. *Abnormal Types of Speech in Nootka.* Canada Geological Survey, Memoir 62, Anthropological Series, no. 5. Ottawa: Government Printing Bureau.

———. 1917. "Do We Need a 'Superorganic'?" *American Anthropologist* 19:441–47.

———. 1921. *Language.* New York: Harcourt, Brace and Company.

———. 1949a. "Cultural Anthropology and Psychiatry." In *Selected Writings of Edward Sapir,* edited by David G. Mandelbaum, pp. 509–21. Berkeley: University of California Press.

———. 1949b. "Psychiatric and Cultural Pitfalls in the Business of Getting a Living." In *Selected Writings of Edward Sapir,* edited by David G. Mandelbaum, pp. 590–97. Berkeley: University of California Press.

———. 1949c. "The Unconscious Patterning of Behavior in Society." In *Selected*

*Writings of Edward Sapir,* edited by David G. Mandelbaum, pp. 544–59. Berkeley: University of California Press.

Scheflen, Albert E. 1973. *Communicational Structure.* Bloomington: Indiana University Press.

Schieffelin, Edward L. 1985. "Performance and the Cultural Construction of Reality." *American Ethnologist* 12:707–24.

Shotter, John. 1992. "Bakhtin and Billig: Monological versus Dialogical Practices." *American Behavioral Scientist* 36:8–21.

Silverstein, Michael. 1976. "Shifters, Linguistic Categories, and Cultural Description." In *Meaning in Anthropology,* edited by K. Basso and H. Selby, pp. 11–55. Albuquerque: University of New Mexico Press.

———. 1986. "Sapir's Synchronic Linguistics." In *New Perspectives in Language, Culture, and Personality,* edited by William Cowan, Michael K. Foster, and Konrad Koerner, pp. 67–106. Amsterdam: Benjamins.

Spencer, Herbert. 1880. *First Principles.* 4th ed. Philadelphia: McKay.

———. 1893. *The Principles of Sociology.* Vol. 1. New York: Appleton.

Sperber, Dan. 1991. "The Epidemiology of Beliefs." In *The Social Psychological Study of Widespread Beliefs,* edited by Colin Fraser and George Gaskell, pp. 25–43. London: Oxford University Press.

Stallybrass, Peter, and Allon White. 1986. *The Politics and Poetics of Transgression.* London: Methuen.

Steedly, Mary M. 1993. *Hanging without a Rope: Narrative Experience in Colonial and Postcolonial Karoland.* Princeton: Princeton University Press.

Stewart, Susan. 1983. "Shouts on the Street: Bakhtin's Anti-Linguistics." *Critical Inquiry* 10:265–82.

Tedlock, Barbara. 1991. "From Participant Observation to the Observation of Participation: The Emergence of Narrative Ethnography." *Journal of Anthropological Research* 47:69–94.

Tedlock, Dennis. 1979. "The Analogical Tradition and the Emergence of a Dialogical Anthropology." *Journal of Anthropological Research* 35:387–400.

———. 1983. *The Spoken Word and the Work of Interpretation.* Philadelphia: University of Pennsylvania Press.

———. 1990. "From Voice and Ear to Hand and Eye." *Journal of American Folklore* 103:133–56.

———. 1991. "The Speaker of Tales Has More Than One String to Play On." In *Anthropological Poetics,* edited by Ivan Brady, pp. 309–40. Savage, Md.: Rowman and Littlefield.

Thomson, Clive, ed. 1990. *Mikhail Bakhtin and the Epistemology of Discourse.* Amsterdam: Rodopi.

Titunik, I. R. 1984. "Bakhtin and/or Medvedev: Dialogue and/or Doubletalk?" In *Language and Literary Theory, in Honor of Ladislav Matejka,* edited by Benjamin A. Stolz, Irwin R. Titunik, and Lubomír Doležel, pp. 535–64. Ann Arbor: University of Michigan Papers in Slavic Philology.

Todorov, Tzvetan. 1984. *Mikhail Bakhtin: The Dialogical Principle.* Minneapolis: University of Minnesota Press.

Toelken, Barre, and Tacheeni Scott. 1981. "Poetic Retranslation and the 'Pretty Languages' of Yellowman." In *Traditional Literatures of the American Indian: Texts and Interpretations*, edited by Karl Kroeber, pp. 65–116. Lincoln: University of Nebraska Press.

Trawick, Margaret. 1988. "Spirits and Voices in Tamil Songs." *American Ethnologist* 15:193–215.

Tyler, Stephen A. 1987. "On 'Writing-Up/Off' as 'Speaking-For.'" *Journal of Anthropological Research* 43:338–42.

Urban, Greg. 1984. "Speech about Speech in Speech about Action." *Journal of American Folklore* 97:310–28.

———. 1986. "Ceremonial Dialogues in South America." *American Anthropologist* 88:371–86.

———. 1989. "The 'I' of Discourse." In *Semiotics, Self, and Society*, edited by Benjamin Lee and Greg Urban, pp. 27–51. Berlin: Mouton de Gruyter.

Watkins, J. W. N. 1952. "Ideal Types and Historical Explanation." *British Journal for the Philosophy of Science* 3:22–43.

Weiss, Wendy A. 1990. "Challenge to Authority: Bakhtin and Ethnographic Description." *Cultural Anthropology* 5:414–30.

Wertsch, James V. 1985. "The Semiotic Mediation of Mental Life: L. S. Vygotsky and M. M. Bakhtin." In *Semiotic Mediation*, edited by Elizabeth Mertz and Richard J. Parmentier, pp. 50–97. Orlando: Academic.

———. 1991. *Voices of the Mind: A Sociocultural Approach to Mediated Action*. Cambridge, Mass.: Harvard University Press.

White, Leslie A. 1947. "Culturological vs. Psychological Interpretations of Human Behavior." *American Sociological Review* 12:686–98.

Willis, Paul E. 1981. *Learning to Labor: How Working Class Kids Get Working Class Jobs*. New York: Columbia University Press.

Woodbury, Anthony C. 1987. "Rhetorical Structure in a Central Alaskan Yupik Eskimo Traditional Narrative." In *Native American Discourse*, edited by J. Sherzer and A. Woodbury, pp. 176–239. Cambridge: Cambridge University Press.

# ONE

# Dialogic Breakthrough: Catalysis and Synthesis in Life-Changing Dialogue

JOHN ATTINASI AND PAUL FRIEDRICH

## INTRODUCTION: LINGUACULTURE

A basic assumption of this essay is that the many sounds and meanings of what we call "language and culture" belong to a single universe. It is one universe of analysis, and of the discourse and actions of participants. We are talking about a domain of experience that intermingles and fuses three things. First, the vocabulary, words, idioms, and short formulas that work as "conversational prefabs," and also as coordinators for a worldview. Second, the semantic aspects of grammar, which is to say the full meanings of such things as "tense" and "mood" — for example, the nuances of "past" or the subjunctive of "fear" — as these overlap with other cultural meanings. Third, the verbal aspects of culture, which are more readily labeled or discussed than areas that are relatively free of language. We do not agree with Wittgenstein that the limits of one's language coincide with the limits of one's mind.

These sets of language and culture are seen as underlying mental processes while, at another level, they are constantly being used and (re)created by actual people on the ground. In any case, the universe of vocabulary, grammatical semantics, and verbal culture can be called "linguaculture"; to take two concrete examples, Iroquois linguaculture or southern rural Twin State linguaculture. One reason for coining this word is to transcend the decades-long balancing act between "language *and* culture," "language *in* culture," and other phrasings (as in Hoijer 1954); "culture in language" would be useful as well. The linguacultural phenomena in question constitute the common ground of much of our ongoing research. What are some of the main traits and varieties of this linguaculture, in light of the problem before us?

## FIVE FEATURES OF DIALOGUE À DEUX

Within any linguaculture we find a boundless interplay of dialect styles and individual voices. Of such polyphony (Bakhtin 1981: 259) there are many fascinating examples: the literal polyphony of certain conversational styles, especially in the Caribbean, in "New York Jewish" culture, and in other cultures where it is often appropriate for two or more participants in a conversation to articulate their ideas at the same time, or to interrupt each other frequently as a way, among other things, of reaffirming emotional solidarity (Tannen 1981). A quite different polyphony pervades the ambiguity of most texts, notably such elaborately orchestrated literary works as the Old Testament and the novels of Proust, which operate on many interacting symbolic levels.

Within these and other kinds of polyphony we think that an exceptional status accrues to the obvious element of dialogue. By this we do not have in mind metaphorical uses and misuses, as when Lévi-Strauss says that anthropology is "a dialogue between man and man," nor even the theoretically viable title of this collection, "the dialogic emergence of culture." What we refer to is the actual exchange and sharing of words and sentences in a natural language. This is theoretically in tune with Peirce scholars and with Peirce himself, who wrote, "We must not begin by talking of pure ideas . . . but must begin with men and their conversations" (cited in Singer 1984: 74). But we are cutting even narrower and beginning with conversations between two human beings in a small space, including such limiting cases as the Rorschach interview, Socrates' ironic pedantries, talk with a friend and, of course, between anthropological field-worker and field-worked native consultant. Or, as Lyons puts it more precisely, dialogue or "the canonical situation of utterance . . . involves one-one, or one-many, signalling in the phonic medium along the vocal auditory channel, with all the participants present in the same actual situation able to see one another and to perceive the associated non-vocal paralinguistic features of their utterances and each assuming the role of sender and receiver in turn" (Lyons 1977, 2:637). Except that we are dealing only with "one-one." In this natural albeit culture-bound sense, let's ask just what differentiates dialogue both from the all-encompassing polyphony of the surrounding linguaculture and from the universe of the so-called monologue, which is always a dialogue with an imagined other (Singer 1984: 80).

Dialogue, in the sense of Two-Folk-Speak, seems to be informed by at least five interrelated features which describe something real and also have heuristic value. First, tête-à-tête dialogue involves language and the use of language that is in several senses primal; that is, it includes exclamations, gasps, audible breathing, visible movements of the lips, tongue movement, and variations in pitch, tempo, and dynamics that bespeak the body and often belie or simply bypass reason and logic (Goffman 1978). Thus, by the term *language* we include speech, idiosyncratic behavior, and all similar overt symbols with their deep sources in reason, emotions, and motivations. These things are interconnected with or partly included by linguaculture, although not identifiable with it.

Second, dialogue in the concrete sense used here can be motivated by a partly physical or corporeal attraction or empathy that promotes agreement and harmony. But dialogue can also be activated by antipathy and agonistic feelings, and veer toward hatred and aversion, toward tearing-down and polarizing. All human relations are to some extent ambivalent, and there has to be some differentiation of the parties to the dialogue as well as identification; positive and negative forces are always present; both have creative as well as destructive functions; both can generate synthesis and transcendence or chaos and destruction. (In the same way, all expressions in language are to some extent ambiguous.) From another angle, a given dialogue is always, potentially, headed toward harmony or order, and, potentially, toward disorder or chaos; chaos always lurks beneath order, and vice versa. But whether the feelings are plus or minus, sympathetic or antipathetic, ordered or chaotic, the tête-à-tête, the Two-Folk-Speak, is opposed fundamentally to the narcissistic and the egoneurotic. It is fundamentally different from inner or interior speech (of which the only valid example may be the dream, or at least some dreams).

Third, since two interlocutors are never completely equal and since they are often politically nonequal, the sort of dialogue we are adumbrating often involves a fundamental change in power, with one party becoming more empowered or at least the power structure between the two changing deeply. That is one dimension of the point made below, that such dialogues are analogues of parent-child or sibling relations. Anthropological dialogue invariably involves profound differences in power or at least individuals coming to each other from profoundly different power universes, hence politics is always present.

Fourth, while there is not too much typicality in the dyadic, tête-à-tête sort of dialogue, it is obviously congruent with a large set of venues, some of which have been alluded to: the meal à deux, bridges, intersections, secluded beaches, and other places where the rest of humanity is absent, or flowing by indifferently. On the other hand, the peculiar intensity of the phenomenon in question make it possible for it to happen despite the physical milieu—just as poems, when they must, get written in the most unlikely places.

Fifth, in terms of Dwyer's (1977) geometrical figure of two centers, dialogue brings the edges of the two interlocutors into contiguity and then into partial mingling and fusion. Or, to switch metaphors, dialogue can result in partial *communis* or 'emotional commonality'. Obviously, the two centers can never coincide; if they seem to then the dialogue has ceased to be dialogue and has become the mutual narcissism just referred to, a *folie-à-deux* 'an illusory communitas'; like that experienced by the primate, raised in the home of a physical anthropologist, which for a brief but blissful time imagines that it belongs to the same species as its foster parents. But the impossibility of coincident scope does not greatly weaken the significance of partial overlap and sharing. Dialogue is thus essentially or at least typically liminal, involving a "betwixt and between" (Turner 1967: 76–79).

Dialogue is liminal in a second way as well: it creates a special, semi-private space and time shared by the two interlocutors to the partial exclusion of the rest of the world. Because of these two kinds of liminality, the act of dialogue, like so many liminal phenomena, can change and even transmute the participants, can be the catalyst of a relation that may endure for a lifetime or, perhaps more often, the quietus to a relation that has endured too long (Paul Simon's *Dangling Conversation:* "a superficial smile. . . . The borders of our lives"). Either of these, the cementing or the rupture, instances what we call "dialogic breakthrough" (or "pronominal breakthrough," as in Friedrich 1979: 95). Such breakthrough is allied to cure in psychotherapy, to religious conversion, and sudden insight in science.

Let us sum up the discussion to this point. Dialogue, unlike discourse in general, is (1) partly corporeal; (2) driven and energized by shades and blends of emotional affinity and of antagonistic feelings; (3) involves some changes in political empowerment; (4) lacks strong typicality but does tend to take place in certain likely venues, which interact with the sometimes exclusive psychological space around the interlocutors; (5) is a matter of boundaries and partial merger, a transient intercommunication between two centers that leads to some overlap or fusion, or toward the destruction of such qualities.

## DIALOGIC BREAKTHROUGH
## IN ANTHROPOLOGICAL FIELDWORK

The above abstract characterization can be illustrated by the prototypical anthropological situation: fieldwork. To get reasonably full data one needs to initiate, entertain, and draw on many kinds of dialogue. At the level of the system of a culture, language, or linguaculture, the ethnographer talks with individuals, some of whom are typical or representative, and with specialists in various fields of endeavor. He or she also takes an active part, both verbally and physically, in many if not most of the games, work routines, social networks, and the like. At the level of behavior, the ethnographer needs to collect massive census and other quantitative data, to study and map distributions and processes of various kinds, and eventually achieve a concrete-behavioral, techno-economic, and microstatistical grasp of the local scene. Such a grasp is a sine qua non of situational competence in the culture of a community. For example, your conversation with a large fraction of the normal adult working-class male population of the United States will break down if you turn out to be ignorant of things like fishing jigs, catalytic converters, or slotbacks and Texas Leaguers, that is, with certain sports (as practiced professionally), mechanics (particularly automobile mechanics), and "huntin-n-fishin." (It is significant that almost no social or linguistic anthropologists—including self-consciously populist ones—are fully conversant with all three of these universes of discourse.) At a more personal level, the anthropologist collects texts, through dialogue, which can serve for biographies, psychological characterizations, and so forth. On a yet more personal level, the anthropologist collects, internalizes, or variously experiences imagined or purely potential information, such as the dreams, daydreams, speculation, slander, gossip, lies of all kinds, and paranoid fantasies that form part of the content and sometimes the gist of many dialogues. Indeed, the complexity and validity of the anthropologist's description and interpretation of a linguaculture depend on the varieties of dialogue in which s/he is prepared and willing to engage—in other words, on the depth and scope of his/her dialogic eclecticism.

The diversity of dialogue in versatile and rich, "good" (as opposed to mechanical, model-dependent) fieldwork highlights our contention about dialogic values, about what is really going on when we enter a culture to participate in it, ask it questions, and find out what *its* questions are. Among the conventional values or outputs of such fieldwork, we might begin with the inventory of rituals or with the texts of myths or with the transcripts of conversations about gossip or hog raising. Written texts and magnetic tapes of such things can become part of an ethnography or serve as the raw materials for metaethnography.

The kindred problems of collecting diverse information and mastering diverse universes of discourse have tended to obscure a fascinating and fundamental flaw in the most prevalent models of the speech or communicative event (which originate in Bühler 1934). These models make the speaker and hearer, the so-called addresser and addressee, analytically coordinate with such relatively shallow and limited—if not trivial—variables as the topic of conversation or the particular text of a particular message. The flaw is revealed and reflected in the many pragmatic or sociolinguistic analyses that typically say nothing at all about the addressers and addressees beyond naming them: Mr. Smith and Sr. Gómez. But one or even several dialogues between Smith and Gómez are but brief, puny, transient instances or manifestations of something vastly larger and more significant. This larger significance, the phenomenological center of (the) dialogue, occurs in the meeting of the imaginations (or minds, personalities, ideas, and feelings) of the speakers or interlocutors themselves—for example, a field-worker and a native speaker. The interaction and transitory symbiosis between these imaginations is the core of the dialogic speech event. These neurologically, psychologically, and culturally unique imaginations are infinitely more complex and interesting than is the evidence for them that is provided by a transcript of the words spoken over a few minutes or even many hours. To focus on the words in the text to the practical exclusion of the imaginations that they partially reflect is to promote a pragmatism that is a pseudopragmatism, an anti-Peircian pragmatism that has been called "mindless" but that actually is not so because it does turn out to promote a mind—that of the brilliant, analyzing, explicating anthropologist.

The ultimate emergence of shared feelings, understandings, and intuitions and the corresponding semantic weightings of words and phrases (that is, a sort of minimal linguaculture) between the field-worker and the native consultant is a psychologically special, usually asymmetrical, and essentially limiting case of the generic phenomenon of dialogue that concerns us here. This generic dialogue within the de facto polyphony and multidialectalism of any given culture ranges along a gradient between two experiences that are fundamentally different from each other.

Of less concern to us is the relatively repetitious, formulaic, routine, even banal and vacuous sort of dialogue that makes up the great majority of conversations: two mechanics discussing a broken catalytic converter, for instance, or two professors of anthropology discussing the departmental foreign language requirement. Many of these routine dialogues, on the other hand, while mainly repetitious, do have a degree of originality and emotional effectiveness (Schegloff 1986). These ordinary dialogues serve mainly to maintain a status quo in friendships, families, and neighborhoods. Culture emerges from such dialogues only as a matter of statistical drift, which is not at issue here, despite its importance. Such dialogues shade through many degrees along many dimensions into the essentially intimate and tense sorts of dialogue which are the concern of this essay.

## FIVE STAGES OF DIALOGIC BREAKTHROUGH

The kind of dialogue that concerns us here is a catalyst of change between "dialoguing imaginations." Let us start with an example. After a field-worker has reached the point of reasonable fluency in the language and knows the basic patterns and processes, she or he is operating with vague, largely unformulated hypotheses of how the linguaculture works. Then come one or more (sometimes many) memorable dialogues that approximate conversion experiences, in which a fundamental realignment and reevaluation takes place. The steps in these life-changing dialogues seem to be five in number:

1. There are minutes or hours or even years of convergence in the cognition, emotions, and motivation of the two parties, a psychological affinity that may be narrowly intellectual (or narrowly emotional) or comprehensive.

2. A point or span of time, beginning with some sort of initial turbulence and resulting in some sort of cathexis, usually over some theme or issue, or a word, or an intellectual problem, from the social to the mathematical, that may be extremely complex (in fact, the shared concentration on such a problem partly accounts for the breakthrough effect).

3. This is followed by a rapid, sometimes split-second, realignment of myriad psychological values in the minds of the interlocutors, or by a more drawn-out and gradual interlocking—a sort of shift to a new state in which there is greater coordination or calibration between the two minds.

4. The new alignment is solidified and reinforced through further dialogue and additional experience; a new point of view is synthesized.

5. The dialogue continues to exert its force through memory or repeated, even habituated, recall and reinterpretation because, depending on the individual or culture, the realignment may be on the spot (sudden insight) or not be realized at all until later and then grow through the months or years (e.g., through flashbacks). While some realization does occur at the time it would be a fallacy of rationalism to claim that there was full understanding. Similarly, some individuals who are relatively open or mature may realize more fully at the time what is happening, whereas a more inhibited or complex person may totally repress the significance at

the outset. The onset or growth of understanding also depends heavily on the subject matter: a problem in science, where there is a shared, explicit notation, or in "relationships," where there is all too much verbalization, may be (over) realized at the time the dialogue is taking place, whereas other themes or subjects, for which formulas are lacking, may entail a long series of reflective realizations. In other words, dialogues, including life-changing ones, are partly governed by culture and are part of the systems of ritual and spontaneity in terms of which the individual lives. Unfortunately, they often also alienate the native consultant from his or her culture, just as they often alienate the anthropologist from his or her native culture.

## THREE DIALOGUES: TARÁSCAN, MAYAN, RUSSIAN

While the reader may justifiably be leaping to the conclusion that the dialogues in question primarily involve Freudian or Jungian factors, let it be countered right off that the issues may be formally abstract perceptual or cognitive dynamics. For example, Friedrich's fieldwork has in part concerned the Taráscan language of Mexico, and, in particular, the general structure of the sound system and the nature of variation between dialects in Taráscan phonology. What follows is an abridged quotation from *A Taráscan Phonology:*

The lack of phonetic consistency in one's interlocutors, coupled with certain features in many idiolects . . . gradually became a source of considerable difficulty in inferring the phonology, and of some personal anxiety as well.

It was with some relief, after nine months in and out of . . . the Taráscan area . . . that I welcomed the opportunity to interview two recognized storytellers from Cocucho . . . a (notoriously ethnocentric) town high on the flank of a mountain of the same name . . . deep in the *Meseta Tarasca* (Taráscan highlands). . . . One of the two visitors was particularly well-known . . . because he had won a New Years Day story-telling contest several years earlier. . . . He had never lived outside Cocucho, had had only two years of schooling there, and was not too fluent in Spanish.

From the first it was clear to me that this man . . . stood in a very sensitive relation to Taráscan; he tended, for example, to correct my placement of the dorsovelar nasal and the retroflex r and ṣ, and my intonation, and to point out various syntactic ineptitudes. [Indeed, it was only a few seconds — maybe a minute — into our first conversation in the presence of his hosts that he corrected my pronunciation in a peculiarly irritating and yet also inviting way.]

On his second visit to San José, a three-day sojourn, I walked him [in a pouring rain] down [the four miles of] the almost impassably muddy road to . . . the county seat . . . and then went to Zamora, where we had a memorable lunch and lunchtime conversation in a dirty restaurant while watching a cat torment a large, pathetic rat. At the termination of the meal, and of the rat, I translated a final line from a play by Pisarev: "What's a game for the cat, is tears to the rat." This stirred up Feliciano. In Zamora that afternoon we reviewed my entire list of Taráscan roots, checking, in particular, the placement of the dorsovelar nasal and the retroflexion of *r* and *ṣ*. Thereafter the people in San José affirmed that I spoke Taráscan like someone from Cocucho, and this was correct because I had been "converted."

Personal empathy with this unusual native speaker—a natural grammarian—became synthesized with the process of an illuminating re-evaluation of an abstract system—leading to a breakthrough to a point of view that guided my many subsequent months of analysis. (Friedrich 1975: 15-17)

Let's take a second fieldwork example from Mexico. The life-changing dialogue in anthropological fieldwork can begin as a structural insight into grammar, but widen ultimately into a lifelong decision. In exploring the Chol Mayan emphatic particles *che* and *ku,* Attinasi realized that he was seen as more fluent to the degree that he mastered the phatic partial repetitions that end with either particle and create a bond of attention, understanding, and consensus between interlocutors. During one particular conversation with Sebastián Pérez (S.P.) in this style, the content began to turn to the relationships between Ladinos (outsiders who speak Spanish) and the Chol. Being both an outsider and an aspiring Chol speaker seeking nativelike competence, Attinasi (J.A.) was indirectly a topic. The dialogue covered economic and friendship associations, and at one point Sebastián said, "When they come to Chiapas to buy our coffee at cheap prices or sell us something expensive, the *kashlan* [from 'Castillians'] call us brother, but do not have the time even to say '*che-ku-yi.*'"

The dialogue continued as follows:

S.P.: More and more the *kashlan* come to our land.
J.A.: They come, *ku.*
S.P.: *Che,* more and more.
J.A.: *Che-ku.*
S.P.: *Che-ku-yi.* [They do. They sure do.]
S.P.: And they want to buy from us cheap.
J.A.: *Che* to buy.
S.P.: They turn around and sell their goods at high prices—pure exploitation.
J.A.: Pure, *ku.*
S.P.: *Che-ku-yi.*
J.A.: *Che-ku.* [Pure and simple. Yes it is. Really.]
S.P.: They say they're going to work to build for the pueblo, but the work doesn't appear. They even speak our language. They call us brother and ask for our vote. They claim they're part of us but they don't even take the time to *che-ku-yi.*

J.A.: *Che-ech.*
S.P.: *Che-chi.* [So it is. It is so. Just so.]
S.P.: The campesino suffers and the *kashlan* is doing well, not just here but all over the pueblos, because they are exploiting us.
J.A.: *Che-ku-yi.*
S.P.: *Che-ku.* [It is so. It is.]
S.P.: But the campesino has a patient heart. We know the land; we will not die of hunger, we know how to work the land to eat.
J.A.: Work the land, *ku.*
S.P.: Work, *che.*
J.A.: The land, *ku.*
S.P.: *Che-ku-yi.*
J.A.: *Che-chi.*
S.P.: They have money, but they can't eat their money.
J.A.: Cannot, *che.*
S.P.: Cannot, *ku.*
J.A.: *Che,* not at all.
S.P.: Campesinos are the richness of the land. They have patient hearts.
J.A.: Patient, *ku.*
S.P.: Patient, *che.*
J.A.: *Che-ku-yi.*
S.P.: *Che-chi.*
J.A.: *Che-ech.*
S.P.: *Che-ku,* brother.
J.A.: *Che-ku.*

For the field-worker, the decision to continue to engage in a committed science sprang from that dialogue: Phatic brotherhood implied interactions that would never take any commodity, including language data, without a mutually empowering, or at least beneficial, outcome. All this, not simply from a grammatical set that has no lexical reference but from a dialogue that included *che* and *ku* at syntactic and pragmatic, linguistic and metalinguistic levels.

Let us take a third and more accessible example from world literature: Tolstoy's *War and Peace.* Two close friends, Pierre and Prince Andrew, both at troubled times in their lives, have a long conversation at a synergistic confluence of liminal symbolism: a ferry between the banks of a wide river at sundown. This conversation changes both interlocutors forever, nudging them into a newer and more meaningful philosophy. The fact that both are soul-searchers only intensifies the force of the example. But let's let Tolstoy speak:

> But Pierre and Andrew, to the astonishment of the footmen, coachmen, and ferrymen, still stood on the raft and talked.
>
> "If there is a God and future life, there is truth and good, and man's highest happiness consists in striving to attain them. We must live, we must

love, and we must believe that we live not only today on this scrap of earth, but have lived and shall live forever, there, in the whole," said Pierre, and he pointed to the sky.

Prince Andrew stood leaning on the railing of the raft listening to Pierre and he gazed with his eyes fixed on the red reflection of the sun gleaming on the blue waters. There was perfect stillness. Pierre became silent. The raft had long since stopped and only the waves of the current beat softly against it below. Prince Andrew felt as if the sound of the waves kept up a refrain to Pierre's words, whispering: "It is true, believe it."

He sighed, and glanced with a radiant, childlike, tender look at Pierre's face, flushed and rapturous, yet shy before his superior friend.

"Yes, if it were only so!" said Prince Andrew. "However, it is time to get on," he added, and, stepping off the raft, he looked up at the sky to which Pierre had pointed, and for the first time since Austerlitz saw that high, everlasting sky he had seen while lying on that battlefield; and something that had long been slumbering, something that was best within him, suddenly awoke, joyful and youthful, in his soul. It vanished as soon as he returned to the customary conditions of his life, but he knew that this feeling which he did not know how to develop existed within him. His meeting with Pierre formed an epoch in Prince Andrew's life. Though outwardly he continued to live in the same old way, inwardly he began a new life. (Tolstoy 1966: 422–23)

This and the related sorts of dialogue which the great page above serves to distill, most usually and normally take place in the context of relationships sociologists call primary and that we could call primordial or intimate. Such dialogue resonates with the deep structural affinities, conflicts, and identifications of the nuclear family and other, similar groups: friends and siblings, brothers and their analogues, parent and child and their analogues, healer and patient and healer, teacher and student.

It is a curious fact that, of all the professions, entry into linguistics seems to involve the most conversion conversations: The instance that is probably best known to anthropologists is of the young Edward Sapir, fresh from the then Germanic philology, deciding after a dialogue with Franz Boas that he had "everything to learn about language" and that he would do so under the tutelage of his interlocutor (Mandelbaum 1949: vii). Such dialogues and the resultant dependencies, on the other hand, not infrequently suffer from maudlin, authoritarian, and otherwise obnoxious ingredients. But in all the types cited above the analogy to a primal familial situation creates psychic energies that can be enormously constructive.

## PARADOXICAL CIRCUMSTANCES IN SOUTH DAKOTA

Life-changing dialogues may take place under a variety of paradoxical circumstances. In one case it is between total strangers of markedly different social class who hardly see each other and never meet again. Think, for example, of the nocturnal reminiscences and confessions of a driver to a hitchhiker he is taking from Mobile, Alabama, to New Orleans. Or the dialogue may not be participated in at all actively, but overheard involuntarily, as when you learn that your neighbors on the other side of the wall love each other or hate each other; such insights are not all that infrequent in fieldwork, given the closeness of the quarters in many sleeping arrangements.

An extraordinary example of how life is changed through an accidentally overheard dialogue occurs in *Giants in the Earth*, of which we cite a few excerpts below (the full passage merits meticulous sociolinguistic analysis, preferably of the Norwegian original). It was chosen not only because Rölvaag's genius illuminates the entire issue here but also because of the obvious contrasts and complementarities with the selection from Tolstoy above. Notice, in each case, for example, the concluding shift to (lyrical) monologue, as actually happens in real life often enough.

The leading female protagonist, Beret, has gradually been driven half insane by the blizzards, cold spells, droughts, plagues of locusts, and other dimensions of homesteading in a "soddy" in the "utter desolation" of the then treeless vastnesses of eastern South Dakota. One horrifyingly frequent response of a pioneer woman at this point was to kill her children together with herself. Apprehensive, Beret's husband's best friend, who is a moral as well as a physical giant, pays a visit to him one day, not aware that Beret is an unintended eavesdropper on the other side of a wall. He offers to adopt the new baby boy:

> "There are so many things we don't comprehend. . . . I certainly ought to know Beret . . ."
>
> . . . "I doubt that very much," interrupted Per Hansa, "though you are an observing man. I have lived with her all these years, yet I confess that I don't know her. . . . She is a better soul than I have ever met. . . . The finest castle on earth I was going to build her—and here we are still living in a mole's hole. . . . But this I've decided, that she shall keep the baby—though I thank you for the offer."
>
> Beret listened no more; she walked away in a dream of happiness; she did not know where she was going or what she did. In the southern sky floated transparent little clouds; rainbow ribbons hung down from them. She saw the rainbow's glow; her face was transfigured; she walked on in ecstasy. . . . "Are there signs for us in the sky? . . . That is the Glory of the Lord now. See! . . . The whole heavens are full of it! . . . There . . . and there again . . . everywhere!" (Rölvaag 1929: 416–17)

So Beret kept her little boy, Peder Victorius, and, through knowledge of her husband's faith in her, she was able to regain her sanity.

Quite different dialogues were overheard many decades later in 1987 by Friedrich while breakfasting in a truckers' café on the western edge of Madison, South Dakota, within sight of a reconstructed "Prairie Village" and not far north from where the real-life models of Per Hansa and his doughty friend had eventually watered "the great plain with the blood of Christian men." Directly in front of Friedrich, in a booth, sat a gaunt, work-worn farmer of about fifty, grinning well nigh sheepishly while he nibbled at a cinnamon roll and listened to a paunchy, red-shirted banker (or similar creditor) say, "I'm not going to tell you whether or how to raise corn and soy beans," and the like. To Friedrich's right, at the same counter, sat three men, one an ex-farmer and dealer in spare parts, the other two middle-aged Norwegian-American family farmers. The three drifted into a complicated discussion of corn prices, various machine parts (not including catalytic converters), and ways to continue to block the big corporations from controlling more land through measures like the "corporation exclusion act" (pioneered by South Dakota in 1974). By the time the two conversations had ended after about fifty minutes and all the parties had exited, the unintending, double-timing, now mind-boggled listener, who had been about to give up field-working the "midwestern farm crisis," went back to his job with renewed resolve. Many life-changing dialogues in anthropology involve finding or selecting a good field site or a "key informant," or a decision to leave the field or at least to move on within it.

Overheard dialogues such as the above have a unique truth value in that they are unmonitored, without adjustment to the anthropological inquirer. (On his midwestern trips, Friedrich, suitably attired, was usually taken for a hunter, trucker, or the like.) Overheard dialogues solve the problem mentioned above of the paucity of unmonitored texts (granted that it is usually impossible to record them on the spot).

The distinctive thing about this gamut of life-changing dialogues is that they catalyze or somehow create a realignment or a reinforcement that is fundamental in the point of view, even the depths of the imagination of at least one of the interlocutors. Almost always it is just one who is profoundly changed, magnifying the personal aspect of the experience. Thus solitary and lyrical qualities characterize a life-change which began in dialogue.

## DIALOGUE AND THE LYRIC MODE

The experience we're driving at — which might also be called primary dialogue — can be illuminated from another standpoint — that of Bakhtin. This theorist of language, especially the language of sociolinguistics and cultural poetics, helped to clarify the difference between two fundamen-

tally different kinds of dialogue. The first consists of the ordinary polyphonic universe of language in society, with its myriad, interdependent
voices, styles, and dialects, which we have already discussed and which
could be further illustrated ad infinitum from novels and plays as well as
ethnographies and biographies.

The second kind of dialogic language experience, about which Bakhtin
says little, is the highly marked, relatively monophonic language of the
song or the poem, which, in many cultures, comes at you out of silence;
we hasten to add that this silence is metaphorical, since potential or hypothetical dialogue is always an undercurrent. In many cultures, of course,
such as all Eskimo ones, the song or poem or song-poem, while composed
in isolation, is usually recited to a group, often as part of a ritual event.

What Bakhtin and others of his cast of thought have neglected is what
we have been calling life-changing dialogue, a language experience that
occupies an interstitial ground between his two fundamental and apparently antithetical spheres of language. In this life-changing dialogue, the
necessary liminality and alienation of the individual gets connected with
the reality and the metaphorical extensions of the social field: you feel
the levels of discourse weaving and pulling together. There is both a play
of dialect and related intimations of sociolinguistic complexity, and, on
the other hand, the full intensity of the lyrical mode. The lyric within
the dialogic is brought to the surface, or dialogized, and at the same
time the polyphonic is concretized, condensed, and, as it were, lyricized.
The dialogic-polyphonic is synthesized with the monologic-lyric; life-
changing dialogues often are "found poems." It is the power to represent
this which characterizes many of the dialogic breakthroughs in many of
the life-changing dialogues in Bakhtin's favorite writer, Dostoevsky.

These are not simple correlations; they aren't even correlations. There
is, it is true, some connection between the verbally formulaic and the situationally routine, and, on the other hand, between the verbally innovative
and the situationally extraordinary. But it is also true that the situationally extraordinary, because of personal factors such as anxiety, may veer
into the maximally formulaic: the clichés of stress. Moreover, the formulaic at the phrase and clause level may be combined with great creativity
in conversation (Tannen 1987)—and, for that matter, in T'ang poetry and
in Homer! All these kinds of discourse, rather than being fundamentally
different, involve different balances and combinations of similar or identical underlying modes and tensions that are present in talk, just as we say,
not that signs are indexical or symbolic, but that the underlying modes of
indexicality and symbolism are combined in actual signs.

While dialogic breakthrough as characterized here would seem to be diametrically opposed to the relation between speaker and audience in the media, the two situations differ only in degree. At one extreme there sound the impersonal or at least unidentified voices of the weatherman and the commercial advertiser, but, at the other end, whatever it is that transpires between Garrison Keillor and many individuals in his audience is emotionally in the same ring as the "life-changing dialogue." Many of Keillor's so-called monologues on "The Prairie Home Companion" radio show have in fact been life-changing dialogues for thousands and perhaps tens of thousands in his audience. Processes of deep personal identification are working here, where the phonics of voice are, through the channel of radio, both artificially isolated and incredibly powerful and persuasive. Speaking more generally, dialogic breakthrough involves enormous numbers of combinations of the variables in the speech act that have been made familiar through the theorizing of Bühler (1934), Jakobson (1960), Hymes (1974), and many others: addresser, addressee, message, code, channel, context, and so forth.

## LIFE-CHANGING DIALOGUE IN SOCIAL CHANGE

Let us turn from these extreme examples to the role of life-changing dialogue in the linguaculture and linguacultural change of everyone, because in a changing world—and it has always been in flux—to engage in such life-changing dialogue is part of being human. This is partly because the dialogic process and language itself and culture itself are a complex blend of realities that are emotional and motivational in addition to the more familiar cognitive and perceptual. This psychology of linguaculture, or linguacultural psychology, is not shared and transmitted for the most part at the national and state level, but in dialogue between friends, fellow workers, relatives, and the like. The way such dialogues interconnect varies but the dialogues are a crucial part of the processes of change. There is some evidence that when a linguaculture shifts structurally—to a different religion, political ideology, or even a foreign language—it does so mainly, perhaps, through bits of information and statistical drift reflected in or created by the mass media. But the change also occurs as the result of thousands of life-changing dialogues that call into play the affective and corporeal energies of the participants in the history of their times. Here, once again, the realistic novel and play may give us more insight and raw information than social science, partly because they realistically and persuasively report what speakers would think as well as what they would say when dialoguing with each other (Fabian 1979). One virtue of *The Quiet Don* is that, in its depiction of the revolution and the civil war among the

Don Cossaks, it includes some of these mind-changing conversations between ordinary individuals: between urban workers and Cossak farmers, between rich and landless Cossaks, between White and Red Cossaks.

What do we actually know in terms of explicit social science about such dialogue? To start with a negative case, psychological analysis and therapy, both Freudian and Jungian, specifically sets itself the task of changing life through dialogue (often something verging on a monologue which is carefully attended to), but the concern is with lives and therapy, with a process that inducts the person being analyzed into an ideologically formed consciousness of one of the natures of dialogue. The psychoanalytical dialogue provides an arena for a quasi-spontaneous process which is often disrupted or submerged in everyday life. Its concern is thus not mainly or even very frequently with the nature of dialogue, to say nothing of life-changing dialogue in the full context of linguaculture. On the other hand, to turn to a more positive case, many of the data and ideas advanced above could be fit, variously, into the framework of phenomenology, ethnomethodology, Zen studies, or gestalt psychology. In fact, if one could assemble—or better, experience—a considerable number of such dialogues from one culture during a field trip, it would certainly be worthwhile to explore them in maximum qualitative depth—the crannies of conversations working as some sort of dialogic analogue to the nooks and crannies and interstices in the cellars, rooms, and garrets in Bachelard's (1969) tours-de-force of phenomenological practice.

## THE CHALLENGE OF LIFE-CHANGING DIALOGUE

Life-changing dialogue and related kinds of dialogue in socially or politically charged situations have been explored courageously by Kevin Dwyer (1982) and in some of Oscar Lewis's work (1959). These explorations antagonized various fastidious or paranoid individuals in the anthropology establishment, (1) partly because dialogical anthropology in its entanglement with dialetical anthropology is obviously threatening in some ways, and (2) partly because these pioneers, or some of them, moved into zones that were marginal, illegal, risky, or hard to study, to describe, or to measure methodically. The variegated fortunes of Lewis suggest that dialogical data ipso facto and dialogical anthropology in a more inclusive sense have powerful, built-in tendencies to veer into socially and politically sensitive, problematic, and explosive territories even while they often veer away from anthropology in most of its purposes.

One reason for the general ignorance of the cultural side of life-changing dialogue is that such dialogues must arise spontaneously amid all the predictability and unpredictability of real life in streets and houses;

they cannot be programmed or prefabricated. It is the acute difficulty of assembling sets of full data or of making lots of precise measurements that make it so hard to deal scientifically with the onset of dialogic turbulence; how much harder will it be to account for the emergence of new orders and new *coherences* in points of view in the individual or the group? The problem is intensified when, as in this essay, we deal from a universal point of view as well as, for example, Taráscan or Chol indigenous culture or Russian aristocratic culture. The facts and problems of life-changing dialogue question the limits of all conventional social science and suggest new standards and goals for anthropology—particularly poetic, psychological, and political anthropology.

### DIALOGUES IN ETHNOGRAPHY, BIOGRAPHY, AND HISTORIOGRAPHY

Dialogues, to say nothing of intimate or primal ones, are not found in many ethnographies, and some ethnographies, as Tedlock has correctly observed, contain only a few words uttered by native speakers (Tedlock 1983: 321–39). This is hardly surprising, since our earlier models and strategies for research—linguistic, social anthropological, sociological, historical— stressed texts, social behavior patterns, historical events and processes, and macrotheory, and there was little or no room for Two-Folk-Speak. Yet dialogic material of various kinds is scattered about in the anthropological literature, and we have the brilliant work of Griaule (1965), Haviland (1977), and, recently, of Behar (1993), Abu-Lughod (1993), and others. Empirical analysis of dialogue is feasible, and life-changing dialogues can become evidence because of the fact that life-changing dialogues can be recalled, sometimes almost verbatim, just as life-changing dreams can be recalled indefinitely—can become part of one's permanent consciousness. Another good source for such dialogues, as noted above, is the often highly realistic exchanges found in films, in novels, and, perhaps above all, in the theater; realistic, life-changing dialogue is often the crux of drama. Even when such literary data are not literally realistic in terms of wording, repetition, hesitation, and pace, the verbal artist's attempt at realistic construction can always give us valuable new ideas. All in all, life-changing dialogue is a peculiarly sensitive and revealing phenomenon that could well become a subfield of the historical, oral historical, poetic, political, and psychological anthropology to which we are variously and differentially committed. Or a field of its own (with, we hope, adequate standards for relating dialogue data and theory to the cultural values, the political economy, and other fields or systems). The immediate issue, however, is not to create or even speculate about a systematic, empirical field of study, but to bring the phenomenon of life-changing dialogue to the working consciousness of anthropologists and perhaps other social scientists.

We do not know if the simple idea of life-changing dialogue is a cross-cultural universal. On the one hand, we have been told that it is nearly or practically absent in areas such as those alluded to at the outset, where people are almost always in groups, submerged in a constant flux of talk and other noise. Even in the vast expanses where the modern European languages are now native and where the simple idea seems natural enough, we do not find conventional words or idioms to hand; our "life-changing dialogue" is a neologism. Nevertheless, it is difficult for us to imagine that the simple idea is totally absent in any society. Even without prefabricated labels, it comes as a natural conceptual category in the linguacultures of which we have personal experience and/or some knowledge through study: European (e.g., English, French, Russian), American (including, for example, the Hispanic and Greek communities), Israeli, Mayan and Taráscan (and many other American Indian cultures, not excluding the Yaqui), Japanese, East Indian, and, perhaps most of all, Chinese (where, for example, in T'ang times it plays a crucial role of which poets were particularly aware). As a literary model the idea is widely spread in the Orient, in Buddhism, and in the West, as in Martin Buber. To make a comparison, the simple idea of a vision quest is no more universal than life-changing dialogue, and yet who could deny its widespread distribution in the cultures of the world and its enormous theoretical import? Further attention to Two-Folk-Speak—or better, Two-Folk-Speak-Listen (because [the art of] listening is almost as essential here as speaking)—would give us not only greater honesty about fieldwork but an ethnography with as much wisdom as structure, composed not only of codes and messages but of human dialogue in a richer and more significant complexity—and one that faces up, too, to the dialogic catalysis and synthesis within that complexity.

## CONCLUSIONS

We have tried to approach dialogue through fairly conventional definitions, not only as conversation but as the sharing and exchange of ideas and emotions through natural language. We also tried to explore its corporeal, emotional, catalytic, political, situational, and bridging aspects. In part we did so by conceptualizing dialogue within the larger context of "linguaculture," a de facto domain of experience that crosscuts and synthesizes vocabulary, the semantic components of linguistic structure, and the verbal aspects of culture. We focused, not so much on the *idea* of dialogue or the competing theoretical constructs of dialogue, but on actual, concrete exchanges, on what we called Two-Folk-Speak, as exemplified by convincing and realistic pages in world literature and by cases from anthropological and linguistic fieldwork. And we focused, not on routine, relatively redundant conversation, but on the sorts of interchange and interinfluence that greatly restructure one's attitudes, feelings, cognitive evaluations, and so forth, or that even fundamentally alter one's emotional, philosophical, motivational, and political set—dialogues in cafés and at intersections and on rafts and the many other locations to which we have alluded where dialogic breakthrough takes place—granted that there is relatively little typicality and that such dialogues can take place under very diverse circumstances. Such dialogues, while hard to catch on the wing, can be evidenced through happening upon them, like startled pheasants taking off, during intensive and extensive fieldwork, or through the more or less vivid recall and reiterated reinterpretation that seems to characterize them much of the time. The meaning of such dialogues is hardly or rarely realized at the time but emerges dynamically as they are ruminated on, reduced, expanded, reactualized, and rerepresented, often with reversal or slowing down of tempo, and otherwise transformed through subsequent imaginings, like the biographical routinization of charismatic experience. Life-changing dialogue can also be captured or evidenced through representations and interpretations in works of verbal or cinematic art, particularly those in the more or less realistic or psychologically realistic traditions. This life-changing dialogue, partly because it makes us go beyond the conventional parameters, paradigms, and perimeters of social science, could lead us to valuable truths about human interrelations, about anthropological (and similar) fieldwork, and about qualitative change, especially political and religious change, in the linguacultures of the world. Other valuable truths would emerge from examining the connections of life-changing dialogue to the cognate experiences of religious conversion, political persuasion, psychotherapy, and "sudden insight" or illumination in personal relations and in science.

## NOTES

For their critical comments on various stages of the manuscript we stand indebted to Dwight Bolinger, Jean DeBernardi, Deborah Friedrich, William Hanks, John Leavitt, Bruce Mannheim, Emanuel Schegloff, Milton Singer, Deborah Spitulnik, Deborah Tannen, Dennis Tedlock, and Steven Tyler.

It should be acknowledged that this analysis reflects the personal preferences of the senior author for the dyadic sort of interaction. It also tends to emphasize the creative individual and the creative act. The essay is thus culturally and idiosyncratically structured, as are all statements. Further work on life-changing dialogue from other perspectives would clearly lead to additional generalizations.

## REFERENCES CITED

Abu-Lughod, Lila. 1993. *Writing Women's Worlds: Bedouin Stories.* Berkeley and Los Angeles: University of California Press.

Bachelard, Gaston. 1969. *The Poetics of Space.* Translated by Maria Jolas. Boston: Beacon Press.

Bakhtin, M. M. 1981. *The Dialogic Imagination.* Translated by C. Emerson and M. Holquist. Austin: University of Texas Press.

Behar, Ruth. 1993. *Translated Woman.* Boston: Beacon.

Bühler, Karl. 1934. *Sprachtheorie.* Jena: Fischer.

Dwyer, Kevin. 1977. "On the Dialogic of Field Work." *Dialectical Anthropology* 2:143–51.

———. 1982. *Moroccan Dialogues: Anthropology in Question.* Baltimore: Johns Hopkins University Press.

Fabian, Johannes. 1979. "The Anthropology of Religious Movements: From Explanation to Interpretation." *Social Research* 46:4–35.

Friedrich, Paul. 1975. *A Tarascan Phonology.* Chicago: University of Chicago Department of Anthropology.

———. 1979. "Structural Implications of Russian Pronominal Usage." In *Language, Context, and the Imagination: Essays by Paul Friedrich,* edited by Anwar S. Dil, pp. 63–125. Stanford: Stanford University Press.

Goffman, Erving. 1978. "Response Cries." *Language* 54:787–815.

Griaule, Marcel. 1965. *Conversations with Ogotemmêli.* London: Oxford University Press.

Haviland, John. 1977. *Gossip, Reputation, and Knowledge in Zinacantan.* Chicago: University of Chicago Press.

Hoijer, Harry, ed. 1954. *Language in Culture.* Chicago: University of Chicago Press.

Hymes, Dell. 1974. *Foundations in Sociolinguistics.* Philadelphia: University of Pennsylvania Press.

Jakobson, Roman. 1960. "Closing Statement: Linguistics and Poetics." In *Style in Language,* edited by Thomas A. Sebeok, pp. 350–77. Cambridge: Technology Press; New York: John Wiley.

Lewis, Oscar. 1959. *Five Families.* New York: Basic Books.

Lyons, John. 1977. *Semantics.* 2 vols. Cambridge: Cambridge University Press.

Mandelbaum, David G., ed. 1949. *Selected Writings of Edward Sapir in Language, Culture and Personality.* Berkeley and Los Angeles: University of California Press.

Rölvaag, Ole E. 1929. *Giants in the Earth.* Translated by Lincoln Concord and the Author. New York: A. L. Bart (with Harper and Brothers).

Schegloff, Emanuel A. 1986. "The Routine as Achievement." *Human Studies* 9:111–51.

Singer, Milton. 1984. *Man's Glassy Essence, Explorations in Semiotic Anthropology.* Bloomington: University of Indiana Press.

Tannen, Deborah. 1981. "New York Jewish Conversational Style." *International Journal of the Sociology of Language* 30:133–39.

————. 1987. "Repetition in Conversation as Spontaneous Formulaicity." *Text* 7:215–43.

Tedlock, Dennis. 1983. *The Spoken Word and the Work of Interpretation.* Philadelphia: University of Pennsylvania Press.

Tolstoy, Leo. 1966. *War and Peace.* Edited by George Gibian. Translated by Louise and Aylmer Maude. New York: W. W. Norton.

Turner, Victor. 1967. *The Forest of Symbols: Aspects of Ndembu Ritual.* Ithaca: Cornell University Press.

# TWO

# Women's Voices: Lima 1975

## BILLIE JEAN ISBELL

### INTRODUCTION

I invite you to observe a family drama; one that is unusual only because I, as Juana the anthropologist, play a minor role in the cast. It was at my urging that the scenes set out below took place. Nevertheless, I can imagine similar dramas occurring all over the world as members of families find it necessary to translate their experiences to one another as they join the mobile populations that move across traditional ethnic territories and even international boundaries. Such is the case with the three women in this particular drama. They are three generations of one family that share with tens of thousands of other migrants the transforming experiences shaped by continual migration from their small villages of origin in the hinterlands of the Andes to urban centers of their own nations and, increasingly, those of the global world. Andean diaspora, motivated by the increased political violence in Peru in the 1980s, has reached such unlikely places as Paterson, New Jersey, and San Francisco, California. These stories from the lives of the three women presented below are situated in the period just prior to the mass exodus from Chuschi, the village of origin of the two older women, in 1985. The three women tell me their stories in my house in Lima in 1975.

Following Dennis Tedlock's suggestion, I have set these dialogues out in the form of a two-act play. Pauses are indicated by dots and loud passages by small caps. Juana, my *nom d'anthropologie*, is a character in the play. The first act is "Francisca's Marriage." Francisca tells her story in Spanish but her mother provides commentary in Quechua. The structure of the storytelling resembles that of Quechua stories: Virginia contradicts her daughter and provides an alternative version; she also intensifies the emotional moments of her daughter's tale. In act 2, there are two scenes.

The first, "Virginia's Rustlers," takes place in Quechua as Virginia regales us with one of her famous tales while her daughter provides the necessary commentary, as well as translated synopsis from time to time. The latter breaks the flow of Quechua storytelling. In act 2, scene 2, "Anita's Hopes and Dreams," Virginia's granddaughter sets forth her aspirations. Her mother and grandmother have almost nothing to say at all. There are no responses, no commentary. Is it because Anita's aspirations are so foreign both to her mother and her grandmother that they cannot participate with her as she creates a vision of her hoped-for future? Or is it simply that the future cannot be dialogically constructed? Virginia and Francisca negotiate their realities through their dialogues about their shared past experiences. But Anita, on the other hand, looks to the future and elicits my cooperation in constructing her vision.

## CAST OF CHARACTERS
### Francisca

A woman of about thirty-six or thirty-seven years of age who looks ten years older. She is short and heavy-set with fair skin. Her body shows the signs of eleven births accompanied by little medical attention. But her freckled cheeks and bright eyes give her face a youthful appearance except that when she smiles, several missing teeth attest to years without dental care. She is dressed in a gathered blue cotton skirt, a white blouse, and cheap plastic sandals. She is always hatless. A small gold cross on a chain around her neck contrasts with the plainness of her clothing. When she is nervous, she has the habit of touching the cross with her right hand. Her dark, thick hair is cut short, parted on the side and pinned back out of her face. When she talks, her hands are always busy—mending some article of clothing, shelling corn, or knitting. She sits with her knees together but never crossed and when she walks she takes the small, hurried steps of a woman who has learned to carry her children on her back, one of the few highland habits she has maintained in Lima.

### Virginia

Francisca's mother, who is sixty-two or sixty-three, is thinner than her daughter and appears in better health. She has a strong-looking body and all of her teeth. She is dressed in the typical highland dress of the Río Pampas region of Ayacucho: several long, full, wool skirts held in place by a beautifully hand-woven belt with the specific designs from her home village. Virginia, unlike her daughter, customarily squats on her heels, using her skirts as a low stool, with her knees wide apart and her numerous skirts pulled down to her feet. Under her *lliqlla*, the alpaca wool carrying cloth that also bears local designs in intricate patterns, shines a bright pink satin blouse that buttons on one side. Her ensemble is topped off by a black felt hat that has seen many Andean winters. On her feet she wears lace-up black plastic shoes and no socks. Even though the coastal spring has arrived and it is quite warm, Virginia prefers her highland costume even though she could pass as a coastal farm wife if she were dressed differently because of her light skin and hazel eyes. Like her daughter, her hands are also always busy—spinning wool. She tucks the raw wool, spindle and completed thread in her top skirt, which is tucked up to make a large pouch in front. Also in her skirt is toasted dried corn that she continually munches on as she listens to her daughter's and granddaughter's stories.

### Anita

Francisca's daughter, seventeen years old. Pretty with a heart-shaped face, intense, intelligent, dark brown eyes. Her yellow blouse, blue jeans, multicolored sneakers (and no socks) are the after-school uniform of the multitude of students who attend the free state schools. She has the same fair complexion and a few freckles span her nose and cheeks. Her hair is shoulder-length and permed. She wears large gold-plated earrings but no makeup. Her hands are also always busy but not with the same kind of activities that occupy her mother and her grandmother—she bites her painted nails. When she talks she pokes at an imaginary target in front of her face with the index finger of her right hand and keeps her brow furrowed as if she is concentrating on what she wants to say. She sits crossed-legged or paces around as her mother and grandmother talk.

### Juana

An American anthropologist the same age as Francisca. Tall, blond, and blue-eyed—a typical, pleasant-looking *gringa*. Her hair is long and caught up above her ears in two ponytails that fall over her shoulders when she scribbles in her ever-present notepad. Even though it is now the mid-1970s she has a 1960s air about her. She wears glasses which she periodically pushes back up the bridge of her small nose. She wears a cotton skirt of hand-printed silk-screen cotton in a pre-Colombian design that she made from yardage. Her white cotton blouse is soft and practical. She wears American-made leather sandals. She tries to keep her hands busy—writing and working the tape recorder because Virginia and Francisca often make fun of how useless her hands are—she doesn't know how to spin, knit. They tell her that she is slow at even children's tasks such as shelling corn or peeling potatoes.

## ANTHROPOLOGICAL REFLECTIONS

All of the women who speak here also played major roles in an earlier publication of mine, *To Defend Ourselves: Ecology and Ritual in an Andean Village* (Isbell 1978). First of all, three chapters in that volume, those on kinship, reciprocity, and the migrant community in Lima, draw heavily on the same family. What is different here is that, presented by dialogues, the three women emerge as unique individuals. They are not submerged into the collectivity. You do not get a picture of a typical extended family from the village of Chuschi in the department of Ayacucho nor do you get an overall image of the migrants from that village in Lima. The reader is offered glimpses of the lives of women as they recount their unique experiences and therefore what is lost at the level of generalizations is gained in human depth. Virginia is not the typical humble, monolingual, illiterate, Quechua-speaking peasant woman that forms the major image of Andean women for English readers. She is an intelligent, funny, strong woman who learned to negotiate the demands of two very different worlds: the rural life of Chuschi where she farmed her lands and tended her herds with the assistance of her blind son and his young wife and that of the urban squatter settlement where she pushed Francisca and her husband into participating in the invasion that gained her property and a small income. By and large Virginia is content with her life. Her sense of her self-worth has remained high throughout her life. She does not express a sense of belonging to an underclass.

Both her daughter and granddaughter do however: Francisca holds a fatalistic view and relies on religion to change her life; Anita, on the other hand, is hopeful that she can control the events of her life to a sufficient degree to escape the hardships that she believes her mother and grandmother have suffered. She declares that she will escape the misfortunes they recount, but she also realizes that some calamity may derail her plans. Nevertheless, no one expects to arrange a marriage for her; nor will they dictate how many children she must have.

Francisca conforms fairly closely to the image presented in the anthropological literature on mestiza women caught between two worlds. Thrust into a marriage not of her choosing, denied the education she hoped for, she has great aspirations for her eldest daughter. As is the case for many women who are caught in between two cultures, Francisca bemoans her life and hopes for better possibilities for her children. It seems that the death of her first child is an emblem for the suffering that is her lot in life. She recounts the many dreams she never realized: getting an education, becoming a nun, learning to play the piano. These aspirations are placed before her daughter, Anita, who, by becoming educated, also rejects the type of life that comes with arranged marriage and dedication to one's family and community. For Anita, as for many young women like her, education is a radicalizing experience in many ways. For one thing, she wants to control the number of children she will have, and for another, she has a broader view of society. For Anita, membership in society includes a sense of belonging to a nation and even the world at large, views not shared by either her mother or grandmother.

One of the striking aspects of this dialogical text is the loss of the anthropological authoritative persona; the one who never speaks directly but who lifts dialogue out of its context to the level of generalizations. Notice that I am able to insert that kind of authority with interpretations that Juana presented to the audience. Nevertheless, in the dialogues themselves the reverse is true; my voice is seldom heard. I am the least revealed and the least developed character in the stories. After all, these women were translating their shared lives to each other. I was a mere catalyst for the process of the creation of shared realities. Of the three women, only Anita engaged me in dialogue because she not only wanted to make a political point by asking "Why should you make my mother remember?" she also thinks that I share her reality to a greater extent than does her grandmother, but the last scene, which contains the greatest dialogue between the anthropologist and her subject, differs from that recent genre of anthropological confessions in which the author bares his or her soul and the so-called informants either fade into the background or become characters in the drama of the anthropologist. In the dialogues presented below, I occasionally impose a structure or a question upon the interactions of the other three women but I am never asked to tell *my* story. Perhaps this is one of the reasons why we have seen so little dialogue in the anthropological literature: It reveals how little we, as outsiders, interest our interlocutors. Ironically, I become their unexplored "anthropological other" while Virginia and Francisca, as unique individuals, create their shared realities through dialogue. As our story ends, Anita's reality is unrealized as she looks to the future.

## ACT 1: FRANCISCA'S MARRIAGE

*Juana's place, a modest combination living-dining room. The walls are made of cement blocks; a stairway to the second floor is off to the left and an open door gives a partial view of the kitchen, patio, and laundry area. Noise from the arriving and departing jets of the international airport as well as street noise invades the house. Some of the sounds include specific whistles and calls of the numerous vendors who ply the neighborhood: meat, fish, bread, milk, fruit vendors, knife sharpeners, rag and bottle collectors all have particular*

*sounds that their customers learn to listen for. Children can be heard play-*
*ing soccer in a small park nearby. The furniture consists of odds and ends*
*borrowed and rented from various sources so nothing matches. Francisca and*
*Anita sit on a somewhat run-down, bright floral print sofa; Juana sits in a*
*straight-back chair next to a small dining table where the tape recorder and*
*microphone are. A nondescript reading lamp and an electric Singer sewing*
*machine are also on the table. A battered copy of a colonial leather chair is*
*against the opposite wall across from the sofa and its mate is on the other*
*side of the couch. Both are covered with alpaca saddle blankets. The walls are*
*decorated with large, unframed, color photos of Andean scenes familiar to all*
*of the women.*

*Juana comes through the doorway with a large tray holding four small*
*plates, glasses, a small tray of warm cakes and a large pitcher of chicha*
*morada. Capitalizing on one of the few skills the other women admire, she*
*has baked small sweet cakes and made the cold, nonfermented drink prepared*
*from dried purple corn to welcome her guests. She fills the glasses with the*
*purple drink and invites her guests to serve themselves from the large plate of*
*cakes. The two younger women do so, but Virginia shakes her head no so she*
*is served by her daughter. After admiring the sewing machine, Virginia sits*
*in front of one of the leather chairs on the floor using her multitude of skirts*
*as a low stool. She takes her spinning from the fold of her skirt and places it*
*in her lap. Alternately, she munches on her toasted corn and takes small bites*
*of the sweet cakes on a plate in front of her.*

*Juana steps forward, takes off an apron and addresses the audience while*
*the other two women look at the photos, chat, serve themselves and settle*
*down on the sofa.*

JUANA: I have invited these three women to my house near Catholic
University where I am teaching. I have known Francisca and her mother,
Virginia, for about eight years. I met Francisca in 1967 during my first
fieldwork in Peru as an undergraduate; she was on one of her annual trips
from Lima to Chuschi to help her mother with the harvest. I soon learned
that by returning every year Francisca retained her access to agricultural
lands which supplemented her family's urban income. Virginia is a widow
and the only child that remains at home is her youngest son, Felix, who
is blind.

Over the years, Francisca and I have developed a friendship as two
married women of about the same age with children. She is the expert,
however, and I am the novice: she has ten children ranging from three to
twenty and I only have one—a ten-year-old girl. My mother spent a year in
the village during my first fieldwork and even though she spoke no Spanish nor Quechua, she and Virginia "conversed" for hours about everyday

affairs. I remember a particular conversation my mother reported that she had with Virginia about the origin of the village chickens with feathers that seemed to grow the wrong way. I checked on my mother's version of the conversation with Virginia and found that they somehow communicated. Virginia verified that, indeed, these wrong-feathered chickens had been introduced by a market vendor about ten years ago. It's too bad that my mother returned home; she would have helped me in this current project.

Francisca is defined by her mother as "moderna" (she uses the Spanish word for modern) — Francisca says she will never return to the harsh life of the highlands. But, she keeps up her ties to her family (and to the lands she had been promised as part of her inheritance) by helping her widowed mother. Virginia pushed Francisca and her husband into participating in the invasion that established the squatter community where they now live. Virginia knew the woman who had spearheaded the invasion in 1963; she made it a point to be present in Lima during the initial land takeover. She took possession of a small plot, built a shelter that grew into a house, and now, in 1975, she is enjoying the rent it earns from relatives who come to Lima on sundry business.

I have just come down from the highlands and I am working in the squatter settlement where Chuschinos are settled. Francisca has offered to introduce me to the migrant community and I have just met her seventeen-year-old daughter, Anita, for the first time. I arrived with two of her "country cousins" from Chuschi who hope to study in Lima. As the oldest daughter of ten children, she is required to shoulder the responsibility of much of the housework and care of her younger siblings, even though she is a full-time student who had just completed her secondary education and had won a scholarship to study at the national university. Anita had never visited Chuschi, the birthplace of her mother and her grandmother. Moreover, she knows only a few phrases of greeting in Quechua. Even though Virginia has become a frequent visitor to the squatter settlement, these meetings at my house are the first occasions that granddaughter and grandmother have conversed with one another about their lives.

Francisca works long hours in the family's small store, which is a major center of activity for the migrant community. It features a television set powered by electric lines illegally carried up to the squatters on the hill from a commercial urbanization project down below. She charges a few centavos for each hour of viewing but her main business comes from the sodas, beer, and snacks people consume as they watch hours of "telenovelas" — "soaps," sports events, American or Mexican movies, and sometimes, but not too often, the news. The family's quarters are three rooms upstairs and a kitchen behind the store. We decided that the hectic routine in the store and living quarters was not conducive to taping their stories. I suspect that they also felt greater liberty outside of their home and community. Logistics are a major issue: we have to hold our sessions when one of Francisca's sons can watch the store for an afternoon. The trips to my house by bus require four transfers — an hour and a half during off-hours and as much as three hours at peak times.

*(Juana withdraws from center stage and a spot lights Francisca sitting on the couch.)*

FRANCISCA: We arrived from Lima during school vacation. We came to change our mourning black in honor of my mother-in-law. Well. We were in her house all night, singing.

VIRGINIA: Mmm.

FRANCISCA: My father asked me, "Well, do you know Don Albino?" Well it was funny. He is the older brother of my husband. All of the relatives were in Chuschi for the ceremony.

VIRGINIA: They are both alike. They like to drink.

FRANCISCA: They knew. My mother knew that night, well .... they .... well ... We didn't know ... Fortunato and I didn't know.

VIRGINIA: Nuche, nuche bastidiando a ver. Nuche, nuche bastidiando. "No quiere, no quiere," dice. Mmmm, pero, pero tarde, tarde tambien bastidiando ... Waq warmi papa mama ya .... Kanchu kawsakunqa, Papa mama ya Tudo ya empeñado.

FRANCISCA: They arranged it for both of us.

JUANA: So, they went to his house every night? That's how it is?

FRANCISCA: Yes, that's how it is.

VIRGINIA: She was sixteen. At sixteen she was married.

FRANCISCA: I had not even seen him yet. That Sunday when I left church we saw each other from afar. I was taking a turn around the plaza to go up the hill to my house — you know — where the school is — when my mother said to me: "See that young man on the corner? I'm going to give you over to him with a rope. *(laughter)* You are going to marry that young man." I said: "M-A-M-Á!! Why would you do such a thing to me? Why am I going to get married . ? ." I was so surprised. I didn't suspect anything.

*(Both women interrupt their story, pause and laugh together. Anita gives them an angry look and mutters something.)*

FRANCISCA: They had given their word. They didn't ask either one of us. It was just between them.

VIRGINIA: I said: "Be quiet daughter. We have been looking for a good son. — .. in .. I mean husband for you."

FRANCISCA: That's the way it was. Well. They told me. And when I tried to escape they wouldn't let me leave the house. They forced me to marry. When I was sixteen.

JUANA: Did you return with him to Lima?

FRANCISCA: No, we stayed for two years … After marrying, we suffered a lot. Sad suffering. It was like this, there wasn't enough work to even put clothes on our backs, we left.

VIRGINIA: They worked in the fields with us.

FRANCISCA: But working in the fields only gave us enough to eat. We couldn't even buy clothes. During that time we went to Ayacucho for a year to work.

VIRGINIA: Yes, to Ayacucho.

FRANCISCA: He was a mason's helper and I sold fruit in the market. We did that for a year and then we returned to Chuschi.

FRANCISCA: It is a very private thing …. *(Long pause. She looks down at her hands and talks quietly.)* But I will tell you. It died. Counting that one, I have eleven children in all. One is missing.

JUANA: Eleven?

FRANCISCA: It is so sad when babies die … *(sobbing)* when my first baby boy died. Cuando mi primerito murió. So sad. So-o-sad. *(Her voice trails off and she keeps repeating "so sad" in the cadence of a Quechua funeral dirge. Long pause.)*

VIRGINIA: No, no, no … MMM MUJERCITA WARMIWAWA-M! A LITTLE GIRL!

FRANCISCA: A little girl? That's right … a little girl …

*(A long pause—Francisca continues to sob.)*

JUANA: A little girl?

FRANCISCA: Her name was Valeria.

VIRGINIA: A little girl.

FRANCISCA: She was only a month and a half old when she died.

*(Now both mother and daughter are sobbing. Francisca, taking out a handkerchief from her skirt pocket, begins to cry in earnest.)*

JUANA: Did you know what the baby's illness was?

ANITA: The baby died of hunger. Because it was her first and she was inexperienced. It starved to death, that's why the baby died. When she remembers, she becomes very sad and cries. Why should you make her remember?

JUANA: Ah, ah, a … I, ah, don't mean to cause her pain.

FRANCISCA: When I remember how my little daughter died. She was so tiny ...

*(She begins to sob loudly and Virginia sobs with her, their sobs turn into funeral wailing. As the emotional tension heightens, the dialogue between Francisca and Virginia takes on the quality of a Quechua storytelling session whereby a dramatic event necessarily is responded to by a listener in such a way that a rapid and intense rhythm is created. Francisca's statements are made in a low voice and Virginia's loud commentary creates an emotional intensity that is absent in Francisca's voice quality.)*

FRANCISCA: There wasn't even a health worker in those days.

VIRGINIA: NOT EVEN A HEALTH WORKER! Pus formed here .... *(she points to her nipples)* AND ONE DAY SHE BLED!

FRANCISCA: I couldn't nurse. The baby couldn't suck. She was starving. She turned into a skeleton.

VIRGINIA: LITTLE MOTHER! PAIN! SHE WAS IN TERRIBLE PAIN!

FRANCISCA: The little bitty one. She suffered. My mother tried to nurse her. She was nursing my sister, Justa.

VIRGINIA: J-E-S-U-S!

JUANA: Was she able to give milk to the baby?

FRANCISCA: She nursed her but it didn't do any good .. In those days there were no baby bottles with nipples. When she died, I cried a lot. Sure, I have lots of kids, but I always remember; it makes me cry to think of how my first little baby died. Just like ... just like ... a little dried-up skeleton. After suffering for a month and a half she died. Perhaps it's not like when a grown-up dies. I don't know, her little eyes rolled back, her little hands, with just her tiny skin and nothing more. I couldn't even nurse her because it hurt so much.

JUANA: And the milk didn't come?

FRANCISCA: No. We gave her anise water and chamomile tea.

VIRGINIA: She didn't have a chance to live and there was no way that we could cure her.

FRANCISCA: There is this belief that ... Could it be true? That this happened because a sick man arrived at my house? ... and stayed in my kitchen ... When I was still living in the house of my father-in-law, he arrived one day and stayed in the corner of the kitchen. That's where he got sick. And they say that because I looked at his suffering while I was pregnant .... I saw how he suffered ... he twisted and turned like this *(she twists her body to demonstrate)*. And because he was from the uplands — he didn't even know how to pray. He only asked for a drink of liquor when he was dying.

VIRGINIA: For courage, ani—m—o o ... coca ...

FRANCISCA: That's right, coca and trago in order to die.

VIRGINIA: Adults and babies alike need trago, coca and cigarettes to die.

FRANCISCA: Just like him, my baby was born just like him. Because I looked at him perhaps my baby got his sickness. I looked at him. He died there in the corner. I looked at him. His wife just looked at him.

JUANA: Just like him?

FRANCISCA: Just like him. Her eyes rolled back. She twisted. Exactly the same. Just like the man I saw die. Exactly the same. Here in the sierra, ... we have this belief that when you see something ... the same thing can happen. Then ... then ... could it be true?

JUANA: Could it have happened that way?

FRANCISCA: My first baby made me suffer a lot. And because my breast was infected the baby couldn't nurse. Even now I have problems nursing my babies. But when I get the same infection, I can get an injection and I don't swell up. I buy medicine at the pharmacy.

VIRGINIA: So much expense.

FRANCISCA: I remember with the first .... I remember why the baby couldn't nurse—the milk formed a hard mass. It hurt so much that I cried and screamed all day and night. The pain was like a hot arrow. It wouldn't stop night or day. Then my husband took a razor blade .... no .... he broke a bottle and took a piece of glass and cut my breast, here, just under the nipple where it was swollen. I have a little scar. Here (she draws a fine line on right breast with her index finger). Pus poured out.

VIRGINIA: CHAYPI PUSO—O—O! THERE WAS PUS IN THERE!

FRANCISCA: But the pain, day and night.

VIRGINIA: IN THOSE DAYS NOTHING!! NO DOCTOR, NO HEALTH WORKER —NOTHING .... NOTHING!

FRANCISCA: The hard lumps hurt so bad I cried all the time. They tied herbs on me but that didn't help. Then my breast burst and the lumps came out through the cut. I still have a hole where they were. My husband and father-in-law kept lancing my breast. Trying to get the infection out. Each time they would put a bit of salt in the wound. Sometimes a bit of sugar too. Every time they would take off the scab, pus would come out.

JUANA: MY GOD! THAT MUST HAVE HURT!

FRANCISCA: I was getting weaker and weaker. I didn't have the strength to cook, to do anything. And every day, my baby got worse and worse. For the lack of food ...

JUANA: Worse and worse.

FRANCISCA: She was drying up ... turning into a skeleton.

VIRGINIA: Nothing. We could do nothing.

FRANCISCA: Then she died. *(She whispers this over and over again until finally you can only see her lips moving forming the phrase.)* Every time I get pregnant, I have what feels like a tumor right here. *(She points to the scar on her right breast.)*

ALL: Mmm mmm

FRANCISCA: When I was pregnant with my eldest, Teodolfo, you remember, the one who came last night, we ...

JUANA: Ah ah

FRANCISCA: ... came to Lima. We didn't have anyone except Fortunato's sister who lives in San Pedro. We stayed there for a while. My husband had been living in Lima with his conviviente—his, you know—girlfriend ... with his .. señora. He had a child with her. That was when he was single. He worked in the hospital: It was a good job. He returned to that job. He's been there twenty-two years.

JUANA: And what did you do?

FRANCISCA: I sold fruit from a cart with my son on my back in my lliqlla. Then my father, who's now dead, got me a stall in the Fray Martin market.

JUANA: How did he get it?

FRANCISCA: The owner went back to Chuschi and he sold it to us.

JUANA: How much did it cost to buy a stall?

FRANCISCA: They sold it for 250 soles.

JUANA: Ah hah.

FRANCISCA: I worked there nine years. But by that time three of my children were born and I couldn't sell in the market. So, we took part in the invasion of the barriada and I started my business here. I didn't like tending animals or working in the fields. I prefer to be here in Lima or in Ayacucho. I also wanted to go to school. The first time that I came to Lima I was only eight.

JUANA: So you decided to come to Lima when you were eight years old?

FRANCISCA: Yes, I worked in the wholesalers' market with the cousin of my mother. She sold fruit. No, mamá?

VIRGINIA: Yes, with Margarita, her sister, and her brother.

FRANCISCA: They came to Lima when they were little, no mamá? They were orphans.

VIRGINIA: Yes, since they were little. They must still be alive. I never see them anymore.

FRANCISCA: Tomasa comes to see me all the time.

VIRGINIA: I don't even know where they live.

FRANCISCA: Margarita was very good to me. She was going to put me in school. I lived with them for a year. I helped their cook in the kitchen.

The cook had a boyfriend from Huancayo. He came over all of the time and she spent her time with him and I had to do her work: make the beds, clean the floor, and help in the kitchen. The husband of my aunt gave me one sole for my work. *(laughter)* My aunt didn't know how much I was doing. One day, my uncle Agripino came from Chuschi to visit. I think my mother had sent him to check up on things. The husband of my aunt came home. He was a fat guy by the name of Bedoya.

VIRGINIA: *(Laughing)* UN GOR-DA-SU—U—U! A REAL FATSO! *(puffing out her cheeks and gesturing with her hands to indicate a big belly)*

FRANCISCA: The cook told him I was not doing my work in the kitchen. He scolded me saying: "Do you think you are a visitor on vacation?" But he didn't hit me. My uncle, Agripino, went home and reported that I was being treated like a slave. My parents sent for me to come home.

VIRGINIA: What were they doing to my daughter?

FRANCISCA: I came home and right away my mother put me in a school in Ayacucho. I attended school for a year. I lived with my grandmother's sister then I went to live and work in the store of another aunt in Ayacucho. She promised to put me back in school. I worked for them for about a year. She was a good person but her husband was real bad. One day I was washing dishes and a silver spoon escaped down the drain. For such a little thing my uncle began to hit me and just as if I were his woman, he gave me several hard kicks. When my father found out, he took me out of there. I came back to Chuschi but couldn't get used to tending the animals or working in the fields. I wanted to go to school. So I begged my parents to put me in the convent, Santa Clara, in Ayacucho. I said I would enter as a servant to the sisters: I would sweep the floors—do anything to be inside.. I could learn to play the piano in the convent. We came to Ayacucho with my papá to find out. They said there were no vacancies at Santa Clara. We asked at La Merced, but they wouldn't accept me either.

JUANA: How did you get the idea to enter a convent?

FRANCISCA: I don't know. Ever since I was little, I had faith in God. I liked to pray. I liked catechism classes ... to study ...

JUANA: How much did it cost to enter, you know ... the dowry ... el dote?

FRANCISCA: My father asked the sisters at Santa Clara and I asked the Mother Superior at La Merced how much it cost to enter. At the time the dowry was about one thousand soles. A lot of money then. We were so embarrassed, we had 200 soles and two sacks of potatoes.

JUANA: What a shame. So then what happened?

FRANCISCA: Well, there was a man that my father knew who was a sculptor. His wife helped him make ceramic nativity scenes and statues of saints. Manas reqsinmanchu? Perhaps you know him?

*(Virginia and Juana continue in Quechua until Francisca resumes her story in Spanish.)*

VIRGINIA: Do you know him, Juana, he lives in Cangallo?
JUANA: No, I don't know him.
VIRGINIA: You must know his wife, Olivia.
JUANA: I don't think so.
VIRGINIA: She lives in Chuschi in a house with a tin roof?
FRANCISCA: Mamá, she doesn't know her.
VIRGINIA: How can she not know her. She has a daughter, who had two daughters .... one died .... the other teaches in Ayacucho.
JUANA: Maybe ... She lives in a house on the corner with a tin roof?
VIRGINIA: Mmmm.

*(In a tone of some impatience but with satisfaction) ...*

FRANCISCA: My father went to him and asked him to teach me as an apprentice. I liked the idea. They had a piano. His wife said she would teach me to make baby clothes as well. My father agreed to bring food from our fields every month — potatoes, corn, habas, quinua, and cheese. Sometimes he brought saddle blankets for the couple to sell in Cangallo. All of this was for my expenses. So my father left me in their house for a year to learn to be a sculptor, to play the piano, and to learn to sew baby clothes. All because we didn't have the 1000 soles for me to enter the convent ..
VIRGINIA: Chaykunapiña churaniku paytaqa. We put her in all of those places. *(In a sad, almost wistful tone of voice.)*
FRANCISCA: They promised my father to teach me .... to be a sculptor .... to play ... the piano .... *(her voice fades ... a long pause)* The only thing they taught me was to cut and then to sew baby clothes by machine. She taught me maybe a half an hour a day ... no more. I was just their maid. I cleaned, helped the cook, went to the market, carried water .... I was just their maid and my parents were paying them! CARAJO!!
VIRGINIA: IT'S TRUE! CARAJO!
FRANCISCA: After a year, I began to buy material and make baby clothes on my own. I left their house in Cangallo. I traveled from village to village to Huarcaya, Tomanga .... to sell my baby clothes. It was a hard life. I traveled with a señora who was selling also. She looked after me.
JUANA: How old were you?
FRANCISCA: I was fourteen. No, mamá?
VIRGINIA: Yes. And when you returned to Chuschi, we made the agreement with your husband's parents that you two were to get married.

## ACT 2

### Scene 1: Virginia's Rustlers

*Several days later in the patio-garden area in the back of Juana's house. A small herb garden, tomatoes, lettuce, and chili peppers are planted in the flower beds. All four women are seated on the circular walkway that defines the garden, shelling dried corn from a large handwoven alpaca sack. Clothes are drying on the lines. The cast cement wash basin, scrubboard, and cake of lye soap are visible to the right of the door that leads into the kitchen. A lone metal chair is against the wall of the servant's quarters—one room with a bath—in the back of the garden. The street and airport noises are even more pronounced. The scene opens with the sounds of the high whistle of the knife sharpener growing louder as he approaches on his bicycle cart and diminishing as he passes. Virginia has taken off several of her skirts and is wearing only one wool skirt. Her battered wool hat is on the ground beside her. Juana is wearing cotton slacks and a shirt, the same sandals.*

JUANA: *(addressing the audience)* I have grown fond of Virginia. She is intelligent, quick, and has a wonderful sense of humor. What's more, she is patient with my attempts to learn Quechua and she understands that I am here to write about her culture. It is largely through her influence that I am tolerated at her family's celebrations and gatherings. She says that I am next to useless but funny to watch. Often when I am helping her with planting or harvesting, she points out to everyone that Felix, her blind son, works better than I do. She is especially disappointed that I have not learned to spin or make alpaca saddle blankets, like the one covering that chair. Virginia sells them to Ayacucho market women who come to Chuschi.

Virginia is a renowned storyteller and she relishes listening to her own stories on the tape recorder. But, repeatedly, she has declared that I and my tape recorder don't know enough to listen and Anita doesn't even understand Quechua. Francisca is a good listener: she knows when to comment, when to add information, and most of all, when to give encouragement at appropriate moments in the story. She has a special role in our meetings—she acts as the translator for Anita and sometimes for me too. I have already asked Virginia a series of typical anthropological questions—the names and places of origin of her parents, how many siblings she had, when she got married, how many children each of her siblings had, and so forth. In my mind, I am guided by an invisible genealogical chart of her kin relationships—living and dead. She isn't very interested in my line of query but I did learn that she had five sisters and one brother. Only the brother had any schooling. I was surprised to learn that she couldn't remember the number of siblings that had died. She answered with —

VIRGINIA: How many could there have been?

JUANA: But you say you have one brother and five sisters, right?

VIRGINIA: That's right. I am the second to the oldest.

JUANA: How old are you?

VIRGINIA: I must be about fifty.

FRANCISCA: My mother was born in 1913. I have her baptismal certificate.

JUANA: Let's see, ... that makes her sixty-two. Why did she say she was about fifty?

VIRGINIA: My brother went to school but all five of us were ignorant. I didn't even know how to sign my name until Francisca taught me. How many years did you say you studied to be a professor?

JUANA: Years in the university?

VIRGINIA: U .. mmm.

JUANA: Ten.

VIRGINIA: TEN?? *(in exaggerated disbelief—nervous laughter from the other three women)* Ten years of studying and as far as I can tell you are absolutely useless. You can't spin, grow crops; you've only had one child and I'd be afraid to leave my herds in your care ... TEN YEARS?

FRANCISCA: Mamá, por favor ..

*(But Francisca breaks into laughter while Virginia dumps ears of dried corn in Juana's lap.)*

VIRGINIA: Let's see if you can shell this corn I have brought you from my fields before tomorrow morning.

JUANA: May god repay you for your generosity, señora. I will do my best.

VIRGINIA: My sisters and I were in charge of pasturing the animals. We had lots. At one time we had almost 1,000 head of sheep, cattle, alpacas, and llamas as well. I spent all of my time with the herds.

FRANCISCA: Of the five sisters my mother was the bravest. Mamá, tell her the story of the time you shot those rustlers!

VIRGINIA: Sí, pues. Robando, robando animales ... *(A long pause; a jet screams overhead as it approaches to land.)* Cuatro sillada, cinco ... revolvillaña ...

FRANCISCA: The riders were all armed. But she had a revolver too — she carried it in her skirts — here.

VIRGINIA: Sí, pue .. e ... *(A look of consternation crosses her face as she searches for the right words but her Spanish fails her.)*

JUANA: Tell me in Quechua ... how it happened .. how old you were ... and ...

VIRGINIA: That day, they came with guns while I was tending the herds. First there appeared a lone rider over the hill and then the others came. *(As if calling to herders)* EEEE E E E! *(shouting)* THERE WERE A LOT OF HERDERS IN THE PASTURES THAT DAY! *(Almost whispering)* The thieves cut the herd into two equal bunches and began driving them back over the hill to a ravine. Three, then eight riders appeared around the side of the hill called Lachuq Kuchu. They always robbed us the same way. I hitched up my skirts and ran and ran up on the ridge above the ravine. When I got there, there was one sole rider left with the cattle. So, I loaded my pistol, aimed, and shot.

FRANCISCA: She shot at them to defend herself and her family's animals.

VIRGINIA: He left two animals behind but got away with the rest.

FRANCISCA: She only saved two animals.

VIRGINIA: The thieves got away with the rest of the herd. We followed them for several days but they climbed up the mountain on a different trail. When we got to the top we could see them in the distance; one fat bull was straggling behind because it was so fat that it couldn't walk. Our riders kept after them. The rustlers got off of their beasts and began to fight with us.

FRANCISCA: They began to fight with them.

VIRGINIA: There were many broken heads ....

FRANCISCA: With stones. The rustlers must've run out of bullets because they threw stones.

VIRGINIA: Yes, stones. *(She stands up and shows how she drew her gun out from under her skirts.)* I crept nearer and fired my revolver again. PAM! I fired again! PAM! I made a couple of holes, I did. I wounded two of them. Some of the rustlers were killed. I hit one of them in the knee and he couldn't get back on his horse. He couldn't keep hold of the reins. The other rustlers scattered when I fired—they rode off and left him there. He didn't have a poncho, a hat; he didn't have anything. He was bleeding. One of the other ones caught the reins of his horse and led it off.

FRANCISCA: She fired at them!

VIRGINIA: The rustlers killed one of our people—

FRANCISCA: One, they killed one ...

VIRGINIA: ... the guy with the broken head .. there wasn't anything alive in him anymore. They were coming closer to where I was. I said to myself: "If they reach me, they'll take my gun away," so I ducked down and tried to take aim. They rode past and when they were riding up, up, up the mountain, my young thoughts called out: "Hey!, don't rob cattle anymore! Stay here and marry me!" I raised my skirts and showed them my gun that was tucked here just over my buttock! I ...

*(Laughter of the other women cuts her off.)*

FRANCISCA: That's what she said ..

VIRGINIA: Ay, me, ... the life I had in the high pasture lands. As he was escaping .. that's what I said ... wounded ... he was ... wounded.

FRANCISCA: He was wounded.

VIRGINIA: I was so young.

FRANCISCA: She was young.

JUANA: How old were you when this happened?

VIRGINIA: I was just a young thing beginning to flower.

JUANA: *(Turning to Francisca)* How old was your mother then? She was still single, right?

FRANCISCA: Yes, she was single.

VIRGINIA: .................... I was just a young thing.

## Scene 2: Anita's Hopes and Dreams

*The national zoo in Lima, which is also located near the airport but among archaeological ruins. Parts of ancient adobe walls are visible along with huge clay replicas of pre-Colombian ceramics. Off to one side is a three-foot board with a well-known Peruvian folk legend printed in large block letters and brilliantly colored illustrations. At the back of the stage is a large curved sign over the entrance of the zoo that reads: Parque de las Leyendas. The screams of jets combine with human and animal noises. The zoo is a favorite place for working-class families to take outings. The women are gathered for a Sunday picnic which is also a good-bye party for Juana and her daughter. The debris of the picnic are scattered on the grass with two large washtubs in the foreground. All of the women are busy wiping the faces and hands of some ten children of various ages. Two additional women are among the group. One child is tall, lanky, and blond. The others are dark haired but a few are fair in complexion. After cleaning up the children, the women gather the utensils, dishes, pots, and pans and stack them near the washtubs. Then they settle down on blankets spread out on the ground. Virginia takes out her raw wool and thread and begins the rhythm of spinning—dropping her spindle and carefully winding the finished thread around the thumb and pinky of her left hand; Francisca is knitting on a child's sweater and Anita writes in what looks like a diary. The children are shepherded by two women down a path and offstage. Juana rises and walks to front, center stage and addresses the audience:*

JUANA: Francisca's sister and sister-in-law are taking the children to see the monkeys. *(She points to the two washtubs.)* That was a tub of strawberry jello and the other one was full of soft drinks. We carried them from the Pueblo Joven on the bus—four changes and almost two hours in transit. We must have looked like a motley urban matrilineal tribe: an elderly matriarch, four middle-aged women, one teenager, and ten children lugging two large washtubs and pots and pans of food. Francisca insisted on bringing all of it because it is a good-bye party for me and my daughter. We are returning to the U.S. in a few days.

*(She walks over to Anita, sits beside her, and turns on her tape recorder. Anita carefully shuts her notebook.)*

JUANA: How is your club going?

ANITA: We have twenty-two members but my father threw us out of the house. He won't let us meet on the roof any more.

JUANA: Why?

ANITA: He says bad things about our club. He says it's not like the adult club. You know—El Club Santa Rosa de Lima? He says that my brother and I can't belong anymore. He says it's the "Club for Lovers" that all the young people want to do is fool around—but not on his roof. He says we're lazy that we don't help our parents. It's terrible. He doesn't understand. We have a plan to give talks on health to mothers. To hold sports events for the kids. We're not ready to give the talks yet but we have done something. We've bought one volleyball and one soccer ball, and a blackboard. We plan to organize a small pharmacy and get medical students to help us. Now my father has ruined everything. We have to find somewhere else to meet.

JUANA: That's too bad. Congratulations on your fellowship! Your mother told me you won! Tell me about it.

ANITA: The fellowships are given to the two students who have maintained the top grades during all five years of secondary school. The fellowships were created in 1970. In every state high school two fellowships are awarded and the winners can go to whichever university they choose without taking the entrance exam and without paying one cent!

JUANA: How marvelous! Where are you going? What are you going to study?

ANITA: I'll go to San Marcos University. I put chemical engineering as my first choice. We had to list five choices in all. I put engineering, medicine, biology, pharmacy, and linguistics.

JUANA: Linguistics?

ANITA: Who knows? I know I don't really want to study medicine. Everybody starts out in medicine. My grades are good enough but I don't have the economic means to finish nine or ten years of study to become a doctor. Besides, I would like to be an engineer. One of my friends is studying chemical engineering and he said that seventy men and ten women started in his class. It is a career for men, he says. But I don't think so. I think that I am capable of doing it. He says it's hard. So what. Getting the fellowship was hard.

JUANA: So when you finish and you are a PROFESSIONAL — you'll be a chemical engineer.

ANITA: Yes. This is the year of the Peruvian woman. There is a revolution for women happening. A great step forward has been taken with obligatory military service for women. Before it was only for men. Only a right that men had ... to serve our country. Women didn't get any preparation for the possibility of war. Now we are being trained. We are becoming equal to men. Right?

JUANA: Umm. Equality to go to war?

ANITA: Women are less bellicose than men. If women were governing, they would attempt to mediate. In contrast, men, out of pride, always want to win, to fight, to go to war. They don't compromise.

JUANA: Tell me. Where will you be in two years?

ANITA: Studying. For now, marriage is not in my plans. Certainly, falling in love. That can happen. But not with the idea of getting married. I don't plan to marry. Not yet, anyway.

JUANA: How many children would you like to have?

ANITA: Me? .... One or two, no more. Life is very difficult. I look at my father, at my whole family .... Our family is too large. There are ten children. With two, with three ....

JUANA: So you want to have two or three children?

ANITA: I know that I have to study because my whole family is counting on me. My mother continually says: "Daughter, you have to do it, I have hope in you." She encourages me, my father also, but not like my mother. She has blind faith in me. It would be terrible if I had to betray that faith.

JUANA: What kinds of things could happen? What are you afraid of that would stop your studies, your career?

ANITA: The things that happen .... you know .... for example if my father were to die and we were left orphaned. Ten children. I don't even know how to work. I only know how to do housework.

FRANCISCA: Dios Mío.

*(She and her mother both cross themselves. Francisca clutches her gold cross.)*

VIRGINIA: Don't talk about death!

FRANCISCA: Yes, just think what happened to your aunt Rosa. She is now a widow with small children.

ANITA: Yes, that was terrible. Last Sunday, when her husband was roofing their house, he fell from the first floor. Only the first floor. They say that blood was coming out of his ear .... He had an internal hemorrhage.

They operated on his brain. Right here. *(She points to her head.)* HE DIED! He was unconscious two or three days and then he died.

JUANA: How many children does she have?

THE OTHERS: Four, four little ones.

ANITA: The oldest is only seven and the youngest doesn't walk yet. She is probably about ten months old.

JUANA: How old was the father?

ANITA: Young. He was MUCH younger than my aunt. She's about thirty-two and he was probably twenty-eight. And the señora that the club is trying to help? Her husband was killed when he fell out the back door of the bus because it was so crowded. He fell under the wheels and was killed. The president of the Santa Rosa de Lima club is helping her collect his social security. Without the club's help, it would take years and she has SIX children!

JUANA: Yes, I know. The club has asked me to make a video documentary of her and her family to show to the department of social services. We'll present the film along with a signed petition from all of the Chuschinos. Meanwhile, all the families have contributed something to help her out.

FRANCISCA: She cannot escape now. She has her children.

*(A long silence, then the shouts of the excited children float from backstage like a prophetic affirmation of Francisca's flat and matter-of-fact statement.)*

ANITA: I will escape! I ... will ... I will ... I will ...

*(Her voice fades to a whisper and she stares off toward the sound of the children. Virginia looks up from her spinning and shakes her head back and forth slowly as she watches Anita.)*

## REFERENCES CITED

Isbell, Billie Jean. 1978. *To Defend Ourselves: Ecology and Ritual in an Andean Village.* Austin: University of Texas Press. Reprinted 1985. Prospect Heights, Ill.: Waveland Press.

# THREE

# Video Production as a Dialogue: The Story of Lynch Hammock

### ALLAN F. BURNS

"We talked a little bit before about this lynching over in Newbury." With this matter-of-fact statement, Charles Watson and his family began a narrative about a tragedy in north Florida. Charles was a minister in a small rural church. With him were two remarkable women who were responsible for the health of many throughout the region: his great aunt Elizabeth, who was a practical nurse, and his grandmother Rose, a midwife. Charles and his family were videotaping a few hours of reminiscences and family stories for the church, which was about to hold a day of honor for his great aunt Elizabeth. I had been asked by Charles to videotape the family for the day of honor because of my interests in the community, in applied anthropology, and in locally relevant videotape productions. These are the issues discussed in this essay.

The conversation about the lynching is discussed here as an illustration of the work of dialogic anthropology. The conversation itself has conceptual and linguistic features of dialogue, and the event of the family videotape production itself was a dialogue between the family and myself. In the following analysis, the dialogic base of the event will first be discussed, then the narrative of the lynching will be presented with an analysis of the forms of speech and the content of the conversation. The goal here is not so much to provide a set of tools or methods for doing anthropology through dialogue as it is to bring forth an interpretation of rural culture in the southern part of the United States through a presentation of a conversation within a family, the dialogues between whites and blacks within the story, and the dialogue between anthropology and contemporary community life.

At first glance, the story about a lynching some seventy years ago in a rural hamlet of north Florida sounds like an oral history anecdote, one that can be validated through written sources and so become part of the historic record. My approach is not one of oral history or folklore, however. The story of Lynch Hammock is related through multiple voices, including the participants, myself, and now a videotape. The event is an interplay of all of these voices, such that the meaning or message of the story itself is a result of the primary speakers' interest in preserving family history, a grandson's interest in honoring his great aunt, my own interest in black and white relationships in the South, and a videographer's interest in local production. The conversation about Lynch Hammock can be interpreted from all of these points of view. The text itself can be carefully read so that readers can see the subtle ways in which the interlocutors bring in ideas and interpretations. The point of view of any of the speakers can be taken in the reading so that their own concerns and interests in the event are apparent. The event itself can be understood from the point of view of the clients who requested the videotape or the team that made it. For the former, the resulting videotape was a religious and family artifact, in many ways similar to the religious and medical artifacts used in midwifery and curing by the women who tell the story. The videographer and myself were drawn to the event by the opportunity to learn more about a local community and the status that accrues to people within it. Further, the use of videotape, not only as a means of "taking notes" but also as a means of expression, was an important part of the methodology. Marcus and Fischer describe a similar technique when they talk about a "poetic" presentation of ethnography: "How much more interesting . . . to retain the different perspectives on cultural reality, to turn the ethnographic text into a kind of display and interaction among perspectives. Once this is done . . . the text becomes more acceptable to readerships other than the usually targeted professional one" (Marcus and Fischer 1986: 71).

The story of Lynch Hammock is not a monologue but a conversation among many people. The qualities that arise from the interplay of these different voices result in meaning that is apparent only after one becomes engaged in the different goals and voices of the event. This talk about a lynching is arranged here first in terms of verbal and cultural dialogues, second as local videotape production, third as the story of the lynching, and fourth as a discussion.

## VERBAL AND CULTURAL DIALOGUES

At the literal level, dialogues are verbal exchanges. In their most concrete form, they are made up of conversations between people in ordinary circumstances. At least two people must participate in the event, and some shared words must pass between the participants. Unlike monologues, dialogues are characterized by the emergence of forms through negotiation, elaboration, interruption, and other forms of exchange. The linguistics of dialogues is not very well known; indeed, many researchers look at dialogues as if they were monologues. If, as I found in the case of the Yucatec Maya (Burns 1983), even narrative speech is normally the product of at least two people, then a linguistics that claims to be based on speech must begin from the foundation of speech production as a shared activity, not from what a single individual does when producing the sounds and words of a language.

At another level, dialogue can be more abstract than words and exchanges between speakers. It can be an extended communication between groups of people, as in a political dialogue, or the beginning of negotiations in cases of risk and danger. The content and form of these more abstract kinds of dialogue may have a formal verbal structure or routine, as in an exchange of ambassadors, but beneath the formality are the possibilities and even probabilities of sudden shifts in action and spontaneous changes in rules. This is especially apparent in the dialogues of personally dangerous circumstances, such as hostage crises or violent confrontations, when a shift in dialogue can lead to sudden and often tragic violence. Under such circumstances dialogues switch from verbal communication to communication through physical force. The cultural dialogue of the lynching is an excellent example of this form.

Dialogic anthropology, as discussed in this volume, has an even more abstract level. It makes explicit what ethnographers have noticed for generations: what an ethnographer writes is partly her or his own and partly belongs to the people studied. Dialogic anthropology brings the joint character of this venture to the forefront, often in ways that lay bare the conversations that lead to ethnographic accounts, as in the case of Dwyer's (1982) work on Morocco.

One of the common narratives that circulate in black communities in north Florida concerns a confrontation between a black man and a white sheriff under the volatile conditions engendered by racial distrust, poverty, and hunger during the early part of this century. The story is a cultural dialogue between blacks and whites, encompassing an accusation of theft by the sheriff, an attempt to arrest the alleged thief, the death of the sheriff, and the lynching of several women in retaliation. This is a cultural dialogue that begins with words and ends with shootings and lynchings. The event was so terrifying that the woods where the lynchings took place are known to this day as "Lynch Hammock." (In the physical geography of north Florida, a hammock is a thick growth of natural vegetation.)

The profundity of African Americans' concerns about interethnic relations can be seen in narratives like this one about Lynch Hammock. Although the event took place over seventy years ago, the regularity of its retelling in family conversations makes it a benchmark in the history of black and white relations. Struggles dating from the times of slavery and emancipation are basic topics in rural black family conversations. The events and anecdotes described are not told in the street vernacular of the black idiom described by linguists such as Labov (1972b), but in a formal or "high" style of speech. Labov himself discredits the high style in his early work, referring to those who speak it as "lames" (1972a) and making an elaborate case on the basis of one example in order to show that the style is characterized by "padding" and "verbosity" (Labov 1972b: 198). The high style of careful enunciation, slow delivery, exaggerated tone contours, elongations, and stress is heard in the speech of African American preachers and politicians. The Reverend Jessie Jackson used this style extensively in his bid for the Democratic presidential nomination during the 1988 elections. The style itself may have been an outgrowth of two kinds of creole developed during the slavery period: house creole and field creole. Material collected at the very end of the Civil War by the Hampton Institute, for example, provides examples of courting speech in this high style. A young man might respond to the question of a young woman about how he spent the day in this way: "I spent the day as an elephant spends it. I played, as a player of backgammon. The elephant is lame, they shot him. The pat is mown down, they waled it. A nice bottle of bird-seed is food for birds. The wide fig tree and the menlanger tree are ornaments of a house. In the East we are the children of the hippo. In the West we are the children of the Governor" (Waters 1983: 205).

The high style is better known from studies of language use in the Caribbean. Anthropologists and linguists have recognized that Caribbean creoles or "nation languages" exist along a continuum from a careful, decorous, and polite style, often confused with standard British English, to a boisterous, creative street style. Abrahams (1983) has described the system at great length, including the existence of informal schools or "colleges" where the high style is learned, and "tea meetings" where it is used. During tea meetings different experts at "talking sweet" take their turn in performances of oratory and poetry which are judged by assembled community residents. The importance of the high style in the speech of blacks in the United States has not been recognized. Here too, it is a form that is consciously learned and practiced. A colleague recounted that he was taught to talk in the formal register by his parents in rural north Florida. They sat at the dinner table in the evening and had him practice verb declensions and pronunciation so that he would be able to speak with dignity and clarity. The development of this high style could easily be seen as predating the slavery experience, having roots in African formal poetry and oratory.

The story of Lynch Hammock, as told by Elizabeth LeCompte, her older sister Rose Davis, and Charles Watson, with myself present, is not so much a story or item of contemporary rural folklore as much as it is a conversation in this formal register or "high style" of speech.

In many conversations, one person completes the thoughts and sentences of another. In more formal contexts, including oratory, this feature of "dual thinking" is spurned and thought of as inappropriate to the flow of speech, or as rude. But the record of spontaneous, dialogic speech recorded around the world is clear: multiple conversations, interruptions, and the finishing of sentences by interlocutors are very common in vocal communication. Caribbean speech communities serve as excellent examples of multiple conversations. Marshall Morris, for example, in his *Saying and Meaning in Puerto Rico* (1981), reports that "In ordinary daily experience in Puerto Rico, there is much 'confusion' of what would be kept separate, in, say, an Anglo-Saxon society" (ibid.: 61). He goes on to give an example of how people there listen to and "appropriate" the conversations of others: "There are six people in the room, in two conversations, four in one, two in the other. The conversations are about different things. At one point I answer 'No' to a question in the conversation in which I am participating. A person in the other conversation hears me say 'No' and asks, 'Why not?'—but why not in terms of her *own* conversation. She had crossed over the line between the conversations, apparently without noticing it, and applied what I said to her own line of thought" (ibid.: 61, emphasis in the original). It is only in the more frozen and formal monologic style of oratory, lectures, or the printed page that what would otherwise be multiple conversations take on the character of interruptions.

The emotional impact of the killings and the relationship of people today to them is balanced by a slow delivery and the dignified presentation of the event during the videotape production.

In rural communities like Brooker, where this narrative was videotaped, it is customary to celebrate the achievements of the black community through an honorary church service. Such services are compliments paid to the strength of individuals who have made particular contributions to their communities. Elizabeth LeCompte was to be honored at the Shiloh Baptist Church for her years of help to the community as a "practical nurse." A practical nurse is a local health worker who cares for people who are infirm or close to death. Elizabeth's older sister, Rose, had been one of north Florida's most famous midwives before her retirement some fifteen years ago. Rose is close to ninety years old now, and is not as verbose as her sister Elizabeth, although she, like Elizabeth, continues to exhibit a warm, sparkling manner in public. Rose's grandson Charles, who is the minister of Shiloh Baptist Church, had asked me to videotape his great aunt and his grandmother talking about their lives. He wanted to use the videotape in the church service so that the congregation could see and hear for themselves the wisdom and wit of Elizabeth within her family context. Charles also wanted a record of his elder relatives, and saw the videotape as an important home artifact to be treasured along with his grandmother's medical equipment and family photographs.

## DIALOGUES THROUGH LOCAL VIDEOTAPE PRODUCTION

The project videographer and myself enjoyed the opportunity to produce the videotape that Charles had requested. I suggested that he also be included in it as testament to his interest in his family. The videotape production was a chance to record his family history and an opportunity to apply a dialogic approach to anthropology in the community. In this case, my clients were an important but poor family of the region, in contrast with the kind of applied anthropology in which the clients are government agencies or corporate sponsors. Applied anthropology is not just an excuse to use statistics in anthropology or engage in social engineering as many practitioners would have it. It is an orientation toward anthropology that places primary emphasis on careful study and analysis to help people.

The production of a videotape is well suited to working in small communities like Brooker without many resources: equipment costs are low, the videotape itself is inexpensive, and the production can be carried out with ease. With careful work, the resulting videotape can be produced "in camera" without expensive editing costs. The immediate presence of videotape is also an advantage. Although videotaping can be an intrusive "extra eye" in an event, it can also be enjoyable for all the participants, with the person behind the videocamera being as much a part of the interaction as other participants. As soon as taping was completed, Charles asked to see a portion of it. We connected the equipment directly to his own television and reviewed some of the videotape. Comments were made about how each of the people on the tape looked and the family expressed its approval of the venture.

The way in which the videotape production was developed is illustrative of applied anthropology based on participation and dialogue. I had met Charles and his family while I was engaged as a consultant to a number of community forums in the town of Brooker. The Florida Endowment for the Humanities had awarded a community grant to Brooker to hold a series of meetings about the past, present, and future of the small community. The forums were a chance for the residents to come together each week and talk about who they were as a community and the problems of life in a small town in the 1980s. As the organizer and moderator of the forums, I had entered into a dialogue with the many people who came each week to this public entertainment. Charles was one of the people who had been suggested to me as a panelist for one of the weekly forums. He spoke on the topic of family; I chose him because he was recently divorced and was able to provide a counterpoint to the other members of the panel, who gave glowing reports of married life and nuclear families in the community. The forums were being videotaped so as to provide a community archive of the events, and it was because of this that Charles asked if I could make a videotape of his family.

## VIDEOTAPING THE EVENT

Most uses of professional videotaping belong to a broadcast mode of production, in which multiple cameras, production teams, editing studios, and wide public distribution are the rule. In contrast, a local production mode uses a single camera and portable equipment, and is aimed at a specific audience who will see the product through a home VCR. Local production video is sensitive to the residents of the local community in which it is made, and is not hindered by the intrusion of the values of the broadcast industry, which demand fast-paced editing, variety in camera position, and composition of the image, all aimed at producing a general level of understanding. In broadcast productions, the director and editor of a piece decide who is to talk and when, in effect imposing a monologic process on a dialogic event.

In a local production mode, the videotaping itself becomes a part of the dialogic process. The participants have editorial control over the end product from the moment of the activity itself. They are free to stop the production, get up and walk around to show the audience some important artifact of the home, and talk with the videotape audience as personal friends who happen to be visiting. In other words, in a local production mode, the videotape of an event is not a means of acquiring ethnographic data, as Mead (1975) and others have thought. Instead, the videotape is the interpretation of that event, the final product of applied anthropology, and as such is planned and executed with the idea of documenting the conversations and dialogues within a local community. Videocassette players have become a ubiquitous feature in the United States; they are almost an obligatory feature of public institutions such as churches, libraries, schools, and clubs. The number of videocassette players and the variety of their community contexts makes a local production mode a viable and important way of returning the power of documentation to local people.

The town of Brooker is situated twenty-five miles from my home in Gainesville, Florida, so I was able to arrive early in the morning for the production. Finding Charles's house was easy. He had given excellent directions for finding it: I was to take a dirt road off of the main highway through town and look for a green frame house on my right. Charles met me at the door and apologized briefly for the condition of the house. It was an old house with a neat lawn and gardens. Charles noted that the family had been in better financial conditions before, but since both his grandmother and his great aunt had stopped working full time it was difficult to keep the house up. Still, the house and area around it were pleasant and cheerful. A six-year-old girl came by as we walked into the house and asked for "little mother." Charles explained that his grandmother still cared for neighborhood children. In Brooker and north Florida in general, "little mother" is a term of reference and endearment used by children for the women who share child rearing with their biological mothers.

The videotape equipment was set up in the living room of the house, as the sun was too hot to allow us to film outside. The living room was small, about fourteen by sixteen feet, and the walls were painted green. There was only a floor lamp and a bare bulb hanging from the ceiling, so we had to open the dark curtains that were hanging on the windows. The furniture in the room included a long sofa, where Rose sat down; an armchair, taken by Elizabeth; a coffee table; and a television. There were several religious pictures on the walls, together with photographs of family members. Charles brought out two kitchen chairs, one for me and the other for himself. After arranging ourselves and the equipment, we discussed what general topics we would talk about. For several reasons, I had asked Charles to be the principal interlocutor. First of all, I was an acquaintance of his grandmother and great aunt, but I did not have any knowledge of their lives or family histories; Charles was much more likely to encourage important topics than an outsider like myself. Second, Charles, as minister of the Shiloh Baptist Church, was an integral part of the day of honor for Elizabeth, his great aunt. Third, he had a keen interest in his own family history. The videotape would be a context in which he would learn more about his family. His engagement in the conversation was an important aspect of his great aunt's and grandmother's motivation to talk. He had taken time during the week before to write out a series of ideas about the family, and had found several birth and death certificates and other family documents that he wanted to use during the filming as points of reference for his grandmother and great aunt.

Elizabeth came into the room dressed in a plaid dress and sat directly in front of the camera, with Charles and myself to her right and her sister Rose to her left. Rose wore a dark red dress, and Charles noted to me that she would not be talking too much during the taping as she was having trouble remembering things. Also, she had worked all morning as a volunteer at a home for the elderly, and so was tired. Still, she wanted to be part of the conversation that was to be recorded.

Elizabeth and Rose both had a warm, serene manner accompanied by a dry wit. Rose had used her skills and knowledge throughout her lifetime to assist in the births of several thousand Floridians, while Elizabeth had used her own skill and knowledge to help people who were ill and often about to die. As the discussion began, both Elizabeth and Rose recounted how they learned their skills from their mothers, who lived in the times of slavery, and that their mothers had learned curing skills from their mothers before them. As the conversation continued, Elizabeth talked slowly and directly, often looking straight at the camera as if to include it in the conversation. The camera and videographer were not an intrusion into the living room, just other features of the event. Elizabeth did the majority of the talking, although Rose joined in from time to time and Charles and I asked for clarification of several points.

The principal topics of the conversations were the difficulties of surviving through the years since freedom and the unique qualities of different relatives. Elizabeth and Rose talked about some individuals with unusual physical features, such as dark hair that never turned grey or feet that appeared like those of cattle, and others with great mental abilities, including ministers and nurses. Elizabeth related how her grandfather had come from France at the turn of the century, which explained why her last name is French. It was soon after this that Charles brought up the subject of the lynching. The transition to the story of the lynching was, like most of the segments of the conversation, initiated by Charles. He was an inquisitive grandson, a respected minister, and the intermediary between his older relatives and ourselves. He had written down a list of topics he wanted to cover that day, but very few of them were discussed. The lynching, though, was one that he had on his list. Elizabeth accepted the topic but integrated it into the longer discourse on family and kinship relationships that had characterized the event from the beginning.

## THE DIALOGUE OF THE LYNCHING

The general story of the lynching is well known throughout the region. In her version of it, Elizabeth not only makes a connection to her family but links the event to the landmarks of several present-day towns of the region, making it a part of the cultural geography of the area. In the transcription, I have used several conventions to signal interaction, including brackets when a second person talks at the same time as the one already speaking, and an equal sign to signal the immediate connection of chains of speech. Loud words are indicated by capital letters, pauses by line breaks, and other features of voicing are indicated in parentheses. For more details, see the transcription note at the end of this work.[1]

| | |
|---|---|
| Charles: | Ah, we tálked a little bit befòre abòut, ah |
| | this LÝNCHING over in ⌐Nēwbury. |
| | Do you remember thát? |
| Rose: | Yès. |
| Elizabeth: | └Yēah, I remēmber. |
| | That was in Níneteen Hundred and SIXTÉEN. |
| | And uh, when uh, BÓISE LÓNG |
| | killed the high sherìff of Gāinesvìlle, |
| | two dēputies |
| | and wòunded one or ⌐twò |
| Rose: | (lower voice, almost ⎸as an aside) |
| | └She can remember further |
| | back than Í càn. |
| Charles: | Yēah. |
| Elizabeth: | (Genuinely laughing) |
| | Há há há há. |
| Rose: | (Quietly) |
| | She can remember hēr wày. |
| Elizabeth: | Hā hā. |
| | WELL, I remémber because I was living in |
| | Jacksonvìlle. |
| Allan: | You were living in Jácksonvìlle? |
| Elizabeth: | Úhùh. At that tìme. |
| | And uh … George WÍNN, his sistèr. |
| | You knòw we half-cropped alòng his sister's |
| | plàce.= |

Charles begins this section of the production with a statement that refers to a conversation he had with his great aunt a few days before. Although his utterance is a statement, it functions in the dialogue as a question, prompting Elizabeth to shift the topic of the conversation to the lynching. Elizabeth, quick to respond, is already finishing Charles's sentence by joining in with the date and name of the protagonist of the event. Before she can set the stage by naming all of the people who were killed in the first part of the event, Rose legitimizes the narrative so far recounted by commenting on Elizabeth's excellent memory.

Elizabeth continues by noting her relationship to the story and in that way suggesting the reason why she remembers the details so well. She also indicates that the crime to be recounted was not a simple event, but one complicated by black and white relations at the turn of the century. Elizabeth notes that she was sharecropping (she uses the term "half-cropping") on land that belonged to the sheriff's sister. These brief statements preview several aspects of the crime: the circumstances will involve agriculture and, through the reference to the institution of sharecropping, hunger on the part of those who must sharecrop. The crime will also involve the institutional power and threat of violence embodied in the position of the high sheriff.

| | |
|---|---|
| Allan: | =Uhuh. |
| Elizabeth: | =Down in Kāmochà. And uh, |
| | so he was, he GOT TO BE hígh shériff from |
| | Gainesville behind sheriff RĀMSÈY, if |
| | I aín't mistàken. |
| | Anyway, |
| | he was the sherìff |
| | when we were living, FÁRMING on his place, |
| | MCCLÉAN'S plàce. |
| | You knòw, Miss MCCLÉAN and George Winn were |
| | sísters and brothèrs. |
| Rose: | Yeah. |
| Elizabeth: | And Dick Wríght, |
| | SÁM Wright was, he was their ÚNCLÈ. |
| | Uh, George Wínn was Díck's and Sám's unclè, |
| | 'cause they were Miss McCléan's SÓNS. |
| Rose: | Yeah, I know Dick and Sam was Miss McCléan's |
| | sòns.= |
| Elizabeth: | =Uhuh. |
| Rose: | ⌐I know that. I don't know nothing about the |
| | u   u<sub></sub>unclè. |
| Elizabeth: | └And uh, LĪLAH, Eva, and Lilah and ÉFE. |
| | ⌐Those |
| Rose: | └Those were the three gīrls. I remember their |
| | nàmes. |
| Elizabeth: | =Uhuh, but they áll was Miss McClean's |
| | childrèn. |
| Charles: | Were they one of the people that was lýnched? |
| Elizabeth: | ⌐Nò. Nò, nò. |
| Rose: | └Nò, that was |
| Elizabeth: | The people that was LÝNCHED was |
| | uh, BLĀCK PÈOPLE. |
| Charles: | Uhuh. |

In this section of the dialogue Elizabeth reinforces her own connection to the white landowners of the region, especially the ones of her own age whom she knew through her family's labor on their land. Rose supports the short kinship lesson, but notes that she did not know the connection with the uncle. Elizabeth continues to outline the family tree of the sheriff, much to the confusion of Charles and myself, who do not quite understand these relationships as they are spoken. Charles asks if the women that Elizabeth is talking about are the ones who were lynched, and in this way previews the subsequent violence of the event. Elizabeth, somewhat surprised at her nephew, points out that the people who were lynched were black people, not the whites she had been describing.

In keeping with her style throughout the videotape production, Elizabeth connects the narration to the two guideposts of place and kin. In this section she and Rose elaborate on the relationships of their family to the sheriff by naming the sheriff's sister and all of her children. The story of the lynching, heard throughout the region, suddenly becomes a family story involving Rose, Elizabeth, and Charles.

| | |
|---|---|
| Elizabeth: | See, there was the DĀVISES, (quietly) and |
| | whò èlse? The Lóngs, |
| | and uh |
| | mý gósh, and BÁSKINS! |
| Rose: | Josh Baskins= |
| Elizabeth: | =Josh Baskins. They killed two wōmen |
| | and a màn. One màn. |
| Allan: | Now, what was the círcumstànces. Why did he |
| | kill the high sheriff, and= |
| Elizabeth: | =WELL nòw, I can't say whether it was trūe or |
| | fàlse. |
| | There was some HÓG STEALIN' goin' on back out thère. |
| | And ùh |
| | the sheriff went to Boise Long's |
| | HÓUSE. And ùh |
| | when they KNOCKED at the dòor, |
| | they kept knóckin' and tellin' him it was the shériff. |
| | And he had his wife to open the DÒOR. |
| | When they open the DOOR and he CÓME ÍN, |
| | they say he had a high powered rìfle. |
| | (quietly) And he begun to pump the bullets in |
| | to thèm. |
| | KILLED George Wìnn, |
| | two of |
| | the deputies that was with hìm, |
| | and woūnded some more peoplè. |
| | Then HÉ GOT AWĀY. |
| | And |
| | so they CÓME BÁCK thèn. |
| | they got his wìfe. |

>They got her sīster-in-làw
>(quietly) and there was an old preacher,
Rose: Josh Baskins=
Elizabeth: =Josh Baskins. They got HÍM. They LỲNCHED
THÈM.
Charles: Thrée?

Elizabeth and Rose began this section of the dialogue by recounting the family names of the black people who were lynched. This provides a balance to the previous section and again underscores the importance of kinship in the social activity of north Florida. I ask for a synopsis of the actual event at this point, which cuts short Elizabeth's recounting of the kinship relationships for the moment. Elizabeth then begins the account of the circumstances of the lynching with a disclaimer, stating that she does not know if Boise Long was actually guilty of hog stealing. But noting that there was some hog stealing, Elizabeth phrases the event in the context of the hunger of rural black people at the turn of the century. There were large numbers of feral hogs in the woods of north Florida at that time, a source of food for both black and white hunters. The escape of domestic hogs was a common occurrence. Indeed, the present city of Gainesville was first known as "Hog Town."

The confrontation between the rural black man, Boise Long, and the white sheriff from the city is tragic. It begins with the summons by the sheriff at Boise's door. The personal danger to Boise Long is critical, only obliquely referred to in the account when Elizabeth mentions that they kept knocking on his door. When Boise's wife opens the door, he shoots the sheriff. What had begun as a verbal dialogue between the sheriff and Boise suddenly became a dialogue of violence.

Elizabeth told this part of the story in a straightforward, matter-of-fact style. The laconic recitation of the events of the shooting ends with a statement that three people were "lynched." The word "lynched" in this context refers to mob violence that took place in retaliation for the killing of the sheriff.

Elizabeth: Yeah.
And this uh, Denise màn,
what wàs his=
Rose: =Bill=
Elizabeth: =Bíll Dénise?
Rose: Uhùh.
He was wàlkin',
comin' out of the country into Newbùry.
And they SHÒT HIS BRAINS ÒUT,
they jùst

He was wàlkin' alòng the road and they jùst
rode along by and SHÒT hìm.
Oh, they kílled several peoplè, I can't
    remember áll of thèm, but now this
    was
was in one familỳ.
And uh, they lōcked up
Mirah Denise had a little bábỳ.
(quietly) Óh, two or three days òld.
They didn't KILL HER.
They LÓCKED her up in jàil.
And ùh
She ùh,=

Rose:    =Dídn't they kill a wómán?
Elizabeth:    Húh?
Rose:    Dídn't they kill a wóman?
Elizabeth:    Yeah. They killed MÁRY DÉNISE, dón't you
        remémber?
Rose:    Ōh.
Elizabeth:    And Mariah's sistèr.
Rose:    Uhuh.
Elizabeth:    Uhuh. And JÓSH BASKÌNS. And then they
        killed BÓISE's màmà.
        Her name was MARỲ.
Rose:    Uhuh.
Elizabeth:    She didn't
        BÓISE's mamà,
        and Máry Deníse. THEY LÝNCHED THÉM WÍTH
        JÒSH BÁSKINS.
Rose:    Uhuh.
Elizabeth:    And uh, NÉAL DENÌSE, they SHÓT HĪM.
        Góing into Néwburỳ.
Charles:    Whāt ever happened to Mary's babỳ? She
        ever=
Elizabeth:    =Nōw she was down there in the jail hòuse when
        some whíte women from Newbury went dòwn
        thère
        and BÉGGED them to turn her OÙT and go back to
        her bàby
        because (quietly) her breasts was, you know, oh,
        she was just in miserỳ.
        Ánd they tell me they TIED her behind a "Ť"
        model and drùg her=
Charles:    =Uhuh.=
Elizabeth:    =(quietly) and out of the citỳ limit
        and tūrned her lòose. She went home.

BUT WHÉN
When Boise heard abòut they lynched his wífe,

Charles: Uhuh.

Elizabeth: HE GAVE, HE GAVE HIMSELF ÚP. (quietly) They hùng him too.

Charles: Uhuh.

The full force of the event now becomes evident. The unnamed group begins by killing two women and a minister and then, not satisfied, shoots a man walking down the road. Rose brings him into the narration with a short recollection and Elizabeth finishes the description. Then Elizabeth brings up the case of Mariah Denise and her new baby. In other accounts of the event, she is lynched with the others and spontaneously aborts her baby. In Elizabeth's account, she is locked up and released through the intervention of some white women of the town, further underscoring the complexity of relationships between whites and blacks at the time. As a final indignity, however, Mariah is dragged out of town behind a car. Almost as an afterthought, Elizabeth adds that the original protagonist, Boise, turned himself over to the police at that point, and was hung.

Elizabeth: (quietly) But he give himself ùp.=

Charles: =She dídn't=

Elizabeth: =And this BÁBỲ
that his WIFE
LEFT.
his AUNT RAISED HIM.
And he used to bè
the MECHÁNIC to the JÓHN DEERE place in Newbúry.

Charles: Uhuh=

Elizabeth: =(quietly) He was a mechanic there, oh, a long, long time, 'TILL HE DÍED.

Charles: Uhuh.

Elizabeth: ⌐And uh, RÁNDALL

Charles: ⌊Do you rēmember

Elizabeth: His name was Rándàll.

In this section Elizabeth brings the event up to date by placing the young child in the context of his later life as a mechanic at a farm implement store in the same area where the lynching took place. In keeping with the strong sense of personal relations which permeates her account, Elizabeth names the child even as Charles begins to ask for more clarification.

Charles: We talked once about à
a lynchìng, I don't know if it was this lynching,
but a MÁN came up and CUT a màn in the

           BĀCK or something
           for a whip or sòmething.
           Dó you remember thát?

Elizabeth:  OH YEAH. NO, THAT WAS JOSH BÁSKINS, the
           MÁN. After they cut him DÒWN,
           the man cut a STRIP out of his—he was a jet-
           black man, just about the color of these
           pànts—of the CENTER of his báck bòne.

Charles:  Uhuh.

Elizabeth:  And said he was going to make a "CRACKÈR"=

Charles:  =For his hòrse.=

Elizabeth:  =For his
           cōw whīp.

Charles:  Uhuh.

Elizabeth:  And he stooped DÒWN.
           I MÉT him since I been back from Geórgià, I met
           him several times in
           in GAINESVÌLLE.
           Ánd he stooped dòwn and cut that strip out of
           that Negro's bàck and he never straightened
           up no mòre.

Rose:  Never díd.

Elizabeth:  Nev̄er did straighten up no mòre.

The last feature discussed in this dialogue is the retribution visited upon one of the whites for his horrible behavior. Charles brings the episode up in sketchy form. He and I had talked with Elizabeth about this part of the story once before. At that time, Elizabeth described how the sky turned dark and a huge wind came up as the white man cut a strip out of the dead minister's back, and, as in this description, he became a hunchback. This time, she is content with mentioning the result itself, not the circumstances. Although no special emphasis was given to the term "cracker" in the dialogue, whites in Florida and Georgia are often called "crackers." The folk entymology of the term refers to cowboys cracking their whips as they rode into small rural towns. An alternative explanation often given is that migrants from the mid-Atlantic states after the Civil War brought tins of crackers with them. The term, as used in this part of the dialogue, reinforces once again the racial division between blacks and whites at the end of the event.

In keeping with her style of bringing the dialogue up to the present, Elizabeth mentions that she had met the person who did this ugly deed in Gainesville. The mention of this place further connects the dialogue to the present; it is the city where I live and the home of many of Rose's other grandchildren. At the end of this part of the videotape Rose rejoins the dialogue by underscoring that the man never did straighten up from the incident. With this statement the dialogue ends.

## DISCUSSION

There are few examples of the high or prestigious style of speech of rural black women to be found in the literature on Black English. This short transcription of a videotaped dialogue calls attention to the importance of this form in communities such as Brooker. The style is not oratorical in that it is not limited by the constraints of public performance before a large audience. At the phonological level, the style is characterized by careful enunciation of words, including inflectional endings that are often deleted when the "low" or street style is used. Vocabulary is elaborate. Words are chosen with care and elaborate utterances are constructed: "When they KNOCKED at the door, they kept knockin' and tellin' him it was the sheriff. And he had his wife to open the door. When they open the door and he COME IN, they say he had a high powered rifle. And he begun to pump the bullets in to them. KILLED GEORGE Winn, two of the deputies that was with him, and wounded some more people." In this example some tense markers are deleted in verbs such as "open" and "come in," but others are included, including "kept," "begun," "killed," and "wounded." The syntactic elaboration associated with this high style is also present in the above example. Sentences that begin with subordinate phrases, such as the first and third, implied subjects used for emphasis, as in the last sentence, and thematic elaboration, seen in the third and fourth sentences, are a few of the syntactic features of the style. The sociolinguistic features of the style include family settings such as these where events of family history are recounted by people in older generations. Interruptions are expected and taken in stride. Appropriate themes include the time of freedom (soon after the abolition of slavery), the time of slavery, and morality. Like Martin Luther King, Jr.'s famous speech, "I have a dream," the dialogue about the lynching in Newbury draws upon the inequities of racial discrimination and hatred in a manner directed at understanding and bettering the relationships. The feeling conveyed at the end of the story of the lynching is one of sadness and of hope that such violence will not happen again.

These are only a few of the characteristics of this high style. My point here is to illustrate its existence and to show that it is not merely "standard English" spoken in counterpoint to African American English. It is a style that is one of the registers of African American English. It is not a style that is necessarily learned in school in contradiction to "Black English," but is a style available to people, such as those introduced here, who have very little formal education.

From a discourse perspective, the text is a dialogue, not a monologue, and it is not structured by rhyme or extended repetition as much as oratory is. The prestigious style transcribed here relies on the curious and interested group of interlocutors found in a family where members are used to talking to one another. At the end of this part of the videotaped dialogue, a ten-year-old girl walked into the room, sat down on Elizabeth's lap, and looked up to listen to what she was saying.

The episode itself is unsettling. The account does not provide a clear-cut reason for the original shooting, nor does it elaborate on the reasons for the furious vengeance that was visited upon Boise Long's family afterwards. Even at the turn of the century, such a wave of violence against the family of a criminal would have been unusual. The fact that the actions are not fully explained points to a feature of dialogue. When a story is told in a dialogical context such as this one, the participants create the text by emphasizing, questioning, and leaving unsaid different portions of what might be said. The emphasis at the end of the story on the fate of a minister, for example, arose out of a question by Charles, himself a minister. In contrast, monologic storytelling traditions, or dialogic traditions reduced to monologues for the printed page, are evaluated by hearers or readers on how fully a plot is elaborated by a single performer. In this sense, monologues present culture predigested, as it were, and dialogues present it emerging, flowering.

The production of the videotape involving Elizabeth, Rose, Charles, and myself is an illustration of a dialogic approach to the work of anthropology. In producing the videotape at Charles's request, I engaged in a conversation with them about their family history and culture. Although his original plan was to videotape his aunt Elizabeth for the church service, the actual production included all of us, and in this way underscored the interconnections between Elizabeth, her family, and the community. The dialogue about a lynching was only a small part of a two-hour tape. Other sections included recollections of different family members, descriptions of the community and north Florida through the years, and recipes for health and curing. Elizabeth and Rose had complemented one another throughout their lives, Rose working as a midwife and Elizabeth as a practical nurse. Between the two of them they had brought thousands of people into the world and held them here as long as they could. In their conversations for the videotape something of this wide-ranging community is brought out, through the names of places and people all across north Florida and Georgia. Although Rose's participation in the dialogues was limited by her health and the work she had already accomplished that day, her presence and comments balanced those of Elizabeth.

The lynching episode was a tragic event for people in north Florida when it happened, and remains so today even as a place name on the highway. The explosive racial violence of northern cities during the 1920s had its north Florida counterpart in events like this. The violence remembered today by Elizabeth is a testament to the difficulties of living a life in service to other people. The fact that such stories are recounted without obvious bitterness speaks to the strength of people like Rose and Elizabeth and also to the dialogue they had with birth, illness, and death in their lifetimes. Rose mentioned during the videotaping that in all of her sixty years as a midwife, she had never lost a baby. Notice that in the part of the conversation presented here, reference is made to Boise Long's wife, Mary, who was taken to jail while nursing a baby. Elizabeth laughed during another passage, when she remembered the anger of one of her patients as he approached death. I asked her how she could bear such anger. She said she just "soaked up" the anger and pulled it from him so he would not feel so bad.

The videotape made with Elizabeth and her family, especially the excerpt transcribed and presented here, shows how the interpretation of community life in rural Florida takes place within dialogues. The questions, responses, and affirmations concerning the story of Lynch Hammock make clear the social relations between whites and blacks, the role of kinship in those relations, and the important role of senior females in the continuity of community life and culture. It also illustrates some important qualities of a dialogic style of social discourse. Among these are the emergence of cultural understanding through talk. The questions that Charles raises, the comments that Rose makes, and the story told by Elizabeth do not make up a complete account of an event, but rather produce approximations of it, approximations finely tuned to the circumstances of the particular day the tape was made. The dialogue is never entirely finished; any future day might present the opportunity for Charles or anyone else to say, "We talked a little bit before about this lynching … ," and in this way open a further interpretation of rural life for the participants. I have presented this excerpt in order to enlarge the record of cultural discourse, but where Geertz hoped that interpretive anthropology might "make available to us answers that others, guarding their sheep in other valleys, have given" (1973: 30), the dialogic anthropology I practice here can claim only to raise the questions that others have raised in their conversations. By showing readers or viewers how participants produce a text, it points to the possibility of multiple readings of that text.

The conversation within the story of the lynching and the conversation between the participants at the time of the videotaping were linked through the verbal skills of Elizabeth, as she elaborated on kin relationships and place names. A seventy-year-old event suddenly took on new life and meaning as we were each drawn into the dialogue. Before that came a dialogue between Charles and myself within the series of town meetings held in Brooker, during which we developed a contract for the videotape production. Had not Charles recognized the utility of local production video as a way of elaborating his planned celebration of his aunt's contribution to the community, the tape could not have been made. This was then an instance of applied anthropology that took its impetus from the questions and interests of local residents.

## NOTES

I would like to thank the Florida Endowment for the Humanities for sponsoring the town meetings that led to this videotape. Also, Elizabeth LeCompte, Rose Davis, and Charles Watson, of Brooker, are a fine family and made this project possible. I have disguised their names and the name of their town to ensure their privacy. The University of Florida Department of Anthropology has generously made videotape equipment available for projects such as this, and, together with the Universidad Complutense de Madrid, has provided the time and circumstances necessary for the writing of this essay. Discussions with Alan Saperstein and Denise Matthews, two independent filmmakers, were important in developing the idea of the local production mode. Karen Ross is to be thanked for excellent videography on the project. Her rapport from behind the camera helped make the event successful. The editors of this book, Bruce Mannheim and Dennis Tedlock, are to be thanked for their insights and suggestions about dialogic anthropology, as are many colleagues in Spain and the United States with whom I have discussed similar issues.

1. Ordinary spelling (as opposed to a technical orthography) has been used in the transcription so as to keep the meaning of the utterances in view at all times. Several discourse transcription conventions have been added to highlight conversational overlap and the paralinguistic features of this high, formal style of conversation. I have followed Sacks, Schegloff, and Jefferson (1974) in using a single bracket ([) at points of overlap of two or more voices. For example, the beginning of the dialogue has a short summary of the action told by Elizabeth which includes a comment by Rose about Elizabeth's memory. Rose begins talking as Elizabeth says the word "two:"

> (E.)    and wounded one or ┌two
> (R.)                          └She can remember further back
>          than I can.

An equal sign (=) is used to signify the immediate start of a new utterance without a pause. Late in the dialogue, Elizabeth is not sure of a name. Rose supplies it and

Elizabeth immediately repeats it without a pause between the utterance of Rose and her own:

(E.) and BASKINS!
(R.) Josh Baskins.=
(E.) =Josh Baskins. They killed two women

Paralinguistic features including voice quality, accent, and utterance length are also signaled in the transcription. Some vocal qualities such as quietness are signaled by parenthetical remarks, while changes of line indicate pauses:

(E.) Mirah Denise had a little baby.
(quietly) Oh, two or three days old.

Short pauses within a line are indicated by three dots. Capital letters indicate stress on particular words through increased loudness:

(E.) SAM Wright was, he was their UNCLE.

Pitch contours and a relatively slow delivery give this formal register its characteristic sound. The use of rising, steady, and falling tones has been noted for Caribbean creoles; the high style used here is not as "lilting" as they are, but it does involve the use of pitch contours for emphasis. I include the pitch markings in the transcription only when they deviate markedly from common American English usage. See Bolinger (1978) for a general discussion of intonation contours. In the present formal register intonation is used at the level of individual words, often in conjunction with stress or loudness. Rising, falling, and steady pitches are indicated, respectively, by an acute accent ( ´ ), a grave accent ( ` ), and a long mark ( ¯ ):

(E.) Úhùh. At that tìme.
And uh ... George WÍNN, his sistèr.
You knòw we half-cropped alòng his sister's
plàce.

In general I have tried to keep the transcription as readable as possible, yet detailed enough to show how conversation and narrative are organized in this high style of African American speech.

## REFERENCES CITED

Abrahams, Roger. 1983. *The Man of Words in the West Indies.* Baltimore: Johns Hopkins University Press.

Bolinger, Dwight. 1978. "Intonation across Languages." In *Universals of Human Language,* vol. 2, *Phonology,* gen. ed. J. Greenberg, pp. 471–524. Stanford: Stanford University Press.

Burns, Allan F. 1983. *An Epoch of Miracles: Oral Literature of the Yucatec Maya.* Austin: University of Texas Press.

Dwyer, Kevin. 1982. *Moroccan Dialogues: Anthropology in Question.* Baltimore: Johns Hopkins University Press.

Geertz, Clifford. 1973. *The Interpretation of Cultures*. New York: Harper and Row.

Labov, William. 1972a. *Language in the Inner City: Studies in the Black English Vernacular*. Philadelphia: University of Pennsylvania Press.

———. 1972b. "The Logic of Nonstandard English." In *Language and Social Context*, edited by Pier Giglioli, pp. 179–215. Baltimore: Penguin Books.

Marcus, George E., and Michael M. J. Fischer. 1986. *Anthropology as Cultural Critique: An Experimental Moment in the Human Sciences*. Chicago: University of Chicago Press.

Mead, Margaret. 1975. "Visual Anthropology in a Discipline of Words." In *Principles of Visual Anthropology*, edited by Paul C. Hockings, pp. 3–10. The Hague: Mouton.

Morris, Marshall. 1981. *Saying and Meaning in Puerto Rico*. Oxford: Pergamon Press.

Sacks, Harvey, E. Schegloff, and G. Jefferson. 1974. "A Simplest Systematics for the Organization of Turn-Taking for Conversation." *Language* 50:696–736.

Tedlock, Dennis. 1972. *Finding the Center: Narrative Poetry of the Zuni Indians*. New York: Dial Press.

Waters, Donald, ed. 1983. *Strange Ways and Sweet Dreams: Afro-American Folklore from the Hampton Institute*. Boston: G. K. Hall and Co.

# FOUR

# The Voices of Don Gabriel: Responsibility and Self in a Modern Mexicano Narrative

## JANE H. HILL

In "Discourse in the Novel," Bakhtin identified a central question for the study of responsibility in discourse: the moral choice required of the speaker among the terministic and linguistic possibilities presented by the "heteroglossia" of any community of speakers. For Bakhtin, this choice constituted a formative moment in the emergence of consciousness, which "everywhere . . . comes upon 'languages' and not language. Consciousness finds itself inevitably facing the necessity of *having to choose a language*. With each literary-verbal performance, consciousness must actively orient itself amidst heteroglossia" (Bakhtin 1981: 295).

In order to explore this problem of choice, Bakhtin proposes a thought-experiment: He asks us to imagine a peasant. At first, Bakhtin's peasant, although immersed in a variety of language systems (of course he is a Russian peasant, so we may imagine that he spoke some local Russian variety, heard his priest pray in Old Church Slavonic, and dictated to the local scribe petitions to officialdom couched in the local "paper" language), does not coordinate these dialogically. Instead, "each was indisputably in its own place, and the place of each was indisputable" (ibid.: 296). Bakhtin proposes that for this peasant there will come a moment which is identical to the moment of formation of literary consciousness, when "a critical interanimation of languages began to occur in [his] consciousness . . . [when] it became clear that . . . the ideological systems and approaches to the world that were indissolubly connected with these languages contradicted each other and in no way could live in peace and quiet with one another . . . [when] the inviolability and predetermined quality of these languages came to an end, and the necessity of actively choosing one's orientation among them began" (ibid.: 296).[1]

The present study follows Bakhtin's directive to "examine a peasant." It explores the practices by which a speaker of modern Mexicano claims a moral position among conflicting ways of speaking, weighted with contradictory ideologies, by distributing these across a complex of "voices" through which he constructs a narrative about the murder of his son.

Don Gabriel was said to be the last speaker of Mexicano in San Lorenzo Almecatla, a town of about eight hundred inhabitants which crowns the top of a small hill about five miles north of the city of Puebla, just west of the bustling industrial suburb of Panzacola. We went to interview him on a hot Sunday afternoon in the dry season, when dust and fumes from the factories blew through the rutted lanes around the house where he lay dying. In his great *sala* it was dim and cool, with only the buzzing flies to remind us of the outdoor heat. Emaciation and the pale ivory of his skin after months of illness and shade gave the old man the face of a Quixote. Pneumonia was gathering in his lungs, and coughing and spitting punctuated his speech. Indeed, though, to speak Mexicano with our young interviewer would be *cē lujo* 'a luxury'. So the tape recorder was set up beside him on the bed, and the interview began. Don Gabriel's life had been full, with hard work and community service. He held fervent opinions on the contrast between the *rigor* of the old days and the softness of today. God be thanked, he had never suffered any accident, never been ill. The interviewer, pressing for text on this "danger of death" question, a standby of sociolinguistic interviewing (Labov 1972), tried to verify this claim:[2]

| | |
|---|---|
| INT: Huān cē acci'dente 'āmo 'quiēnman? | And never any accident? |
| DG: 'Mm? | Mm? |
| INT: 'Cē acci'dente. | An accident? |
| DG: Acci'dente 'ni lo 'quiera 'Dios. | No accident, by God's will. |
| INT: _Aah. | Aah. |
| DG: 'Āmo. \Āmo āmo] acci'dente 'āmo,]$_{P,INT}$ > 'sola⁻mente,]$_{1N}$ | No. No, no accident, no, only]$_1$ |
| >ōquimic'tihqueh | they murdered |
| 'cē nomu^chacho.]$_{2N,S}$ | my son.]$_2$ |
| ... Qui'piāz 'como: ... como si'ete ... como 'ocho nueve 'años.]$_{3N}$ | ... It will be like ... like seven ... like eight, nine years.]$_3$ |
| Zan por in 'dicha 'fábrica ōquitlā'lihqueh.]$_{4N}$ | They left him right by that factory.]$_4$ |

## Episode 1.A

Huān ōqui'chīhqueh 'cē: ...
'cē con´venio 'entre in
den ni⁻cān, .. den ´mismo
⁻pueblo,]₅ₙ
que ccala'quīzqueh cē ´carro 'de:
... de pa'saje.]₆ₙ
Huān ōqui´nōtzqueh 'de:
... 'ser teso'rero
īmi´nāhuac]₇ₙ,ₐ
neh ācmo 'ōniccā'huaya,
porque]₈ₚ lo ´mismo 'ōyec
presi'dente.]₉ₙ
INT: _Aah.
DG: Huān niqui⁻lia,
ʰ\"Ācmo ximocomprometerō;
ʰ\xiccāhua, hijito.
ʰ\Nōn xiccāhua."]₁₀ₙ,Q

And they made a ...
an agreement among
those here, .. of the same
town,]₅
that they would put in a
passenger bus.]₆
And when they called him to
... to be treasurer
among them,]₇
I did not give him permission,
because]₈ he was municipal
president as well.]₉
Aah.
And I tell him,
"Don't make any more commitments;
leave it, son.
As for that leave it."]₁₀

## Episode 1.B

In carre⁻tera, por \yeh ōmotlapoh
nōn.]₁₁ₙ Hasta ⟩divi´sión
'ōyec.]₁₂ₙ,T
INT: _Aah.
DG: Hasta ōquitlatī'lihqueh in
īal'mīāl.]₁₃ₙ ʰ\Bueno,]₁₄ₙ,ₚ
tonteʰ\rías
ōquichīhuāltihqueh.]₁₅ₙ,ₚ
Huān qui⁻lia, ʰ\"Ācmo
nimocalaquīz."]₁₆ₙ,D ⟩Pero 'todas
ma'neras ōquitlāni´lihqueh 'in
īvolun⁻tad.]₁₇ₙ,T ʰ\Siempre ... ō-
... ⟩ō'calac.]₁₈ₙ,ₚ,T

It was opened up by way of the
highway.]₁₁ There was even
a quarrel.]₁₂
Aah.
They even burned his fodder
stack.]₁₃ Well,]₁₄
it was foolishness
that they did to him.]₁₅
And he tells him, "I won't
go in anymore."]₁₆ But after
all they won from him his
agreement.]₁₇ Always ... he,
... he went in.]₁₈

## Episode 1.C

'Ya 'yōne'miya 'yōquichī'huaya
ne'gocio, para 'nōn
compro'misọ.]₁₉ₙ Pero, ...
des´graciadamente 'nīnqueh
cris⁻tianos, in āquin
ōquipi'ayah ambi'ción de 'nōn ... de
'nōn tra⁻bajo,]₂₀ₚ,ₙ ōqui⁻milih,
"\Bueno, in āquin 'nequi ´nōn,
quēnin nanqui'nequih, .. 'nōn:,
´nōn 'sobra, .. o 'nōn: ... 'nōn

Now he was going about doing
business, for that
agreement.]₁₉ But, ...
unfortunately these
people, who
had ambition about that ... that
"work,"]₂₀ when he told them,
"Well, whoever wants that,
how do you all want it, .. tha-a-t,
that surplus, or tha-a-t ... that

aˉhorro, ¹cā´nin
caˉlaquīz"?]₂₁ ₙ,ᴅ (clears throat)
Quihtoah in yehˉhuān, "Pero ´para
in 'pōxahtli, 'no. ⟨Āmo de
'nōn."]₂₂ ₙ,ₐ Porque bas'tante
'feo coˉrázōn.]₂₃ ₚ Con rá´zōn
quihtoah in 'gente in ˉpueblo, que
timote'huiah īpan in 'cargo por
'base de inteˉrés.]₂₄ ₚ,ᴮ
INT: _Mhm.
ʰ\Āmo.]₂₅ ₚ "Xicpensa'rōcạn
ˉcualli, huān 'mā motē'maca
ʰ'luz."]₂₆ ᴄ Pues ´nēci āmo
'ōquimpadeˉceroh]₂₇ ₚ
ōcuīqui'lihqueh ven'taja.]₂₈ ₙ,ₚ

savings, where
will it go in"?]₂₁
They say, "But for
'the pocket,' no. None of
that."]₂₂ Because of such
ugly hearts.]₂₃ With reason
the people of the town say, that
we fight one another about a
job due to personal interest.]₂₄
Mhm.
No.]₂₅ "Think you all
well, and let people be given
light."]₂₆ Well it seems that it
did not appear to those]₂₇
who took advantage of him.]₂₈

## Episode 2.A

Ōcuīquili'lihqueh ven'taja huān
cē 'tōnal ... ]₂₉ ₙ,ₚ
WOMAN: De ʰ\pura política.
DG: ⟨'Qué?] (unintelligible reply)
De ma´nera ōˉninen]₃₀ ₙ
huān ocachi 'īhcih, ōnah´cico]₃₁ ₙ
nēchi'liah 'este, ..
"Xicmecharhuīʰ'lihqui cē 'taco
noʰ\nāhuac"]₃₂ ₙ,ᴅ Niquilia,
"Aʰ\yāmo nimaʰ\yāna]₃₃ ₙ,Q ´Cān
ōticcāh in mocˉnīh, para
in, in yōl´cāmeh?"]₃₄ Q
Quihtoa, "Pos 'hasta ōmpa
ōni'cuālcāh'tēhui, para
⟨quinhuā´līcāz."]₃₅ ₙ,ᴅ Niquilia,
"´Mā niquin'chia.]₃₆ ₙ,Q ¹´Cān
tiyāz in 'te̲h?"]₃₇ Q Este,
"ˉChiāhueh 'Tlāx'cuāpa."]₃₈ ᴅ "Para
ˉtlen?"]₃₉ Q "ˉChiāhueh,
ticttāˉtīhueh 'este ... este
ticcāhua'tīhueh in toˉmín, 'den:"
... ]₄₀ ᴅ ʰ\Tlenōnōn
ōnēchilih?]₄₁ ₚ (clears throat)
"Ticcāhua'tīhueh in 'tomín
'para in: ... pues para in perˉmiso,
vaya, para in ˉplacas, o: ..."]₄₂ ᴅ
ʰ\Āmo niquilnāmiqui quēn
ōnēchilih.]₄₃ Niquilia, "ᶜʰ\Bueno,

They took advantage of him
and one day ... ]₂₉
Nothing but politics.
What? (unintelligible reply)
For some reason I went walking]₃₀
and early, when I arrived,]₃₁
he told me uh, ...
"Come have something to eat
with me."]₃₂ I say,
"I'm not hungry anymore.]₃₃ Where
did you leave your brother, for
the, the animals?"]₃₄
He says, "Well I went to leave
him over that way, for
him to bring them."]₃₅ I tell him,
"Let me wait for them.]₃₆ Where
are you going?"]₃₇ Uh,
"We're going to Puebla."]₃₈ "What
for?"]₃₉ "We're going
in order to see about uh ... uh
to go leave the money, fo:r"
... ]₄₀ What was it
he told me?]₄₁
"We are going to leave the money
for the: ... well for the permit,
I mean, for the plates, o:r ..."]₄₂
I don't remember what
he told me.]₄₃ I say, "Well,

a'dios."]₄₄ ₙ,Q ⟨ˡ "Ps āmo
tihueh'cāhuah."]₄₅ D ⟩ "ʰ\Āmo."]₄₆ Q
⟩Yō'yahqueh, .. 'mero den: .. 'īpan:
... 'īpan: ... 'īpan cēm´pōal huān
chicuacen 'tōnal de: ... de: 'julio,
Nuestra Se'ñora Santa 'Anạ.]₄₇ ₙ
(spits)

goodbye."]₄₄ "Well we won't
be long."]₄₅ "No."]₄₆
He went, .. exactly on: .. on:
... on: ... on the twenty-
sixth of-f ... of-f July,
the day of Our Lady Saint Ann.]₄₇

## Episode 2.B

⟩´Tonz cē tōnal 'antes,] ō'yahqueh
ō'huāllah oc´cē 'tōnal.]₄₈ ₙ
Ō'huāllah cē desˉpues,]₄₉ ₙ
nēchi'lia este ...
"Timotlapia'lītịh?"]₅₀ ₙ,D =
Niquilia, "ʰ\Quēmah niquimpiatih
in yōlcāmeh.]₅₁ ₙ,Q ´Nēchilia, "Mā
ti'ācạn īhuān noc´nīh,]₅₂ ₙ,D huān
'ōncān ni'cuālcāh'tēhuāz.]₅₃ D
Xicmoma'quilī cē 'vuelta ītech in
'campo."]₅₄ D Ōˉniah]₅₅ ₙ ⟩huān
ōni'huāllah lo 'mismọ.]₅₆ ₙ
Quemeh ´nīn hora 'ye,
ticcha'rohtoqueh in ī'tacọ]₅₇ ₙ
nēchilia, "Xonhuālʰ\moīca,
tiquecha'rōzqueh cē 'taco."]₅₈ ₙ,D
= Niquilia, "ʰ\Ah, hijo, aʰ\yāmo
nimaʰ\yāna.]₅₉ ₙ,Q In moc'nīh
ō'mocah ītech in 'campo."]₆₀ Q
Niquilia, "Nic´chia mā
'huāllāz."]₆₁ ₙ,Q Huān este, "Ps,
ʰ\cān tiyāz?"]₆₂ Q Quihtoa
este, .. " 'Chiāhueh
yōtcarregla'rohqueh in
a'sunto,]₆₃ ₙ,D ya no más zan
mocā'huatih in toˉmīn,]₆₄ D huān
este, monom'brarōz in direc'tiva,
de ´nōn a'suntọ."]₆₅ D (spits)
Ni´quilia, "Pues ʰ\tlen diario
āhueliti nancarre'glaroạh?"]₆₆ ₙ,Q
"\Está bien quēmạh."]₆₇ D
Toz niquilia, "Aʰ\yāmo xiā," o
"ʰ\Āmo xiā."]₆₈ ₙ,Q (clock begins
tolling music and 11 A.M.) Quihtoa,
"ʰ\Āmo, ⟨pero
yōnimocomprome'teroh."]₆₉ ₙ,D

Then one day before, he came and
went another day.]₄₈
When he came some time
later,]₄₉ he tells me uh ... "Are
you going to go shepherding?"]₅₀
I tell him, "Yes I went to watch
the animals."]₅₁ He tells me, "Let
you and my brother go,]₅₂ and
I will be staying over there.]₅₃
You go take a walk around the
fields."]₅₄ I went]₅₅ and
I came back the same way.]₅₆
Like at this hour now, when we
used to go to eat something,]₅₇
he tells me, "Come, let's have
something to eat."]₅₈
I tell him, "Ah, son, I'm not
hungry now.]₅₉ Your brother
stayed in the fields."]₆₀
I tell him, "I'll wait until he
comes."]₆₁ And uh, "Well,
where are you going?"]₆₂ He says
uh, .. "We are going
to take care of the
business,]₆₃ just
to go leave the money]₆₄ And
uh, to name the directors,
of that business."]₆₅
I tell him, "Well it can't be you
all have to take care of things
every day?"]₆₆ "It's O.K., sure."]₆₇
Then I tell him, "Don't go now," or
"Don't go."]₆₈
He says,
"No, but I have an
appointment."]₆₉

ʰ\Pos yah yeh.]$_{70\ O}$ ⟩" 'Āmo, tlen hora 'tihuītz?"]$_{71\ Q}$ ʰ\"Āmo."]$_{72\ D}$ "⟩/Cualcān?"]$_{73\ Q}$

Well he went.]$_{70}$ "No, what time will you come back?"]$_{71}$ "No."]$_{72}$ "In the morning?"]$_{73}$

### Episode 3

Como ni'cān, zoā'tzīntli ōmopahti'aya ⁻Puebla,]$_{74\ N}$ huān zan 'neh ni'cān ōni'catca nochi in no-, noni'etas.]$_{75\ N}$ (coughs) Ō'huāllah (coughs, spits) 'cē nozo'āmōn de 'nē 'lado de 'cē nomu'chacho ^máyōr.]$_{76\ N,S}$ (Clock stops tolling 11.) Nēchilia, "Pápā ā'yāmo timēhtzī´noa?"]$_{77\ N,E}$ Niquilia "Ā'yāmo."]$_{78\ N,Q}$ Nēchi'lia "Xic'mottil 'tlen yōnic'ahcic."]$_{79\ N,E}$ Niquilia "ʰ\Tlenōnōn?"]$_{80\ N,Q}$ Nēchilia "'Yōnic'ahcic cē 'carta."]$_{81\ N,E}$ "'Āquin ōccāʰ'huaco?"]$_{82\ Q}$ "'Quién 'sabe,]$_{83\ E}$ nōn neh ōnic'ahcic ītla in, ītla in 'puerta den 'záguān."]$_{84\ E}$ "A ⁻ver,]$_{85\ Q}$ 'xicuā'lica ni'quittāz."]$_{86\ Q}$ Ye ni'quittā.]$_{87\ O}$ (clears throat) Quih'toa este, "Nimitzonanticiparhui'lia]$_{88\ N,F}$ xiconit´tā in 'moco⁻nēh, porque]$_{89\ F}$ yō'quimic⁻tihqueh]$_{90\ F}$ huān ⁻huetztoc, ītech in carre'tera de Tlax'cala, ah, ōmpa 'cerca de San Fe'lipe."]$_{91\ F}$ ⟩'Nēci quen 'āmo ōnicnel'tocac]$_{92\ O,P}$ como ´āmo qui'piāc.]$_{93\ O,P}$ ʰ\Cpāctiaya alguna cosa.]$_{94\ O,P}$ Pues ʰ\āmo ōnicneltocac.]$_{95\ O,P}$ INT: ⟨'Aaah. DG: 'Āmo,]$_{96\ P}$ pero de 'toda ma'nera niquih⁻toa "'A ver]$_{97\ O,Q\ or\ R}$ ʰ\mā niquittā."]$_{98\ Q\ or\ R}$ =

Well the lady here had gone to the doctor in Puebla,]$_{74}$ and I was here with all my, my granddaughters.]$_{75}$ My daughter-in-law on that side, my elder son's wife, came over.]$_{76}$ She says to me, "Papa, you're not up yet?"]$_{77}$ I say to her "Not yet."]$_{78}$ She says to me, "Look at what I have found."]$_{79}$ I say to her, "What is it?"]$_{80}$ She says to me "I found a letter."]$_{81}$ "Who came to leave it?"]$_{82}$ "Who knows,]$_{83}$ I just found it under the, under the door to the courtyard."]$_{84}$ "Let's see,]$_{85}$ bring it for me to see."]$_{86}$ Now I see it.]$_{87}$ It says uh, "I am warning you,]$_{88}$ see your son, because]$_{89}$ they have killed him]$_{90}$ and he has fallen on the highway to Tlaxcala, ah, over there near San Felipe."]$_{91}$ It seems like I did not believe it]$_{92}$ like she did not have it.]$_{93}$ He'd been happy about something.]$_{94}$ Well I did not believe it.]$_{95}$ Aaah. No,]$_{96}$ well in any case I say, "Let's see,]$_{97}$ let me see about it."]$_{98}$

## Episode 4.A

⟩Ō⁻niah]₉₉ ₀ huān nicnā'miqui
'cē mu'chacho te'quīti
'Puebla]₁₀₀ ₀ huān /huītzeh lo
mismo de ⁻yoac.]₁₀₁ ₀ Huān
niqui'lia este, "Īc ´ōncān
'nan´huītzeh 'den
carre⁻tera.]₁₀₂ ₙ,Q ʰ\Āmitlah
ōnanquittāqueh?"]₁₀₃ Q
Quihtoa "ʰ\Āmo Don Gabriel,
⟨\āmo.]₁₀₄ G ⟩⁻Tlīca?]₁₀₅ G
Niquilia "ʰ\Xquitta nīn
carta."]₁₀₆ ₙ,Q = Quihtoa "ʰ\Ay,
carambas!]₁₀₇ ₙ,G ʰ\Āmo, āmo,
para ʰ\tlen tictōzqueh
ōticttāqueh?]₁₀₈ G = ⟨ʰ\Āmo,
nōn 'tlenōn.]₁₀₉ G
´A ver]₁₁₀ G ʰ\xonyah
xontlahtlanī."]₁₁₁ G

I went]₉₉ and I met
a young man who works in
Puebla]₁₀₀ and comes home the
same at night.]₁₀₁ And
I tell him uh, "You came over
there by way of the
highway.]₁₀₂ Didn't any of
you see anything?"]₁₀₃
He says, "No Don Gabriel,
no.]₁₀₄ Why?"]₁₀₅
I tell him, "Look at this
letter."]₁₀₆ He says,
"Ay, carambas!]₁₀₇ No, no,
why would we say
we saw it?]₁₀₈ No,
nothing like that.]₁₀₉
Let's see,]₁₁₀ you might go
and make inquiries."]₁₁₁

## Episode 4.B

⟩Ōnictlahtla'nīto in īcu'ñado]₁₁₂ ₀
⟩ye 'nōn ōcatca
presi'dent̲e̲,]₁₁₃ ₀ ⟩in
īcu'ñado.]₁₁₄ ₀ (spits) que lo
'mismo quil a´yāmo huītz.]₁₁₅ ₚ,H
Toz neh ōnicmalpen'sarōh
como]₁₁₆ ₙ,P ō'catca 'fuerte in ..
in po'lítica den yeh⁻huān.]₁₁₇ ₙ,P
Niquihtoa "A lo 'mejor ⟨'xāmo
ōquinmā'gaqueh.]₁₁₈ ₙ,R ⟨īpan 'yoal
ōquimispia'rōhqueh.]₁₁₉ R A ´ver
ʰ\tlen sudērihui.]₁₂₀ R ʰ\Āquin
nictlahtlanīz?"]₁₂₁ R

When I went to ask his brother-
in-law,]₁₁₂ the one who had been
president,]₁₁₃ his brother-in-
law,]₁₁₄ it was the
same, that he "hadn't come."]₁₁₅
Then I didn't like him since]₁₁₆
their uh .. politics used
to be fierce.]₁₁₇
I say, "Most likely maybe
they beat him up.]₁₁₈ At night
they spied on him.]₁₁₉ Let's see
what happens.]₁₂₀ Who
will I ask?"]₁₂₁

## Episode 4.C

Y 'ōnitlahtla'nīto este, . in
'īchān, como]₁₂₂ ₀ in 'īchān
āmāca ⁻chānti]₁₂₃ ₀
ōquihtlani'lihqueh pa
co'legio.]₁₂₄ ₀ Como ´huēi in
⁻pieza]₁₂₅ ₀ tlani'lihqueh pa
co⁻legio]₁₂₆ ₀
⟨āmo ōc'tēmacac.]₁₂₇ ₀ "Mā
nitlahtla'nī"]₁₂₈ R aʰ\yāmo ayāmo

And when I went to inquire uh, at
his house, since]₁₂₂ at his house
nobody is home]₁₂₃
they went to inquire at the
school.]₁₂₄ As the room is
large,]₁₂₅ when they asked at the
school]₁₂₆
nobody answered.]₁₂₇ "Let me
ask"]₁₂₈ still still

ācah cah.]$_{129\,O}$ Ōni´huāllah | nobody there.]$_{129}$ When I came
occēppa nicān]$_{130\,O}$ | here again]$_{130}$

ācah cah.]$_{129\,O}$ Ōni´huāllah
occēppa nicān]$_{130\,O}$
nitlahtlanīco]$_{131\,O}$ āmo āmo
tle¯nōn.]$_{132\,O}$ "›ˡToz ´tlen
pa'noā?"]$_{133\,R,T}$ Hasta al ´cabo de
rato 'este, .. niqui´lia, "Pues ¯āmo
ācah ¯nēci.]$_{134\,O,R}$ A ´ver]$_{135\,R}$
occēppa 'mā niquit´tā,]$_{136\,R}$
ōmpa ītech in 'īchān 'xāmo
ōcoch¯huetz,]$_{137\,R}$ huān
ōmo¯catcac]$_{138\,R}$ huān
āhueliti]$_{139\,R}$ ʰ\vaya."]$_{140\,R}$
‹Āmo motlapoa in ^puerta.]$_{141\,O,S}$

nobody there.]$_{129}$ When I came
here again]$_{130}$
when I came to ask]$_{131}$ not not
anything.]$_{132}$ "Then what
is going on?"]$_{133}$ After a
while uh, .. I tell him, "Well it
seems there's nobody.]$_{134}$ Let's
see]$_{135}$ let me see again,]$_{136}$
if he might be asleep there at his
house]$_{137}$ and the door being
closed]$_{138}$ he can't
hear,]$_{139}$ O.K."]$_{140}$
The door does not open.]$_{141}$

*Episode 4.D*

Ō¯niāh]$_{142\,O}$ yō´nicah'cito in ..
¯maestra,]$_{143\,O}$ niqui'lia este,
ōnictla´paloh,]$_{144\,O}$ niqui'lia,
nēchon´maca rázōn]$_{145\,O,Q}$ āmo
'cah, 'āmo ōncān cah in
¯dueño."]$_{146\,Q}$ Quihtoa, "›'Āmo,
‹ʰ\āmo āmo."]$_{147\,O,I}$ "ʰ\Está
bien."]$_{148\,Q}$

I went]$_{142}$ I went to find the ..
teacher,]$_{143}$ I tell her uh,
I greeted her,]$_{144}$ I tell her,
"Tell me why]$_{145}$ he's not
there, the householder isn't
home."]$_{146}$ She says, "No,
no no."]$_{147}$ "It's
O. K."]$_{148}$

*Episode 4.E*

Nic'maca ¯vuelta]$_{149\,O}$
huān 'ōncān in 'plaza
nimotēl¯quetzā,]$_{150\,O}$
huān nitla´chīxtō ihquīn īc
tla¯tzīntlan]$_{151\,O}$
cuāc ōni'quittāc.]$_{152\,O}$
´Yōah'cico ōme 'cōchix.]$_{153\,O}$
(spits) "ʰ\Āquinonōn
huelīz?"]$_{154\,R}$ (clears throat)
´Cē noher'mano quipia in
'īcōchix]$_{155\,N,P}$ chānti de
'nē, 'nē, 'lado de
co'lonia.]$_{156\,N}$ Nēchi¯lia,
"´Tlen 'ticon'chīhua]$_{157\,N,J}$
'cualcān yō'tonmēh."]$_{158\,J}$
Niquilia, "Pues cuāndo
precisa´rihui 'ihcōn."]$_{159\,N,Q}$
Nēchilia este, .. niqui¯lia, ih¯cōn]
"'Cuando 'tiyā ti¯huītz,]$_{160\,N,Q}$
'āmo tiquit´tā 'algo, 'ōmpa den

I'm walking around]$_{149}$
and I'm standing
over there in the plaza]$_{150}$
and I went to look down
below this way]$_{151}$
when I see it.]$_{152}$
Two cars came.]$_{153}$
"Who
can it be?"]$_{154}$
My brother has a
car,]$_{155}$ the one who lives on
that, that, that side of the
town.]$_{156}$ He says to me,
"Hello]$_{157}$
you got up early."]$_{158}$
I tell him, "Well when it's
necessary, I do it."]$_{159}$
He tells me uh, .. I say to him,
thus "When you went out]$_{160}$
did you not see anything, there on

carre⁻tera?"]161 Q Nēchilia,
"ʰ\Āmo,]162 N,J ⟩⁻tlīca?"]163 J
Niqui´lia, "Tic⁻matīz,]164 N,Q
⟨quil yō'quimic'tihqueh
in no'conēh.]165 Q
⟨ʰ\Xquittā nīn āmatl."]166 Q
O'quittāc.]167 O Quihtoa, "⁻Ah,
pues ticon'matīz,]168 N,J pero,
ōtite⁻mōcoh,]169 J
ōtiquit⁻tāqueh]170 J
pero ʰ\āmo āmo.]171 J
⟨ʰ/Āmo yen yeh."]172 J Niquilia,
"ʰ\Cómo no?"]173 N,Q "ʰ\Āmo
yeh."]174 J "ʰ\Cómo no?"]175 Q
'Mati ōnē'chilih īca 'cē
'suéter, ⁻gris.]176 N,J Niquilia,
"'Āmo,]177 N,Q 'cē cami'solas
de ⁻tana, īca 'nīn īpan'tálōn
casi⁻mir, huān
īzapa'toshuān.]178 N,Q
ʰ\Ha de ser yen yeh."]179 Q (spits)
Quih'toa "Pues ʰ\fácilmente
ticonmatīz inīn."]180 N,J
"ʰ\No cabe duda ha de ser yen
yeh."]181 Q "Pues, ⟩ti'āhueh]182 J
⟩xon⁻tlehcō]183 J ʰ\tiāhueh
ttātīhueh."]184

the highway?"]161 He says to me,
"No,]162 why?"]163
I tell him, "You'll see,]164
they say they murdered
my son.]165
Look at this paper."]166
He saw it.]167 He says, "Ah,
well you'll find out,]168 but when
we came to go down,]169
we saw him]170
but no no.]171
It isn't him."]172 I tell him,
"Why not?"]173 "It's not
him."]174 "Why not?"]175
I think he told me about a
sweater, grey,]176 I tell him,
"No,]177 a tan
vest, with his cashmere
slacks, and
his shoes.]178
It has to be him."]179
He says, "Well it's easy for you
to find out about this."]180
"There's no doubt that it's
him."]181 "Well, let's go]182
climb in]183 let's go
see."]184

## Episode 5

⟩Ōti⁻ahqueh,]185 O,T ⟩ʰ\de
melāhuac yēcah
gente nē.]186 O,P,T Este,
⟩´vaya yōte'mōcoh in 'yehhuān, ..
⁻miēcqueh]187 O,T ⟩huān oc'cēqui
mu'chachos,]188 O,T ⟩huān
yōni'temōc]189 O,T ⟩'niah,
'niah īncui⁻tlapan,]190 O,T ⟩huān
ō'catcah cēqui zoā'tzitzīn]191 O,T
huān nēchi'liah este, \quiliah in
nocnīh este, "ʰ\Tlenonōn nōn
señor?"]192 O,T,K Qui'lia este,
⟨"Este ī^pāpā."]193 O,S,J "ʰ\Āmo
xiccāhuacan mā mopacho,]194 K
ʰ\āmo xiccāhuacan!"]195 K ⟩Neh
'zā niman ōni⁻quīxmat.]196 O,T

When we went,]185 for
sure then there were a lot of
people there.]186 Uh,
well when he went down they were
.. many]187 and some
boys,]188 and
when I went down]189 I went,
I went up behind them,]190 and
there were some women,]191
and they tell me uh, they tell
my brother uh, "Who is that
gentleman?"]192 He tells her,
"This is his father."]193 "Don't
let him come close,]194
don't let him!"]195 As for me
I knew him at once.]196

⟩'Zā niman, 'zā niman
ōni⁻quīxmat.]₁₉₇ O,T
⟨" 'Teh."]₁₉₈ Q ····
Ih´quīn ōquite^cāqueh,
īpan 'cē:, īpan 'cē: ´tetl 'nōn de,
de ca'mīchis,]₁₉₉ O,S huān
ōquilpal'tihqueh cē 'náilōn,]₂₀₀ O
ōquīxtlapa'choqueh īca in
'náilōn.]₂₀₁ O ʰ\Ōmpa ihcōn
ōquiyēctēcāqueh.]₂₀₂ O,P
Ni \modo este.]₂₀₃ R
\Āmo ōnēchcāhqueh.]₂₀₄ O,P Ye
nēchilia, "Ps, 'ya, 'ya /āxan
quēmah yō'mottāc."]₂₀₅ N,J
´Niquilia pues 'este,
"⟩⁻Ya."]₂₀₆ N,Q ⟨"´A ver]₂₀₇ Q
\tiāhueh ticttātihueh.]₂₀₈ Q
/A ver]₂₀₉ Q ʰ\tlen Dios
quimihtahuilīz."]₂₁₀ Q ⟩Neh 'nicah
'casi ya la^crado.]₂₁₁ O,S

At once, at once
I knew him.]₁₉₇
"You."]₁₉₈ ····
They had laid him down this way,
on a, on a rock of, of
camichis]₁₉₉ and they had covered
him with a plastic sheet,]₂₀₀
they had covered his face with a
plastic sheet.]₂₀₁ Thus they had
laid him down nicely.]₂₀₂
Nothing to be done.]₂₀₃
They didn't permit me.]₂₀₄ Now
he tells me, "Well, now, now, now
for sure he's been seen."]₂₀₅
I say well uh,
"Done."]₂₀₆ "Let's see]₂₀₇
let's go see.]₂₀₈
Let's see]₂₀₉ how God
will dispose."]₂₁₀ I'm
almost destroyed now.]₂₁₁

## Episode 6

´Yō-, yōti'huāl'lahqueh para
ni'cān.]₂₁₂ N ... Este, ōni´cānaco
algo 'de to⁻mīn.]₂₁₃ N Este,
ōah´cico nōn 'den judi⁻cial.]₂₁₄ N
Nēchilia "´Tlen
ticonchīhuāz,]₂₁₅ N,L
xicomprepararō in
cen'tavos,]₂₁₆ L huān ōmpa ton´yā,
ītech 'in:, 'ītech in
espec⁻ción."]₂₁₇ L
"ʰ\Está bien."]₂₁₈ Q (spits)
⟩´Yōnihuāllah.]₂₁₉ O,T
⟩Niquinnāmiqui 'cēqui de
⟩judi´cial ni'cān
in sa'lida̱.]₂₂₀ N,T
⟩´Pues zan
'ōtēchtēmo'ihqueh,]₂₂₁ N,T ··
⟩ōtēchtla'tēmo⁻lihqueh.]₂₂₂ N,T
Nēchi'lia:, in 'jefe den judi⁻cial,
nēchilia, "⁻Teh,"]₂₂₃ N,M nēchilia,
"ˡIn teh'huātzīn ton'tētah den
mu⁻chacho?"]₂₂₄ N,M Niquilia,
"ʰ\Quēmah."]₂₂₅ N,Q Quihtoa "ˡ'Tlen

We, we came by
this place.]₂₁₂ ... Uh, I came to
pick up some money.]₂₁₃ Uh,
that official came.]₂₁₄
He tells me, "What
you'll do,]₂₁₅
is get the money
ready,]₂₁₆ and you go there
to the, to the
inspection."]₂₁₇
"O.K."]₂₁₈
I went.]₂₁₉
I met some
officials here
on the way out of town.]₂₂₀
Well they just inquired of
us about the matter,]₂₂₁ ··
they made inquiry of us.]₂₂₂
He tells me:, the chief official, he
tells me, "You,"]₂₂₃ he tells me,
"Sir, are you the father of the
young man?"]₂₂₄ I tell him,
"Yes."]₂₂₅ He says, "Why

ōnemiya arˉmado?"]226 N,M Niquilia
"ʰ\Aīc.]227 N,Q ›Aīc ōquino-,
ōccono'ceroh alguna 'arma de
‹qui'nemi, ‹qui'nemīz.]228 Q,T
Desde in 'tiempo que 'ōyec por
eˉjemplo]229 Q ōyec nom'brado
como autori'dad]230 Q 'āmo
ōqui'pāctih."]231 Q "Pues,
ˡt'cahxilihqueh 'cē pis'tola,]232 M
'īca .. ('mati 'ōnē'chilih) cē ōme
'carˉtucho.]233 M,(N)
Ōctlaˉtihqueh,]234 M huān 'cēqui
'tiros īhtec in īˉpōxah."]235 M
Niquilia, "\Āmo, de ʰ\nōn
āmo."]236 N,Q "ʰ\Está bien."]237 M
›Cuāc nēchi'lia]238 N
ōnēchcāhtē'huilih in
a'punte.]239 N,S ... Nēchilia "Tlā
'algo 'mitzonofreˉcerōz,]240 M
este, (spits) nimitzon'chia en tal
'lugar."]241 M ʰ\Mati
ōchāntiya ītech cē hotel
parece.]242 P "\Ōmpa
nimitzon\chia."]243 M
"\Está bien."]244 Q ›ʰ\Āmo, 'āmo
ōni'catenˉderōh,]245 O,P
o'cachi ōni'caten'derōh in
‹'cuerpo.]246 O

did he go armed?"]226 I tell him,
"Never.]227 He never knew any
weapon for walking around with,
to walk around with.]228
Since the time that for example
when he was,]229 when he was
named an authority]230 he didn't
like it."]231 "Well,
we found a pistol,]232
with .. (I think he told me) a few
cartridges.]233 They'd been
fired,]234 and some
rounds in his pocket."]235
I tell him, "No, it
can't be."]236 "O.K."]237
Then he tells me]238
he left me an
address.]239 .. He tells me "If
I can do something for you,]240
uh, I'm at your service in such-
and-such a place."]241 I think
he lived in a hotel, it seems
like.]242 "I'm at your service
there."]243
"O.K."]244 No, I didn't
pay any attention to him,]245
I was thinking more of the
body.]246

## Episode 7

Zan 'niman ōmoquīx'tihqueh para, ..
para in 'pántiōn.]247 N
›Chīhuī'lihqueh in
operaˉción.]248 N ›Ōtcuāl'cuepqueh
ya ye 'tiōtlac.]249 N 'Occē tōnal
a, .. casi 'āmo, . 'āmo
ō'motlāl'lāquih,]250 O,P por
'cues'tión de famˉilias.]251 O,P
xitīn'toqueh,]252 O,P
ōhuālˉlahqueh,]253 N
›ōtquin'chīxqueh,]254 N,T
›ōmosepul'tarōh.]255 N,T
ʰ\Todavía āmo ōnēchilihqueh
quemeh.]256 P ‹A los (mati) a los
'ocho o nueve ˉdías,]257 O

Then they took him to, ..
to the cemetery.]247
They did the
operation.]248 We returned him
already by afternoon.]249 The next
day uh, .. they almost didn't, .
didn't bury him,]250 because of
the relatives.]251
They were scattered,]252
they came,]253
we waited for them,]254
he was buried.]255
They've never told me
how.]256 After (I think)
eight or nine days,]257

nicreco'gerōz in ī'ropa.]$_{258}$ O      I was to collect his clothing.]$_{258}$
⟩ʰ\Āmo ōnicrecogeroh, ⟩ʰ\āmo.]$_{259}$      I didn't collect it, no.]$_{259}$
P ⟩ 'Ihcōn 'este, ⟩ 'solo nōn      Thus uh, only that
fra'caso, ⟩'ōnēch'panǭc.]$_{260}$ P =      mistake, happened to me.]$_{260}$

### Coda

⟩\Ah pues, ⟨ayāmo tlen 'huehcah lo      Ah well, not long ago it was the
'mismo.]$_{261}$ P ⟩Cē nomu'chacho      same thing.]$_{261}$ My oldest son
'máyōr ni'cān 'chānti̲.]$_{262}$ N Lo      who lives here.]$_{262}$ The
'mismo]$_{263}$ N de que      same thing]$_{263}$ that some one
'nemi īca in . borra'chera      going around . drunk
como]$_{264}$ N te⁻quiti]$_{265}$ N (spits)      as]$_{264}$ he was working]$_{265}$
quibalacea'rohque̲h.]$_{266}$ N      they shot him.]$_{266}$
⟩Ccalaqui'lihqueh tres 'tiros,      They put three bullets into him,
'ya me'rito̲.]$_{267}$ N,T ⟩Pero      just like that.]$_{267}$ But
ōnimāvi'vāro̲h.]$_{268}$ N Pues, este,      I survived.]$_{268}$ Well, uh,
ʰ\ōyec sano hasta āxan.]$_{269}$ P      he was healthy until now.]$_{269}$
ʰ\Ōyec sano.]$_{270}$ P \Nada más      He was healthy.]$_{270}$ It's just a
\cosa de 'neh,      personal thing,
nopersonali'da̲d.]$_{271}$ P      a personal matter.]$_{271}$
'Quihtōz āquinonōn,      If somebody should ask,
"'Algún accidente?"]$_{272}$ P,INT      "Some accident?"]$_{272}$
\Āmo ... ʰ'Āmo 'āmo.]$_{273}$ P      No ... No, no.]$_{273}$
INT: ⟨\Aaaaah.      Aaaaah.

To tell his son's murder, Don Gabriel must address an ideology, the capitalist idea of doing "business for profit," that is antithetical to the values of reciprocity and community solidarity which people in towns like Almecatla hold sacred. Don Gabriel's son was murdered for what local people call *envidia*, a destructive form of envy which leads to revenge against its object. Dow (1981) proposes that *envidia* is seldom directed against those who prosper in the ordinary way, through hard work in domestic production and exemplary citizenship within the traditional order. Instead, *envidia* targets those who practice true capitalist accumulation, thereby tipping the delicate balance of reciprocity by which towns like Almecatla "defend themselves" against the tightening vise of appropriation of their resources. In order to speak about the murder, then, Don Gabriel must invoke the ugly lexicon of dealings for profit, which for Mexicano speakers is drawn entirely from Spanish. This lexicon remains for him alien, and his struggle with it—a principal source of dysfluency in the otherwise eloquent flow of his narrative—supports Bakhtin's intuition that in intertextual practice in the heteroglossic speech community there will always be words which "cannot be assimilated into [the] context and [will] fall out of it; it is as if they put themselves in quotation marks against the will of the speaker" (Bakhtin 1981: 294). To analyze this struggle, I look closely at his narrative, focusing on the voice system.

I adapt from Bakhtin (1984, 1981; also Voloshinov [1986 (1930)] and Silverman and Torode [1980]) the concept of a system of "voices" as the site of consciousness and subjectivity in discourse. This voice system must be recognized as a new subsystem in what Woodbury (1985, 1987) has called "rhetorical structure" of discourse.[3] While reported speech is an important site for the study of the voice system,[4] the system is realized as well through other rhetorical strategies. The voice system is the field for dialogue and for conflict, where authorial consciousness attempts to dominate and shape the text through its chosen voices. The voice system interacts with prosodic structure; prosodic strategies, particularly intonation, are important to its development and a prosodic interruption, the break through the narrative voice of an "intonational shadow" which may index "artless" emotion, will be shown to pose a paradox for a search for a subject, a "self" which might be the locus of consciousness and choice in narrative. Lexical choice and language choice are clearly important components of "voices," as is the distribution of these across the large structures of the discourse such as episodic structure, plot structure, and systems of oppositions in geography, gender, and the like. In order to assimilate (at least partially) the Spanish lexicon of business-for-profit into his narrative, while making clear that his "own" moral position is firmly grounded in the peasant communitarian value of reciprocity, Don Gabriel constitutes the voice system of his narration along a moral axis (supported by a moral geography), and distributes this lexicon among voices which are far removed from the moral center of his text. When the lexicon of profit penetrates close to this center, he tries to dominate it with a euphemism.

The problem of the voice in speaking directs us to inquiry as to how the self should be understood. Other authors have shared Bakhtin's intuition that individual consciousness is constituted through a choice of voices, although not all of these authors have shared his view that responsible, choosing consciousness, rather than an affected, emotion-producing entity, is the core of individuality. Goffman (1974) found in reported speech and other multivocal phenomena his most important clues that the "everyday self" can be considered as a framed dramaturgical presentation; I employ his taxonomy of the laminations of voices in conversational narrative, which for Goffman demonstrated that the "glassy essence" of the self[5] is in fact a kaleidoscope. Singer (1980), drawing on the work of Charles Peirce, sees the self semiotically, as a dynamic system of signs distributed by communication across a "loosely compacted person." Becker

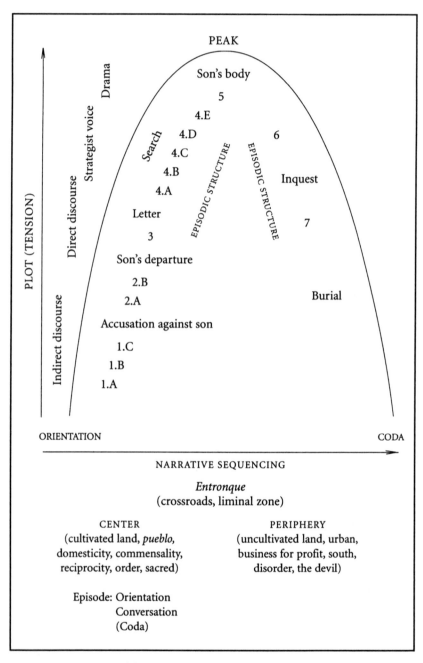

Figure 4-1. Dimensions of the text structure.

(1979, 1983) has suggested that the self is an intertextual entity, the product of a text-building process. Similarly, I show that the "Don Gabriel" constructed through his deeply felt narration is a complex construction, which cannot be seen as mere elaboration around a single "essential" core of the self.

The artful practices of lamination of frames through which Don Gabriel constructs the voice system, the principal moral axis of his narrative, can only be understood within the context of the other rhetorical strategies in his narrative. These include the construction of a system of oppositions, the most important being a moral geography; a sequential or narrative system; and a system of tension or plot. These are organized by an episodic system. The voice system is distributed across these other systems, and is both constrained by and constrains them. These systems are diagrammed in figure 4-1; the detailed diagram of the voice system itself is found in table 4-1.

## THE MORAL GEOGRAPHY OF THE NARRATIVE

Warman (1982) argues that although the peasants of Mexico are incorporated within capitalism, they retain a substantial autonomy, with distinctively peasant forms of production, ideology, and consciousness. Taussig (1979) shows that Latin American peasants represent their opposition to the values of individual gain which are central to capitalism by attaching these to the dominant symbol of the devil, the force of darkness which resides particularly in money and its exchange for profit. Taggart (1977, 1982, 1983) has pointed out that among the Nahua speakers of the Sierra de Puebla, the region immediately to the northeast of the Puebla-Tlaxcala valley, the opposition between the orderly human realm and the domain of the devil is often constituted geographically as a contrast between a center and a periphery. Folktales represent this contrast by telling of the journey of a hero, who survives a passage out from the center into the periphery, the devil's world. Don Gabriel assimilates his narrative to this journey form in order to create a moral geography in which spaces associated with peasant communitarian values are contrasted with spaces associated with danger and business-for-profit.

In Don Gabriel's narrative, the episodes which occur before the peak (Longacre's [1976] term for the moment of plot climax) in episode 5 take place entirely in the "center," the community of Almecatla itself, which symbolizes safety and order. However, Don Gabriel's text is ironic, for even in this center the worm of greed—action "para in pōxahtli" 'for the pocket' (private profit) (22),[6] rather than "para den pueblo" 'for the community'—has appeared. The peak and postpeak episodes take place outside the town, in a peripheral realm where disorder prevails. The moral geography is constructed through three devices: by the specification of physical locations of episodes, by the themes of the conversations which are the core of each episode, and by the journey of Don Gabriel as he searches for his son, finds him, and buries him.

Early episodes locate characters in or near their homes. In conversations between father and son they speak of fields and animals—the core of the peasant way of life—and of commensality between family members. In episode 3 commensality is again a theme, albeit a presupposed one, for when Don Gabriel's daughter-in-law arrives, local hearers know that she has come to prepare his breakfast, a duty which falls to this relative when a wife is away. (In Almecatla, an eldest son will set up his household next door to his father's home, so the daughter-in-law does not have a long journey.) In this episode, where a wife, granddaughters, and a daughter-in-law are mentioned, Don Gabriel is in a realm of women; women are considered to be particularly *Mexicano* and so stand for peasant values (cf. J. Hill 1987). But a stunningly ironic note is struck when the daughter-in-law, representing domestic conformity and tradition, brings to the old man the anonymous letter which informs him that his son is dead.

In episode 4 the journey motif begins, and sections A through E trace the geography of the community, the moral center, as Don Gabriel wanders from house to house, eventually reaching the central plaza. Again we see irony, for during the journey doors are closed to Don Gabriel that should be open, and he must reflect on the politically based enmity between relatives (in 4.B). An ironic note is struck again when, precisely in the center of the town, the plaza, in episode 4.E, Don Gabriel learns from his own brother where his son's body lies.

The peak episode, 5, where the body is found and identified, and the postpeak episodes take place outside the town in the dangerous peripheral realm. Don Gabriel and his brother leave the town in a car,[7] and find the son's body laid out at the edge of the highway. The description of the site at (199)—"Ihquīn ōquitēcāqueh, īpan cē, īpan cē tetl nōn de, de camīchis" 'They had laid him down this way, on a, on a rock of, of "camīchis"'— is the most detailed specification of physical setting in the narrative, and makes clear that because of the rocky degraded soil—*camīchis* (probably *caliche*, hard, lime-encrusted earth)—we are in *monte* 'uncultivated land', and not a cultivated field, part of the peasant order of things. In this dreadful place a crowd of women, symbols of Mexicano tradition, try to keep Don Gabriel from the sight of his son's body; again, as in the episode of the letter, women mediate a revelation of horror.

In the first postpeak episode, 6, the conversation with an official (a representative of an external and clearly dangerous order) takes place in a liminal zone, the "salida" 'exit' (220), the road out of town. The burial takes place in a peripheral realm, the cemetery on the edge of town.[8] In the episode of the burial the broken moral geography of Don Gabriel's family is made clear: "xitïntoqueh" 'they were scattered' (252) and could hardly even gather for the interment. This constitutes a sharp contrast with the domestic intimacies of the prepeak episodes.

The physical flow of information and participants in the narrative also follows the center-periphery axis. The initial conflict is a matter of "mismo pueblo" 'the community itself' (5), but the climactic events take place in the periphery, and disorder—in the form of people who cannot answer Don Gabriel's questions—flows into the center from this periphery. Thus Don Gabriel questions a young factory worker returning from the night shift (in 4.A), and the teacher arriving from the city to open the school (in 4.D); neither can help him.

While in Taggart's narratives from the Sierra de Puebla *monte* is the most important feature of the periphery, in Almecatla the city, and the Spanish way of life which it represents, are also part of the peripheral realm of death and disorder. The city of Puebla, where Don Gabriel's son goes to do business, lies only five miles south of Almecatla (Taggart has pointed out that the south is the devil's realm). The dry-farming lands which once surrounded the town have largely given way to soil erosion, shantytowns, and the spread of industry. From the plaza of Almecatla one looks west into the storage lots of the Puebla Volkswagen plant, the largest factory in Latin America. Nearby to the east and south several plants make products such as glue and chemical fertilizer; fumes from these installations drift continually over the town. While the people of the region value the factories for the wage labor they provide, they consider themselves *campesinos* 'cultivators', and are deeply suspicious of the city, which is seen as a place where criminals run free to prey on the meek, and as a source of real physical pollution, *esmog* 'smog'.

The fundamental plot complication in Don Gabriel's narrative is his son's involvement in the establishment of a bus line which will link Almecatla closer to the city. Don Gabriel's son is murdered along the road which the buses travel. Roadsides, and particularly *entronques* 'crossroads' are liminal zones, and crosses are planted there to ward off danger. *Entronques* with major highways are of particular significance; in 1982 the Virgin appeared miraculously at the *entronque* between the road from the town of Tenancingo and the new Vía Corta, the expressway from Puebla to Santa Ana Chiauhtempan. Don Gabriel's son's body is found at the *entronque* where a minor road from Almecatla joins the main Puebla-Tlaxcala highway, near the reeking factories, on barren rocks amid lurking demons.

## THE SEQUENCING OF EPISODES
## AND THE BUILDING OF PLOT TENSION

The central moral axis of the text, constructed through moral geography and the voice system, is crosscut by the systems of narrative sequence and plot tension. The sequential skeleton of the narrative is constituted first by the sequence of narrative verbs (Labov 1972). In Mexicano the unmarked narrative verb is perfective, and is prefixed with the antecessive ō-; an example can be seen in *ōquichīhqueh* 'they made it' in sentence (5), the first sentence on the narrative main line. In Don Gabriel's narrative many verbs lack the antecessive prefix and are examples of the historical present. These verbs lend immediacy by constructing a "presentness" of events, while temporal sequence is sustained by an agreement between narrator and listener about the sequential nature of turn-taking in conversation. Most of these historical-present forms are locutionary verbs, such as *niquilia* 'I tell him' in sentence (10), but some nonlocutionary verbs also appear in the historical present. Here listeners may infer that sequence is represented unless there is evidence to the contrary. Thus episode 4, the search, begins with a perfect verb *ōniah* 'I went' (99). But the next verb, in (100), is *nicnāmiqui* 'I meet him', a historical-present form. The main narrative line is sustained entirely by historical-present locutionary verbs until the end of the subepisode. Episode 4.B then begins with a perfect verb, *ōnictlahtlanīto* 'I went to ask him', at (112).

A higher-level sequential system is the sequence of episodes. Each episode is framed by a brief orientation, which establishes time, place, or other relevant background. Often this contains imperfect verbs marked with the suffix *-ya*, which mark material as being background for the narrative main line (Labov 1972). Many of the episodes are terminated with a brief coda, including moral evaluation of the events just recounted. Thus, at the end of episode 1.B, the coda is the judgmental "Siempre ō-, ōcalac" 'Always he went in' (18), evaluating the conduct of the son. Concluding the letter episode, 3, is a coda at (92–95) in which Don Gabriel observes that the letter was so shocking that he could hardly believe that it existed. The core of each episode is a conversation, through which a new complication is established. Each of these, except for the three brief interchanges in episode 4, builds to a climax of mimetic "drama" (Longacre 1976), in which utterances are exchanged without locutionary verbs.

Overlaid on the sequence of events and episodes is the trajectory of the plot, structured through tension. Plot builds to a peak and "untangles" (ibid.) in postpeak events. This trajectory is repeated each episode and subepisode, so that the large wave form of the building of tension to peak is partially constituted by the sequence of smaller waves. Tension builds

from the presentation of the first conflict—the son agrees to become involved in the bus line—to the peak when his father sees his dead body.
The plot "untangles" in the postpeak episodes of the inquest and burial.

Don Gabriel uses several techniques to develop plot tension. First is the
increasing frequency of historical-present verbs on the narrative main line.
Second is reported speech. Episode 1 has relatively little reported speech,
and what appears is mainly in indirect discourse, as in (5),(6), and (7).
As peak is approached, reported speech constitutes a larger and larger
proportion of each episode. In some subepisodes of episode 4, reported
speech alone constructs the narrative line, and an inner voice that Goffman (1974) called a "strategist" takes over the narrative (this can be seen
in clauses [118–21]). A subtechnique in the deployment of reported speech
is a shift from dialogue, where the exchanges of conversational turns are
marked by sequences of locutionary verbs, to drama, where these verbs
disappear. This can be seen in (173–76), and (181–84) in subepisode 4.E.
The peak of the narrative, sentence (198), is constituted by a single word
in dramatic speech, *Teh* 'You!' spoken at the moment of recognition of
the son's body.[9] This is the only instance in the narrative where no turn
sequence is established by a previous sequence of locutionary verbs. The
speaking by a single voice, with no reply, is a powerful representation of a
confrontation with death.

A third technique for the building of tension is "change of pace" (Longacre 1976). This can be seen at peak. The climactic sentence of the narrative
(198), is the single word, "Teh" 'You!' Preceding it at (196) and (197) are two
short, repeated sentences, spoken very rapidly; one contains also an internal repetition: "zā niman ōniquīxmat. Zā niman, zā niman ōniquīxmat"
'At once I knew him. At once, at once I knew him'. Preceding and following
these brief sentences at peak are the long, intricate compound sentences
which begin the peak episode (185–92), and the equally elaborate sentence
describing the laid-out body and its location (199–201) which follow the
long pause after the moment of recognition at (198). The long sentences
at (199–201) which attend so closely to material details (the only time in
the text such attention occurs), contrast sharply with the mimetic drama
of peak at (198).

Yet another tension-building technique is "concentration of participants" (ibid.). Except in the climactic scene, only two people are on stage
at any time. But the discovery of the body occurs in a veritable mob—
young men, women, the brother, Don Gabriel—and at least three people
are speaking. The cry of the women, "Āmo xiccāhuacan ma mopacho"
'Don't let him come close' (194–95) seems to come from several throats as
Don Gabriel pushes his way through the crowd.

## THE VOICE SYSTEM

Don Gabriel's narrative is, to use Bakhtin's (1981) term, "polyphonic" in its attention to verbal detail. At least twenty voices are compressed into the seventeen minutes of the text; they are listed in table 4–1. There are snatches of vernacular wisdom, a quotation from the Bible, threats from hard and corrupt men, the inauthentic concern of officialdom, the gentle respect of a young woman for her father-in-law, the evasive conversations of a father and son at odds.

Many of these voices are what Goffman (1974) has called "figures": personages created by the speaker (who functions as what Goffman called an "animator," a machine for speaking), represented in both direct and indirect discourse. Other voices are laminations of some self belonging to the animator: in order of their distribution along the moral axis of the voice system from its center out (Goffman [1974] has called such a center the "addressing self," suggesting its fundamentally dialogic nature), these are the intonational shadows (S and T), the evaluator (P), the father (Q) (a "protagonist" [ibid.] who intersects between the system of self-lamination and the figure system), the "strategist" (R, Don Gabriel's inner voice which appears briefly in episode 4 and at peak, and which is also a reported-speech voice which intersects with the figure system), and two narrative voices, the involved narrator (O) and the neutral narrator (N).

In addition to the novelistic polyphony of the figure system and the self-lamination system, the voice system includes at least two different "languages" (which constitute encodings of ideology, following Bakhtin's usage). These represent the fundamentally opposed ideological positions of peasant communitarianism and the economics of reciprocity in the Mexicano-speaking community on the one hand, and the pursuit of individual profit in the Spanish-speaking world of the marketplace on the other.

I have pointed out above the importance of irony in the system of moral geography. This trope also organizes the voice system, for the entire narrative can be seen as an ironic "interruption" (Silverman and Torode 1980) of a word, *accidente* 'accident' proposed by the voice of the interviewer, who asks: Had Don Gabriel ever been so ill, or in such a bad "accident," *accidente*, that he thought he would die? Don Gabriel's opening line incorporates this word by echoing and then denying its terms: "Accidente ni lo quiera Dios. Āmo. Āmo āmo accidente āmo" 'No accident, by God's will. No. No no accident no'. The interruption is the narrative, an elegant trajectory of episodes which trace the dimensions of life's contradictions in Almecatla, leading to the culmination, of Shakespearean intensity, in which the tragedy foretold in the opening lines is realized as Don Gabriel

Table 4-1. The Voice System of the Text

---

1. The "Figures": Reported Speech of Others
   A  The voice of son's business partners, murderers "voice A"
   B  People of the town
   C  Ephesians 5:14
   D  Son
   E  Daughter-in-law
   F  Letter (may be voice A)
   G  Young worker
   H  Son's brother-in-law
   I  Teacher
   J  Brother
   K  Women in the crowd
   L  First official
   M  Second official
2. Self-laminations of Don Gabriel
   N  Neutral narrator
   O  Involved narrator
   P  Evaluator
   Q  Father (center of point-of-view; intersects with system of "figures")
   R  Strategist (Don Gabriel's "inner voice," also intersects with system of "figures")
3. Intonational shadows (so called because they "cast a shadow" on the voices with which they appear)
   S  *Cantante* ("singsong" intonation marked with ^)
   T  Desperate (high pitch, voice breaks)
4. Languages encoding ideology
   Spanish
   Mexicano

---

gazes on the murdered body of his son. In the final lines (272–73) Don Gabriel again offers the interviewer his own word: "Quihtōz āquinonōn, 'Algún accidente?'? Āmo. Āmo āmo." 'Would someone say, "An accident?"? No. No no'. Indeed, in Almecatla the death of sons is no accident.

This ironic use of the voice of the interviewer to frame the narrative is excellent evidence for Sperber and Wilson's (1981) proposal that irony is best understood as a dialogic phenomenon, as the representation of "What someone else might say." And the sustaining of this frame across an "interruption" of seventeen minutes attests conclusively to the artful attention of the narrator to structural tension at the most abstract level, and to the possibilities for very large-scope structures in oral discourse.[10]

## THE DIALECTIC OF STRUCTURE AND DISCOURSE

The problem of defining the function of the voices in narrative is part
of a more general issue: can these voices, manifestations of the order of
intertextuality at the level of discourse—Bakhtin's "centrifugal" order—
be discussed in terms of the abstract and timeless systems of structure—
Bakhtin's "centripetal" order—or do they themselves constitute this order?
The voices do have a constitutive function, but their polyphonic play
occurs within a dialectic field which includes the systems of sequence and
plot, and the syntactic organization of individual sentences. These systems are part of a level of context-free, reiterable structure that Bakhtin
saw as being in dialogic interaction with the order of the contextualized,
immediate, unreiterable utterance.[11]

The voice system, particularly the system of figures, constitutes the core
of each major episode as a conversation. The sequence system is carried
by these conversations, through the sequence of locutionary verbs and
through the convention of turn-taking. These conversations also build tension in the plot system, through the shifts from dialogue to drama, and in
the one-word conversation at peak, *Teh* 'You!' (198) where we must draw
on larger conventions about life and death to understand who is speaking.

Dialogic interaction between the narrator (N, O) and evaluator (P)
voices shapes episodic structure. The narrator establishes material orientation, while the evaluator draws moral conclusions in codas. The evaluator
voice introduces explicitly moral terms, such as *desgraciadamente* 'unfortunately' (20), and "loaded" words such as *ambición* 'ambition' (20)
or *ventaja* 'advantage' (28, 29). The strategist (R) voice also functions
as a moralist, expressing suspicion against the son's political enemy, his
brother-in-law (118–19). Other figure voices are also used in this evaluative
function. When the young worker is shown the anonymous letter, he ex-
claims in horror, "Ay carambas!" 'Oh my heavens!' (107). When the father
learns that the son must go again to the city on business, in episode 2.B, he
says "Pues tlen diario āhueliti nancarreglaroah?" 'Well it can't be that you
all have to take care of things every day?' (66).

Reported speech is a particularly appropriate site for the embedding of
evaluation. It is a domain of flexibility and openness, which can be exploited to a variety of purposes. In addition, as Tannen (1980) and Clancy
(1980) have pointed out, reported speech lies on a different "world line"
from the propositions of the main narrative line, so its truth is less accessible to question by the hearer.

While voices in reported speech can be exploited as sites that are open
to evaluation, their appearance is constrained by the systems of the episodes, plot, and clause-level syntactic structure. The first constraint, at the

episodic level, is part of the construction of point-of-view (Chafe 1976). Point-of-view is centered in the voice of the father (Q), the only figure which appears in every episode to engage other voices in conversation. The figure of the strategist (R) (which may shift point-of-view "inward" from voice Q) is more restricted, appearing only in the search, episode 4, except for one line at peak, "ni modo este" 'nothing to be done' (203), which may belong to this voice (it is possible that [207–10] are also voice R, the strategist, but I have assigned them to voice Q). However, the search episodes are in turn constituted by this voice, gaining their sequential and plot-level coherence by having the movement of the father in the episode motivated by the inner speech voice of the strategist.

The son (D) is second to the father in amount of dialogue and in number of episodes in which he speaks; he appears in episode 1, and becomes the ideologically dominant voice (although point-of-view does not shift from the father) in episode 2.B. The daughter-in-law (E) appears only in episode 3, as does the voice of the letter (F) (although the latter is implicitly present in episode 4 as people react to it). The brother (J) appears in episode 4.E, and has two lines in the polyphonic peak episode (193 and 205). The official (there may be two, with the first appearing in [215–17], the second later, so I have distinguished official voices L and M) appears only in episode 6. There are no foreshadowings of these voices, and no flashbacks to them except indirectly, as in the reactions to the letter in episode 4, and the remark by the evaluator in the coda to episode 3: "Cpāctiaya alguna cosa" 'He had been happy about something' (94).

The appearance of the two narrative voices and the evaluator is constrained at the intra-episodic level. The evaluator appears primarily in the codas of episodes, identifiable by its direct-address intonation contours and by its use of morally loaded terministic choices. This voice occasionally appears outside the codas (e.g., in the "orientation" at [8] and [20]), and is perhaps the most interruptive of the voices, interjecting contradictions to other voices, as at (23) or (92–93). However, even in these interruptions, the appearance of the voice is constrained by clause-level syntax or by restriction to the periphery of clauses.

The distribution of voices by clause structure can be seen in the long sentence which includes clauses (7), (8), and (9): "Huān ōquinōtzqueh de ... ser tesorero īmināhuac]₇, neh ācmo ōniccāhuaya, porque]₈ lo mismo ōyec presidente]₉," 'And when they called him to be treasurer with them, I would not give permission, because he was municipal president as well'.

In (7), the protasis of the sentence, the narrator N and voice A appear, with voice N uttering the locutionary verb *ōquinōtzqueh* 'they called him', a perfective verb on the main narrative line. Voice A utters its complement, appearing as reported speech in indirect discourse, and is identifiable by

the switch into Spanish business language in "de ser tesorero" 'to be treasurer' (this switch, which occurs in violation of Gumperz's [1982] Verb-
Verb Complement Constraint, is discussed in J. Hill 1985). The interruption by the evaluator, at (8), is recognized by the presence of the negative
ācmo 'no longer' (negatives were noted by Labov [1972] as an important
component of evaluation), and by the imperfect verb ōniccāhuaya 'I allowed him'; Labov has also pointed out that imperfect verbs signal evaluation by departing from main-line sequencing. The voice of the narrator,
using characteristic nonterminal "sequencing" intonational contours, resumes in (9).[12] This sentence has a very intricate voice structure, but gains
coherence through syntactic organization in which each voice is assigned
its own clause.

Clause structure is not perfectly constraining on the voice system; a
number of lexical items, for instance, are almost certainly "double-voiced"
(Bakhtin 1981). To illustrate, in (10) voice Q, the father, utters the expression "Ācmo ximocomprometerō" 'Don't make any more commitments'.
Voice A may also be present, since at some point his business partners
must have said to the son, "Ximocomprometerō" 'Make a commitment!'
However, since this lexical item is used by everyone locally, and almost
certainly could be used by Don Gabriel himself without suggesting any
special ideological tone, I have not indicated the possible presence of voice
A at (10). Further examples of voice interaction at the lexical level are
discussed below.

A second syntactic technique which Don Gabriel uses to embed the
voice of the evaluator into narrative sentences is to take advantage of the
flexibility of the preverbal complex (Hill and Hill 1986). Malinche Mexicano is a verb-initial language. The position before the verb functions as
a site for connective, expressive, and relational particles, for topicalized
arguments of the verb (arguments which are not topics or otherwise in
focus are represented only by verbal prefixes), and often for locative or
manner adverbial phrases. For instance, solamente 'only' in (1) plays a relational role, signaling that the speaker will interrupt the interviewer's voice,
and an expressive role as ironic mitigation of the tragedy which will be
narrated. The preverbal complex is a favored site for the appearance of the
evaluator voice. Thus in (14-15), the preverbal complex has two elements.
The adjective bueno 'good' functions as a POP element (Polanyi 1982); it
signals a return to the main narrative line from a brief digression. This
element is in the evaluator voice with direct-address intonation. However,
it also has an ironic "expressive" force, since what has gone before is in
no sense bueno 'good'. (The topicalized object tonterías 'foolishness' is also
ironic. It refers to the burning of the almial, the rack of dried corn stalks
which is used to feed stock through the dry season, a middle stage in the

escalation of *envidia*. Surely such arson, with the attendant danger of the spread of the fire to buildings and trees, and the loss of winter fodder, is more than "foolishness.") The evaluator voice in the preverbal complex is also heard at (18) where the evaluative preverbal element *siempre* 'always' is in this voice.

A very intricate preverbal complex occurs in (20) in episode 1.C. Here, the connective relational element, *pero* 'but' belongs to the evaluator, and interrupts the previous sentence which takes "going about doing business" to be quite ordinary. The weighty adverb *desgraciadamente* 'unfortunately' includes in its scope all of the rest of the sentence. Following this expressive adverb is a long and complex topicalized object, which includes a relative clause of a rare and highly hispanized type (Hill and Hill 1981, 1986), in which *in āquin* 'the ones who' appears as a relative pronoun with the overt nominal head *cristianos* 'people' (this may be an ironic choice of terms, but *cristianos* is often used in Malinche Mexicano to mean simply 'human beings', rather than 'Christians' in the narrow sense). The narrator appears only at the verb *ōquimilih* 'he told them' (21), after which the voice of the son is embedded as direct-discourse reported speech.

A third linguistic technique employed by Don Gabriel to embed evaluation and to dominate voices in the figure system is to exploit the Mexicano particles *mati* and *quil* to comment upon indirect discourse. *Mati* 'it seems' makes evidential reference to the form of representation, and means that, since the speaker cannot remember exactly how something was said, no claim is made for the fidelity of the representation. The evidential *quil* implies that the speaker is faithfully representing form, but is questioning the veracity or accuracy of its propositional content. Instances of *mati* are found in the conversation with the brother at (176) in episode 4.E, and in the conversation with the official at (233) in episode 6. It appears also in (242), bracketing with *parece* 'it seems', a Spanish form, a somewhat nonfaithful representation of a speaking attributed to the official. *Quil* can be seen in (115) in episode 4, where it casts doubt on the veracity of the brother-in-law's claim that the son had not returned home. I have tried to capture this in the translation by placing the brother-in-law's speaking in quotation marks. *Quil* appears again at (165) in episode 4.E, where its use suggests that Don Gabriel, telling his brother about the letter, has still not accepted its claim that his son is dead.[13]

*Quil* and *mati* can appear only when reported speech is represented in indirect discourse. This constraint on the occurrence of these evidentials in Mexicano supports the claims noted above by Tannen (1980) and Clancy (1980) that direct-discourse reported speech establishes a new "world line" that is not accessible to anaphoric constraints, or to truth conditions which operate in the world of the main narrative line. Thus, reference to truth conditions can be accomplished only if reported speaking is drawn into the narrative line syntactically, by representing it as indirect discourse, using the deixis of the narrative-line world.

In codas, the evaluator voice usually has as its scope an entire sentence, as in the conclusions of episodes 1.B, 1.C, 3, 5, 6, and 7. But even in codas the evaluator is sometimes in complex interaction with other voices. An example is the odd rhyme which links (23), "porque bastante feo corázōn [koráso:]" 'because of such ugly heart(s)', to the immediately following "con rázōn [ko:ráso:]" 'with reason'. In Malinche Mexicano word-final [n] variably disappears (the stress in these forms is on the penultimate syllable, as in Mexicano). This rhyme links the evaluator to voice A and to the "people of the town," and will be discussed further below.

The two narrative voices appear throughout the text. The second narrative voice, O, appears as peak approaches, and is distinguished from voice N, the more neutral narrative voice, by a higher frequency of sharply dropping terminal sentence contours (which do not seem to be accompanied by pause), by the frequent use of historical-present narrative verbs, and, in the peak episode 5, by a series of short, "excited" clauses (at 187–92). The narrator voices interact with other voices, functioning to orient episodes and speak locutionary verbs under which reported speech is embedded. Many examples of this framing technique can be found in the text. Usually the shift from the narrative voice of the locutionary verb to the reported speech involves the shifts of deixis, and attention to the form of the purported original according to conventions of "fidelity" (Leech 1978), characteristic of direct discourse. However, the text also contains examples of representation of reported speech as indirect discourse, in which the reported voice is dominated by the point of view of the narrative voice. Sometimes such indirect speakings are embedded, not under true locutionary verbs, but under other so-called metapragmatic verbs (Silverstein's [1985] expression for verbs which refer to speech acts and events and their purposes). For instance, in (6) the clause "que ccalaquīzqueh cē carro de pasaje" 'that they would put in a passenger bus' is the complement of "ōquichīhqueh cē convenio" 'they made an agreement'. This is not explicitly locutionary, although it clearly represents an event where speech occurred. Similarly (7), "de ser tesorero īmināhuac" 'to be treasurer with them' is embedded under "ōquinōtzqueh" 'they called him', an inflection of *nōtza* 'call, speak with purpose'. What is represented must have been a speech event, and the content, although not the form, of that speech can be reconstructed.

## INTERACTION BETWEEN VOICES

The voices in Don Gabriel's narrative interact not only with narrative sequencing, episodic structure, plot, and syntactic structures but with one another, in at least five major ways: dominance of the evaluator voice noted above, lexical interactions, conversational interactions, intonational breakthrough, and in the several types of confrontation between the Mexicano voice of peasant ideology and the Spanish voice of business-for-profit.

### Lexical and Topical Interactions of Voices

The level of lexical and topical interaction involves harmonic or antiphonal relationships between the terministic choices of different voices. Silverman and Torode (1980) point out that word choice can commit one voice to participation in a premise established by another. This participation can be the echo or repetition of words uttered by another voice, or the use of relational particles which acknowledge that utterance, even though the expressive force of the particles may be contradiction.

An excellent example of intervoice lexical interaction is seen in the repetition of the verb *calaqui* 'go in', which is endowed early with a fatal resonance. This verb first appears in (6), where it is transitive, referring to "putting in" a bus line in an indirect-discourse representation of voice A. In (16), the son states in direct discourse, "Ācmo nimocalaquīz" 'I won't go in any longer'. But in (18) we hear the verb again, this time in the coda offered by the evaluator: "Siempre ō-, ōcalac" 'Always he, he went in' (technically, what is repeated is the antecessive particle ō-, not the third person, but it is impossible to render this in English). Thus, even though in (16) the son denies that he will "go in," he is speaking within the terministic framework established by voice A, a voice which is probably that of his murderers. The intonational complexity of (18), and the dysfluent repetition of ō-, may derive from the confrontation of the evaluator voice with this verb, which has been rendered problematic by being the terministic choice of voice A. Next, the verb appears in a pivotal speech by the son in (21): "Cānin calaquīz?" 'Where will it go in?' a reference to the cash surplus which he, as treasurer, must deal with. In its reply, voice A implicitly echoes this term by ellipsis, in the accusation at (22) which specifies where the surplus might "go in": "pero para in pōxahtli, no" 'but for the pocket [embezzlement], no'. The next, and final, instance of the verb is in the last coda, the brief subnarrative about the recent murder of Don Gabriel's eldest son: "Ccalaquilihqueh tres tiros" 'They put three shots into him' (267).

The interaction of voices can also occur at the level of topic. Mutual acknowledgment of a topic can suggest a unity of purpose between two

voices. For instance, in the initial stages of the conversations between the
father and the son in episodes 2.A and 2.B, the topic of conversation,
about the location of the other son (family solidarity) and the pasturing of
the animals (the peasant way of life) is mutually established. Both voices
use the same crucial terms, such as the verb *tlapiatia* 'to pasture, care for
animals' (50–51). The conversation in 4.E, between Don Gabriel and his
brother about the identity of the body which the brother has seen, is also
of this type, as is the conversation with the official in episode 6, about
whether or not the son carried a gun. This kind of cooperation about
a topic can be sustained even though the conversation represented is an
argument, as in the latter two examples.

In the representations of argumentative conversations we must distinguish between two types of negative responses. Cooperative negatives
acknowledge and reply appropriately to questions, while agonistic negatives attempt to establish new conversational terms. For instance, when
the father is represented as replying to the son's invitation to eat with
"ayāmo nimayāna" 'I am not hungry now' (33, 59), this answer, while not
affirmative, acknowledges the question and cooperates with its topic.

Voices can appear in disharmony or antiphony as well as in harmony,
and in such cases we see agonistic negatives. Examples are found in (69)
and (72). Here, in the conversation between father and son, the son's negatives are not appropriate topic-acknowledging replies to yes-no questions.
In (69) the first negative, *āmo* 'no' is an inappropriate reply to a negative imperative, *āmo xiā* 'Don't go!' (68), but it is followed immediately
by a 'cooperative' particle with negative force, *pero* 'but', which seems to
acknowledge the imperative. However, by (72) the voice of the son is represented as abandoning any attempt at cooperation, replying *āmo* 'no' to a
question about what time the son will return from the city.

Perhaps the most ominous examples of agonistic negatives are uttered
by voice A in (22). Here, the first *pero* 'but' is not cooperative; it is a reply
to a request for specific information, rather than to a proposal or a command which might appropriately be answered with "but." Its use implies
that an inappropriate proposal was made. The strong Spanish negative
*no*, which is vanishingly rare in Malinche Mexicano usage (*āmo* 'no' and
*quēmah* 'yes' are strongly preferred to Spanish *no* and *sí*)[14] completes this
utterance. In the coda negatives voice A repeats itself with still more negatives: *āmo de nōn* 'none of that'. The expression "not for the pocket" is a
local cliché; "for the pocket" is embezzlement. Thus, this speech by voice
A is intricately intertextual. It is allied with the indirect discourse attributed to the "gente den pueblo" 'people of the town' immediately following
at (24), where "por base de interés" 'on the basis of (personal, conflicting,
illicit) interest' would be known to a listener to be also a cliché. It is also

allied by the rhyme between "feo corázōn" 'ugly heart' (23) — a property assigned by the evaluator to the people who could make such an accusation — and "con rázōn" 'with (ugly?) reason', a property assigned to the people of the town. The vox populi is clearly an ambivalent one.

## Conversational Interaction

The second type of interaction of voices involves the dominance and subordination of conversational roles.[15] The shifting balance of domination between figures is seen in the conversations between the father and the son represented in 2.A and 2.B. This is the only pair of episodes which is not clearly sequenced. Episode 2.A concludes with the sentence (47): "Yōyahqueh .. mero den: īpan: ... īpan ... īpan cēmpōal huān chicuacen tōnal de: ... de julio, Nuestra Señora Santa Ana" 'They left exactly on, o:n ... o:n ... on the twenty-sixth of July, Our Lady Saint Ann'. The careful attention to detail in this sentence suggests that on this day the son departed, never to return. But in 2.B he appears again in conversation with the father. Don Gabriel tries to accomplish episodic sequencing by some corrective measures, such as the explicit sequential connector *tonz* 'then' (from Spanish *entonces*) at (48), and an explicit allusion to temporal order, "cē tōnal antes" 'one day before'. This fragment, delivered in the sharp down-drop intonation contour usually used by the evaluator voice, is apparently an attempt to establish coherence with 2.A, and suggests that Don Gabriel is backtracking to a day before July 26. But the narrative voice then enters with the orientation, "ōyahqueh ōhuāllah occē tōnal" 'they went they came (they made a journey) another day' (48), which might suggest that the episode is sequenced after 2.A. This problem can be resolved if we consider episode 2.B to constitute an overlay (Grimes 1972), an expansion and replay of 2.A, with new embellishments and a subtle alteration of the relationships between the two figures of father and son.

The first conversational topic in both episodes is "taking care of animals." In 2.A, the conversation begins with the father's refusal of food (at 33), which makes him dominant. The father continues in dominance by posing a question (asking the son where he has left his brother and the animals [34]) which by both sequential and ritual constraints requires an answer. But in episode 2.B the son asks the first question (at [50]), and tells the father to go to the fields with the brother (52–54). Thus, the son is in dominance in this conversation, although the topic, about animals and food, is the same as in 2.A. The impact of the shift in dominance in 2.B is heightened by a change in position of the talk about animals and fields. In 2.A, this comes after the son's invitation to the father to have a snack, while in 2.B it appears at the beginning of the episode, before the invitation. Since the main evaluative work accomplished by these conversations is an assertion that both father and son follow a peasant way of life, which is threatened by the son's fatal involvement in business for profit, the shifting of dominance relationships between 2.A and the overlay in 2.B is of great interest.

The talk of commensality and the care of animals in the countryside in 2.A and 2.B contrasts sharply with the second major conversational topic in these episodes: the son's business in the city. In 2.A, the father controls this topic, introducing it with the question in (37). In (38), the son tries to evade the full pragmatic force of the question, answering only that he is going "to Puebla." The father then forces a reply by his question at (39) "para tlen?" 'for what?' In 2.B, the father again introduces the topic, at (62), and the son replies with a full account of the business. The father challenges the need to do the business, at (66) (but adopts the son's terministic choice, the verb *arreglaroa* 'arrange'); the son refuses to accept the challenge. After this refusal, conversational harmony breaks down. In 2.A, at (45), the son is represented as assuring the father that he will not be gone long. In 2.B, we encounter the agonistic negatives of (69) through (73), as the father becomes more and more indirect in his challenge, moving from the imperative "Don't go" (at 68) to the question "When will you return?" (at 71), to the even more open-ended question, "[Will it be] in the morning?" at (73). The son refuses to answer even this courteously vague plea.

The subordination of the voice of the father in episode 2.B is particularly clear when this conversation is compared to the long interchange between the father and his brother in 4.E. Here also there is an argument, but the brother utters only cooperative, not agonistic, denials of the father's proposals. The father controls topic choice throughout, and completes the conversation with a strong assertion, the authoritative hispanized utterance at (181), "No cabe duda ha de ser yen yeh" 'There is no doubt, it must be him'.

### Intonation and Intonational Breakthrough

Intonation provides a third device which Don Gabriel exploits to express interaction between voices. Intonational rhyming suggests harmony between voices, intonational opposition suggests disharmony, and intonational shadows can break through other voices to suggest an additional layer of presence in the text.

While Don Gabriel's diseased lungs present some problems for his control of pitch, in his narrative, as in all Mexicano narratives which I have examined, the "faithful" reproduction of intonational contours is a focus of the representation of reported speech. Mexicano storytellers attend to intonation as much as English speakers attend to pitch (and Mexicano speakers hardly attend to the latter at all). Only attention to language choice (cf. K. Hill 1985) receives as much attention as intonation contour.

The details of the notation for intonation in the text are given in note 2. The major components of intonation represented by speakers are contour amplitude, the direction of terminal contours, undulation or sharp drop of the total contour, and relative pitch level. Contour amplitude is the distance between the highest and lowest pitches of the intonational contour. In Mexicano, high amplitude (represented in the text by superscript h) seems to be an index of interlocutor solidarity, low amplitude (represented by superscript l) an index of neutrality and distance. Mexicano high-amplitude contours can be quite striking; in greetings by women, they begin with a falsetto squeak and fall to creaky voice. Male contours are less extreme, but still exhibit far more amplitude than any common contours in English.

Terminal contour can fall, rise, or remain level. Terminal contour direction in Mexicano matches the intonational universals proposed by Bolinger (1978). Sharp terminal fall in Mexicano signals finality and elimination of tension, while level or rising contours signal increasing tension. In narrative, relatively level contours mark the ongoing narrative sequence. Absence of any terminal fall signals a dependent clause prior to a main clause. Very high terminal contours are an index of extreme tension, and mark impolite prodding questions, desperation, or threat.

Total contour quality contrasts undulation or sharp drop. Undulating contours exhibit a series of falling pitch accents (represented as ' in the text), and tend to have a slight down-step at each new fall (actually a rise-fall when such pitch accents follow one another). It should be noted that Mexicano long vowels have a slightly lower pitch than surrounding syllables when they occur within the domain of a ´ or ¯ pitch accent, which complicates contours; these slight drops are predictable and so are not noted in the text notation. Undulating contours are characteristic of ongoing narrative. Sharply dropping contours are used to mark direct address, both in conversations represented in narrative and in "real life" conversations. In their extreme wide-amplitude version, as noted above, these contours index great solidarity between speaker and hearer.

Finally, Mexicano relative pitch reflects a pattern which is fairly common in the languages of the world, with low pitch often indicating threat and ominousness, while high pitch indicates fear, desperation, and the like.

Intonation is an important marker of voices in the system of self-laminations. The two narrator voices are contrasted by intonation. The narrator voice N is characterized by low amplitude, moderate terminal fall, moderate undulation, and pitch in the middle range. Relative pitch tends to be elevated slightly at the beginning of episodes and at other major structural breaks. This pattern can be clearly seen in the early sentences and orientation of the first episode (1–6). The first sentence is interrupted by an intonational shadow which I have labeled the *cantante* 'singsong' contour, which will be discussed below. The moderate amplitude of the N voice distances it from the hearer, signaling that no reply is required, and the moderate fall on terminal contours signals that the sequence of the narrative will continue.

The narrator voice O appears at the moment of a particularly important complicating action, the discovery of the letter, at (92–95). Unlike the undulating sequences of falling pitch accents preferred by the narrator N, the O voice often uses sharply falling contour dropping to low pitch, marked by \. This voice builds involvement on the part of the hearer in at least two ways. The sharply falling contours are characteristic of intimacy and direct address, and thus invite attention and reciprocity. The low finals of the terminal contours suggest finality, even though the sequence of the narrative will continue. Thus the listener can find each new clause in the narrative sequence somehow surprising, which increases tension and the sense of collaboration in the narrative work as the surprise is accepted.

Wide-amplitude undulation and/or sharply falling contours, as opposed to the slightly undulating downstep of narrative sentences, are characteristic of Mexicano direct address, particularly in such speech acts as greetings, invitations, questions, and commands. Sharply falling contours express great politeness (the most extreme examples, with a fall from falsetto to creaky voice, are used between ritual kin, especially by women). These contours can perhaps be accounted for in terms of Bolinger's (1982) claim that relatively flat intonational contours are an icon for control of tension. If this is the case then, by contrast, the sharp fall can index solidarity so great that there is no tension to control.

Don Gabriel's narrative contains several representations of speech with quite sharply falling total contour, and the voice of the evaluator uses it. Examples of the contour in the representation of reported speech can be seen in the conversation in episode 4.E, where the father and his brother argue cooperatively in a reciprocal exchange of total contours which fall sharply from high to low pitch, at (173–75) and again at (179–81). In 4.A, at (104) and at (107–11), the figure of the young worker uses this contour in his replies to Don Gabriel, indexing his deferential cooperation with the old man's purpose. The use of the contour by the evaluator voice P can be seen in the word *siempre* 'always' in (18). The use of this contour by the evaluator voice is immediately followed by a response from the interviewer, which supports the suggestion that the evaluator is in some sense a direct-address voice instead of a narrative voice *sensu stricto*.

While very sharply dropping contour with the scope of an entire utterance is one form which wide-amplitude intonation can assume, other patterns are possible, such as undulation within utterances. A good example of such an undulating wide-amplitude contour within a sentence is in (33), in the father's reply to the son's invitation to eat. To the English speaker, the contour of (33), "a^h\yāmo nima^h\yāna" 'I am not hungry now', sounds whiny, even rude. However, in Mexicano it is very polite. I have often heard children use it to reply to questions from parents, who accept the contour without taking any redressive action. Like the high-low contours, this wide-amplitude contour apparently suggests solidary absence of tension and a concordance of views, and forthcoming cooperation or obedience.

While wide-amplitude speakings suggest politeness, solidarity, and relaxed cooperation, low-amplitude contours, particularly in direct address, suggest great tension. They are at best distancing, and can be threatening. The flatter the contour, the greater the tension. An example of a low-amplitude speaking by the son occurs at (21), when the son asks his business partners what he should do with the money. Here, the low-amplitude contour suggests tension between the interlocutors. The drops at the moments of dysfluency (represented here by the falling pitch accent ', since their scope is over single words) may come from interruption by an intonational shadow which rejects the attempt to use a term for business-for-profit by signaling finality before the term is reached. Another example of an unexpectedly flat contour can be seen at (37), where the father first asks the son where he is going.

An excellent example of the contrast between solidary and tense contours can be seen in the two representations of almost the same sentence in episodes 2.A and 2.B. In 2.A, in the first representation of the conversation between the father and the son about the son's business in the city, the father asks the son at (37), "^l'Cān tiyāz in 'teh" 'Where will you go?', with a relatively flat contour, as noted above. In the replay at (62), the father asks the same question with a very sharp high-low total contour. The difference between these two representations is part of the shift in dominance between the two figures discussed above. In 2.A, the father is in control, free to disapprove frankly of the son's business. In 2.B, the father has become the supplicant, pleading with his son and trying to establish a common ground for discussion. Additional examples of flat, tense contours can be seen in episode 6, at (224) and (226), where the official speaks to the father. Here these contours indicate the dominance of the official and the great social distance between him and the father. The official's statement at (232), "Pues, t'cahxilihqueh cē pis'tola" 'Well, we found a pistol', exhibits a very slight terminal rise on the final high pitch accent in *pis'tola;* this makes the question very ominous indeed. The reply by the father is represented with very deferential high-low contours in (236). And the official, apparently satisfied, echoes this in (237).

High rising terminal contours, noted with /, signal great tension. At (73), the father uses the high rise to plead for an answer which he does not expect to receive. At (172) the brother insists, of the corpse he has seen, "⟨ʰ/āmo yen yeh" 'It isn't him' (the son); the contour suggests that he is, in fact, uncertain of this conclusion.

Other types of high pitch are also tense. Both appearances, at (105) and (163), of the question "⟩¯Tlīca?" 'Why?', are uttered on a high, flat note; such a question is intrusive, and the nearly falsetto pitch is "tense," or "negative" politeness (Brown and Levinson 1978), as opposed to the solidary, positive politeness of the high-low drop. Low pitch can be seen in (22) and (194), which are both warnings.

The intonational contours reviewed above appear in rhyming and non-rhyming relationships in the representation of conversation in the narrative. The example of intonational rhyming between the father and his brother at (173–75) has been noted above. The intonational rhyming heightens the sense of the solidarity of these figures.

Harmonic, rhyming intonational patterns contrast with patterns of intonational dissonance, which show lack of cooperation in conversation. For instance, in episode 2, the intonational patterns of the father and the son consistently fail to achieve rhyming. Where the father's are tense and flat, the son's show sharp high-low drop. Where the father has wide amplitude, the son exhibits low amplitude. In 2.B, we see an increasing dissonance of contours. The negatives at (68) and (69) share high-low contour, but in (69) the polite negative is followed by the low-pitched refusal to break the appointment in the city: "⟨pero yōnimocomprome'teroh" 'but I have an appointment'. But in (72, 73) the contours themselves go in opposite directions. Dissonant contours can also be seen in the conversation between the father and the official in episode 6. The official maintains relatively flat low-amplitude contours, while the father uses a relatively deferential wide-amplitude drop in his replies. Only at (236–37) and in the final exchange in (243–44), where the official invites the father to come and see him if he needs any help, do the contours begin to rhyme. However, at (245), in the evaluative coda, the evaluator and narrative O voices make it clear that the invitation was ignored. An inhabitant of Almecatla would be foolish to involve himself with such an official beyond the minimal requirements of the law. Don Gabriel notes that he even failed to collect his son's clothing, probably to avoid the risk which attends contact with the police. The dissonance of intonation contours throughout this conversation may, then, represent the fundamental distrust which people like Don Gabriel feel for officials of governments beyond the community.

## The Breakthrough of Intonational Shadows

The intonational shadows are apparently "artless" voices that interrupt the artful allocation of intonational patterns to sustain plot tension and sequencing. Two major intonational shadows appear in the text. The first, the S shadow, is the *cantante,* marked by ^. This contour is a stereotype in vernacular Mexican Spanish, where it is especially common in joking among men. Mexicano speakers use the contour, but the environments for its use are restricted and its functions have changed: its appearance seems to signal negativity, anguish, or ominousness. In Bolinger's (1982) terms, the sharp control over the down-drop of terminal contour which is the special mark of the *cantante* intonation signals extreme tension "under control." This contour appears at several points in the narrative. The first appearance is at (2) "ōquimic´tihqueh 'cē nomu^chacho" 'They killed one of my sons'. It appears again at (76), when we learn that the daughter-in-law is the wife of Don Gabriel's eldest son, " 'cē nomu'chacho ^mayōr." Of course in the brief coda at (262–69), we learn that this son was also murdered. The contour appears very clearly in (211), the evaluative coda of the peak episode: "⟩Neh 'nicah 'casi ya la^crado" 'I'm almost destroyed now'.

The second intonational shadow is a "desperate" voice, which exhibits very high pitch and a weak, breathy, almost tearful voice quality. This shadow appears at points of no return in the plot. It first appears in (18), the coda sentence of the first episode, where it interrupts the utterance by the evaluator voice, "ʰ\Siempre ... ō- ... ⟩ō'calac" 'Always he, he went in'. This brief utterance has a very intricate contour, which terminates on a less-than-usual drop from the final ' pitch accent. The desperate shadow appears again in (196) and (197), where the narrator describes the moment of recognition of the son's body: "⟩Neh 'zā niman ōni⁻quīxmat. ⟩'Zā niman, 'zā niman ōni⁻quīxmat" 'As for me I knew him at once. At once, at once I knew him'. It appears at (206), when the father "accepts" the death: "⟩⁻Ya" 'Done'. It is seen again at (219), where the narrator says "⟩´yōnihuāllah" 'I came'—to go through the ordeal of the inquiry by the officials—and at (228), as the father tries to convince the official that the son never carried a weapon. Here, this "voice break" shadow appears on an unusually low pitch and accompanies an interesting switch from a present-tense to an irrealis verb form, ". . . ⟨qui'nemi, ⟨qui'nemīz" 'for walking around with, to walk around with'. At (133) the inner voice, the strategist, is interrupted by this voice, when, after repeated inquiries which have failed to yield any information, the strategist asks, "⟩ˡToz ´tlen pa'noā?" 'Then what is going on?'

At least two interpretations of the intonational shadow voices may be advanced. They may represent moments where the work of lamination between the animator and the voices which this animator establishes breaks down, and the grief and emotion of some core of the self pierces the layers at moments of special significance. If this account is correct, then we cannot consider the direct-address voice of the evaluator, the "addressing self," as the core, but must see this voice instead as artfully managing the task of moral evaluation, while the desperate intonational shadow is somehow the "real" Don Gabriel, the parent devastated by the death of a child. However, even the intonational shadow voices perhaps should be considered "artful." No one who hears Don Gabriel's narrative can fail to be affected by the agony which ·penetrates lines (196) and (197): "›Neh 'zā niman ōni⁻quīxmat. ›'Zā niman, 'zā niman ōni⁻quīxmat" 'As for me I knew him at once. At once, at once I knew him'. The sense of "lack of control," constructed partly by the breakthrough of the high pitch, is part of the intensity of this narrative moment. The possibility that this intonational shadow should be understood as another manifestation of Don Gabriel's art, rather than some kind of breakthrough of an authentic self, perhaps can be supported by contrasting this moment of tragedy in (196–97) with the reading of the letter at (88–91). At the end of episode 3 (92–95) the evaluator tells us that the letter was so horrible that Don Gabriel did not even accept its reality. As late as episode 4.E, the voice of the father still refers to its contents under the evidential particle *quil*, which questions the veracity of its content. When the father "reads" the letter (88–91), the reading is represented in a very flat, singsong tone which lends great immediacy—it is precisely the sound of a person who does not read much reading a text for the first time, there before the listener. The flat contours also suggest the lack of full comprehension of the meaning of the letter. (The reading of the letter can also be usefully compared to the use by the evaluator voice of the biblical quotation at [26]. This is represented with a very earnest tone, suggesting the strong commitment of the evaluator to this message [which is probably Ephesians 5:14, where people are urged to turn away from darkness, as seen in corruption and bad feelings between people, and receive Christ's light].) The "reading" of the letter shows that part of the art of fidelity to intonation in the narrative is the reproduction of precisely the emotion of the moment, even though the "real" Don Gabriel has had, at the time of the telling of the narrative, ample time to reflect on the horror of the letter. Thus, the "intonational shadow" of the desperate voice may be equally a faithful representation of emotion in the narrative world, not in the world of the "I-before-you."[16]

Both the reading of the letter and the breakthrough of the desperate shadow may be examples of the art of creating the type of frame which Goffman (1974) has called "insider's folly": "a glimpse behind the scenes [to induce] the belief that you are seeing the backstage of something" (ibid.: 475). If this analysis, that the intonational shadows are laminated by an "insider's folly" frame, is correct, then we cannot claim that the "addressing self," the moral center from which our vernacular theory of personality suggests the text must emanate, is in fact represented overtly anywhere in the voice system. We hear only the animator, and must ask, "Who is Don Gabriel?"

### The Moral Orientation of Narrative Consciousness

Having sketched in the major systems of the narrative: structural opposi- tions, episodic sequencing, plot, and the voice system, we can turn to the problem raised at the outset, Bakhtin's formative moment of literary con- sciousness, when the author must choose an orientation among the moral and ideological implications of the voices of the heteroglossic world.

Don Gabriel must address two central problems: the fact of the murder and the motives for it. His handling of the two problems contrasts strik- ingly: the fact of the murder is narrated with great fluency, but when Don Gabriel addresses the problem of motive, serious tensions in composition appear: in Bakhtin's terms, the alien lexicon of business-for-profit "falls out" of the voice system of the narrative and resists assimilation to it.

The lexicon of business-for-profit in the Malinche is Spanish. Malinche Mexicano usage incorporates an enormous amount of Spanish material at all levels of the borrowing hierarchy, from nouns to particles and other "function" elements, and exhibits substantial convergence with Spanish (Hill and Hill 1986). The syncretism with Spanish is viewed with pro- found ambivalence. Malinche speakers often say that "mixing" has pol- luted Mexicano, and Spanish itself is assigned an ambivalent functional role, being the language of elevated public spheres such as religion and government but also of drunkenness, cursing, and insincerity. It is, par ex- cellence, the language of the market economy: buying, selling, the making of profit, the counting of money. The Spanish lexicon of business in the marketplace provides a "vocabulary of motives" (Mills 1940) which Don Gabriel cannot avoid, even though this lexicon carries with it the ide- ology of the urban, individualistic, profit-seeking sphere which is anti- thetical to the peasant values of communal reciprocity which Don Gabriel clearly places at the center of his narrative structure.[17] The most impor- tant strategy which Don Gabriel uses to handle the moral dilemma posed by the necessity to use this lexicon is to assign "speaking of business-for- profit" to figures in reported speech, and, in the system of self-lamination, to the neutral narrative voice, the voice farthest from the moral center of this part of the voice system. When a voice which is very close to this center, the evaluator, must speak of business-for-profit, it is done in euphe- mistic terms. However, even with this strategic allocation of terms, there is considerable evidence in the narrative of struggle and resistance against "speaking of business," particularly manifested in lexical dysfluencies.

First, let us consider the distribution of speaking of business-for-profit along the moral axis of the voice system. I have shown that the narrative contains two major classes of voices: laminations of the animator and figures, with the protagonist, the figure of the father, and the strategist, Don Gabriel's inner voice, belonging to both categories. In the first group, the narrator voice N is distinguished from the others by being neutral, divorced from the I-thou world of direct address and belonging entirely to the narrative world, functioning to sustain the narrative main line and to give material orientation. The other voices in the self-lamination system are all located closer to the I-thou world and hence to the moral center of the narrative work. They provide overt moral commentary or engage in direct address (as in the case of the evaluator voice), or they use techniques of immediacy, such as sharp down-drop terminal contours separating sentences in the narrative sequence, or historical present verbs, as in the case of the narrator voice O. The father is the focus of point of view in the narrative. The father's voice is at the intersection of the self-lamination system and the figure system, and seems to be at the moral center of the latter. Among this group of voices, Don Gabriel's self-laminations, only the distant, neutral narrator N speaks of the son's business affairs. Examples of the treatment of business by this voice are seen at (5) and (19), which are part of the orientations to episodes 1.A and 1.C respectively. Here the voice uses Spanish terms: *convenio* 'agreement', *negocio* 'business'. In episode 4.B, at (116–19) the narrator N voice addresses the related question of *política* 'politics' (I take *fuerte* in [119] to be the evaluator's word).

Most of the discussion of business is handled by two figures, voice A, the voice of those who were envious of the son and who may have caused his murder, and the son himself. In (7) voice A, represented in indirect discourse, uses the code-switched expression *de ser tesorero* 'to be treasurer'. But most speech about business-for-profit is assigned to the son, in sharp contrast with the father, who never uses this lexicon. The son's voice first addresses the business at (21), using the terms *sobra* 'surplus' and the explicitly financial *ahorro* 'savings'. In the conversations in 2.A and 2.B, the son uses a fully developed vocabulary of business, discussing *tomín* 'money', and various papers, at (40) and (42). In the replay conversation, the son discusses *asunto* 'business' and money at (63–65). A third reported-speech voice which is exploited briefly to make a moral judgment about business-for-profit is the indirect-address representation of voice B, the "people of the town" at (24), which evaluates the motive for fighting: "que timotehuiah ïpan in cargo por base de interés" 'that we fight one another over the job due to personal interest' — that is, for personal gain.

It is easy to imagine different distributions of the vocabulary of the profit motive. For instance, the voice of the father could spell out the details of the "business" in its accusations and questions, or the voice of the evaluator could elaborate and comment about the "business" in rendering judgments about it. But these voices never mention the "business," and their comments on it derive meaning only by being adjacent to more explicit statements assigned to other voices.

In one instance the evaluator cannot avoid mentioning the "business" as this voice makes a moral judgment. The problem is solved by euphemism. This occurs at (20), where the evaluator voice appears in a very intricate preverbal complex, which makes a moral judgment about the presumed origin of voice A: "nīnqueh cristianos, in āquin ōquipiayah ambición de nōn, ... de nōn trabajo" 'these people, who had ambition about that ... that work'. We can be sure that this is the evaluator, because of the expressive sentence adverb *desgraciadamente* 'unfortunately' and the negatively loaded term *ambición* 'ambition'. The term *trabajo* 'work', used here for the business, is a euphemism for *asunto* or *negocio,* terms which are used by the son and the narrator N. The business, of course, is the bus system. In the Malinche towns, bus systems are private enterprises, and the son is involved with a group of partners who are seeking permission from the urban government to run the system. For a number of years in the 1960s and 1970s, while gasoline prices were still very low in Mexico, partnership in a community bus system was a virtually certain route to wealth. The right to participate in such partnerships was intricately intertwined with local politics, because of the need for official permissions. Thus, the bus system was clearly an *asunto* or *negocio,* a business for profit (although the partners would claim that it was for the good of the town), and its affairs were *política* 'politics' (a term which has the same negative resonance for Mexicano speakers that it has for many English speakers). Don Gabriel represents himself as having urged his son to stay out of the business as an illegitimate conflict of interest with his legitimate public service as municipal president.

Mexicano has no indigenous terms for business-for-profit. The term which is used for enterprise in the peasant way of life is *tequipanoā* 'pass along by work', often translated into Spanish as *mantenerse* 'to maintain oneself'. The element *tequi* in this verb appears in other expressions. As a possessed noun it means "responsibility, concern" in a very general sense, such that the Mexicano expression *āmo notequi* translates into English as 'it's not my responsibility' (but not as 'it's none of my business'!). The nonpossessed (absolute) noun *tequitl* is usually translated by Mexicano speakers as *trabajo* 'work'. In Classical Mexicano the *tequitl* was the work done to pay the tribute, the portion collected from the peasantry by the state. All other terms which intersect with the English notion of "work" have very specific designations in Mexicano (for activities such as cultivation, woodcutting, animal care, carpentry, kitchen tasks, and the like), and are usually referred to collectively with the Spanish term *oficio* 'occupation'. Such *oficios* are occasionally referred to as *trabajo*, but *trabajo* is prototypically wage labor. It is certainly not routinely used, as "work" is often used in English, to mean the pursuit of business for profit. Thus, the usage of this term by the evaluator at (20) is a rare extension of the word into this realm, and should be considered a euphemistic terministic choice, which preserves the moral distancing of the evaluator voice from the words of the realm of business-for-profit.[18]

The assignment of the lexicon of "business" to reported speech voices or to voices far from the moral center of the self-laminations does not entirely overcome the resistance of Don Gabriel's speaking to the incorporation of this lexicon. Most of the major dysfluencies in the text appear when "business" is mentioned, and these dysfluencies can occur regardless of which voice is in play. An example can be found in the speech of the evaluator in the passage at (20) discussed above, where there is a dysfluent repetition and pause in "de nōn ... de nōn trabajo" 'about that ... that work'. Dysfluencies also occur in the voice of the narrator N. Thus, at (5) there is a dysfluent repetition and pause: "cē: ... cē convenio" 'a:n ... an agreement'. Such dysfluencies even occur in representations of the voice of the son, as in (21): "nōn:, nōn sobra, .. o nōn: ... nōn ahorro" 'tha-a-t, that surplus, .. or tha-a-t ... that savings' (in Mexicano it is the final /n/ which is lengthened, not the vowel of *nōn*).

The most dramatic breakdown in fluency occurs in an attempt to represent the voice of the son in episode 2.A. Here, the son is explaining to his father what he will do in the city, so the details of the "business" must be mentioned. The son begins speaking at (40), in response to the father's insistent questioning; his utterance contains hesitation forms (*este, den*) and pauses. Then he is interrupted completely by what seems to be the evaluator, at (41), who says "Tlenōnōn ōnēchilih?" 'What did he say to me?' This interruption is particularly startling, since elsewhere in the text qualifications about fidelity are expressed with particles such as *nēci* or *mati* 'it seems'. Elsewhere, of course, Don Gabriel represents quite complex texts, such as the text of the letter, with little dysfluency or hedging about his memory. After this interruption, Don Gabriel again tries to represent the voice of the son, at (42), and again encounters extreme dysfluency. Finally, at (43), the evaluator voice rejects the matter entirely, saying "Āmo niquilnāmiqui quēn ōnēchilih" 'I don't remember what he told me'.

I have pointed out above that episode 2.B appears to be an overlay or replay of episode 2.A, but that in episode 2.B the son, not the father, is in dominance in the reported conversation about business. Strikingly, in the representation of the son's discussion of business in 2.B, there is none of the dysfluency which was so apparent in 2.A.

The narrative is very fluent overall. The only dysfluencies in it, other than those encountered upon "speaking of business-for-profit," are of the "accounting" type. Examples of "accounting" dysfluencies appear at (3), where Don Gabriel tries to remember exactly how many years ago his son was killed, at (47), where he tries to remember a date, and at (199), where the hesitation is associated with a search for the correct word to describe the kind of rock his son's body lay upon.

The "accounting" dysfluencies are important, for they present evidence for how we should think of dysfluencies in general, and particularly those which occur in connection with the mention of "business." Dysfluencies are not easily assigned to narrative art, and it is tempting to adopt a naive Freudian approach to dysfluency that assumes that it reveals for us the presence of an authentic subconscious locus of affect, the self. But accounting dysfluencies suggest a different interpretation. The self which produces these is a responsible self, which attends to precise representation. Thus dysfluencies in connection with terms for "business" may represent precisely responsibility, a property not of the emotional unconscious but of the active, choosing consciousness to which Bakhtin directs our attention. It is this consciousness which may lie at the moral center of the narrative, and the dysfluencies index its presence. This is an important hypothesis, since anthropological literature has focused on the self as the locus of some continuity of emotional response, and not a continuity of responsibility. Mauss (1985), in his famous essay "A Category of the Human Mind: The Notion of Person, the Notion of Self," suggested that during the last two hundred years westerners have tended to unite the two qualities — the notion of the "responsible" legal person and the notion of the "emotional" person with an inner life, in a single socially relevant entity. The present analysis suggests that the close study of oral discourse may be an important research site for exploring the relationship between these two very closely related properties of human actors.

The murder itself, in contrast to the motives for the murder, offers no resistance to assimilation into Don Gabriel's narrative. The English speaker imagines that the great problem for such a narrator might be to come to grips with the horror of the violent death of a child. However, passages having to do with the death are among the most artful and fluent in the narrative. While morally central voices never address "business-for-profit" directly, almost all discussion of the murder and the body is assigned to the morally central figure, the father. The evaluator, the morally central voice in the system of self-laminations, also discusses the matter. Other

Table 4-2. Distribution of Topics of Business-for-Profit and Death
among the Voices

|  | Business | Death |
|---|---|---|
| Moral Periphery |  |  |
| Anonymous letter |  | 90 |
| Voice A | 6,7 |  |
| People of town | 24 |  |
| Son | 21,40,42,63,65 |  |
| Narrator N | 5,19,116,117,213 | 2,266,267 |
| Narrator O |  | 196,197,199,200,201,202,246 |
| Evaluator | 20(euphemism) |  |
| Father |  | 165 |
| Moral Center |  |  |

figures, including the daughter-in-law and the several figures which appear in episode 4, the search, never use the verb *mictia* 'kill' or nouns such
as *cuerpo* 'body', which is used by the evaluator at (246), in the coda to
episode 6. The distribution of the topics of "business-for-profit" and the
murder among the voices is shown in table 4-2.

In contrast to "business-for-profit," there is little dysfluency associated
with discussion of the son's death. Instead of dysfluent pausing and repetition, in discussions of the murder we find breakthrough by intonational
shadow voices, such as the *cantante* shadow at (2) and (211), or the "desperate" shadow at (196–97), (206), and (211). A brief dysfluency appears at
(192) in the climactic scene: "nēchiliah este, quiliah in nocnīh este" 'They
tell me uh, they tell my brother uh', but this seems to be an "accounting"
dysfluency having to do with attention to accuracy in managing the peak-
marking strategy of "concentration of participants," and is not related to
any problem of incorporating the lexicon of murder into the art of the
narrative.

Don Gabriel can speak the death of a child. What resists his voice and
"falls out" of his fluent narrative art is the language of business and profit.
This resistance, demonstrated through the close analysis of his narrative,
is additional evidence which supports the contention of Taussig (1979),
Dow (1981), Warman (1982), and others that a peasant consciousness is at
least partially constituted as a domain of ongoing ideological resistance
to a capitalist ideology. This resistance persists even in communities like
Almecatla, which dependency theorists would consider to be fully incorporated into the peripheral capitalist sector. There could hardly be more
dramatic evidence for the persistence of this consciousness than that given
us by Don Gabriel, who can report the moment when he gazed upon

the murdered body of his son with elegiac elegance, but who stammers when he must speak the motives for that murder in the Spanish lexicon of gain. The value of this evidence shows the relevance for the great problems of anthropology of close analysis of oral narrative which has been developed in recent years by scholars such as Labov (1972), Hymes (1981), Tedlock (1983), and Woodbury (1985, 1987). The narrative reveals a veritable kaleidoscope of "emotional selves," which are all art, distributed in fragments across the rhetorical systems of the narrative. But the narrative does give us evidence of the integrity of another self, the "responsible self" which we may call consciousness, and allows us a privileged glimpse of the moment of "active choice" when this consciousness orients itself as a voice in a heteroglossic universe.

## NOTES

This work was supported by grants from the National Endowment for the Humanities, the American Council of Learned Societies, and the Phillips Fund of the American Philosophical Society. Thanks are also owed to Bruce Mannheim, Ellen Basso, Dell Hymes, and Kenneth C. Hill, with whom I have discussed this and related work.

The term "Mexicano" has been used for nearly five hundred years for the Uto-Aztecan language also known as Nahuatl or Aztec. "Mexicano" is strongly preferred local usage; for speakers, it stands for a claim of prototypical citizenship in the Mexican state.

1. Interest in Bakhtin's concept of the dialogic interaction of voices (which can be seen, for instance, in Silverman and Torode [1980] and Bruner and Gorfain [1984], as well as in the present work) advances a tradition of concern for the development of a unit of discursive consciousness, found in the work of Sapir (in a number of papers in his *Selected Writings* [Mandelbaum, ed. 1949]; see discussion in J. Hill [1988]), and particularly in work by Hymes, who has argued that the "voice," the manifestation of the "individuality" which must develop communicative competence, must be a fundamental unit of linguistic study (Hymes 1979), and that "vocal realization" is an important system of representation in oral literature (Hymes 1981). Friedrich (1986) has suggested that the properties of the individual voice are best captured by considering it as a poetic "imagination." Subjectivity has been proposed as a basic unit of linguistic and discourse analysis by Benveniste (1971), Lyons (1982), and Banfield (1973, 1981, 1984). The present study draws on this work, but takes as central Bakhtin's "voice," which defines subjectivity as dialogic in its essence, and, most appropriately for the topic in this volume, as the locus of "active choice" and responsibility.

2. Notation of the text uses the following conventions:

Right bracket ], followed by subscript numbers, approximates the units of the voice system (sometimes these are clauses, sometimes utterances with more than one sentence). In order to avoid proliferating brackets, by convention I have not separated off locutionary verbs (uttered by one of the narrative voices, N or O). It is impossible to bracket clearly the structural units of the voice system, since often quite short utterances contain several voices in a multidimensional array. Brackets without numbers occur occasionally to mark the end of intonation contours.

Subscript letters following brackets and numbers. These refer to "voices" listed in table 4–1 in the text, and indicate (roughly) the voices which participate in the bracketed units. Marking direct-discourse reported speech clauses with a subscript for one of the narrative voices means that that voice is assigned to the locutionary verb which introduces the reported speech.

Where speakers other than Don Gabriel (DG), such as the interviewer, are speaking, their voices are indicated in capital letters before their contribution.

The transcription of Mexicano-language material follows the usage of Karttunen (1983); a macron over a vowel indicates a distinctive long vowel. Spanish loan words have distinctive long vowels at the location of Spanish-language stress; to avoid proliferation of diacritics beyond what is absolutely necessary I have not indicated these vowels as long, except where stress has shifted, e.g., *rázōn* 'reason' at (24). Spanish loans are spelled as in Spanish, except in such cases. Note that the Spanish acute accent is placed over the vowel, e.g., *fábrica* 'factory' (4); when the acute accent marker is before a vowel, it indicates rising pitch accent, as discussed below. Native Mexicano words, with very few exceptions, are stressed on the penultimate syllable.

Colon following a vowel or consonant indicates extra length, e.g., *nōn:* (21), where final /n/ is extra long as the speaker hesitates.

Unspaced dots, e.g., "cē: ... cē convenio" (5) indicate noticeably long pauses. The number of dots reflects the length of the pause. Other notations for pause phenomena include comma and period, which are normal clause-final and sentence-final pauses accompanied by characteristic terminal pitch accents.

= is used to indicate absence of pause where punctuation such as ? is required due to content, or where an episode ends but is not accompanied by a pause. Examples are at (106), (109).

Notational conventions for intonation contours are as follows:

a. Pitch accents appear on tonic syllables: the penult, e.g., "ōqui´nōtzqueh" 'they called him' (7), rarely on secondary-stressed syllables (the penultimate before the penult, e.g., "ōni'cuālcāh'tēhui" 'I went to leave him' [35]), or sometimes on some other syllable prior to this, for reasons which are not clear to me; an example is " 'ōquimpade¯ceroh" 'it appeared to them' (27), and on syllables with long vowels where the word contains a single long vowel which is not the penult, e.g. "ni¯cān" 'here' (5). Pierrehumbert (1987) suggests that pitch accents will always fall on "stressed syllables"; the accommodation of this proposed universal to Nahuatl metrics is beyond the scope of this essay.

b. Three pitch accents are noted:

1. ´ is rising pitch. After this pitch accent, pitch remains high until another pitch accent or tonal contour occurs. High pitch accent is not interrupted

by brackets, commas, or periods. An example can be seen at (130), where the high pitch accent in "ōni´huāllah" 'when I came' initiates high pitch which continues until the fall on " 'tle⁻nōn" in (132).

2. ⁻ is a high flat "nonterminal" contour. Pitch rises to high (or remains high after rising pitch accent), and remains high only until the end of the word on which the pitch accent is marked. Pitch is low at the beginning of the following word; this new low pitch is not marked. Pitch remains low until the next marker.

3. ' is a rise-fall or fall. If pitch has been low (as after ⁻ or a previous '), pitch will rise on the marked syllable and fall again to low on the immediately following syllable. If pitch has been high (as after '), it will remain high on the marked syllable and drop to low on the following syllable. Pitch remains low until the next pitch accent marker occurs. A sequence of ' pitch accents will exhibit down-step; this is not marked. This occurs, for instance, in (48), where the overall fall from the preverbal complex marked with ⟩ (a non-numbered bracket marks the domain of the ⟩) is as striking as in the ʰ\ contour type, but is not identical with it since the undulation of the sequenced ' pitch accents is clearly audible.

c. Three special intonational contours are indicated: \, /, and ^. \ indicates an uninterrupted fall from high to low which continues until the following comma, period, right bracket, or next pitch accent or contour marker, whichever comes first. / indicates a rise from low to high with the same domains. ^ is the *cantante* contour; the first syllable following the marker is high, while the next drops slightly to a flat pitch which is much higher than a normal terminal contour. An example is seen at "nomu^chacho" (2). The next clause then begins with low pitch, which is not marked.

d. An underlined vowel after a ' pitch accent indicates that the fall is not as "low" as normal, although the flat quality is not as striking as in the ^ contour, e.g., "presi'dent̲e" (9). Underline at the beginning of a word, e.g., "_Aah" (uttered by interviewer in opening conversation) indicates a low contour with a slight fall-rise.

e. ⟩ indicates that pitch is unusually high. ⟨ indicates that it is unusually low. The unusual pitch level continues until the end of the bracketed section in which it appears.

f. Superscript ʰ indicates a high-amplitude contour. This is most commonly seen with \, e.g., "ʰ\Ācmo ximocomprometerō" (10) (in opening conversation); this contour indicates respectful courtesy to the interlocutor, and is very common in Mexicano direct address. Superscript ˡ indicates a low-amplitude or unusually flat contour; this may indicate tension between interlocutors. Both high- and low-amplitude contour markers can also occur with regular pitch accents to indicate an overall strongly undulating or unusually flat quality to the sequence. The domain of these is until the end of the bracketed element where they appear.

3. The analytical framework here, of a system of rhetorical practices which includes narrative sequence, plot tension, and the voice system, owes much to several recent studies. Hymes (1981) has distinguished plot and incident as aspects of

content, and poetic form, rhetorical form, and vocal realization as aspects of presentation. Woodbury (1985) has proposed "rhetorical structure" as the practices which organize systems of text-building such as prosody, particles (which I have neglected in the present discussion), and syntax. Hymes distinguishes his concept of "vocal realization" from the more usual notion of reported speech, since it includes what I have here called "fidelity" and "drama," as well as audience response. This concept seems close to, but not identical with, what I have here called the voice system.

4. Major recent studies of reported speech in oral discourse include Larson (1978), Longacre (1976), Hymes (1981), Sherzer (1981), Silverstein (1985), Coulmas (1986), and Lucy (1993). Labov and Fanshel (1977) have explored voice differentiation in therapeutic discourse. Leech (1978) has examined the implications of reported speech for formal pragmatics and semantics.

5. Singer (1980) borrows the term "glassy essence" for the self from C. S. Peirce, who in turn took it from Shakespeare.

6. The numbers in parentheses refer to clause numbers in the text, found immediately after the right-facing brackets (]).

7. Hymes (personal communication) has suggested that some features of the text suggest ambivalence on Don Gabriel's part about wealth. In a comment on J. Hill (1985), he proposes that the switch in (7) to the Spanish *ser tesorero* 'to be treasurer' may signal pride in the son's career, as well as being a representation of voice A and of Spanish market ideology. The mention of the brother's car at (153) and (155) is additional evidence for the correctness of this suggestion. At this period a car, perhaps more than any other material possession, signaled that a person was a *rico* 'a rich person'. Don Gabriel's substantial house also suggested that his family was quite wealthy relative to the Malinche norm. The entire narrative might be seen as an assertion that, in spite of his wealth, Don Gabriel insists that he is committed to peasant values; the framing in such a case would become even more complex than has been suggested here.

8. The movement of cemeteries to the edge of town is an innovation in the Malinche region. Traditionally the dead were buried in the churchyard itself, at the center of town, but crowding in these areas, and concerns for sanitation, led priests and national health administrators to insist on the installation of new cemeteries outside the habitation zone. Many people on the Malinche object to the new cemeteries and indicate that they wish they could be buried in the churchyard beside their ancestors.

9. The form *teh* is perhaps best translated 'thou'; it is a "T-form" (Brown and Gilman 1960) which is contrasted to the "V-form" *tehhuatzīn* and, in Mexicano, to an even more formal pronoun, *momahuizotzīn* or *īmahuizotzīn* 'your reverence', 'his/her reverence', respectively.

10. Much of the cognitivist attention to discourse structure has focused on units at the lowest level, as in the exemplary work of Chafe (1980). Phenomena like the sustaining of an ironic frame in the present text (and indeed Chafe's own work on short- and long-term memory structures [1973]) suggest that important cognitive systems at the long-term memory level as well might be investigated through the study of oral discourse.

11. Silverstein has suggested that in Chinookan narrative "descriptions of speech interactions . . . constitute the very textuality, the cohesion and framework, of the narrative art" (1985: 145). He criticizes the tendency for narrative analysts to start with higher-level narrative structures (ibid.: 144). Here I take higher-level narrative structures to have an independent systemic existence, and I assume an interaction between these and the voice system, perhaps shaped by a rhetorical structure as suggested by Woodbury (1985, 1987).

12. Note that in numbering the sentences I have followed a convention proposed by Silverman and Torode (1980), and assigned the complementizer *porque* 'because' to the evaluator voice in (8), which plays the role of making logical or moral connections, instead of to the narrator voice in (9), which plays a temporal sequencing role. This assignment does not match the intonational system of Mexicano, where clause-final flat terminal contour does not include these elements, which instead drop to low following the word containing the flat contour, just like other unmarked clause-initial words.

13. In addition to the particle *mati* 'it seems' and its Spanish (rough) equivalent *parece* 'it seems, it appears', a hesitation form *este* appears in the text. *Este* may be the voice of the "animator," the "machine for speaking" suggested by Goffman (1974). However, it might also be assigned to the same "responsible" voice which is the source of dysfluent hesitation and is discussed in the section "The Moral Orientation of Narrative Consciousness." While *este* is a very important element, I am not sure of how to analyze it, and so have not assigned it to a separate voice in the marking of the bracketed units. It is possible that *mati* and *parece* should be grouped with some instances of *este* as lexical choices of the "responsible" voice.

14. The avoidance of Spanish *sí* and *no* may perhaps be explained in terms of politeness theory (Brown and Levinson 1978). Spanish is a language of power and distance on the Malinche. A negation in particular is a heavy threat to positive face; an appropriate strategy of mitigation would be to utter negations in Mexicano, the language of solidarity. Analysis of many conversations shows that *sí* and *no* occur only when interlocutors are seriously at odds, even exchanging insults.

15. An important technique for representation of conversational interaction, the distribution of voices across turns in the turn-taking system, is not exploited in the narrative. Flores Farfán (1986) has shown that in market interactions in Mexico, Spanish speakers dominate speakers of Indian language by taking all the turns in a bargaining exchange.

16. Dennis Tedlock (personal communication) has pointed out that a breaking of the voice, as in the intonational shadow case, may begin as "uncontrolled," but become, through retellings, a part of the art of a text. Tedlock cites an example from a Zuni storyteller's narrative of the death of his sister.

17. The fact that Don Gabriel centers his narrative on the values of peasant communitarianism does not, of course, mean that making a profit is impossible within a "traditional" way of life, where participation in markets, both local and regional, is entirely in order. Don Gabriel himself was an "upper peasant," with a substantial house and furnishings, many animals, and (at the time of the interview) a venerable flatbed truck. As noted above, "business" is objectionable from this point of view when it brings in extraordinary benefits which are seen as un-

reasonably extracted from the community and never returned to it in the form of redistribution or reciprocity.

18. Chamoux (1986) has recently considered the Nahuatl concept of work, and finds also that the term *tequitl* does not include the notion of business-for-profit, but implies work which especially constructs appropriate gender identification, ritual involvement, and the like.

## REFERENCES CITED

Bakhtin, M. M. 1981. *The Dialogic Imagination.* Translated by C. Emerson and M. Holquist. Austin: University of Texas Press.
———. 1984. *Problems of Dostoevsky's Poetics.* Edited and translated by C. Emerson. Minneapolis: University of Minnesota Press.
Banfield, Ann. 1973. "Narrative Style and the Grammar of Direct and Indirect Speech." *Foundations of Language* 10:1–39.
———. 1981. "Reflective and Non-Reflective Consciousness in the Language of Fiction." *Poetics Today* 2:61–76.
———. 1984. *Unspeakable Sentences: Narration and Representation in the Language of Fiction.* London: Routledge and Kegan Paul.
Becker, Alton L. 1979. "Text-Building, Epistemology, and Aesthetics in Javanese Shadow Theatre." In *The Imagination of Reality,* edited by A. L. Becker and A. A. Yengoyan, pp. 211–44. Norwood, N.J.: Ablex.
———. 1983. "Toward a Post-Structuralist View of Language Learning: A Short Essay." *Language Learning* 33:217–20.
Benveniste, Émile. 1971. *Problems in General Linguistics.* Coral Gables: University of Miami Press.
Bolinger, Dwight. 1978. "Intonation across Languages." In *Universals of Human Language,* vol. 2, *Phonology,* gen. ed. J. Greenberg, pp. 471–524. Stanford: Stanford University Press.
———. 1982. "Intonation and Its Parts." *Language* 58:505–33.
Brown, Penelope, and Stephen Levinson. 1978. "Universals in Language Usage: Politeness Phenomena." In *Questions and Politeness,* edited by E. N. Goody, pp. 52–289. Cambridge: Cambridge University Press.
Brown, Roger, and Alfred Gilman. 1960. "The Pronouns of Power and Solidarity." In *Style in Language,* edited by Thomas A. Sebeok, pp. 253–76. Cambridge, Mass.: MIT Press.
Bruner, Edward M., and Phyllis Gorfain. 1984. "Dialogic Narration and the Paradoxes of Masada." In *Text, Play, and Story,* edited by S. Plattner and E. M. Bruner, pp. 56–79. Washington, D.C.: American Ethnological Society.
Chafe, Wallace. 1973. "Language and Memory." *Language* 49:261–81.
———. 1976. "Givenness, Contrastiveness, Definiteness, Subjects, Topics, and Point of View." In *Subject and Topic,* edited by C. N. Li, pp. 25–56. New York: Academic Press.
———. 1980. "The Deployment of Consciousness in the Production of a Narrative." In *The Pear Stories,* edited by Wallace Chafe, pp. 9–50. Norwood, N.J.: Ablex.

Chamoux, Marie-Noelle. 1986. "The Conception of Work in Contemporary Nahuatl-Speaking Communities in the Sierra de Puebla." Paper presented to the 85th Annual Meeting of the American Anthropological Association, Philadelphia, Penn.

Clancy, Patricia M. 1980. "Referential Choice in English and Japanese Narrative Discourse." In *The Pear Stories,* edited by Wallace Chafe, pp. 127–202. Norwood, N.J.: Ablex.

Coulmas, Florian, ed. 1986. *Direct and Indirect Speech.* Berlin: Mouton de Gruyter.

Dow, James. 1981. "The Image of Limited Production: Envy and the Domestic Mode of Production in Peasant Society." *Human Organization* 40:360–63.

Flores Farfán, José. 1986. *La Interacción Verbal de Compra-Venta en Mercados Otomíes.* México: Cuadernos de Casa Chata no. 103.

Friedrich, Paul. 1986. *The Language Parallax: Linguistic Relativism and Poetic Indeterminacy.* Austin, Tex.: University of Texas Press.

Goffman, Erving. 1974. *Frame Analysis: An Essay on the Organization of Experience.* New York: Harper and Row.

Grimes, Joseph. 1972. "Outlines and Overlays." *Language* 48:513–24.

Gumperz, John. 1982. *Discourse Strategies.* Cambridge: Cambridge University Press.

Hill, Jane H. 1985. "The Grammar of Consciousness and the Consciousness of Grammar." *American Ethnologist* 12:725–37.

———. 1987. "Women's Speech in Modern Mexicano." In *Language, Sex, and Gender in Comparative Perspective,* edited by S. U. Philips, S. Steele, and C. Tanz, pp. 121–60. Cambridge: Cambridge University Press.

———. 1988. "Language, Genuine and Spurious?" In *On the Ethnography of Communication: The Legacy of Sapir,* edited by Paul V. Kroskrity, pp. 9–54. Los Angeles, Calif.: UCLA Department of Anthropology.

Hill, Jane H., and Kenneth C. Hill. 1981. "Variation in Relative Clause Formation in Modern Nahuatl." In *Nahuatl Studies in Memory of Francisco Horcasitas,* edited by F. Karttunen, pp. 89–104. Texas Linguistic Forum 18.

———. 1986. *Speaking Mexicano: Dynamics of Syncretic Language in Central Mexico.* Tucson: University of Arizona Press.

Hill, Kenneth C. 1985. "Las Penurias de Doña María." *Tlalocan* 10:33–118.

Hymes, Dell H. 1979. "Sapir, Competence, Voices." In *Individual Differences in Language Ability and Language Behavior,* edited by C. J. Fillmore, D. Kempler, and W. S-Y. Wang, pp. 33–45. New York: Academic Press.

———. 1981. *"In Vain I Tried to Tell You": Essays in Native American Ethnopoetics.* Philadelphia: University of Pennsylvania Press.

Karttunen, Frances. 1983. *An Analytical Dictionary of Nahuatl.* Austin, Tex.: University of Texas Press.

Labov, William. 1972. *Language in the Inner City: Studies in the Black English Vernacular.* Philadelphia: University of Pennsylvania Press.

Labov, William, and David Fanshel. 1977. *Therapeutic Discourse.* New York: Academic Press.

Larson, Mildred. 1978. *The Functions of Reported Speech in Discourse.* Dallas: Summer Institute of Linguistics.

Leech, Geoffrey. 1978. "Natural Language as Metalanguage: An Approach to Some Problems in the Semantic Description of English." *Transactions of the Philosophical Society of London* 1976-77:1-31.

Longacre, Robert E. 1976. *An Anatomy of Speech Notions.* Lisse: Peter de Ridder Press.

Lucy, John, ed. 1993. *Reflexive Language.* Cambridge: Cambridge University Press.

Lyons, John. 1982. "Deixis and Subjectivity: Loquor, Ergo Sum?" In *Speech, Place, and Action,* edited by R. J. Jarvella and W. Klein, pp. 101-24. New York: John Wiley and Sons.

Mandelbaum, David G., ed. 1949. *Selected Writings of Edward Sapir in Language, Culture and Personality.* Berkeley and Los Angeles: University of California Press.

Mauss, Marcel. 1985. "A Category of the Human Mind: The Notion of Person, the Notion of Self." In *The Category of the Person,* edited by M. Carrithers, S. Collins, and S. Lukes, pp. 1-25. Cambridge: Cambridge University Press.

Mills, C. Wright. 1940. "Situated Action and Vocabularies of Motive." *American Sociological Review* 5:904-12.

Pierrehumbert, Janet. 1987. *The Phonology and Phonetics of English Intonation.* Bloomington, Ind.: Indiana University Linguistics Club.

Polanyi, Livia. 1982. "Linguistic and Social Constraints on Story Telling." *Journal of Pragmatics* 6:509-24.

Sherzer, Joel. 1981. "The Interplay of Structure and Function in Kuna Narrative, or: How to Grab a Snake in the Darien." In *Analyzing Discourse: Text and Talk,* edited by Deborah Tannen, pp. 306-22. Georgetown University Round Table on Languages and Linguistics 1981. Washington, D.C.: Georgetown University Press.

Silverman, David, and Brian Torode. 1980. *The Material Word.* New York: Routledge and Kegan Paul.

Silverstein, Michael. 1985. "The Culture of Language in Chinookan Narrative Texts; or, on Saying That . . . in Chinook." In *Grammar inside and outside the Clause,* edited by J. Nichols and A. Woodbury, pp. 132-71. Cambridge: Cambridge University Press.

Singer, Milton. 1980. "Signs of the Self: An Exploration in Semiotic Anthropology." *American Anthropologist* 82:485-507.

Sperber, Dan, and Deirdre Wilson. 1981. "Irony and the Use-Mention Distinction." In *Radical Pragmatics,* edited by P. Cole, pp. 295-318. New York: Academic Press.

Taggart, James. 1977. "Metaphors and Symbols of Deviance in Nahuat Narratives." *Journal of Latin American Lore* 3:279-308.

———. 1982. "Animal Metaphors in Spanish and Mexican Oral Narrative." *Journal of American Folklore* 95:280-303.

———. 1983. *Nahuat Myth and Social Structure.* Austin: University of Texas Press.

Tannen, Deborah. 1980. "A Comparative Analysis of Oral Narrative Strategies: Athenian Greek and American English." In *The Pear Stories,* edited by Wallace Chafe, pp. 51-88. Norwood, N.J.: Ablex.

Taussig, Michael. 1979. *The Devil and Commodity Fetishism in Latin America.* Chapel Hill: University of North Carolina Press.

Tedlock, Dennis. 1983. *The Spoken Word and the Work of Interpretation.* Philadelphia: University of Pennsylvania Press.

Voloshinov, V. N. 1986 [1930]. *Marxism and the Philosophy of Language.* Translated by L. Matejka and I. R. Titunik. Cambridge, Mass.: Harvard University Press.

Warman, Arturo. 1982. *We Come to Object.* Baltimore: Johns Hopkins University Press.

Woodbury, Anthony C. 1985. "The Functions of Rhetorical Structure: A Study of Central Alaskan Yupik Eskimo Discourse." *Language in Society* 14:153–90.

———. 1987. "Rhetorical Structure in a Central Alaskan Yupik Eskimo Traditional Narrative." In *Native American Discourse,* edited by J. Sherzer and A. Woodbury, pp. 176–239. Cambridge: Cambridge University Press.

# FIVE

# Rage and Redemption: Reading the Life Story of a Mexican Marketing Woman

RUTH BEHAR

In recent years the life history, as a cultural text and a form of writing, has come under critical scrutiny from a wide range of psychological, phenomenological, hermeneutic, and feminist perspectives.[1] Widely ranging as these works are, they converge in their view of the field of life history writing as one of unrealized potential, what James Freeman and David Krantz have called "the unfulfilled promise of life histories." In the words of Freeman and Krantz, which are the words of many who have examined life histories, the promise of life histories has not been fulfilled because of the tendency "to force life histories into a Procrustean bed of conventional social science principles. . . . If there is a promise, it is in evolving new standards and perspectives in which life histories can be more appropriately interpreted and analyzed on their own terms." While the task of evolving new standards and perspectives is, to put it simply, easier said than done, one key component suggested by Freeman and Krantz must certainly be for life history studies to evenly integrate "an adequate theory with a comprehensive narrative that brings to life the narrator as a person" (Freeman and Krantz 1979: 1). Following their lead here, I want to explore new ways in which to articulate the interplay between theory and narrative in life history writing, to begin fulfilling the promise of an enterprise that continues to interest, challenge, and trouble so many of us in cultural, literary, and feminist studies.

## READING AND WRITING LIFE HISTORIES

The anthropological life history, as an approach that assumes an eventual written product, offers a paradox to the anthropologist as author: on the one hand, there is the desire and temptation to leave the account wholly in the native voice, in imitation of the literary autobiography that it is not; on the other hand, there is the anthropological imperative to place the account in a theoretical/cultural context, to provide some sort of background, analysis, commentary, or interpretation, so as to mediate between the reality of a life lived and inscribed elsewhere but wedged between book covers and read here. In performing this delicate act of mediation, the anthropologist is obliged to let the reader know, somewhere, most frequently on the margins of the text in a preface or afterword, just what the micropolitics of the situation was in which the life history was obtained and the ways in which the anthropologist was personally involved in, and even transformed by, the intense one-to-one relationship of telling and listening.

Torn between these voices, the life historian/author usually settles for a segregated, often jarring combination of the three: the native voice, the personal "I was there" voice, and the authoritative voice of the ethnographer. The difficulties inherent in making music out of these three "voices" or "discordant allegorical registers" (Clifford 1986a: 109) also pose the key challenge: by mediating between, or counterpointing, different linguistic tropes or registers, the ethnographer can potentially create a text that is as much an account of a person's history as it is an account of how such a history is constituted in and through narrative—the native's life story narrative and the life historian's telling of that narrative. A life history narrative can set the stage for a double telling, in which both the native and the anthropologist, side by side, act as narrators, readers, and commentators.

As a problematic genre, the life history narrative invites critical reflection as part of the current anthropological project to rethink and refashion ethnographic representation (Marcus and Fischer 1986). There are two directions in which I think it would be promising to take the genre of life history. First, fixing on the "life" part of the equation, toward an elaboration of the concept of the actor as engaged in the meaningful creation of a life world. Second, looking at the "history" part of the equation, toward an elaboration of the relationship between history and its textual representation, looking at history as story. I call this work a life story rather than a life history to emphasize the fictions of self-representation, the ways in which a life is made in the telling and "an ordered past imposed by a present personality upon a disordered life" (Titon 1980: 290).[2]

As Sherry Ortner points out, there has been an overwhelming tendency in anthropological accounts to spotlight the "thingness" or objectivity of social forms once they are created, in the process displacing the actor's part in world-making. Anthropologists need to forge, she suggests, more imaginative tools based in a theory of practice in order not only to reinsert but to place (or re-place) the actor in the center of their accounts of other histories and cultures. "History," in her words, "is not simply something that happens to people, but something they make" (Ortner 1984: 159). Elsewhere she notes the importance of viewing symbols—gender symbols in particular—not as inherently meaningful but as invested with meaning by social actors (Ortner and Whitehead 1981: 5).

An actor-centered practice approach would seem to be an obvious starting point for life history. Rather than looking at social and cultural systems solely as they impinge on a life, shape it, and turn it into an object, a life history should allow one to see how an actor makes culturally meaningful history, how history is produced in action and in the actor's retrospective reflections on that action. A life history narrative should allow one to see the subjective mapping of experience, the working out of a culture and a social system that is often obscured in a typified account.

Ironically, many life histories, despite the fact that they focus on individual actors, fail to do just this. The problem lies in the nature of the frame that the ethnographer feels called upon to produce to lend weight, meaning, and credence to the native's words. The purpose of such a frame is, too often, to show that while the account bears the signature of a single actor, it ultimately is representative of, undersigned by, some larger social whole. Thus Marjorie Shostak enlists Nisa, the articulate and highly intelligent !Kung woman who is the subject of her life history, to metonymically represent women in !Kung society and thereby to provide us in the West with a primitive model of the ideal of sexually liberated womanhood (Shostak 1981).

Life history writing, as a subgenre of ethnographic writing, falls prey to the same general view of holism as typification, which has been described as "perhaps the most sacred of all the cows of traditional anthropological theorizing and description" (Appadurai 1986a: 758). One common problem in life history writing is that the typifying narrative or frame provided by the ethnographer as an authority on the culture often speaks past, rather than to, the native narrative. Oscar Lewis prefaced some of the most moving life history narratives ever collected, in *Children of Sanchez* (and elsewhere), with dubious theoretical generalizations about "the culture of poverty" and its production of "badly damaged human beings" (Lewis 1963: xxx) that, in the end, said little about the multiperspectival texts they were meant to introduce—and even, I would say, did violence to them by showing so little regard for what his subjects actually had to say. (I will return to this theme of the violence of representation shortly.) Marjorie Shostak introduced each chapter of Nisa's narrative, which she reorganized into such general categories as economy, gender, and religion, with ethnographic generalizations that preceded Nisa's own words; but rarely is there an analysis of the words themselves or a serious attempt to come to terms with how Nisa constructed her life as a story using indigenous notions of oral performance or even notions of commodity exchange modeled on the long history of Western contact with the !Kung (Pratt 1986: 45–46). Shostak's agenda continually acts as a barrier to our really hearing what Nisa is saying. While Nisa speaks in detail of sexual violence and wife-beating, Shostak insists, in her ethnographically authoritative voice, that the !Kung have highly egalitarian gender relations.

This speaking past the text, rather than to the text, is the product of a common misconception about life history texts: namely, that they "speak for themselves," as though transparent, existing outside or beyond a particular reading. As Michael Young, criticizing this tendency, remarks: life history texts "are frequently offered as self-evident 'cultural documents' rather than as texts to be interrogated and interpreted" (Young 1983: 480; see also Hoskins 1985). Gelya Frank, who provides an especially cogent critique of the tendency to let life history texts pass untheorized, notes that the assumption behind not analyzing the text is that "every reader already has a sense of how to understand another person" (Frank 1979: 76). On the one hand, "the common denominator" of life histories is the primary act of readership by which a reader identifies with the subject of the narrative. Yet, on the other hand, "the natural attitude of readers towards biography," like "the social science approach," wrongly assumes that the life history is "a direct representation of the informant's life, something almost equivalent to the informant's life" (ibid.: 72, 77). The text is, in fact, not the person, but a version of the self constructed by a subject to present to the anthropologist: "The text falls into the background as a neutral tool or medium for the 'phenomena' (the events of a person's life as experienced) to shine through. Autobiographical texts appear to offer a truer experience of the subject's life, a direct outpouring of consciousness, but here too certain conventions are invoked to structure the narrative" (ibid.: 83). These conventions stem from native traditions of storytelling, but they are also, significantly, unique forms that emerge in discourse with the anthropologist. As Frank suggests, the biographer-ethnographer must gain a clearer sense of the making of the life history text as a text, so as to denaturalize the link between text and person. In this manner, we can begin to read and to write life histories differently, in more imaginative and theoretically rich ways.

What we need to do more of in life history work is basically to read—or think about how to read (and write) — the native text. Neither the presentation of transcripts of the raw dialogues (as in Kevin Dwyer's *Moroccan Dialogues*) nor edited and recombined pieces made to flow "like a novel" (as in Oscar Lewis's various family autobiographies) are solutions to the dilemma of having to read the text. The life history text is not meaningful in itself: it is constituted in its interpretation, its reading. Reading a life history text, and then writing it, calls for an interpretation of cultural themes as they are creatively constructed by the actor within a particular configuration of social forces and gender and class contexts; and, at the same, a closer analysis of the making of the life history narrative as a narrative, using critical forms of textual analysis and self-reflexive (rather than self-ingratiating) meditation on the relationship between the storyteller and the anthropologist.

Of course, calling a life history a text already reflects a particular analytic move and, in a sense, a particular colonization of the act of telling a life story. With deconstruction we have learned that the border between the "spoken" and the "written" is a fluid one. Thus it is not orality versus textuality that I call into question here, with the image it conjures up of the ethnographer salvaging the fleeting native experience in the net of a text (Clifford 1986a: 113–19). The more relevant distinction for me is Walter Benjamin's distinction between storytelling and information. Information, in Benjamin's analysis, is a mode of communication linked to the development of the printing press and of capitalism; it presents itself as verifiable, it is "shot through with explanation," and it is disposable because it is forgettable (W. Benjamin 1969: 89). Storytelling, on the other hand, is "always the art of repeating stories," without explanation, combining the extraordinary and the ordinary; most important, it is grounded in a community of listeners on whom the story makes a claim to be remembered by virtue of its "chaste compactness," which inspires the listener, in turn, to become the teller of the story (ibid.: 91). It worries me that one does violence to the life history as a story by turning it into the disposable commodity of information. My, at least partial, solution to this problem has been to focus on the act of life story representation as reading rather than as informing, with its echoes of surveillance and disclosures of truth. And I try to make clear that what I am reading is a story, or set of stories, that have been told to me, so that I, in turn, can tell them again, transforming myself from a listener to a storyteller.

## WOMAN READING (AND REPRESENTING) WOMAN

In this essay I explore ways of reading the life story narrative of a Mexican marketing woman, a *marchanta,* as an account of culture-making

and story-making. I borrow the notion of "reading woman" from Mary
Jacobus, who uses it to develop a theory of how "woman" is constructed
"within a multiplicity of shifting selves . . . endlessly displacing the fixity
of gender identity by the play of difference and division which simultaneously creates and uncreates gender, identity, and meaning" (Jacobus
1986: 23–24). The focus on reading places the accent on the constructed
quality of woman as subject, whether "reading woman" (that is, women or
men—especially in Freudian analysis—constructing woman as different
in their texts), or "woman reading woman" (that is, women interpreting as women the texts or self-constructions of other women). I use the
notion of reading here to ask anthropological questions about issues of
representation, and what it means for me as a Western woman to read
(and thereby constitute) the life history text of another (Third World/Latin
American/Mexican) woman.

Esperanza Hernandez (a self-chosen pseudonym), the subject and co-
producer of the narrative, fits all the typologies of lower-class Mexican
womanhood—battered child, battered wife, abandoned wife, female head
of household, unwed mother, "Indian" marketing woman, believer in
witchcraft. Yet I want to see (read) her not as a type but as she sees (reads)
herself, as an actor thrust in the world seeking to gain meaning out of
the events of her life. Similarly, while such general topics as male/female
relations, notions of exchange, healing, witchcraft, women's power, and
cosmology can be pulled out of the account, I will view them not as typified objects but as constructs emerging out of Esperanza's experience as
presented in her story of how she made herself within the limits of her
world. The limits of her world are, indeed, those of the social class and gender to which she was born, but they are limits which she herself reproduces
in terms meaningful to her. Culture, gender, and class are simultaneously
constructed in Esperanza's life story.

The recent critique of the notion of "place" in anthropology can be expanded to a critique of the place women have been given to inhabit both
in writing on Latin American women and, more generally, in life histories
of women (Appadurai 1986b). In both these literatures, there is a vexed
part/whole relation of women to the larger male-dominated society which
constrains their possibilities for action and defines the limits of what constitutes culture. In life history writing, accounts by women have often been
collected to provide the "women's view" of societies that have already been
described from a "holistic" (read male) typifying view, or even to supplement previously collected life histories of men, as when Nancy Lurie wrote
*Mountain Wolf Woman, Sister of Crashing Thunder* (1961) in response to
Paul Radin's *Crashing Thunder: The Autobiography of an American Indian*
(1983 [1926]). That "female experience could ever explain the whole cul-

ture or even a central aspect of it" is outrightly denied, for "women unlike men are not seen as true representatives of their societies" (Watson and Watson-Franke 1985: 164). Even as they occupy the role of central protago- nists in their own life history narratives, women tend to be cast as Adamic fragments, part-people and part-societies, with limited and slanted views of their world. Certainly we need to go beyond this view of women's social action as supplementary, as reacting against a male world, rather than as creatively constructing a complete social world.

In work on women in Latin America, the part/whole problem surfaces in another form. There, the incompleteness of women as social actors is shown in the overwhelming emphasis placed on the political and eco- nomic aspects of women's experience. Accounts focus on women's eco- nomic exploitation and political muting, or point to the ways in which women gain consciousness and a voice in their society at the cost of great emotional and often physical hardship.[3] Esperanza's narrative suggests that there are other possibilities for seeing Latin American women as actors that expand the categories of women as wives and mothers, workers, doers, and political activists. It suggests that, if looked at from a cultural per- spective, Latin American women can emerge as thinkers, cosmologizers, creators of worlds.

The challenge of trying to write about Esperanza in this way is that one is constantly forced to come to terms with, and counter, the fact that Mexico—and the Mexican lower-class woman in particular—exists in academic as well as mainstream reporting as a pretheorized reality, an already-fixed representation. Listen, for example, to the half-disgusted, half-pitying description of a Mexican lower-class woman offered by a femi- nist folklorist:

> Of all the impressions I received while in Mexico, one stands out sharply from all the rest. Everywhere I went, whether to the market places in the provinces or the elegant Zona Rosa of Mexico City, I saw the same scene: a very, very young woman, at the most seventeen, holding by the hand a child who looked to be no older than two. In her arms she carried a tiny baby tightly wrapped in a *rebozo*, and always her belly was big with child. . . . I spoke to many women about their situation, and always their sadness dis- turbed me. They were not joyful in their motherhood, they were resigned. (Cardozo-Freeman 1975: 14)

Octavio Paz, speaking of Mexican womanhood from an interest in "Mexicanness," instead romanticizes the image of the Mexican woman as long-suffering victim "who remains behind the veil of her modesty and immobility," "passive and secretive," "an idol," "a victim hardened and insensible to suffering," yet one who being "sinful from birth . . . must be subdued with a stick" (Paz 1961: 36–39)—stick being used here, one supposes, in the literal and sexual sense of the word. This image of the long-suffering Mexican woman closely matches Oscar Lewis's depiction of the impoverished "ordinary Mexican" as feminized by a "great capacity for misery and suffering" (Lewis 1963: xxx).

We have here a set of classical images which reduce, by means of representational conventions, the marginal Mexican to object status: on the one hand, the abject mother, passive, resigned, mothering unwillingly; on the other hand, the fatalistic, yet heroic, poor Mexican caught tight in the grip of the "culture of poverty" by unfortunate "attitudes" and "value systems" (terms used by Lewis). This object status is reinforced by the fact that these people are said to suffer so much that they are beyond pain, beyond feeling, beyond being. They are not granted subjectivity, agency, and critical consciousness. These images are the representational axis of an analysis that is forged within a context of a First/Third World balance of power, a balance which, I must add, exists internally within the "third world," too, as evidenced in the First World style of theorizing of Octavio Paz. A critical ethnographic narrative—within which I include the reconceptualized life history narrative—should instead seek to destabilize this balance of power and knowledge so that the self-understanding and critical practice of specific actors can come to the fore.

As Chandra Mohanty remarks with respect to universal images of the "third world woman" as *"the veiled woman, the powerful mother, the chaste virgin, the obedient wife,"* images generated by Western feminist analyses, such images "perpetrate and sustain the hegemony of the idea of superiority of the West . . . setting in motion a colonialist discourse which exercises a very specific power in defining, coding and maintaining existing first/third world connections" (Mohanty 1982: 352).[4] By representing, as Mohanty points out, the average Third World woman as leading "a truncated life based on her feminine gender (read: sexually constrained) and being 'third world' (read: ignorant, poor, uneducated, tradition-bound, domestic, family-oriented, victimized, etc.)," Western feminists have engaged in implicit, discursive self-representation of themselves as "educated, modern, as having control over their bodies and sexualities, and the freedom to make their own decisions" (ibid.: 337).[5] Inverting this tendency to view the women they study as passive victims, and perhaps overcompensating, some feminist anthropologists have lately stressed the existence of female cultures of resistance, thereby extending the Western feminist self-representation to their subjects.[6] Clearly, any ethnographic representation—and I include my own, of course—inevitably reflects a self-representation and a certain economy of representation. Even more subtly, the act of representing, as Edward Said points out, "almost always involves violence of some sort to the *subject* of the representation," using as it must some degree of reduction, decontextualization, and miniaturization (Said 1985: 4). "This is one of the unresolvable problems of anthropology," as Said tells us (ibid.: 5). Yet I think there is hope insofar as we realize that ethnographic critique presents us with the paradox, so well put by Linda Brodkey as "the process by which each of us confronts our respective inability to comprehend the experience of others even as we recognize the absolute necessity of continuing the effort to do so" (Brodkey 1987: 74).[7]

Mohanty's sharp critique of Western feminist representational conventions also takes us in a different direction: toward the recent general critique of ethnographic representations exemplified by the papers in *Writing Culture* (Clifford and Marcus 1986). Her critique of how Western feminists have unselfconsciously created a cultural other in their images of Third World women points to the way in which feminist ethnography fits within a larger process of cultural colonization of the non-Western world. This critique of feminist representational forms, which poses the same problems about authority and repression as does ethnography, is a crucial step toward answering the challenge posed by James Clifford in his castigating yet disconcerting remarks about feminist ethnographers not having "produced either unconventional forms of writing or a developed reflection on ethnographic textuality as such" (Clifford 1986b: 21).

Clifford here overlooks one vast terrain of feminist work in which, indeed, unconventional forms of writing and theoretical exploration of ethnographic textuality in the broad sense of the term have figured prominently, radically, and creatively: namely, the terrain of women's autobiography and the complex discussions of women's memory, politics of home, and language use and writing which it has inspired.[8] I think this is a key terrain to which all ethnographers can turn for insights and examples of alternative forms of representation and text-making that combine personal experience with poetic, political, and cultural critique.

In her review of women's autobiographies, Domna Stanton found that "autobiographical" had positive connotations when referring to the works of male authors (e.g., Augustine, Rousseau, Henry Miller), but when the term referred to women's writings it inevitably became linked to negative ideas about women's incapacity for self-transcendence, their presumed inability to rise above the concrete, the daily, the domestic, and the "personal" (Stanton 1987: 4). Internalizing this negativity, women writers themselves, like Colette, could say that women's writings seem a joke to men because "they can't help being autobiographical" (ibid.: 4, 5). Yet if there is a difference in the way women speak and write, it clearly does not reside in some inherent deficiency or limitation, but in the different experience of women in society, and in the specific ways in which the category and idea of the "feminine" is constructed in a given culture. Stanton points out that the purpose of literate women's autobiographies has been not so much to reveal intimate secrets—in fact, they manifest a good deal of concealment and self-censorship—but to conquer identity through writing. These "female autographs" are acts of self-assertion, of giving substance to the female "I" in diverse settings of male domination that render women the inessential other (ibid.: 14).

This view of women's autobiographies as a vehicle for constituting the female subject might be fruitfully extended to women's orally related life histories in non-Western settings as well, and beyond to the ways in which women reflect on their experiences, emotions, and self-construction. From this perspective it is worth taking up as a positive feature, rather than a shortcoming, the idea that women's stories about themselves have a concrete, context-specific texture. As Susan Geiger remarks in an important review essay about women's life histories, "Feminist scholars have revealed that notions of objectivity themselves are andocentric, and that the higher levels of abstraction assumed to present a 'true' picture of 'reality' often represent neither truth nor reality for women" (Geiger 1986: 338). Life histories, in particular, as subjective documents, have rigor and integrity because "they do not claim 'ungendered point-of-viewlessness'" while revealing that "consciousness is not simply the act of interpreting but also of constructing the social world" (ibid.: 338, 348).

Taking up the challenge of writing about female consciousness as world-making, Emily Martin's recent book, *The Woman in the Body*, focuses on the ways in which Baltimore women talk about their experience of living in female bodies in an industrial society geared to a production rhythm that violates the ebb and flow of women's cyclical biology. Martin's analysis builds on Dell Hymes's critique of Bernstein's distinction between elaborated and restricted codes, in which Hymes questions "whether abstract discourse is necessarily the only or even the best way to achieve general understanding" (E. Martin 1987: 196).[9] Martin maintains that powerful and insightful commentaries on the social order are embedded in the concrete, narrative, storytelling form of discourse and she offers the reader a challenge that I want to offer here as well: "It is up to anyone who listens to a woman's tale to hear the implicit message, interpret the powerful rage, and watch for ways in which the narrative form gives 'a weighted quality to incident' [a citation from Hymes], extending the meaning of an incident beyond itself" (ibid.: 201). It is precisely the implicit messages and weighted qualities of Esperanza's tale that I want to ask you to listen and watch for, as I try to work out an interpretation of the rage that simultaneously tears at and empowers her.

## APPROACHING ESPERANZA'S STORY:
## SUBJECTIVITY, VOICE, AND TEXT

Esperanza's history is a story about her life that was constructed very consciously by her as a narrative with herself in the role of central protagonist and heroine, and I would like to take it seriously as a text. Even before I thought to tape-record her life history, she had told me, in compressed form, much of her story. She did this, I realized, not for my particular benefit but because she already had the habit of putting her life in story terms for her children—and especially her two daughters—to hear and learn a lesson from.[10] In telling her story to me, she undoubtedly wanted me to confirm a particular image of herself, and my listening so attentively to her stories did perhaps add moral weight to them, as lessons for her children. But like the story of Youngsu Mother, the Korean shaman about whom Laurel Kendall has recently written, Esperanza's story reminds us "that some among our informants are storytellers in their own lives and that the words they provide have not been given to us alone" (Kendall 1988: 13). When I told Esperanza that I thought her life narrative would make a very good book, she completely agreed, and she took a certain pride in thinking that she alone of all the women in the town had a life worth turning into a text; even, she said, emphasizing her life's supreme textuality, into a history, into a film.

Esperanza views her life as a story, as worthy of making into a story, because of her notion of story, which is based on three intertexts: the Christian narrative as a story of suffering, and particularly of suffering through the body as a vehicle for the release of spirit and divinity; a sense of the melodramatic—a quintessentially female version of the "tragic"—as found in photonovels and television, whose soap operas she occasionally watches on a set that her son has hooked up to a car battery; and cultural myths of women's powers that attribute to women supernatural powers to harm the men who wrong them. Most important for her is the notion of narrative as inscribing a progression from suffering, to rage, to redemption. When I told her that I was also asking other women to tell me their life stories, she was positively shocked when I mentioned among them a younger, respected schoolteacher in the town. "But she, what has she suffered? I never heard that her husband beat her, that she suffered from rages," Esperanza responded. In her view, the rage brought on by suffering, and redemption through suffering, is what gives a woman the right and the need to become a text. Rage and redemption form the poles of her life as text.

Esperanza lives in the small town of Mexquitic, in the arid highlands of San Luis Potosí in north-central Mexico. She is a *marchanta,* a vendor of flowers she herself produces when in season, and of vegetables that she buys at the market and resells door-to-door to her established clients in the city of San Luis Potosí, just a half-hour away by bus. As a self-employed marketing woman, mediating between the rural and the urban world in the informal economy, she depends on her wits and the charm of her style to make a living. Flowers, which she carries in a pail balanced on her head, symbolically mean a good deal to her and speak both to her preoccupation with the revelation of the cosmic in everyday life and the high value given to motherhood in Mexican culture; she says that the Virgin Mary is never absent from a house where there are children and flowers.

Esperanza is the mother of two sons from her marriage and of two daughters and a son born to her later out of wedlock. For her sixty years of age she has a remarkable vitality, almost a girlishness about her; she has a fine sense of irony and, rather than being bitter about a bitter life — as she herself says — she jokes and laughs a good deal. Her voice is rich and strong and she uses it skillfully in storytelling, imitating the voices of all the characters in her tales and modulating her pitch to suit dramatic purposes. She wears her thick brown hair in two long braids and dresses in the apron and shawl that identify a woman as traditional working class and as Indian. She shares a single house compound with her mother, her married son and his wife and child, and her teenage daughters and younger son; each family group has a bedroom of its own, but the cooking space and courtyard are used in common. Their house is on the outskirts of Mexquitic's town center, set on a hill overlooking the town, where the electric wires do not yet reach and running water, recently installed, flows from a single outdoor faucet.

Before I knew Esperanza's own story, I heard the stories about her that circulate in Mexquitic. Esperanza, I learned from various women, bewitched her husband, Julio, after he left her and returned to town with another woman and their children. Cursing him, according to one story, with the words, "So that you will never again see women," she had caused him to go suddenly and completely blind. No one knew exactly how she had done it, but there was some suspicion that she had thrown special powders at him, or gotten a witch to do the work for her in San Luis. She had publicized the rage she felt for Julio, and these rumors seemed to testify to the belief that there was no telling what an enraged women was capable of doing. Doesn't Ecclesiasticus tell us that "there is no wrath above the wrath of a woman?" I also learned, from various people, that Esperanza was a bad-tempered, combative woman that one had to take care not to offend. Her public image was that of a sharp-tongued, aggressive, unsentimental woman, who had gone so far as to throw her eldest son out of the house. For a long time I hesitated to meddle with her.

I finally got to know Esperanza myself when she asked us, out of the blue, to be godparents of the cake for her daughter's coming-of-age rite *(quinceanera)*. Soon after, she came to ask us to be godparents for her Christ child. With this, we became 'co-godmothers' *(comadres)*, linked through ties of ritual kinship. On my first acquaintance with Esperanza, I admit that I was put off by her. She was demanding in her requests rather than deferential as others were. Her two requests for *compadrazgo*, representing significant outlays of money from my husband and me, who were still strangers to her, followed quickly upon one another, and I had the distinct sense of being taken advantage of. These fears quickly abated as I got to know and like Esperanza and realized how much I could learn from her. Certainly, as I got to know Esperanza, I was better able to separate the myth from the woman, but found that she had, in a deep sense, become the myth. However, the fact that I had initially reacted as I had made me realize the extent to which the ethnographic relation is based on power, and that, indeed, I felt uncomfortable when an "informant" was assertive and aggressive, rather than passive and cooperative as informants should be. As has often been the case in other relationships between the subject of a life history narrative and the anthropologist (Mintz 1989), I did not seek out Esperanza, but rather she sought me out. She chose me to hear her story and to take it back across the border, to the mysterious and powerful "other side" from which I came.

Shortly before I was due to leave in 1985, she came to our house for several evenings to tape-record her life history, talking nonstop, late into the night, for three and four hours at a time. She treated her narrative as a string of self-contained stories, segments, or episodes, rather like a soap opera serial. Each night she would ask where we had left off and pick up from there, stringing another story, another bead on her rosary, until she herself thought she had attained some sort of closure. As a performance, her narrative had the quality of a one-woman theater of voices, since she told virtually the entire story in dialogue form. I did not have to "elicit" the account; rather, it was necessary for me to expand my capacities to listen to oral storytelling and performance. On my return trip to Mexquitic in 1987, she told me about the recent events of her life and took me to meet the healer/medium in San Luis who aids her in her continuing struggle with evil. She always came to converse with me accompanied by her son or daughter, often with both, and she told her story as much for their edification as for mine.

### REPRODUCING THE MOTHER IN THE DAUGHTER

*"Comadre,* what a life, the life I've lived. My life is such a long history. My life has been very sad, very sad. Dark, dark, like my mother's life."

With these words, Esperanza begins her narrative, going on to recall her mother's life as she witnessed it during the early years of her childhood. This mother-daughter mirroring is a key theme in her account; often it seems as though she is collapsing time, and through her life giving birth to her mother's life. In childhood, by witnessing her father's brutal treatment of her mother, Esperanza gains a vivid sense of the violence of patriarchal domination. In her words: "My father hit her for any little thing. . . . He would arrive and say to us, 'Why are you making such a racket, you goddamn children.' My father always spoke to us in curses. 'Why do you make so much noise, you sons of ——' [and to her mother] 'You daughter of who knows what, why don't you make them shut up?' Everything offended him." Esperanza recalled how her father would accuse her and her siblings of being "pimps" for their mother, covering up affairs that he was certain she must be having—later, when Esperanza marries Julio he levels the same accusation against her, even while keeping her virtually locked up in the house. If her mother sneaked out of the house and went to grind corn in other houses to earn some tortillas for her family, her father would become furious, accusing her of going to other houses to cry about her troubles. Finally, after a particularly nasty beating, her mother returned home to her mother's house, leaving Esperanza and her siblings behind, uttering the words, "I didn't bring any children with me, and I'm not taking any children with me."

Her mother's escape from this dark, violent, closed, oppressive, male-dominated world is followed by the escape of Esperanza and her siblings, who as small children stole off in the middle of the night with a strip of mutton and a few blankets to rejoin their mother. The escape theme is another key topos in Esperanza's narrative; she too, when her time comes, escapes from the incarceration of marriage (as she herself describes it), rather like the slave, in the slave narrative, made a journey from bondage to freedom through the narrative drive of a text.

After this dark period, Esperanza goes on to describe what she considers to have been the happiest years of her life—the time of her adolescence, when she was independent, working, and self-sufficient. Her mother had sent her sister to work in San Luis as a domestic when she was twelve; Esperanza went to work at the age of ten. The two sisters worked in various houses, and they shared a stint together working in a luncheonette which Esperanza enjoyed because of the easy availability of food. When Esperanza was eighteen she and her sister returned to Mexquitic for the fiesta of Saint Michael, the patron saint of the town, and it was then that she was, almost literally in her description, snared by Julio while she was out in the fields collecting maguey juice.

At this point in the narration, Esperanza turned to me and said, "Now that's the good part. What's still to come. That life eternal. I may even start crying. The life I lived. My life is a history. My life is a film. . . . To suffer just like my mother. Here [pointing to the space between her brows], he kicked me twice. Here [pointing to the side of her head] he threw a machete at me. And I suffered the same life as my mother." It was 1949. It was New Year's Eve. She and Julio argued all night—"he wanting to do his things with me," as Esperanza put it, and she refusing. Esperanza finally followed Julio to his mother's house, where he made a vow to marry her.

When her mother found Esperanza in the courtyard of Julio's house the next day, she refused to say anything more to her than "Get away. Do you have no shame?" Her mother took both Esperanza and Julio to the town court (a frequent pattern when a woman has left the parental house) and said, "Well, if he's such a man and knows how to carry out his word about marrying my daughter, then I want him to go to church right now and make the arrangements." By thus taunting Julio to be a "real man," Esperanza's mother sought to redress the disgrace of her daughter's loss of honor (since she assumed that Esperanza had lost her virginity). Seeking to confer on Esperanza the kind of respectability that she herself had lost leaving her own husband, Esperanza's mother, ironically, pushed her daughter into a marriage that Esperanza had grave doubts about. In the weeks of preparation for the wedding, a townswoman fitted Esperanza for her white wedding dress. Later Esperanza was to recall the prophetic words this woman uttered to her in conversation: " 'So you're getting married, young woman?' 'Yes.' 'Good. But be careful,' she says. 'A white wedding dress is very beautiful but also very punishing.' "

In her narrative, Esperanza plays on this image of marriage as incarceration, as the cross and the curse of the white wedding dress, and as a darkness and a bondage from which she was not able to see the light of day until her emergence into freedom sixteen years later. Her story is built on the contrast between her cloistered life during marriage (a constricting female space) and her later life as an independent woman and a fully public person. A week after her wedding, the reality of her bondage, of being cut off from the world of family and friends, was brought home to her by her mother-in-law. Just as her own mother upheld a social-religious order based on patriarchal domination that had exerted its violence against her, so, too, her mother-in-law turned out to be as brutal as, or more brutal than, Julio in her reinforcement of the idea that women should be subordinate to their husbands in marriage. Even to peek out the door, Esperanza learned early on, was a transgression for her:

> I went to the door to peep out. I took it as a joke that it was the same thing to be single as to be married. I went to the door, just to look out. I'm looking out the door and my mother-in-law is in the other room selling pulque, with the men there. And a man passes by and looks at me. That seemed

funny to me. I just stood there. Suddenly she grabs me by the hair, by the braids, and pushes me inside. We had been married eight days. "Why did you go out? What are you looking for?" It was the first scolding I got from her. After that I was really sorry I had gotten married. But what could I do? So, she finished pushing, shoving, and hitting me. "So that you'll know that from now on things are not the same as when you were single." . . . And she said, "Here you are done with mother. Here you are done with friends. Here you are done with *compadres*. With girlfriends. Here you are done with *comadritas*. Here, you came to know your obligation towards your husband, nothing else." . . . So I tell you. It was a very dark life. During sixteen years. I held out for sixteen years.

## RAGE AND REFUSAL

In 1950, a year after marrying, Esperanza had her first child, a daughter, who lived for only nine months. The child died, Esperanza said, because she had suffered a *coraje*, a very deep anger or rage, after finding Julio with another woman by the riverbanks. Julio had also begun, by this time, to beat her often for anything that offended him about her behavior. While he was continually unfaithful, ending up in jail six times for dishonoring different young women, he suspected her, constantly, of having lovers; yet it was Esperanza's sexuality that was denied as she bore one doomed off-spring after another. After her first child died, she learned from a healer that the child had sucked her anger in with the milk; the anger pent up within her had poisoned her milk, causing her child's death. (With this, Esperanza is initiated into the largely female subculture of illness and healing.) One after another Esperanza's children died. As she put it, she was never without *corajes*, she suffered from one continual *coraje*, a deep welling up of rage that killed the children she gave life to.

*Coraje* is an emotion and illness state especially common to women that is sparked by strife between spouses or between mother and child; as in this case of "angry milk," *coraje* forms part of a feminine ontology of suffering and despair (Finkler 1985: 65 and Farmer 1988). *Coraje* also bears a close resemblance to the rage that Ilongots experience at the death of close kin, moving them to want to expel grief by headhunting (Rosaldo 1984). Even more broadly, rage is a culturally forceful state of consciousness, whether it refers to feminist rage or the diffuse anger that oppressed people feel in colonial settings.[11]

That Esperanza views her married life as the embodiment of a constant, suppressed rage expresses her sense of its disorderliness, of its spiritual and bodily wrongness. Her description of her feelings and interaction with Julio after the death of their third child provides a view of her daily rage, and of its transformation in her account into a narrative of the grotesque:

"She died and she died! And it was my martyrdom! It was my martyrdom as always. I would say to myself, all my children die, it isn't worth it for me to have children. . . . Then he would say to me, furious, 'Well, you swallow them.' 'Yes, I don't have anything else to eat, so I swallow them.' I would answer him like that, and he would slug me." Of the eight children Esperanza bore for Julio, only two sons, her fourth and fifth, survived to adulthood.

The years of her marriage—with its violence, its rage, its toil—are described in great detail in Esperanza's narrative. But I will skip ahead to what Esperanza focused on as a key turning point in her life and her text: the climactic moment at the end of her marriage when she found Julio in San Luis with the woman he would eventually bring to his mother's house as his wife, usurping her:

> When I had my last child with him, a boy named John, he was the last one, when he found the other woman in San Luis. For her he left me. But I grabbed her really well, comadre. No! I had been asleep. He had me tied up, even afraid. And he had me really humiliated. . . . I was eight months pregnant, within days of giving birth, but I found them in San Luis and pounced on them both. I really beat up on that woman! . . . I grabbed her by the hair. With both hands, I pulled at her hair. . . . And I punched her. I said, "This is how I wanted to find you." And to him, "What's new? What do you say to your girl, that you're a bachelor? That you're a young man, a boy? Well, you're wrong. If before you had yours, now I have mine." I changed in that moment and I don't even know how. . . . "Here is your child . . . and we still have another, and how many dead. . . . I'm sick of it." . . . I bring her to her knees with slaps. . . . I pushed her against a window, grabbing her by the hair. I just kept slapping her. The blood dripped down. . . . The woman cried like a child. . . . And I said, "Today you walk. Today you go to court." He says, "Me? Go to court? You're crazy." . . . At that moment I no longer respected him. I no longer respected him as a husband [a subtle linguistic shift takes place in her story at this point; she ceases to refer to Julio as "usted," the formal you, and now begins to call him, "tu," the informal you, used to speak to equals, children, and people of inferior rank].[12] "You have no shame. I respect you as if you were more than my father. And now look how I find you." . . . I kept slapping her and pulling at her. . . . She was wearing a plaid dress, a string of pearls around her neck, and her hair had been permed. I pulled, I tore her dress. That blessed string of pearls went flying. I shook her and gave her a shove. After that I couldn't do more. I let go of her and she ran off.

Esperanza had already begun to see the tables turning before this incident, when a village man threatened to have Julio sent to a stricter jail in San Luis for molesting his daughter (he was in San Luis when Esperanza caught him because he had escaped from jail). But this incident, which allowed Esperanza finally to express her welled-up rage by inflicting pain on the body of the urban woman of pearls (an anti-rosary) and permed hair (both symbols of her non-Indianness), the woman who had won Julio's affection, was the conversion experience that in her narrative turns her into a fighting woman, a myth of a woman, a "phallic woman" (Jacobus 1986: 110–36), powerful enough to blind the man who betrayed and humiliated her. With this rebellion, she takes on the male role, beating up another woman as she herself was beaten by Julio. Here, in her account, another chapter of her life begins in which, forced to work and earn money to support her family, she recovers the independence and autonomy of her adolescence.

After this denouement, Esperanza briefly returned to her mother-in-law's house. She recalls: "He left in May. On the 24th of June the boy was born. . . . With my mother-in-law, I ate my bitter hours. With the *coraje*, the child, suckling with me, had vomiting spells." Shortly before the child died, Julio returned with the new woman and sent a message to his mother that she should get rid of Esperanza. But his mother never got a chance to do that. A week after her child's death, Esperanza went to court in Mexquitic demanding that she be given her husband's plot of *ejido* land. This was land that had been expropriated from a nearby *hacienda* after the Mexican Revolution and redistributed to the people of Mexquitic. The plots in the *ejido* are worked by individual families as their own, but ultimate title to the land resides in the state, which has the authority to take plots away from those who do not work them. Esperanza had legitimate rights to the land because Julio had been away from the town for two years and as his wife Esperanza could lay claim to it. But few women in her position would have gotten up the nerve and the resources to actually have fought to take the land away. A court battle ensued between Esperanza and her mother-in-law and Esperanza won the land. Esperanza viewed the land as being owed to her for her years of labor and suffering in her husband's house; having worked and earned money as a young woman and begun to work again after leaving Julio, she had a keen sense of the value of things. The land was the price of her rage. Having taken away this major source of livelihood from her husband and mother-in-law, Esperanza returned to her mother's house with her two young sons.

The mirroring of mother and daughter receives another elaboration in this part of her narrative. Esperanza remarks: "Because we took the plot away from my mother-in-law, that was when she placed the illness, the evil way, on my mother." It was Esperanza's mother who helped Esperanza to raise herself up, paying to have her plot of land cleared and then sown with corn. Out of spite and envy, Esperanza thinks, her mother-in-law ensorcelled her mother, causing her to be ill for seven years — first with stomach pains, then with pains in the head, and finally with a severe eye infection that left her right eye permanently sunken. With the pain of her own body, her mother paid for her daughter's actions, just as Esperanza suffered her mother's fate. It was through this long illness, however, and their quest for a cure that Esperanza became acquainted with Gloria, a healer and spirit medium in San Luis who subsequently became her guide and oracle in her struggle with evil.

During the long period of her mother's illness, Esperanza began to work as a peddler. She considered it embarrassing to sell in the town where people knew her and decided to sell in San Luis instead. Eventually she found her path: to be a *marchanta*, selling flowers and vegetables door-to-door. In the city, where no one knew her past, she could become another person. Her customers told her that she had an engaging and friendly style, and she soon acquired a set of permanent clients—housewives in a middle-class neighborhood—who expected her flowers and vegetables twice a week. Her ability to sell and thus earn her own money gave her confidence, and Esperanza now makes quite a good living as a self-employed marketing woman, surviving independently of a husband on the margins of the capitalist economy.

## SEXUAL AND SPIRITUAL ECONOMIES

Esperanza had a tremendous longing for daughters and three years after leaving Julio, she began to have an affair with a man ten years younger than she. As soon as the word got out that she was pregnant, her former mother-in-law began to go out with Julio's new woman, introducing her to everyone as a godchild. Then his children by the new woman began to be seen in the street. The eldest child, while out buying beans one day, announced that his father never went out anymore because he was blind. Esperanza's former mother-in-law spread the rumor that Esperanza and her mother had bewitched him. Subsequent events seemed to prove the rumor true. Soon after his mother's death, Julio's new woman took all of her children and packed everything in the house into her brother's pickup truck, leaving Julio.

"She left him with little more than the pants he had on," Esperanza noted, adding, "One pays for everything. Did he think he wouldn't have to pay for what he did to me?" Thus in the spiritual economy of Esperanza's narrative, which is based in the idea that one pays for everything in this world *(todo se paga en este mundo)*, Julio pays for his hubris by turning into a weak, pathetic, castrated figure. She awakens to an intensified seeing, while he retreats into the darkness and dependence in which she was submerged during her years of marriage to him. Aware of the rumor that she bewitched Julio and made him blind, Esperanza does little to counter it, relishing the power it gives her. When I asked her directly about it, however, she laughed and said that only God has such powers, and that Julio's blindness was a payment exacted by the divine for the sufferings he had caused her.

When Esperanza's customers—to whom Esperanza was also in the habit of telling a compressed version of her life story—would ask her why she didn't find another man and marry again, she would reply, " 'No, what do I want men for now? I just beg God to give me a daughter. Because what will I do, alone, with two sons? They will grow up. Sons grow up. We'll lie there in the same place, and I distrust my sons. Because men are men and they grow up. It's fine when they're little, but they grow up. What will I do alone with them?' With your pardon, *comadre,* as the saying goes, what if the devil has horns?" Thus she was happy, she says, when God gave her two daughters, and she saw no need to form any sort of lasting relationship with the man who fathered them.

Esperanza's gender ideology, based in the idea that men are subject to animal desires for sex, including one's own sons once they come of age, is significant in light of a number of incest stories that figure prominently in her narrative. The main story concerns her eldest son, Antonio, who tried numerous times to molest her eldest daughter, his half sister, while Esperanza was away from the house selling. Again her life became a welling up of rage: " 'Who has supported you all these years? Not your father. . . . Why don't you behave properly? . . . You're a man now. If you find it so easy, grab some woman on the street, or get married. I don't want the girl to get pregnant. . . . I couldn't be here alone. Alone with the two of you. Because you grow up, and I a woman alone, I'm sure you would even try to grab me in my sleep by force. . . . Go back to your father. I don't want you like this.' "

In Esperanza's narrative, Antonio comes to seem more and more like his father: cruel, deceptive, obsessed with sex. As if taking up with his half sister had not been ugly enough, he then moved on to a relationship with his own uncle's former mistress, Esperanza's sister-in-law. For Esperanza this was a disgusting act of animal sexuality, but she could not convince Antonio. She later learned from Gloria the healer that the woman got control of Antonio by force, the force of evil, putting magic powders in some guavas she gave him to eat. Thus she likewise has come to see her battle with her son as part of her struggle against evil, a struggle she is still waging. After leaving his mother's house, Antonio rejoined his father, taking up with the prohibited woman in spite of Esperanza's rage. Esperanza has disowned him. She speaks to neither the evil son or the father anymore, though all live in the same small town. She says that she still feels rage against them both, and that she has forgiven neither.

With her daughters, whom she so desired, Esperanza has a sense of profound inner struggle. She doesn't want them to go through what she has — and that is why she relentlessly pounds into their hearts and minds the story of her life — but she profoundly knows that they will. As she puts it, again in the language of a spiritual economy, "One as a mother has to pay for what one did with one's own children. Since I had my failures with another man, one of them will have to do the same." When a woman becomes pregnant outside of marriage or a permanent relationship, she is said to *fracasar*, literally 'to fail or mess up'. The word perfectly conveys the sense of failure, of falling, that a woman is meant to feel when her own body and sexuality betray her. Esperanza knows that she is a fallen woman, and though she realizes that one of her daughters will very likely reproduce her life as she reproduced her mother's life (her mother, too, had children out of wedlock), she still struggles to beat sense — and an awareness of being tied to her, of matrilineal bonding — into her daughters.

When her eldest daughter, Otilia, now eighteen and a domestic in San Luis, refused to support her, saying "Why should I give you money?" Esperanza decided it was necessary to teach her a lesson:

> "No, daughter. That's not the way to think. . . . Many women here have gotten pregnant and their parents have been pimps for them. If you want to follow the wrong path, go ahead, go." . . . And I grabbed a rope and hit her. And she answered back, and again I grabbed the rope. . . . I gave her a few whippings. . . . "I had you so you would help me later on in life, not pull out your nails." . . . No, the girl understood. . . . I whipped her three times. . . . She was gone for eight, fifteen days. [Then she returned.] "Mama." "Has your *coraje* passed?" "Yes, mama." "Behave properly. . . . You are too old to be hit. . . . Look, daughter, I told you, one paycheck is for you, and the other is for me, so that you will support and help me." And so she gave in.

There is a contradictory quality to the words that Esperanza chooses to accompany the violent lesson that she inscribes on her daughter's body. I read them in the light of Esperanza's notions of a spiritual and a sexual economy. Esperanza scolds her daughter for not giving her money, because part of the bargain between them is that her daughter must retain her value by not putting herself into circulation sexually. While Esperanza knows that she must "pay" for her sexual "failing" by seeing one of her daughters repeat her experience, she still wants to fight to the last to prevent this fate, which is the common fate of women of her social class, from unfolding. Having been the provider, Esperanza also wants an economic return from her daughter. This system of exchange is part of a matrilineal economy, in which money flows through the uterine rather than the paternal line. Money has a metaphysical value as a way of showing that there is a bond between women from one generation to the next, a bond that exists outside, and in spite, of paternal control. When her daughter threatened to break this bond, Esperanza had to inscribe it on her body so she wouldn't forget that she, like Esperanza herself, was born of the inscription of pain on her mother's body.

## A WOMAN WITH A MAN'S NAME

Esperanza's beating of her daughter also encodes her effort to carry into practice her own complex and contradictory gender identity. Esperanza has a keen sense of how she has had to be both man and woman to her children, both father and mother, economic provider and nurturer, upholder of the social-religious order and a mirror in which her daughters can read a past that threatens to become their future. "All those years I have been both man and woman to them, supporting them, helping them grow up. . . . I go to work [in the fields]. I use a hoe like a man. I plant. I irrigate. . . . How many woman are there in Mexquitic who use the hoe, the pick? They have their men, their husbands who support them, suffering some rages, perhaps, but supported by their husbands. And me, what man do I have?"

One reads here both a sense of pride in an androgyny that she has managed to pull off and a sense of ambivalence in being a woman who has taken on male roles. "My name is San Esperanzo," she told me, "I have a man's name." I read in Esperanza's narrative a desire to be a *macha*, a woman who won't be beaten, won't forgive, won't give up her rage. A *macha*, too, in the sense of wanting to harness a certain male fearlessness to meet evil and danger head on. It is this *macha* quality that fascinates her about the healer/medium, Gloria, whom she has known since her mother's illness. Gloria, as Esperanza told me, is very manly, *muy hombrona*. When Esperanza took me to meet her in 1987, I had to agree that Gloria was an extraordinarily male female, not a transvestite but a woman who, like a chameleon, seen in one light was a woman, in another light a man, a mystery of androgyny. When Gloria goes into trance one of the spirits that speaks through her is, indeed, the symbol of manly banditry and chaotic power, namely, Pancho Villa. Esperanza told me that Gloria lost all her pregnancies because in her work battling against witchcraft she has to take on too much evil. It is as if her female body rejects its own ability to create life, because she takes on so many "male" qualities to fight evil. In much the same way, Esperanza's children did not survive infancy because the rage they suckled with their mother's milk was so intense as to destroy them.

It is Gloria who has worked with Esperanza in her struggle against evil. On my return in 1987, Esperanza told me about a bizarre and ugly pig that had appeared suddenly one day in the stream by her plot of land where her lilies grow; the pig's feet had been chopped off and it lay in the stream, at first barely alive, and finally, dead and stenching. Esperanza was convinced that the pig had been deliberately placed there to ruin her land and she sought out Gloria's help to clean and heal it. Gloria told Esperanza she would have to remove the pig from the stream herself, which Esperanza did, in a story marvelously told in which the pig virtually becomes a demon against whom Esperanza victoriously struggles. Then Gloria came and "cleaned" the field, making the land burn from within, sprinkling it with certain herbal waters, and reciting prayers over its four corners. This was an expensive cure: it cost Esperanza 240,000 pesos (about $500 at the time), all the money she had in the bank, but it was worth it to her, she says, because otherwise the land would have gone barren.[13] It was worth it, too, to learn from Gloria who had placed the evil on her land; it was her son, Antonio, the rejected son. There is something unresolved about her relation with Antonio, and she must continue to wage a cosmological battle, with her life and her money, to push it closer to some sort of resolution.

## STORYTELLING AND REDEMPTION

Toward the end of our conversations in 1985, Esperanza said to me, "I have made a confession. . . . Now I should confess with the priest. . . . Now you carry my sins . . . because it is as if I have been confessing with my *comadre,* instead of with the priest. You will carry my sins now, because you carry them in your head. Priests confess people, right? . . . Then they confess to the bishops. . . . And the bishops, with whom? With the archbishops. And the archbishops, with whom? With God! Now you, *comadre,* who are you going to get rid of them with? You tell them somewhere ahead so someone else can carry the burden."

This very complex narrative is, ultimately, for Esperanza, an examination of the Christian soul through its inscription in the oldest form of first-person history, the confession. What does it mean that Esperanza has given me a status analogous to the priest as a redemptive listener of her confession?[14] This is a question I will need to ponder as I think about the collaboration between us that produced this text and the complex power relations it no doubt inscribes. One crucial aspect of our collaboration was that Esperanza could offer a different story about herself to me, the anthropologist, than she could tell townspeople in Mexquitic. While they are used to viewing her as an angry woman abandoned by her husband, whose rage exploded in witchcraft, to me, a woman from "the other side," she could tell a different life story: that of a woman who was wronged,

Figure 5-1. Esperanza standing by her home altar. On the far wall is an image of Pancho Villa and below it is another of Niño Tomasito, surrounded by bills. Photograph by Ruth Behar.

Figure 5-2. Esperanza's mother standing by her home altar. Photograph by Ruth Behar.

and whom God, judging well and knowing her faith, has helped to find some degree of triumph and justice. Esperanza's autobiography, by her own definition, is a spiritual chronicle of her soul's journey, and her stories are therefore "sins" for which she hopes to receive atonement. Telling her story, turning her rage into a story, is part of her quest for redemption, the redemption of her past and the redemption of the present she is actively seeking to understand and forge. Her story, like Christ's body, is the currency she offers to pay for her redemption. She told her story to me and I have told it to you. Now you must tell it to someone else, so that eventually the lord and judge of all our actions will hear it, too.

## NOTES

I have presented different, developing versions of this essay to the Ethnography, Literature, and Lunch group, Women's Studies, and the Critical Theory Colloquium, all at the University of Michigan, as well as to the departments of anthropology at the University of California, Santa Cruz and at the New School for Social Research; on all these occasions I have profited from the further readings of Esperanza's text that were suggested to me. I am especially indebted to the following people for their detailed comments and criticism: James Fernandez, David Frye, Linda Gregerson, Susan Harding, Janise Hurtig, Seong-Nae Kim, Barry Lyons, Bruce Mannheim, Sidney Mintz, Deborah Poole, and Teofilo Ruiz. I thank the Society of Fellows at the University of Michigan and the Harry Frank Guggenheim Foundation for their support of my work. Many of the issues explored here in a preliminary way are treated in more detail in my book, *Translated Woman: Crossing the Border with Esperanza's Story* (Boston: Beacon Press, 1993). This essay is reprinted from *Feminist Studies*, 16:2 (Summer 1990): 223–58, by permission of the publisher, Feminist Studies, Inc., c/o Women's Studies Program, University of Maryland, College Park, Md. 20742.

1. The critical literature on life history is quite large, and growing, so I will only mention as key works those of Sidney Mintz (1979), Vincent Crapanzano (1984), Kevin Dwyer (1982), L. L. Langness and Gelya Frank (1981), Lawrence C. Watson (1976), Lawrence C. Watson and Maria-Barbara Watson-Franke (1985), Roger M. Keesing (1985), and Susan N. G. Geiger (1986).

Recent writings in the field of life history have tended to examine closely the context of elicitation of the life history and the nature of the life history text as a literary and political enterprise, connected, on the one hand, to issues of authorship and storytelling, and on the other, to the asymmetries of power stemming from gender and colonial relations. For examples, see Laurel Kendall (1988), Michael W. Young (1983), Janet Alison Hoskins (1985), and Daphne Patai (1988b).

2. Also relevant here is Daphne Patai (1988a: 17–18).

3. In this vein, three different recent life histories of Guatemalan, Bolivian, and Honduran women follow the trajectories by which these intelligent and articu-

late women—who already had gained a reputation for their activism—awoke to a heightened political consciousness of gender, racial, and class domination. Their important and moving accounts are part of a growing Latin American testimonial literature in which Marxist-inspired discourses of liberation figure prominently. See Domitila Barrios de Chungara (1978), Rigoberta Menchú (1984), and Medea Benjamin (1987).

Esperanza's narrative falls outside of this emerging testimonial tradition; from a Marxist perspective, she still has the wool over her eyes. Yet she, too, conceives of her testimony as being about struggle, not a Marxist class struggle, which is foreign to her rhetoric, but a personal struggle against the men who have oppressed her which is embedded within a cosmological struggle against evil. Telling her story, too, as in the case of more politicized Latin American women, is part of her struggle.

4. A related critique can be found in Marnia Lazreg (1988). Lazreg criticizes the reification of such categories as "Middle Eastern women" and "women of the Arab world." This "abstracted empiricism," as Lazreg says, makes it extremely difficult for her, as an Algerian woman, to write about women in Algeria, because "her space has already been defined, her history dissolved, her subjects objectified, her language chosen for her." As she notes, "concrete women (like men) live in concrete societies and *not* in an ideologically uniform space." We need to get beyond the Western gynocentrism that "has led to an essentialism of otherhood." See Lazreg (1988: 95–97).

5. Aihwa Ong, an anthropologist who has worked with Malay factory women, notes that "the non-Western woman is presented as either nonmodern or modern; she is seldom perceived as living in a situation where there is deeply felt tension between tradition and modernity. . . . Although a common past may be claimed by feminists, Third World women are often represented as mired in it, ever arriving at modernity when Western feminists are already adrift in postmodernism" (Ong 1988: 86–87)

6. The feminist notion of counterhegemonic or oppositional structures assumes that in a given time and setting there is a male dominant culture that is operative, against which a female culture of resistance can be constructed, though not without difficulty and not without being paid for by severe repression. This model of female resistance—which places women in an active rather than a passive role— has recently had wide appeal in anthropology, whether the focus is on seventeenth-century Andean women defying colonial structures of domination by creating an oppositional set of cosmologies and rituals, or late-twentieth-century Baltimore women, forging, at times hesitantly, at times vehemently, alternative ways of talking about the experiences of the female body to resist the denigrating notions created by a male scientific establishment. See, respectively, Irene Silverblatt (1987), and Emily Martin (1987).

Esperanza's life history narrative can be read in terms of her struggle to resist male dominance and assert her independence as a "newly born woman." On the domestic level, women's alternatives to patriarchal domination in rural Mexico are few: to remain celibate and live alone; to have various men and make no commitment to any; or to form a female-headed household—all social forms (except for celibacy) that are associated with lower-class standing and sometimes with the "racial" class of "Indian." Esperanza at first chooses marriage, which for her is a season in hell, and ends up escaping only to reproduce her own mother's life as a "fallen," but at least autonomous, woman at the head of her own household. On a more explicitly symbolic level, her highly elaborated cosmological views and notions of witchcraft—which are centered in her continual struggle against evil and her sense that all cruelty and injustice must be paid for dearly in this life or the next—can be read, too, as forming part of a Mexican women's culture of resistance. While this particular feminist reading seems to offer one possible way of reading Esperanza's narrative, it gives me pause. Esperanza certainly has a sense of herself as being oppressed and as resisting, though as a person, not a category. I wonder, also, whether an analysis based on a female culture of resistance tends too much, again, toward the view of women's social action as supplementary, as reacting against a male world rather than as creatively constructing a complete social world. In this particular case, there seem to be yet other readings that have to do with Esperanza's construction of a life and a cosmology for herself out of narrative topoi.

7. I am indebted to Janise Hurtig for this reference, and many others that she has generously shared with me.

8. The literature on this subject is substantial. Elsewhere I hope to consider it in more detail. Some recent important works include Elaine Jahner (1985), Barbara Johnson (1982), Margaret A. Lourie, Domna C. Stanton, and Martha Vicinus, eds. (1987), Biddy Martin and Chandra Mohanty (1986), Sally McConnell-Ginet, Ruth Borker, and Nelly Furman, eds. (1980), Cherrie Moraga (1986), Sidonie Smith (1987), and Patricia Meyer Spacks (1977). For a feminist anthropological critique of Clifford, see Deborah Gordon (1988), and Kamala Visweswaran (1988). On the "awkwardness" of anthropology and feminism as divergent discourses, see Marilyn Strathern (1987).

9. For a critique based on the argument of images and tropes in culture, see James W. Fernandez (1986).

10. As Carolyn Steedman notes in her account of her mother's life as a woman from the English working classes, her mother told her life story to her to teach her lessons, not to entertain, and the main lesson was about "all the strong, brave women who gave me life . . . and all of them, all the good women dissolved into the figure of my mother, who was, as she told us, a good mother" (Steedman 1987: 3)

11. Emily Martin discusses the suppressed anger that women feel as second-class citizens in American society, characterizing this anger as having social causes rather than biological ones. Focusing on the rage that women express premenstrually, she suggests that women seek ways of using this anger constructively. Thus she writes of the possibility of being illuminated with rage, being bright with fury. Finding the causes at the root of this anger, women can join together to turn their anger into the source of liberating change, rather than going individually to the doctor for a cure. In the same context, Martin shows how rage links up with situations of racial and class oppression, citing Audre Lorde's sharp remarks:

"My response to racism is anger. That anger has eaten clefts into my living only when it remained unspoken, useless to anyone. It has also served me in classrooms without light or learning, where the work and history of Black women was less than a vapor. It has served me as fire in the ice zone of uncomprehending eyes of white women who see in my experience and the experience of my people only new reasons for fear or guilt" (E. Martin 1987: 135–36)

12. On the significance of pronouns, see Paul Friedrich (1979).

13. There is much more to be said about Esperanza's relations with the money economy and her ideas about money. In her room (the walls of which are covered with pictures of Christ, the Virgin, various saints, and the pope, all forming an impressive altar), there is an image of a young child, Tomasito, an *angelito* (dead children are always called "angels" because, being sinless, they are thought to enter heaven directly). The picture of Tomasito is framed with bills, which have been placed there as offerings to help her with her selling. Tomasito also speaks through Gloria when she goes into trance and Esperanza says he is "very miraculous."

14. On the idea of "the redemptive power that such derealization of the self in the Other can entail," and "the possibilities for such redemptive listening," see Taussig 1987: 105–6.

## REFERENCES CITED

Appadurai, Arjun. 1986a. "Is Homo Hierarchichus?" *American Ethnologist* 13:745–61.

———. 1986b. "Center and Periphery in Anthropological Theory." *Comparative Studies in Society and History* 28:356–61.

Barrios de Chungara, Domitila. 1978. *Let Me Speak: Testimony of Domitila, a Woman of the Bolivian Mines.* New York: Monthly Review Press.

Benjamin, Medea. 1987. *Don't Be Afraid Gringo, a Honduran Woman Speaks from the Heart: The Story of Elvia Alvarado.* San Francisco: Institute for Food and Development Policy.

Benjamin, Walter. 1969. *Illuminations.* Edited by Hannah Arendt. Translated by Harry Zohn. New York: Shocken.

Brodkey, Linda. 1987. "Writing Critical Ethnographic Narratives." *Anthropology and Education Quarterly* 18:67–76.

Cardozo-Freeman, Inez. 1975. "Games Mexican Girls Play." *Journal of American Folklore* 88:12–24.

Clifford, James. 1986a. "On Ethnographic Allegory." In *Writing Culture: The Poetics and Politics of Ethnography,* edited by James Clifford and George E. Marcus, pp. 98–121. Berkeley and Los Angeles: University of California Press.

———. 1986b. "Introduction: Partial Truths." In *Writing Culture: The Poetics and Politics of Ethnography,* edited by James Clifford and George E. Marcus, pp. 1–26. Berkeley and Los Angeles: University of California Press.

Crapanzano, Vincent. 1984. "Life Histories." *American Anthropologist* 86:953–60.

Dwyer, Kevin. 1982. *Moroccan Dialogues: Anthropology in Question.* Baltimore: Johns Hopkins University Press.

Farmer, Paul. 1988. "Bad Blood, Spoiled Milk: Bodily Fluids as Moral Barometers in Rural Haiti." *American Ethnologist* 15:62–83.

Fernandez, James W. 1986. *Persuasions and Performances: The Play of Tropes in Culture.* Bloomington: Indiana University Press.

Finkler, Kaja. 1985. *Spiritualist Healers in Mexico: Successes and Failures of Alternative Therapeutics.* New York: Praeger.

Frank, Gelya. 1979. "Finding the Common Denominator: A Phenomenological Critique of Life History Method." *Ethos* 7:68–94.

Freeman, James M., and David L. Krantz. 1979. "The Unfulfilled Promise of Life Histories." *Biography* 3, no. 11:1–13.

Friedrich, Paul. 1979. "Structural Implications of Russian Pronominal Usage." In *Language, Context, and the Imagination: Essays by Paul Friedrich,* edited by Anwar S. Dil, pp. 63–125. Stanford: Stanford University Press.

Geiger, Susan N. G. 1986. "Women's Life Histories: Method and Content." *Signs* 11:334–51.

Gordon, Deborah. 1988. "Writing Culture, Writing Feminism: The Poetics and Politics of Experimental Ethnography." In *Inscriptions,* special issue, Feminism and the Critique of Colonial Discourse, 3/4:7–24.

Hoskins, Janet Alison. 1985. "A Life History from Both Sides: The Changing Poetics of Personal Experience." *Journal of Anthropological Research* 41:147–69.

Jacobus, Mary. 1986. *Reading Woman: Essays in Feminist Criticism.* New York: Columbia University Press.

Jahner, Elaine. 1985. "Woman Remembering: Life History as Exemplary Pattern." In *Women's Folklore, Women's Culture,* edited by Rosan A. Jordan and Susan J. Kalcik, pp. 214–33. Philadelphia: University of Pennsylvania Press.

Johnson, Barbara. 1982. "My Monster/My Self." *Diacritics* 12:2–10.

Keesing, Roger M. 1985. "Kwaio Women Speak: The Micro-Politics of Autobiography in a Solomon Island Society." *American Anthropologist* 87:27–39.

Kendall, Laurel. 1988. *The Life and Hard Times of a Korean Shaman: Of Tales and the Telling of Tales.* Honolulu: University of Hawaii Press.

Langness, L. L., and Gelya Frank. 1981. *Lives: An Anthropological Approach to Biography.* Novata, Calif.: Chandler and Sharp.

Lazreg, Marnia. 1988. "Feminism and Difference: The Perils of Writing as a Woman on Women in Algeria." *Feminist Studies* 14:81–107.

Lewis, Oscar. 1963. *The Children of Sanchez.* New York: Random House.

Lourie, Margaret A., Domna C. Stanton, and Martha Vicinus, eds. 1987. *Women and Memory. Michigan Quarterly Review,* special issue 26, 1.

Lurie, Nancy O., ed. 1961. *Mountain Wolf Woman: Sister of Crashing Thunder.* Ann Arbor: University of Michigan Press.

Marcus, George E., and Michael M. J. Fischer. 1986. *Anthropology as Cultural Critique: An Experimental Moment in the Human Sciences.* Chicago: University of Chicago Press.

Martin, Biddy, and Chandra Mohanty. 1986. "Feminist Politics: What's Home Got to Do with It?" In *Feminist Studies/Critical Studies,* edited by Teresa de Lauretis, pp. 191–212. Bloomington: Indiana University Press.

Martin, Emily. 1987. *The Woman in the Body: A Cultural Analysis of Reproduction.* Boston: Beacon Press.

McConnell-Ginet, Sally, Ruth Borker, and Nelly Furman, eds. 1980. *Women and Language in Literature and Society.* New York: Praeger Publishers.

Menchú, Rigoberta. 1984. *I, Rigoberta Menchú: An Indian Woman in Guatemala.* Edited by E. Burgos-Debray. Translated by A. Wright. London: Verso.

Mintz, Sidney. 1979. "The Anthropological Interview and the Life History." *Oral History Review* 7:18–26.

———. 1989. "The Sensation of Moving, While Standing Still." *American Ethnologist* 16:786–96.

Mohanty, Chandra. 1982. "Under Western Eyes: Feminist Scholarship and Colonial Discourses." *Boundary 2* 12, no. 3/13, no. 1:333–58.

Moraga, Cherrie. 1986. "From a Long Line of Vendidas: Chicanas and Feminism." In *Feminist Studies/Critical Studies,* edited by Teresa de Lauretis, pp. 173–90. Bloomington: Indiana University Press.

Ong, Aihwa. 1988. "Colonialism and Modernity: Feminist Re-presentation of Women in Non-Western Societies." In *Inscriptions,* special issue, Feminism and the Critique of Colonial Discourse, 3/4:79–93.

Ortner, Sherry. 1984. "Theory in Anthropology since the Sixties." *Comparative Studies in Society and History* 26:126–66.

Ortner, Sherry, and Harriet Whitehead. 1981. "Introduction: Accounting for Sexual Meanings." In *Sexual Meanings: The Cultural Construction of Gender and Sexuality,* edited by Sherry Ortner and Harriet Whitehead, pp. 1–27. Cambridge: Cambridge University Press.

Patai, Daphne. 1988a. *Brazilian Women Speak: Contemporary Life Stories.* New Brunswick, N.J.: Rutgers University Press.

———. 1988b. "Constructing a Self: A Brazilian Life Story." *Feminist Studies* 14:143–66.

Paz, Octavio. 1961. *The Labyrinth of Solitude: Life and Thought in Mexico.* Translated by Lysander Kemp. New York: Grove Press.

Pratt, Mary Louise. 1986. "Fieldwork in Common Places." In *Writing Culture: The Poetics and Politics of Ethnography,* edited by James Clifford and George E. Marcus, pp. 27–50. Berkeley and Los Angeles: University of California Press.

Radin, Paul. 1983 [1926]. *Crashing Thunder: The Autobiography of an American Indian.* Lincoln: University of Nebraska Press.

Rosaldo, Renato. 1984. "Grief and a Headhunter's Rage: On the Cultural Force of Emotions." In *Text, Play, and Story: The Construction and Reconstruction of Self and Society,* edited by Edward M. Bruner, pp. 178–95. Washington, D.C.: American Ethnological Society.

Said, Edward. 1985. "In the Shadow of the West." *Wedge* 7/8:4–5.

Shostak, Marjorie. 1981. *Nisa: The Life and Words of a !Kung Woman.* Cambridge, Mass.: Harvard University Press.

Silverblatt, Irene. 1987. *Moon, Sun, and Witches: Gender Ideologies and Class in Inca and Colonial Peru.* Princeton: Princeton University Press.

Smith, Sidonie. 1987. *A Poetics of Women's Autobiography: Marginality and the Fictions of Self-Representation.* Bloomington: Indiana University Press.

Spacks, Patricia Meyer. 1977. "Women's Stories, Women's Selves." *Hudson Review* 30:29–46.

Stanton, Domna, ed. 1987. *The Female Autograph: Theory and Practice of Autobiography from the Tenth to the Twentieth Century.* Chicago: University of Chicago Press.

Steedman, Carolyn Kay. 1987. *Landscape for a Good Woman: A Story of Two Lives.* New Brunswick, N.J.: Rutgers University Press.

Strathern, Marilyn. 1987. "An Awkward Relationship: The Case of Feminism and Anthropology." *Signs* 12:276–92.

Taussig, Michael. 1987. "The Rise and Fall of Marxist Anthropology." *Social Analysis* 21:101–13.

Titon, Jeff Todd. 1980. "The Life Story." *Journal of American Folklore* 93:276–92.

Visweswaran, Kamala. 1988. "Defining Feminist Ethnography." In *Inscriptions,* special issue, Feminism and the Critique of Colonial Discourse, 3/4:27–44.

Watson, Lawrence C. 1976. "Understanding a Life History as a Subjective Document: Hermeneutical and Phenomenological Perspectives." *Ethos* 4:95–131.

Watson, Lawrence C., and Maria-Barbara Watson-Franke. 1985. *Interpreting Life Histories: An Anthropological Inquiry.* New Brunswick, N.J.: Rutgers University Press.

Young, Michael W. 1983. "Our Name Is Women; We Are Bought with Limesticks and Limepots: An Analysis of the Autobiographical Narrative of a Kalauna Woman." *Man* 18:478–501.

# SIX

# *Tasting the Water*

## JEAN DeBERNARDI

Throughout the seventh lunar month, Malaysian Chinese celebrate a festival designed to placate and entertain the "Hungry Ghosts." During the
course of these festivities, they offer worship to the Wealth God, who is
an assistant to the King of Hell. The paper statue representing the Wealth
God is a gaudy, macabre image of mourning and death, but paradoxically
he wears a hat on which is written "to see me is great luck."

Sparked by curiosity about this odd conjunction of ideas, I sought exegesis of the meaning of this tall-hatted, opium-smeared hell official, and
soon learned the history of the god. My perspective on the meaning of
the Wealth God was, however, transformed fundamentally when I encountered this god and others as individuals possessing spirit mediums, and I
was drawn into their improvised performances. At the same time, I learned
that some of those who approached this low-ranking bureaucrat in the
"prisons of earth" (as hell is known) were part of a human underworld
that celebrated earthly pleasures: drinking, smoking, gambling, dancing,
undomesticated sexuality, and song.

This essay tells the story of my dialogue with the ritual specialists of
an unfamiliar tradition. It also reflects a dialogue with my own training
in anthropology. When I went to Pinang, I sought cultural virtuosi who
could aid me in my quest for exegesis and insight into the underlying
structures informing Chinese popular religious culture. My Chinese informants, however, advised me to turn to the gods. As they sometimes put it,
"If you want to learn these things, you need to ask someone old, *really* old,
like two hundred years old."

Thus prompted, I asked a god possessing a spirit medium for help in
writing my book. In response, he offered me a dramatically delivered ser-
mon exploring the basic principles of Chinese religion, and I discovered
that the "gods" themselves were to be my most knowledgeable teachers.

The force and meaning of my dialogic interactions with these "gods" as they possessed spirit mediums were not captured easily within the interpretive conventions of structural analysis. Trained in the elucidation of underlying structures abstractly described, I needed to devise a way to explore the play of transformations on a theme in real social settings.

As Tedlock has noted, attention to discourse almost inevitably leads the ethnographer of speaking to become a "speaking ethnographer" (1983: 338). Dialogic analysis is one solution to this dilemma of representation, and I adopt first-person voice here to tell an "impressionist tale" of my unfolding relationship with the Wealth God and his followers (Van Maanen 1988: 101–2). In so doing, I hope to provide insight into the heterodoxies of Chinese popular religious culture. At the same time, I seek to re-create for the reader the experience of arriving at a gestalt understanding of enigmatic cultural forms. I do not take as a primary goal the analysis of my own reactions to the unusual situations in which I found myself, but rather explore ways in which I was written into unfolding scripts not of my own making.[1]

## THE WEALTH GOD

I first saw the Wealth God while studying the lavish celebrations of the Hungry Ghosts Festival (Pudu) in Pinang, Malaysia. Throughout the seventh lunar month ghosts, on vacation from hell, are entertained with food offerings, Daoist incantations, Buddhist rites, nights of Chinese opera, and contemporary pop music and comedy skits in market areas in all parts of Pinang. The King of Hell and his four assistants are honored guests at these events, and their presence aids the people to control the ghosts, who might otherwise fight over the offerings. Brilliantly colored, larger-than-life paper statues represent these underworld bureaucrats (euphemistically referred to as gods) on altars sheltered in an open-sided tent. In front of these altars, worshipers set up enormous tables which they fill to overflowing with offerings of food and drink. Across an open street or courtyard from this carnival hell, a temporary stage lodges the entertainment.[2]

The Wealth God (Caishen) is one of four assistants to the King of Hell (see fig. 6-1). The "Tall One," as he is sometimes known, is displayed together with the "Short One" (who captures souls and brings them to hell), the God of the Earth (Tudigong), and the God of Prosperity (Dabogong). He is also sometimes called the "Inconstant Ghost" (Wuchanggui), or more politely the "Inconstant Uncle" (Wuchangbo). The white-faced paper statue of the Wealth God wears traditional coarse white mourning dress and a tall hat inscribed with the message "to see me is great luck" (yijian daji). Often his tongue hangs out of his mouth, which my Chinese informants interpreted to mean that he died by strangulation. In the festival-opening ceremonies which "open the eyes" of the images and bring them to consciousness, a temple committee member smears the Wealth God's tongue with sticky tar-black opium, the god's favorite intoxicant. In response to my curious questions, members of the street committee for the festival usually explained that the Wealth God was a filial son, and that prostitutes and gamblers worshiped him. This perplexed me on several grounds. First, it seemed odd that a ghost should represent filiality. One expert on Chinese folk religion has suggested that ghosts are representatives of the social category of stranger as opposed to kin (Wolf 1974: 174). Odder still was the connection of wealth and luck with an image of mourning and death, as well as the idea that a filial son would be the patron saint of prostitutes.

While many were acquainted with the god's story, I received the fullest account of his history from a woman spirit medium. This medium (called the "Datuk Aunt" because she was possessed by a Malay spirit politely addressed as "Datuk" or "Uncle") claimed a personal relationship with the Wealth God, and told his history as follows:

> The Inconstant Uncle was a gentleman, but he was unfilial to his parents. He was working in the fields one day, and his mother brought him food. He hit her, and she grew frightened of her son. Then one day he saw young goats sucking milk from their mother, and said, "The mother goat knows how to love her kids, and lets them suck milk. Now I am so unfilial to my mother, and this is not a good thing." . . . He was very unfilial. His mother was frightened until she trembled. She brought rice for him to eat, and still was frightened until she trembled. Even beasts know how to love their mothers.
>
> His mother cooked rice for him very early. He was remorseful, and he ran to kneel before her. She was scared that he would hit her again, and jumped into the well, and died. When his mother died, an ancestral tablet floated to the surface of the water. This is how the Chinese came to use the ancestral tablet. (Datuk Yi, 20 August 1980)[3] [Other tellers of this tale added that the Inconstant Uncle was so grieved by his mother's death that he died. He was then rewarded for his filiality by the Lord of Heaven with a bureaucratic appointment in hell.]

The Datok Aunt concluded by saying that prostitutes worshiped the god, and that his heart was very good. She also mentioned that she had spoken with him more than once through another spirit medium, and she offered to introduce me.

Basing my interpretation on this narrative, I speculated that the visual resemblance between the shape of the god's tall hat, inscribed with the words "to see me is great luck," and the Chinese ancestral tablet (a wooden tablet representing the deceased ancestor that is the object of ritual offerings) was not coincidental. Since death of a parent results in an inheritance for the child, death in this instance could be interpreted as "great luck." My interpretation was met with laughter when I tested it on a maker of the paper statues used in funeral rituals and in the Hungry Ghosts Festival. However, when I suggested this view of death to an educated, Taiwan-born friend, she was shocked. "Jean!" she exclaimed. "An American might say such things, but a Chinese never, never would! The loss of the person is what matters, not the property." At the same time, she admitted that Chinese history frequently told of sons who murdered their fathers in order to usurp their power. My literate informant summed up the pragmatic attitude in a proverb: "When necessary, you don't know your own kin."

She herself knew a version of the god's history that differed in detail from the one retold above, but which is similar in spirit:

> The Tall God and the Short God were brothers. The Elder Brother [the Wealth God] asked the Younger Brother to wait for him under the bridge. The Younger Brother went there to wait, but the Elder Brother was late. In the meantime, the water was rising. However, the Younger Brother was faithful to his word, and he stayed under the bridge and drowned. He represents trust.
>
> The Elder Brother came and discovered that his Younger Brother had drowned. He was desolated by this loss, and hanged himself. He represents faithfulness. The Lord of Heaven, seeing their virtue, awarded them their posts in the underworld.[4]

In both versions of the story, the hero felt painful remorse at carelessly precipitating the death of another and expiated this guilt through his own death. Presumably the "god" was awarded his post in the underworld since his intentions were good (though his original error no doubt ruined his chance for a posting in heaven).

In the Confucian tradition, the "gods" or "saints" were selected and arranged to reflect the Confucian normative order, and to represent solid Confucian values such as filial piety and obedience to parents, trust, faithfulness, and righteousness. Much Chinese historiography was done precisely in order to find heroes from the past who could be canonized and held up to the people as exemplary models (Munro 1977). This inhabitant of hell however is a hero of a rather different sort. The ironically unfilial filial son, who is both a stark image of death and a playful image of luck and good fortune, partakes in the spirit of carnivalesque humor (see Bakhtin 1968: 91). Opposites are confounded in the comic imagery of the Wealth God. He is similtaneously an image of mourning and luck, is both ghost and god, and is someone who was well-intentioned but misunderstood.

Figure 6-1. A paper statue of the Wealth God, festooned with gold "ingots" made of paper and foil. Photograph by Jean DeBernardi.

Figure 6-2. The Wealth God predicts a four-digit lottery number for a client. Photograph by Jean DeBernardi.

Figure 6-3. The Wealth God enjoys a cup of wine. Photograph by Jean DeBernardi.

Figure 6-4. "To see me is to prosper." Photograph by Jean DeBernardi.

Figure 6-5. An opium-smeared statue of the Wealth God on a temple altar. Photograph by Jean DeBernardi.

## ON MEETING THE GOD, AND TASTING THE WATER

In Pinang, the Wealth God is known not only as a symbol of filiality, embodied in an image and a tale, but also as an individual embodied in the spirit medium who "dances" the god. He is part of a pantheon that includes a "mad" monk, a child warrior, and a variety of martial artists and philosopher gods, including the God of War and Laozi (author of the *Daodejing*). Worshipers approach these gods during regular and public trance sessions to seek advice and help with crisis resolution.

In an evening's work, a god might lecture a young man for lack of filiality, advise an elderly woman not to meddle in the business of others, dispense charms to a jealous lover to administer to his fickle girlfriend, and scold a young man asking for lottery numbers (if it appears that his salary is after all quite good) (see fig. 6–2). The god also may offer teaching and advice to the inside members of his temple committee after ordinary clients have left the temple. Chinese who worship the Wealth God no doubt know his image and some version of his story, but these modes of apprehension are insignificant when compared with their personal interactions with him. What, after all, is a paper statue or a secondhand story compared with the vital presence of a witty, urbane god?

The Wealth God's personality as expressed in the trance performance is as ambivalent as the image and story recounted above suggest. Chinese regard him as "crazy" since he likes to joke, but at the same time regard him as a "master" whose omniscient authority is not to be questioned. The Wealth God, like certain dramatic or literary characters, exemplifies an idea. In my view, the idea to which he gives effective voice is not filiality but trust, or rather the impossibility of trust, and the ultimate opacity of human intention. The theme of trust is of course highlighted in the two tales of inconstancy, death, and violent atonement which I have recounted above. It also was an issue raised in my interactions with the god at two allied temples whose spirit mediums "danced" the Wealth God.

I first met the Wealth God at the end of a muddy unpaved path, where I found him possessing a spirit medium at a lively, crowded temple fair. The temple fair had drawn a large and fascinated crowd, who whispered that the god at this temple was very supernaturally effective (Hokkien: *xia*). My landlady measured the god's effectiveness not only by his own achievements in doing salvation work but by the fact that there had been no fighting at the temple fair. All agreed that the event was very exciting.

Well-known recording stars from the capital and a popular comedy troupe performed on an open-air stage facing the temple. Special events included shaving the heads of two boys who were taking Buddhist vows, and the appearance of a pop singer who had been the victim of an acid attack in which she was blinded and scarred. My neighbors whispered that this once-beautiful woman had been the lover of a high-ranking member of a secret society, and that he had ordered the attack when she had refused to cooperate with him in an unknown matter. They believed that she knew her attackers, but that she had never named them in order to protect her child from possible harm. She seemed sad and reluctant. I wondered whether she appeared on the stage willingly, or if her enemy had compelled her to sing in order to demonstrate his fearsome power. I also wondered what connection this temple might have with the secret society whose boss she had apparently attempted to defy.

That was on 24 September 1980. I returned to this temple twice, once to present the three spirit mediums at the temple with photographs of the temple fair and to interview them, then later in the year to attend a special feast commemorating the founding of the temple. The event was small-scale, and primarily designed for inside members. No friends or neighbors were free to accompany me, and I went alone with some trepidation, leaving my camera and tape recorder at home. This part of town was rumored to be controlled by gangs, and I did not entirely trust these spirit mediums.[5]

I arrived upon a splendid scene. The high altar to the Lord of Heaven, decorated with tall stalks of sugarcane, had been set up in the open area in front of the temple. A long red wooden table also stood in this open space. On it worshipers had laid a steamboat filled with simmering chicken broth, and placed around this were platters of raw seafood, pigeon eggs, spring onions, lettuce, and other accompaniments to be cooked in the broth. As well, there were a good many bottles of Anchor beer and Guinness Stout. The small crowd stood, and I recognized among the faces youthful gang members familiar to me from the market. Only two guests sat at the table, the Wealth God and the Vagabond Buddha, both relishing the lavish offerings of food and drink. Their attendants poured them wine from a Chinese porcelain decanter and lit them cigarettes in long ivory holders (see fig. 6–3).

The Wealth God was dressed in a black robe with the Chinese character for wealth *(cai)* emblazoned on the back in gold (see fig. 6–4). His hat was tall, and like the Hungry Ghosts Festival image, it was inscribed on the front with the characters "to see me is great luck," and on the back "to see me is to prosper." The Vagabond Buddha (Jigong) wore the yellow robes of a monk and a brown hat with the character for "Buddha" *(Fo)* written on it. He carried a fan, with which he occasionally chastized people, and he smoked, drank, and was altogether worldly in his demeanor.

The Vagabond Buddha's story is said to date to the Song Dynasty (960–1279), and he is a Robin Hood figure who tricks the rich to aid the poor with a combination of common sense and chicanery. This Buddha, whom some believe to be Maitreya (the Buddha of the Future), is emphatically impure. He eats meat, drinks, gambles, and enjoys the company of women. People delight in saying of him that he "eats black dog," a punning allusion to the Vagabond Buddha's taste for Guinness Stout, which is called "Black Dog" in Pinang Hokkien slang (see also DeBernardi 1987).

When I arrived, it was clear that I had been expected. Bad luck, I had missed the miracle: that morning the god had produced precious gems from a Sunkist orange. The medium's sister fetched the blue and pink oval stones (still mingled with orange pips) for my inspection. But a temple committee member soon called me from my conversation with the women, and invited me to talk with the Vagabond Buddha. This "god" possessed a recently initiated spirit medium who had gone into trance chaotically at the earlier temple fair. At that event, a number of gods, both literary and martial, had possessed him, but now he was possessed consistently by the Vagabond Buddha and the martial artist Baby God.

"Ask him a question!" urged the committee member, so I said: "A friend of mine was badly hurt in a parang [knife] attack in Indonesia. Any suggestions?" Perplexed, the Vagabond Buddha relayed the question to the Wealth God (who possessed his elder brother, an experienced spirit medium). "Tell the god more," said the interpreter for the gods. "His name is Zakir, and he lives in Medan." "What's his birthday?" "I don't know. He's about thirty." My lack of precise information apparently made the question difficult to answer.

Finally the Wealth God exploded with "Mo popo!" "What?" we all said. "One more time!" "Mo popo!" he said again with great authority and conviction, and the worshipers began to giggle. The interpreter apologetically said, "These gods like to joke." In the meantime someone caught on to the fact that the Wealth God was trying to communicate with me in English and was saying, "No problem!" "Fine," I said, "I won't worry then," and I drew back from the table as a third spirit medium, possessed by the Short God (the Wealth God's younger brother), shuffled over to the table to sit by the Vagabond Buddha.

He was driven away by some means, and I was called back. "Ask about your future," the interpreter urged, so I did. The god spoke: "All goes smoothly now, but next year in the Chinese third moon you may have problems. You do a man's job. You are an intelligent foreigner, the first one the god has met. You go to dangerous places in your line of work." "He means like war zones," the interpreter added in English.

The god then said with a smile, "Please have a drink!" "Orange soda, please," I replied demurely. "No, no, have a beer!" insisted the interpreter. Finally I accepted a glass of Anchor. The Buddha took the beer, passed his fan over it several times, took a sip, then handed it to me. I took it and sipped, and the audience waited for my reaction. The medium's sister rushed out of the temple: "How does it taste? Like Black Dog?" "No, like Anchor," I responded a bit dryly, and the interpreter tasted it and handed it back to the god, who once again passed his fan over the beer, giving the handle of the fan a better shake this time. He again took a sip and handed it back to me. Once again I took and tasted it. "Yes, it's different now." Smiles all around. "A bit salty and not sweet now," said the god with satisfaction. I gave the beer to the interpreter, who had a taste. "It tastes like flat beer," he said in English with a grimace.

Once again I stepped back from the table, only to be called over by the Wealth God. "I've spoken with you before," he said. "Yes, that's right, a few months back." He took a sip of wine and a drag on his ivory cigarette holder. "You want to study spiritual arts. If you want to study these things, you have to experience them. You see this glass of water? I can tell you that it's hot or cold, salty or sweet. Do you believe me? If you want to know you must taste it yourself." The committee member interpreted the god's poetic words of advice: "He wants you to go into trance."

The idea that I might go into trance had been brought up months earlier at my interview with this medium and his younger brother. I had not forgotten my promise to consider the suggestion, but was startled when the god himself promoted the idea. My expensive camera equipment was safely at home, so I had no fears there. Still, I was alone. "It might be dangerous," I said. "Don't I need to purify myself by eating vegetarian food?" "No need!" they exclaimed, and finally I agreed.

"Fine," said the Wealth God. "You cannot wear gold when you are entered by the god. Take off your jewelry and give it to someone." Though I knew that mediums were not supposed to wear any sort of metal on their bodies while they were in trance, still I wondered if there was magic by which gold chains were transformed into Sunkist oranges. Sensing my doubt, the committee member reassured me: "Don't worry! My girlfriend can drive you home to leave off your jewelry." The God continued, "And this god," he said, gesturing toward the Vagabond Buddha, "wants to possess you!" "Ah!" I said. I looked at the small gathering of strangers, wondering where this unfolding narrative might lead, and doubting the wisdom of delivering authorship of my life into the hands of these trickster gods. With some lingering regret, I said good-bye and walked away from the feast with the gods, leaving the water untasted.

## "YOU HEAR THE VOICE BUT CANNOT KNOW THE HEART"

I was taken to the second temple by the Datuk Aunt, the spirit medium possessed by Malay spirits who taught me the story of the Wealth God and the origin of the ancestral tablet. At this temple, I did not observe the trance performance, and only had a single opportunity to interview the spirit medium. I learned more about the socially marginal identity of the spirit medium and his followers than I learned about the god himself, and found that these were two pieces of the same puzzle.[6]

The Datuk Aunt was eager to see the god's medium, whom she called Sammy, to ask for his help with a specific problem. Earlier that week, two young boys had robbed her at knifepoint of her antique gold and ruby jewelry. "I am sad about people, not money," she said piously. "I asked Datuk Lai Huat [her possessing deity] what to do. He said that the thieves were heroin addicts, that there was no point in trying to catch them." Despite this pessimistic prediction, she filed a police report, and went to visit Sammy.

As we drove to the temple the Datuk Aunt commented that this spirit medium (like the boys who had robbed her) "ate heroin." "He's a gangster. If I didn't know his mother, I wouldn't dare to go. A while ago Sammy ran into trouble with a Datuk gang [presumably a spirit medium possessed by Datuk spirits and his followers]. I helped him." Sammy owed her a favor, and I guessed that she might be seeking aid in recovering her jewelry.

The temple was lodged in a home in a modern housing estate, guarded with high metal gates. We entered the house through the spacious front shrine room, and I noted that the rank of deities on the altar was unusual. The highest ranked deity was the Holy Mother, rather than Laozi or the Buddha, and above the altar the medium had hung a painting of a Tibetan-looking demon. The statue of the Wealth God was not on the main altar, since he is associated with earth rather than heaven. Rather it was below the altar on the ground, together with the Tiger God and the Earth God.

The spirit medium was a powerful-looking, handsome man. "Who is she?" he asked the Datuk Aunt. "She's the American girl who speaks Hokkien. She's writing a book about Chinese religion and customs. She lives in Lintang village and 'eats Chinese' [follows a Chinese lifestyle]." I gave him my business card. "Do you know the Temple of Ten Thousand Immortals?" I asked. "One of the spirit mediums there also dances the Wealth God." He replied in English: "That's our branch office! Let me look at your notebook to see what you are writing."

Sammy and another man leafed through the book, stopping to read my notes from interviews with a widely known and respected spirit medium and teacher. "I know Master Tan," said the Datuk Aunt. "He sends Datuk possession cases to me." She added, "She's also interviewed Master Lim!" Sammy appeared impressed. "Ah-Bi used to be very famous," he observed. "But when his sister needed $300, she didn't go to her brother. She came to me." He returned the notebook, and invited us to sit in the shaded courtyard, where his wife served us tea and chilled lychee fruit.

After making a gift of used children's clothes to the medium's wife, the Datuk Aunt described the violent theft of her jewelry to Sammy. "This is hard," he said. "The Holy Mother in Bungah Mas is very bad. She makes the gods ashamed." He alluded to a temple close to the Datuk Aunt's house, whose male spirit medium was possessed by the same female deity given highest rank on the altar in Sammy's temple. Sammy did not hold out hope of recovering the jewelry, and I wondered what connection there could be between the Holy Mother and the theft.

"How is your mother?" asked the Datuk Aunt. "I never speak to her," he replied. "She called me a 'thief,' and said she was ashamed to have me as a son. She provoked a fight between my younger brother and me. When I went to a coffee shop with my brother to settle the matter, she called the police. She's bad herself! When I was small, she beat me and cursed me." Sammy addressed me in English: "I'm the black sheep of my family."

The conversation turned to my impressions of Malaysia. "Malaysia is a beautiful country. People in Pinang are very generous . . ." But my words of praise were ignored. "Do people outside know how bad things are here?" he asked bitterly. "The government now forces us Chinese to speak Malay. But Malay is not an international language! English is an international language. Mandarin is an international language. But Malay is not. My children go to Chinese schools, and I speak Mandarin with them. You should write about *these* things so that the world knows what is happening here."

Sammy accused the Malay elite of manipulating government regulations to favor their own business interests, and appeared to have inside information on several recent scams. But he also hinted that he himself had at one time sought illicit gain: "I once did a little speculation and took a risk, but the money was quickly gone. The people I know only use their minds to think up ways to make money through swindles." He added with evident regret that he had wanted to study medicine, but was unable to do so. He expressed conviction in the effectiveness of Chinese herbal remedies, and described several to me.

"May I see your temple?" I asked. We returned to the shrine room, and Sammy drew my attention to evidence of the Wealth God's past successes. "You see these gifts? Grateful clients offered them to the god." Bottles of expensive French brandies and Scotch whiskeys, both empty and full, were displayed on a long table to the side of the altar, together with brightly wrapped imported tobaccos. "May I photograph?" I asked. "You may. But you won't be able to take a photograph of the deity. Something always happens to make the photograph fail." True to his prediction, the photos that I took of the god image, the first two on a new roll of film, were ruined in the process of developing the roll (for a similar god image, see fig. 6–5).

He brought out a photo album, and turned to a picture of himself, possessed by the Wealth God: "The Wealth God is very humble. We call him the 'Old Man,' and he knows many stories. This god is very effective (xia) you know. But Chinese are ungrateful! They come to the god to be healed. Then they pretended not to recognize me when they see me. Indians who come to the temple for healing always wave to me and called me laobeh 'old uncle' [a polite Hokkien term of address for a respected elder] when they see me. But Chinese won't give face."

In looking through his photo album, I noted with surprise that his temple committee was dominated not by men but by women. One of these women was strikingly beautiful, with the glamorous presence of a model or actress. By coincidence, she drove up in an expensive new car as the Datuk Aunt and I were leaving. I thought I detected strain on the face of the spirit medium's wife. Perhaps sensing my curiosity, the Datuk Aunt explained as we drove away: "She bought the house for Sammy. She was a taxi dancer, and married a European. She married him and they had two children, but the Australian abandoned her, and she became a prostitute. Now a Malay prince has bought her a house in Tanjong Bungah."

I recounted this story to another friend (the educated woman who taught me the second version of the Wealth God's story) when we happened to drive past Sammy's temple. "The barber got shaved!" she exclaimed, implying that the woman had separated the prince from his money, but then in turn had been "shaven" by the spirit medium. Temple committee members for the Hungry Ghosts festival had advised me that prostitutes worshiped the Wealth God. Here it seemed I had inadvertently stumbled on evidence that supported this common assertion. Was it the protection of the god or the protection of the medium that she sought? Or was she simply the victim of extortion?

While I was in Sammy's temple, he showed me poetic couplets authored through him by the gods who possessed him. These couplets had been written on large pink cardboard posters, and were conspicuously displayed in the shrine room. Sammy drew my attention to one couplet, authored by the Wealth God: "White rice nourishes black men, / Black waters nourish white fish." "This is sarcastic. You have to reflect to understand it," he advised. Another spirit medium involved in the criminal underworld had used the symbolism of yin and yang to locate himself on the "dark side" of society: "Most people are awake and active in the daytime. I am a man of the night. Taishang [Laozi] teaches that there is white and black, positive and negative. But there is a dark spot on the moon. However perfect you are, there will be one weak point, and however bad you are, there is one bright light. There is always contrast, always comparison, and the devil sits next to god" (DeBernardi 1987: 325). The Wealth God's sarcastic (or, better yet, ironic) poetic couplet also suggests the mutuality and interdependence of opposites. The couplet appears to suggest that the seemingly respectable "white fish" of legitimate society swim in the "black waters" of the "black societies" (as the Chinese secret societies are known in Pinang).

Here is the complete text of this poem:

> There are butterflies in the mountain,
>> But no flowers live there.
> A man speaks eloquently,
>> You hear the voice, but cannot know the heart.
> A man takes a brush to write characters,
>> You see the strokes but cannot see the brush.
> White rice nourishes black men,
>> Black waters nourish white fish.
> A new home holds broken furniture,
>> A new cupboard holds old clothes.
> Sugar is sweet but kills ants,
>> The wheat is ripe but kills birds.
> You will study my poem
>> And know what is in my heart.

The last line is perhaps the most ironic of all. Recall the story of the misunderstanding that led to the suicide of the Wealth God's mother, and the sad tale of the accidental death of the trusting younger brother who faithfully waited under the bridge only to drown. The Wealth God's poem again reminds us of the difficulty of truly knowing another's heart, and the dangers that await us when we fail to understand.

## CONCLUSIONS

In seeking to interpret visual, verbal, and dramaturgical representations of the Wealth God, I have adopted here a dialogic approach that emphasizes social context and event. Let me conclude with consideration of the unique events and individual voices recounted above in light of their relationship to a larger field of meanings.

Chinese popular religious culture expresses the hierarchy of the gods as a system of patterned and stereotyped differences between military and literary gods, Buddhas, and immortals. The divine hierarchy is further ordered into the dualistic ranks of high and low, pure and impure, *yang* and *yin*. The high status spiritual world linked to heaven is one in which beings control their passions and achieve purity. By contrast, the spiritual world linked to hell is much more like the world of humans, and the impure ghosts are filled with desire and attachment.

As this dialogic account demonstrates, spirit mediums in the trance performance express these stereotypical differences as personality traits. Thus the paradoxical impurity of the Vagabond Buddha finds expression in his taste for dogmeat, women, and Guinness Stout (as well as in a refusal to bathe). And the Wealth God, a ruler in the *yin* world of the "prisons of earth," eats opium and shares his followers' passion for gambling. By contrast, when the Holy Mother possesses the spirit medium she expresses her high status by insisting on the purity of her temple and requesting "cooling tea" (in a *very* clean teacup; see DeBernardi n.d.a).

The multileveled hierarchy of gods and ghosts is modeled on human hierarchy, and heaven and hell interpret the contrasting worlds of elites and the homeless poor. The Wealth God (an official in hell) is quite literally worshiped by gamblers and prostitutes, and appears to control a certain territory in the "underworld" of the secret societies. His followers are socially marginal, outside of the law, and are said to live for quick gain and conspicuous consumption. They situate themselves vis-à-vis the englobing society in their worship of a seriocomic bureaucrat in hell, who may epitomize their own ambivalence about their power in the local underworld. The prostitutes, "gambling ghosts," and "opium immortals" who pray to this god are often *not* to be trusted, and a god who doubts the possibility of trust provides an appropriate ideal and law.

But the Wealth God not only represents a stereotyped moral ideal (albeit as a parodic apotheosis of that ideal). As an individual he himself also interprets events, and indeed he might be regarded as the author of events. The meanings associated with a deity such as the Wealth God are emergent, and his biography does not end with the events of his natural lifespan. In a very real sense he continues to live, not only in the imagination of his believers (and one anthropologist) but also as a social actor who influences their lives.

The "gods" who possess spirit mediums engage in dialogue with their human suppliants, and in these dialogues they have the social power of their divine personalities.[7] In the exchange with the gods that I recount above, I am counseled, offered a magically transformed drink, and dared to truly learn spiritual arts by going into trance. Curiosity about a paper statue drew me to back lanes that respectable Chinese avoided. But had I kept to the main road, I would never have met the god, or been challenged to taste the water.

## CHINESE GLOSSARY

| cai | 財 | Pudu | 普渡 |
| Caishen | 財神 | Tudigong | 大地公 |

| | | | | |
|---|---|---|---|---|
| Dabogong | 大伯公 | Wuchangbo | 無常伯 |
| dao | 道 | Wuchanggui | 無常鬼 |
| *Daodejing* | 道德經 | xia [Hokkien] | 口 |
| Fo | 佛 | yang | 陽 |
| Jigong | 濟公 | yijian daji | 一見大吉 |
| Laozi | 老子 | yin | 陰 |
| laobeh [Hokkien] | 老伯 | | |

## NOTES

The research on which this essay is based was conducted in Pinang, Malaysia, from 1979 to 1981, and was funded by fellowships from Fulbright-Hays and the National Institute of Mental Health. A National Endowment for the Humanities Summer Seminar organized by William LaFleur and Stephen Teiser at the University of California, Los Angeles provided me with the opportunity to revise this essay. I have benefited from the comments of Stephen A. Kent, Jeanne Larsen, Bruce Mannheim, Dennis Tedlock, Stephen Teiser, and the anonymous reviewers for the University of Illinois Press. Special thanks are due Professor Chen Yushih for her aid in preparing the Chinese glossary.

1. For a more in-depth account of the content of my dialogues with other spirit mediums, please see DeBernardi (1986, n.d.b). More broadly based analyses of Malaysian Chinese spirit mediumship and popular religious culture include Ackerman and Lee (1988), Cheu (1988), DeBernardi (1987, 1992), Elliott (1955), and Shaw (1973).

2. For a detailed historical and interpretive study of the development of the Ghost Festival and of its connection to Buddhist ceremonies of salvation for ancestors, see Teiser (1988). Other studies include Orzech (1989), Pang (1977), and Weller (1987).

3. Dates given in parentheses in the text refer to the author's field notes.

4. In his ethnographic study of Taiwanese popular religion, Weller recounts a tale that is almost identical to this one. However, in Weller's research community, the two officials in hell are referred to as "Grandfather Seven" and "Grandfather Eight" (1987: 72–3).

5. The dialogue reported in this section is based on field notes written immediately after the event (18 December 1980), and a dialogic analysis written soon thereafter (January 1981).

6. I did not tape my conversation with the spirit medium at this temple, and have re-created the dialogic account presented here from third-person field notes (9 March 1981).

7. The power and persuasiveness of the "god" can be considerable. A skillful medium with a closely bound committee has the power of incontrovertible interpretation, and the "god" may not be contradicted even when his version of the truth is not based in reality. For example, I was told by one medium that I had an elder brother. When I asserted that I had no brothers at all, the men at the temple assured me that my father must have had a mistress of whom I was unaware.

## REFERENCES CITED

Ackerman, Susan, and Raymond L. M. Lee. 1988. *Heaven in Transition.* Honolulu: University of Hawaii Press.

Bakhtin, M. M. 1968. *Rabelais and His World.* Translated by Helene Iswolsky. Cambridge, Mass.: MIT Press.

Cheu Hock Tong. 1988. *The Nine Emperor Gods: A Study of Chinese Spirit-Medium Cults.* Singapore: Times Books International.

DeBernardi, Jean. 1986. *Heaven, Earth, and Man: A Study of Malaysian Chinese Spirit Mediums.* Ph.D. dissertation, University of Chicago.

———. 1987. "The God of War and the Vagabond Buddha." *Modern China* 13, no. 2:310–32.

———. 1992. "Space and Time in Chinese Religious Culture." *History of Religions* 31, no. 3:247–68.

———. n.d.a. "On Trance and Temptation: Images of the Body in Malaysian Chinese Popular Religion." Forthcoming in *Religious Reflections on the Human Body,* edited by Jane Marie Law, pp. 149–61. Bloomington: Indiana University Press.

———. n.d.b. "'The Way That Lives in the Heart': Text and Performance in Chinese Religious Culture." Forthcoming in *Religions in China in Practice,* edited by Donald S. Lopez, Jr. Princeton: Princeton University Press.

Elliott, Alan J. A. 1955. *Chinese Spirit Medium Cults in Singapore.* London: University of London Press.

Munro, Donald J. 1977. *The Concept of Man in Contemporary China.* Ann Arbor: University of Michigan Press.

Orzech, Charles D. 1989. "Seeing Chen-yen Buddhism: Traditional Scholarship and the Vajrayana in China." *History of Religions* 29, no. 2:87–114.

Pang, Duane. 1977. "The P'u tu Ritual." In *Buddhist and Taoist Studies I,* edited by Michael Saso and David Chappell, pp. 95–122. Honolulu: University of Hawaii Press.

Shaw, William. 1973. "Aspects of Spirit-Mediumship in Peninsular Malaysia." *Federations Museum Journal* n.s. 18:71–176.

Tedlock, Dennis. 1983. *The Spoken Word and the Work of Interpretation.* Philadelphia: University of Pennsylvania Press.

Teiser, Stephen F. 1988. *The Ghost Festival in Medieval China.* Princeton: Princeton University Press.

Van Maanen, John. 1988. *Tales of the Field: On Writing Ethnography.* Chicago: University of Chicago Press.

Weller, Robert P. 1987. *Unities and Diversities in Chinese Religion.* Seattle: University of Washington Press.

Wolf, Arthur P. 1974. "Gods, Ghosts, and Ancestors." In *Religion and Ritual in Chinese Society,* edited by Arthur P. Wolf, pp. 131–82. Stanford: Stanford University Press.

# SEVEN

# Waiting for the Mouse: Constructed Dialogue in Conversation

## DEBORAH TANNEN

### INTRODUCTION: REPORTED SPEECH AND DIALOGUE

For Voloshinov and Bakhtin, dialogue is crucial: not dialogue per se, that is, the exchange of turns that is of central concern to conversation analysts, but the polyphonic nature of all utterance, of every word. This polyphony derives from the multiple resonances of the people, contexts, and genres with which the utterance or word has been associated. As Bakhtin (1986: 91) puts it, "Each utterance is filled with the echoes and reverberations of other utterances to which it is related by the communality of the sphere of speech communication."

In exploring dialogue in this broad sense, Voloshinov devotes extensive analysis to reported speech. He introduces this focus as follows: "The productive study of dialogue presupposes, however, a more profound investigation of the forms used in reported speech, since these forms reflect basic and constant tendencies in the active reception of other speakers' speech, and it is this reception, after all, that is fundamental also for dialogue" (Voloshinov 1986 [1930]: 117). Voloshinov criticizes "earlier investigators" for "divorcing the reported speech from the reporting context," which "explains why their treatment of these forms is so static and inert. . . . Meanwhile, the true object of inquiry ought to be precisely the dynamic interrelationship of these two factors, the speech being reported (the other person's speech) and the speech doing the reporting (the author's speech). . . . After all, the two actually do exist, function, and take shape only in their interrelation. . . . The reported speech and the reporting context are but the terms of a dynamic interrelationship" (ibid.: 119). Furthermore, Bakhtin observes that "the speech of another, once enclosed in a context, is — no matter how accurately transmitted — always subject to certain semantic changes. The context embracing another's word is responsible for its dialogizing background, whose influence can be very great. Given the appropriate methods for framing, one may bring about fundamental changes even in another's utterance accurately quoted" (Bakhtin 1981: 340). The essence of this observation is metaphorically expressed in a Wolof proverb which holds, "Everything can be moved from one place to another without being changed, except speech."[1]

My interest here incorporates Voloshinov's notion that the reported speech and the reporting context are dynamically interrelated as well as Bakhtin's that the meaning of the reported speech itself can be — indeed, is inevitably — transformed by the reporting context. Further, I wish to focus attention on the dynamic relationship between the reported speech and the *reported* context. I will question whether the "reported speech" exists at all as reported speech (i.e., as another's words), when divorced from its context of utterance. Rather, when an utterance is repeated by a current speaker, it exists only as an element of the reporting context, although its meaning resonates with association with its reported context, in keeping with Bakhtin's sense of polyphony. In the reporting context, the "reported speech" exists only as the creation of the "reporter." Put another way, the words have ceased to be those of the speaker to whom they are attributed; they have been appropriated by the speaker who is reporting them. This claim is proffered not in counterpoint to Bakhtin, whose chief material is the reported speech of novelistic prose, but rather in counterpoint to American folk wisdom applied to the reporting of the speech of others in daily dialogue, the language of everyday conversation: when told that someone else said something, most Americans believe that the "reported" statement must have been said as reported. In short, I wish to question our literal conception of "reported speech."

## REPORTED CRITICISM IN CONVERSATION

The folk wisdom I have in mind can be viewed in the common act of reporting criticism. One person tells another that a third has said something negative about the addressee. The folk wisdom of daily interaction divorces reported speech from the reported context: On hearing that another has spoken ill of one, few people ask how that comment grew out of, was situated in, or was triggered by, the context in which it was uttered. One rarely considers the possibility that it might have been provoked by someone present at the time, including the reporter, or constructed in the service of some immediate interactional goal — for example, establishing solidarity with one who is present by comparing her favorably to one who is not present, or by sympathizing with a complaint that a present party has voiced about an absent one. The reality of the reported speech is not questioned. Quite the opposite, opinions expressed in one's absence seem to have an enhanced reality, the incontestable truth of the overheard.

The anger and hurt felt in response to such reported criticism is, for Americans at least, typically directed toward the quoted source rather than the speaker who conveys the criticism. (In contrast, an Arab proverb has it that "He who repeats an insult is the one who is insulting you.") For example, a man who works in a large office invests a great deal of his own time to make signs identifying the various departments of his firm. A co-worker tells him that the boss does not like the colors he chose for the signs. The man feels hurt and angry at the boss for his ingratitude, but he never has a chance to say anything to the boss, who did not say anything to him, except to thank him and praise him for his efforts—praise which the man assumes to be hypocritical, taking the report of the co-worker as the truer truth.

The constellation of co-workers and boss is parallel to that of siblings and parents, a configuration which yields innumerable examples of reported criticism. A sister is hurt and angry at her mother because of the mother's disapproval of her boyfriend—which she knows about only because she has been told of it by her sister. A woman ends contact with her parents because they have talked about her in a way that she has demanded they cease—an infraction she learned about from her sister, with whom she does not sever contact. Elsewhere (Tannen 1986a) I discuss these and many other such examples. I refer to the phenomenon here only to provide familiar and easily recognizable evidence that most Americans tend to take literally the act of what is accordingly called "reported speech." That is, they assume that when quotations are attributed to others, the words thus reported represent more or less what was said, the speaker in question being a conduit of objectively real information. The conveyor of information is seen as an inert vessel, in Goffman's (1974: 516) terms, a mere animator: a voice giving form to information for which the quoted party is the principal, the one responsible. I want to claim, with Bakhtin, that there is no such thing, in conversation, as a mere animator (in contradistinction, for example, to someone who reads an academic paper which was written by a scholar who could not be present as scheduled at an academic meeting).

Elsewhere Goffman notes, "We must also be careful to keep in mind the truism that persons who are present are treated very differently from persons who are absent. Persons who treat each other with consideration while in each other's immediate presence regularly show not the slightest consideration for each other in situations where acts of deprivation cannot be immediately and incontestably identified as to source by the person who is deprived by these acts" (Goffman 1953: 41, quoted in Shuman 1986: 23). In this formulation, Goffman suggests that speakers may treat an absent person without consideration because they cannot easily be identified by the aggrieved person. I would suggest, in contrast, that absent persons may be treated without consideration because in that context they are not persons, not perceived as potentially affected by the acts of that context. Rather, absent parties are simply topics of conversation, resources for the important facework required by the immediate context. It is, I think, the view of oneself as not a person but simply the subject of conversation that makes it so discomforting to learn that one has been talked about. But the utterances which may strike an aggrieved party as "acts of deprivation" may not be that at all, until they are repeated in a context in which that party is present.

The folk wisdom about reported criticism in particular and reported speech in general reflects the pervasive American attitude toward language and communication that Reddy (1979) has identified as the conduit metaphor,[2] a misconception which assumes that communication is a matter of exchanging information, and that information is immutable, true or false, apart from its context. In direct contrast with this view, I will claim that when a speaker represents an utterance as the words of another, what results is by no means describable as "reported speech." Rather it is constructed dialogue. And the construction of the dialogue represents an active, creative, transforming move which expresses not the relationship between the quoted party and the topic of talk but rather the quoting party and the audience to whom the quotation is delivered.

It should be noted however that to say the quoted speech may not have been uttered, or may not have had the meaning it seems to have on report, is not to say that it was necessarily not uttered by the speaker to whom it is attributed. Indeed, my claim would not be undermined even by a tape recording "proving" that the words were spoken as reported. It is not that the reporter is lying nor even intentionally misrepresenting what was said but that the spirit of the utterance is fundamentally transformed when the object of the criticism is present rather than absent. This is a particular instance of the general phenomenon that changing the context of an utterance changes its meaning. Barbara Herrnstein Smith (1978: 65) observes that a quotation is a "fictive utterance" because, in quoting another, one presents a "facsimile" of the other's words. Therefore, "The factuality of the subject does not compromise the fictiveness of the tale for it is not the events told that are fictive but the *telling* of them" (ibid.: 128).

I am suggesting, then, that what is called "reported speech," "direct speech," "direct discourse," or "direct quotation" (that is, a speaker casting an account of another's words as dialogue) should be understood not as report at all, but as constructed dialogue. It is constructed just as surely as is the dialogue in drama or fiction. This view does not diminish our image of the individual speaking; rather it enhances it. Bakhtin (1981: 338) observes that "Every conversation is full of transmissions and interpretations of other people's words," and that "of all words uttered in everyday life, no less than half belong to someone else" (ibid.: 339). The act of transforming others' words into one's own discourse is a creative and enlivening one. Following Friedrich (1986), it is a poetic act of the individual imagination. Moreover, and perhaps paradoxically, and this I think is Bakhtin's chief argument, it is a supremely social act: by appropriating each other's utterances, speakers are bound together in a community of words.

In the discussion that follows I first present examples of constructed dialogue from a collection of tape-recorded, transcribed conversational narratives in order to demonstrate that what appears to be reported speech may never have been spoken by anyone. If dialogue does not report speech, what then does it do? To answer this question, I present an entire conversational narrative to illustrate how constructed dialogue creates involvement by making a story into drama.

## REPORTED SPEECH IS CONSTRUCTED DIALOGUE

Following are brief examples taken from narratives recorded by participants in casual conversation with their families and friends. Each example is accompanied by correspondingly brief discussion demonstrating that the dialogue animated in the narrative was not actually spoken by the person to whom it is attributed. In other words, it is not reported speech but constructed dialogue.

### Dialogue Representing What Wasn't Said

Example 1 comes from a conversation in which a young woman tells her friend that when she was a little girl, her father frequently embarrassed her by berating her in front of her peers for not having responded to his orders quickly and efficiently. She represents, in the form of dialogue, what she did *not* say to her father:[3]

(1)                    You can't say, "Well Daddy I didn't HEAR you."

This is a clear example of dialogue constructed rather than reported as the speaker states explicitly that the line of dialogue was not spoken.

### Dialogue as Instantiation

Specific dialogue is often constructed to illustrate an utterance type that occurs repeatedly. Several examples follow.

Example 2 is from a conversation that took place among several women who work together, while they were having lunch in a restaurant. In this excerpt, Daisy animates a line of dialogue in order to illustrate a general phenomenon:

(2)    Daisy:    The minute the kids get old enough
                 to do these things themselves,
                 ⌐that's when
    Mary:    └"You do it yourself."
    Daisy:    Yeah that's when I start to say ...
     →    "Well ... I don't think I'll go in the water this time.
     →    Why don't you kids go on the ferris wheel.
     →    I'll wave to you."

It is clear from the general time frame established, "The minute the kids get old enough" ("the minute" is, of course, meant figuratively, not literally), that the line of dialogue (indicated in the example by quotation marks and an arrow at the left) is offered as an instantiation of a general phenomenon. This becomes even clearer when the context suggested by the dialogue changes before our eyes from "go in the water" to "go on the ferris wheel." Although rhythmically one blends into the other in a single coherent flow of discourse, the scene changes as the general point of the story is instantiated in two different scenarios: from swimming to going on a ferris wheel.

Example 3 is taken from a young man's account of having been punished as a boy. He recalls his mother saying,

(3)            whenever something happened,
     →    then "Oh wait until your father comes."

Although this is certainly the gist of what the mother said, there is no reason to believe that these are precisely the words she always spoke.

Finally, a teacher recounts what he says to a new class when he appears as a substitute:

(4)            I have very strict rules,
            a:nd ... one of the first things I tell them
            after I tell them my name, is ...
     →    "When you follow my rules, you'll be happy,
     →    when you do not follow my rules,
     →    you will be-
     →    Pain and consequences.
     →    You will be very UNhappy."

Once more, it is highly unlikely that these precise words were uttered each time the teacher entered a new class—especially considering the abrupt

cutting off of breath following "be" and preceding the highly stylized inter-
jected phrase, "pain and consequences." But the sense of what he presents
himself as saying to each class is better captured by a particular instance
than it would be by a general summary representing the gist of what he
always says.

### Summarizing Dialogue

Example 5 shows a line of dialogue which is identified as representing the
gist of what was said in a single discourse. The speaker says she was part
of a group having dinner at a Philippine restaurant when one of the members of her dinner party spoke against the restaurant within earshot of the
restaurant staff:

(5)                    and this man is essentially saying
         →    "We shouldn't be here
         →    because Imelda Marcos owns this restaurant."

By using the present tense as well as "we," "here," and "this," the speaker
casts her summary of the man's argument in dialogue. But she describes
it as a summary, what he "essentially" said rather than what he specifically said.

### Choral Dialogue

The next example comes from a narrative that was told by a woman
(who happened to be me) about an experience in the Athens airport: A
Greek woman tried to break into a line in which Americans (including
the speaker) had queued up. The Americans objected to her behavior and
resisted her justifications for breaking into the line until she said that she
had small children with her.

(6)                    And then all the Americans said
         →    "Oh in that case, go ahead."

In this example, the dialogue is attributed to more than one speaker:
"all the Americans." This is impossible, unless one imagines the line of
Americans speaking in unison like a Greek chorus, which is unlikely (despite the Hellenic setting of the story), and, as I can attest, not the case.
Rather, the line of dialogue is offered as an instantiation of what many
people said.

Similar examples are frequent in the narratives collected. Just one more
will be given. In example 7 a woman is telling about having seen two
mothers on the train with their children:

(7)                    and the mothers were telling the kids,
         →    "Hold on to that, you know, to that post there."

Since they are not likely to have spoken in unison, the wording supplied instantiates rather than represents what the *two* mothers said.

## Dialogue as Inner Speech

People often report their own thoughts as dialogue. Example 8 is taken from a narrative about riding the New York subway. The speaker describes a strange man who entered the car and:

(8)            started mumbling about ... perverts,
      →    ... and I thought "Oh God,
      →    if I am going to get
      →    someone's slightly psychotic attitude
      →    on perverts,
      →    I really don't feel like riding this train."

While it is possible that these words actually represent the words the speaker spoke to himself at the time, it is unlikely, especially since the phrase "slightly psychotic attitude" seems stylized for performance effect.

## The Inner Speech of Others

If it is questionable that dialogue in a narrative accurately reproduces what a speaker thought at a time past, it is unquestionable that when a speaker reports what someone else thought, the words thus animated in dialogue do not correspond to the words actually thought by the other person. The animation as dialogue of the thoughts of a character other than the speaker was particularly frequent in a group of narratives told in conversation by Greek women which I have analyzed elsewhere (Tannen 1983). The following example from that study comes from a story a Greek woman told about being accosted by a man late at night in Venice. She says that she drew a rock from her pocket and took a step toward the man while brandishing the rock. The man turned tail and left. She explains his motivation in the words of his (projected) thoughts:[4]

(9)            Sou leei, "Afti den echei kalo skopo."
               [Literally, He says to himself, "She doesn't have a good
               purpose"; idiomatically, "She's up to no good."]

Presenting the thoughts of a character other than oneself is a clear example of dialogue which must be seen as constructed, not reported.

Taken from the corpus of narratives under analysis here, example 10 presents the thoughts of another person as dialogue, but introduces them not so much as what he thought but as what he must have been thinking, judging from his behavior and facial expression. It comes from a story about a baseball game, told by the person who was then the pitcher, describing the batter:

(10)                    And he-you could just see him just draw back like
           →     "Man, I'm going to knock this thing to Kingdom Come."

The word *like* is frequently used to introduce dialogue which, in a sense, is just what it says: not so much what the person said, as "like" what the person said, or as representing what the person felt like. Thus, in example 11, a woman tells of an incident in which her fifteen-year-old sister was riding a bicycle with a basketball under her shirt, giving the appearance of being pregnant. She fell off the bike when she was almost hit by a bus. The narrator says,

(11)                    And the bus driver was like "Oh my go::d!"

She is not suggesting that the bus driver literally said "Oh my god," but that his reaction was such that he might have been thinking something like that.

Example 12 is taken from a story about the experience of a tourist in Japan:

(12)                    and um they didn't tell us, first of all,
                        that we were going into the bath,
                        so we were standing in the room,
           →     and they said "Okay, take your clothes off."
           →     We're like "What?!"
                        and um they gave us these kimono
                        and we put the kimono on,
                        they brought us to this other room,
           →     and they said, "Okay, take the kimono off,"
           →     and we're like "What are you talking about!"

The lines attributed to the speaker(s) who gave orders to disrobe seem to have been uttered, but not in precisely the words represented. (They could not have been precisely those words because two variants are offered: "take your clothes off" and "take the kimono off"; the second is not a repair but simply a marker of return to the story following the backtrack to explain that they were wearing kimono.) There is no suggestion, however, that the speaker and his friends actually said, "What?" and "What are you talking about!" but simply that they felt in a way that would be reflected in such an utterance.

### Dialogue Constructed by a Listener

In the conversational narratives I have examined, a listener often supplies a line of dialogue animated in the role of a character in someone else's story. The listener in example 2, Mary, constructed an utterance in the role of Daisy (or any parent) addressing her children:

Daisy:   The minute the kids get old enough
         to do these things themselves,
         ┌that's when
→  Mary:   └"You do it yourself."

The "you" in this utterance refers not to the conversationalists present but to the children in Daisy's discourse who want to do something adventuresome. In this active form of listenership, the listener's construction of dialogue appropriate to someone else's narrative demonstrates how thoroughly the listener appreciates the perspective of the speaker. When a listener utters a line of dialogue for a story she isn't telling, that dialogue certainly cannot be considered "reported."

Even more extreme is example 13, in which a listener supplies a line of dialogue which is intentionally absurd. This excerpt follows an amusing story told by Lois about how her brother cast a fishing rod and accidentally sunk a lure in their father's face. Lois describes her father arriving at the hospital holding the lure in his face. Joe, a listener, offers a line of dialogue spoken by a hypothetical nurse which satirizes the absurdity of the situation:

(13)      Lois:   So he had the thing.
                  So he's walkin' around ...
→  Joe:    "Excuse me, Sir,
→          you've got a lure on your face."

Encouraged by general laughter, Joe goes on to construct an equally absurd response by Lois's father:

→  Joe:    "Ah ... lure again? [laughter]
→          Boy ... gets stuck there every week." [laughter]

In using Lois's story as material for his performance, Joe is constructing, not reporting, dialogue.

### Fadeout, Fadein

In example 14, an excerpt from a narrative told by a woman about her experience with a dentist, an indirect quotation fades into a direct one:

(14)              It was like he was telling everybody
         →        to "have your wisdom teeth taken out"
                  and I didn't see any point
                  as long as they weren't bothering me.

"Telling everybody to" is the grammatical means of introducing an indirect quotation, but it is followed instead by a direct quotation: "have your wisdom teeth taken out." The speaker might recall what the dentist said to her, but she can't know the precise words in which he spoke to "everybody." Finally, she concludes as if the reported line had been spoken to her ("I didn't see any point as long as they weren't bothering me").

Example 15 is taken from the same story as example 7, about the mothers in the subway car:

(15)         And uh finally the mother opened up the stroller
    →        you know and uh told the kid to "SIT THERE."

As in the preceding example, the mother's speech is introduced with the word "to," suggesting that indirect discourse is to follow. But by assuming the voice quality of a mother giving instructions to her child, the speaker shifts to constructed dialogue.

### Vague Referents

In the next example, which comes from the same discourse as example 1 (in which a young woman tells how her father embarrassed her by ordering her around in front of her peers), the use of vague referents makes it clear that the dialogue was never actually spoken as reported:

(16)         He was sending me out to get tools or whatever
    →        [imitating father] "Go get this
    →        and it looks like this and the other"

If her father had uttered precisely these words, not even he could have expected her to locate what he wanted.

### Nonhuman Speaker

The preceding examples come from conversational narratives. However, discourse need not be narrative to exploit the expressive potential of constructed dialogue. The final example comes from conversation taped at a dinner party. A guest notices the hosts' cat sitting on the window sill and addresses a question to the cat: "What do you see out there, kitty?" One of the hosts answers for the cat:

(17)         She says,
    →        "I see a beautiful world just waiting for me."

He animates the cat's response in a high-pitched, childlike voice. By animating dialogue, the two speakers create a spontaneous minidrama with the cat as central character. The constructed dialogue becomes a resource for a fleeting but finely coordinated verbal pas de deux.

## CONSTRUCTED DIALOGUE
## IN A CONVERSATIONAL NARRATIVE

Having demonstrated that dialogue animated in conversational discourse is constructed dialogue, I now present a complete narrative in order to show how such pseudoquotations work in conversational narrative. The lines of dialogue in the following story were not spoken by the characters to whom they are attributed for the reasons shown in the preceding section. What, then, are they doing in the story? The speaker uses the animation of voices to make his story into drama.

The narrative was told by a young man who came home from his work as a resident in the emergency ward of a hospital, to find a group of his friends gathered in his home, hosted by his wife. Asked whether anything interesting had happened at the emergency room, he responded by telling this story.

1) We had three guys come in,
2) one guy had a cut right here.
3) On his arm? [Listener: uhuh]
4) Bled all over the place, right? [Listener: Yeah]
5) These three guys were hysterical.
6) They come bustin' through the door.
7) Yknow you're not supposed to come in to the emergency room.
8) You're supposed to go to the registration desk, yknow?
9) and fill out all the forms before you get called back.
10) They come bustin' through the door,
11) blood is everywhere.
12) It's on the walls, on the floor, everywhere.
13) [sobbing] "It's okay Billy, we're gonna make it /?/."
14) [normal voice] "What the hell's wrong with you."
15) W-we-we look at him.
16) He's covered with blood yknow?
17) All they had to do was take a washcloth at home
18) and go like this …
19) and there'd be no blood.
20) There'd be no blood.
21) [listener: You put pressure on it.]
22) Three drunk guys come bustin' in,
23) all the other patients are like, "Ugh. Ugh."
24) They're bleedin' everywhere yknow.
25) People are passin' out just lookin' at this guy's blood here.
26) [Listener: Like "We're okay."]

27)     "Get the hell outta here!"
28)     [Listener: Yknow he's got stories like this to tell every night,
        don't you?]
29)     Yeah [Listener: Mhm]
30)     "Get the hell outta here!" yknow?
31)     These three guys-
32)     "What the hell's wrong with you guys.
33)     You don't know anything about first aid?
34)     Hold onto his arm."
35)     ["innocent" voice] "We rai:sed it above his hea::d."
36)     "Oh yeah." shh shh
37)     [Listener: So it bled up.]
38)     Yknow they're whimmin' his arm around
39)     ["upset" voice] "Come here Billy!
40)     No, come here Billy!"
41)     Two guys yankin' him from both sides.
42)     [sobbing] "Am I gonna die?
43)     [loud, sobbing ingress] Am I gonna die?"
44)     He's passed out on the cot.
45)     Anyway so ... [sobbing] "Am I gonna die?"
46)     "How old are you."
47)     "Nineteen."
48)     "Shit. Can't call his parents."
49)     [hysterically pleading voice] "Don't tell my parents.
50)     Please don't tell my parents.
51)     You're not gonna tell my parents, are you?"
52)     [Listener: /?/ "We're going to wrap you in bandages."]
53)     What happened.
54)     Then the cops were there too, the cops.
55)     ["bored" voice] "WHO stabbed dja."
56)     "I didn't get stabbed.
57)     I fell on a bottle." ...
58)     "Come o::n, looks like a stab wound to ME."
59)     [Listener: Well this is Alexandria, what do you think?]
60)     [Listener: Really no shit.]

There are at least five different voices animated in this narrative, and each of these voices is realized in a paralinguistically distinct acoustic representation: literally, a different voice. These are the voices of Billy, his friends, the speaker and other hospital staff, the other patients, and the policeman.

### Billy's Friends

Billy's two friends are represented by one voice, and the quality of that voice creates the persona that the speaker is developing for them. In line (13) they are presented as trying to reassure Billy, but the quality of the voice representing them shows that they are hysterical themselves. It is breathy, rushed, sobbing:

(13)    [sobbing] "It's        we're
                    o
                  kay Billy,       gonna make it /?/."

(39)    ["upset" voice] "Come
                        here Billy!

(40)    N   come
        o,     here Billy"

When the friends protest in (35) that

(35)                              rai:sed          he
    ["innocent" voice] "We     it above his  a
                                     d."

the quality of the voice suggests belabored innocence that is really stupidity.

### Hospital Staff

Another example of more than one person animated in the story as a single voice is the speaker himself, merged with the rest of the hospital staff. The quality of this voice is loud and strident, suggesting frustration and impatience but also reasonableness and calm. Dialogue uttered by this persona is the closest to the speaker's normal intonation and prosody.

(14)    [normal voice] "What        wrong
                        the hell's    with you."

(30)    "Get       outta
            the hell    here!"

(32)    "What       wrong
            the hell's    with you guys.

                                    aid?
(33)    You don't know anything about first

(34)     Hold         a
                onto his   rm."

(36)     "O   ye
              h    ah."

(46)     "How
                old are you."

(48)     "Sh    Can't
              it.              pa
                       call his   rents."

(52)     [Listener: /?/ "We're going to wrap you in bandages."]

Note that in line (52) a line of dialogue is animated by a listener, who assumes a voice quality similar to that adopted by the speaker when he is animating his own voice and that of the staff.

### Billy's Voice

Billy himself is animated in the most paralinguistically marked role-play. The voice representing him is sobbing, gasping, desperate, out of control:

                         I gonna die?
(42)     [sobbing] "Am

                              I gonna die?"
(43)     [loud, sobbing ingress] Am

                              I gonna die?"
(45)     Anyway so ... [sobbing] "Am

(47)     "Nineteen."

(49)     [hysterically pleading voice] "Don't
                              tell my parents.

(50)     Please
                don't tell my parents.

(51)     You're                  par        you?"
                not gonna tell my    ents, are

                 did
(56)     "I    n't get stabbed.

                         bot
(57)     I fell on a    tle." ...

The paralinguistically exaggerated role-play of Billy's voice, and the slightly less marked animation of his friends' voice, contrast sharply with the relatively ordinary quality in which the speaker/hospital staff voice is represented. These contrasting voices create the dramatic tension between the unreasonable behavior of "these three drunk guys" and the reasonable behavior of the speaker/staff.

### Policeman

Marked in a different direction is the stereotypically flat voice of the policeman:

(55)     ["bored" voice] "WHO
                                    stabbed dja."

(58)     "Come        looks                        m
                    o::n,        like a stab wound to    e."

This voice is that of the jaded detective who has seen it all.

### Other Patients

Finally, the other emergency room patients are animated in a single voice:

(23)     all the other patients are like, "U      U
                                    gh.    gh."

                    "We're
(26)     [Listener: Like        okay."]

It is clear in all these examples, for reasons parallel to those explained for the dialogue presented in the first section, that the lines of dialogue in this story are not reported but rather constructed by the speaker, like lines in fiction or drama, and to the same effect. Through the quality of the voices created and what they say, a drama is constructed. The animation of voices breathes life into the characters and their story.

## CONSTRUCTED DIALOGUE
## AS CONVERSATIONAL INVOLVEMENT

Friedrich (1986: 17) observes, "It is the relatively poetic nature of language, formed and articulated through figures of speech, that most deeply and massively affects the individual imagination." Constructing dialogue is a poetic process: It is a figure that fires the individual imagination. The creation of voices occasions the imagination of alternative, distant, and others' worlds.

Rosen (1988) argues for the crucial, transforming, and persuasive power of the autobiographical mode of discourse. As evidence, he cites Hymes's vivid description of a visit to Mrs. Tohet, an American Indian woman, and her account of a traditional Indian story. Hymes emphasizes the animation of dialogue in the woman's performance: "All this in detail, with voices for different actors, gestures for the actions, and, always, animation. For that, as people will be glad to tell you, is what makes a good narrator: the ability to make the story come alive, to involve you as in a play" (Hymes 1973: 14–15). In this account, it is the animation of voices that makes the story come alive, that involves the audience as in a play.

Rosen (1988: 82) takes another piece of evidence not from an exotic language and culture but from a very familiar one: academic discourse. He cites Gilbert and Mulkay's juxtaposition of the way a scientist told about a scientific idea in an interview and the way he wrote about the same idea in a scholarly article. This is how the scientist spoke about his reaction when a colleague first suggested the innovative idea: "It took him about 30 seconds to sell it to me. It was really like a bolt. I felt, 'Oh my God, this must be right! Look at all the things it explains'" (Gilbert and Mulkay 1984). In contrast, "In the formal paper we are told that the experimental results suggested a model which seemed an improvement on previous assumptions and which was, accordingly, put to the test." The drama of the revelation, its emotional nature, is submerged in the scholarly prose. The scientist communicated the emotion in his conversation by casting his reaction to his colleague's innovative idea in dialogue representing his thoughts.

The involving effect of animated dialogue is at the heart of Eudora Welty's location of her beginnings as a writer in the conversational stories she heard as a child in Mississippi. Welty writes that she was first exposed to vivid storytelling in the magic of dialogue when her family acquired a car and took a gossipy neighbor along on excursions:[5]

> My mother sat in the back with her friend, and I'm told that as a small child I would ask to sit in the middle, and say as we started off, "Now *talk*." There was dialogue throughout the lady's accounts to my mother. "I said ..." "He said ..." "And I'm told she very plainly said" ... "It was midnight before they finally heard, and what do you think it *was?*" . . . I might not catch on to what the root of the trouble was in all that happened, but my ear told me it was dramatic. (Welty 1984: 12–13)

In addition, Welty points out the active nature of listenership: "Long before I wrote stories, I listened for stories. Listening *for* them is something more acute than listening *to* them. I suppose it's an early form of participation in what goes on. Listening children know stories are *there*. When their elders sit and begin, children are just waiting and hoping for one to come out, like a mouse from its hole" (ibid.: 14). That listening is a form of active participation is also emphasized by Bakhtin (1986: 68): "The fact is that when the listener perceives and understands the meaning . . . of speech, he simultaneously takes an active, responsive attitude toward it." This is why storytelling is a key element in the establishment of interpersonal involvement in conversation. As Welty points out, the construction of dialogue contributes powerfully to this participation.

One reason for the involving effect of dialogue, especially dialogue animated with the voices of characters, is its particularity. Thus Voloshinov (1986 [1930]: 131) describes the power of what he calls "texture-analyzing" indirect discourse in the novel as a style which "incorporates into indirect discourse words and locutions that characterize the subjective and stylistic physiognomy of the message viewed as expression. These words and locutions are incorporated in such a way that their specificity, their subjectivity, their typicality are distinctly felt." The specificity and subjectivity of a reported utterance are created, even more strongly, in animated dialogue.

Becker (1984, 1988) emphasizes the importance of the particular in discourse as in linguistic analysis.[6] In narration and conversation, the particular enables listeners (or readers) to provide a subjectively real understanding by drawing on their own history of associations. Moreover, this participation in sense-making contributes to the creation of involvement that provides the emotional foundation of understanding in discourse.

## NOTES

Fewer than half of the brief examples discussed in this essay are also presented in Tannen (1986b). The complete narrative analyzed here is also presented in Tannen (1987, 1988). Material in this chapter is incorporated in *Talking Voices: Repetition, Dialogue, and Imagery in Conversational Discourse,* Studies in Interactional Sociolinguistics, no. 6, © 1989 by Cambridge University Press, and is reprinted by permission of Cambridge University Press. I have benefited from discussions of Bakhtin with Ray McDermott, Michael Macovski, and Mirna Velcic. The narratives from which examples are drawn were recorded by students in my Discourse Analysis classes in 1983 and 1987. I am grateful to all of them for recording and transcribing these stories and letting me use them. The narratives from which lines are excerpted here were recorded and transcribed by Gayle Berens, Diane Bickers, Susan Huss, Deborah Lange, L. H. Malsawma, Karen Marcum, Kimberly Murphy, Mary Ann Pohl, Faith Powell, David Robinson, Jane White, Nancy Zelasko, and Wendy Zweben. Names in all stories are pseudonymous.

1. The proverb is "Lu nekk manees na ko toxal, mu mel na mu meloon ba mu des wax." I am grateful to Carrie Kinney for bringing this proverb to my attention and to Hayib Sosseh for translating it.

2. Thanks to Catherine Davies for this observation.

3. Examples are presented in line structure, representing intonation units, to

capture in print the natural chunking achieved in speaking by intonation and prosody. In transcription, punctuation represents intonation, not grammatical conventions. Thus:

| . | indicates sentence-final falling intonation |
| , | indicates clause-final intonation ("more to come") |
| ?! | indicates exclamatory intonation |
| ... | Three dots indicate pause of one-half second or more |
| | CAPS indicate emphatic stress |
| ⌐ | Brackets indicate simultaneous speech: |
| ∟ | Two voices going at once |
| : | Colon following vowel indicates elongated vowel sound |
| :: | Extra colon indicates longer elongation |
| - | Hyphen indicates glottal stop: sound abruptly cut off |
| " " | Quotation marks are added to highlight dialogue |
| → | Left arrows highlight lines key to discussion |
| /?/ | Question mark in slashes indicates inaudible utterance |

When the intonation patterns of individual sentences are discussed, an attempt is made to represent intonational contours using the system developed by Dwight Bolinger: higher pitch and amplitude are represented by array on a higher line.

4. Transliteration of Greek follows conventions established by the Modern Greek Studies Association.

5. In this excerpt, three contiguous dots ( ... ) indicate a pause, as in the original. Three spaced dots ( . . . ) indicate ellipsis: a section is omitted from the excerpt.

6. Alberoni (1983) suggests that falling in love is always a matter of particularity: of acute perception and appreciation of the beloved's specificity, of associations with particular places and times that "produces a sacred geography of the world" (ibid.: 38). I believe that this parallel is not by chance, but rather that the particular is central to the emotional, which is the key to inspiration of all types: cognitive, intellectual, and creative as well as romantic. This idea is also echoed in Mary Catherine Bateson's (1984) recollection that Margaret Mead likened successful academic conferences to falling in love.

## REFERENCES CITED

Alberoni, Francesco. 1983. *Falling in Love.* Translated by Lawrence Venuti. New York: Random House.

Bakhtin, M. M. 1981. *The Dialogic Imagination.* Translated by C. Emerson and M. Holquist. Austin: University of Texas Press.

————. 1986. "The Problem of Speech Genres." In *Speech Genres and Other Late Essays,* edited by C. Emerson and translated by M. Holquist, pp. 60–102. Austin: University of Texas Press.

Bateson, Mary Catherine. 1984. *With a Daughter's Eye: A Memoir of Margaret Mead and Gregory Bateson.* New York: William Morrow.

Becker, Alton L. 1984. "The Linguistics of Particularity: Interpreting Superordination in a Javanese Text." *Proceedings of the Tenth Annual Meeting of the Berkeley Linguistics Society,* pp. 425–36. Berkeley: University of California at Berkeley Linguistics Department.

———. 1988. "Language in Particular: A Lecture." In *Linguistics in Context: Connecting Observation and Understanding,* edited by Deborah Tannen, pp. 17–35. Norwood, N.J.: Ablex.

Friedrich, Paul. 1986. *The Language Parallax: Linguistic Relativism and Poetic Indeterminacy.* Austin, Tex.: University of Texas Press.

Gilbert, N. Nigel, and Michael Mulkay. 1984. *Opening Pandora's Box: A Sociological Analysis of Scientists' Discourse.* Cambridge: Cambridge University Press.

Goffman, Erving. 1953. "Communication and Conduct in an Island Community." Ph.D. dissertation, University of Chicago.

———. 1974. *Frame Analysis: An Essay on the Organization of Experience.* New York: Harper and Row.

Hymes, Dell. 1973. "Toward Linguistic Competence." *Texas Working Papers in Sociolinguistics* no. 16. Austin: Southwest Educational Development Laboratory.

Reddy, Michael. 1979. "The Conduit Metaphor: A Case of Frame Conflict in Our Language about Language." In *Metaphor and Thought,* edited by Andrew Ortony, pp. 284–324. Cambridge: Cambridge University Press.

Rosen, Harold. 1988. "The Autobiographical Impulse." In *Linguistics in Context: Connecting Observation and Understanding,* edited by Deborah Tannen, pp. 69–88. Norwood, N.J.: Ablex.

Shuman, Amy. 1986. *Storytelling Rights: The Uses of Oral and Written Texts by Urban Adolescents.* Cambridge: Cambridge University Press.

Smith, Barbara Herrnstein. 1978. *On the Margins of Discourse: The Relation of Literature to Language.* Chicago: University of Chicago Press.

Tannen, Deborah. 1983. "'I Take Out the Rock—Dok!': How Greek Women Tell about Being Molested (and Create Involvement)." *Anthropological Linguistics* 25:359–74.

———. 1986a. *That's Not What I Meant!: How Conversational Style Makes or Breaks Your Relations with Others.* New York: William Morrow, Ballantine.

———. 1986b. "Introducing Constructed Dialogue in Greek and American Conversational and Literary Narrative." In *Direct and Indirect Speech,* edited by Florian Coulmas, pp. 311–32. Berlin: Mouton.

———. 1987. "The Orality of Literature and the Literacy of Conversation." In *Language, Literacy, and Culture: Issues of Society and Schooling,* edited by Judith Langer, pp. 67–88. Norwood, N.J.: Ablex.

———. 1988. "Hearing Voices in Conversation, Fiction, and Mixed Genres." In *Linguistics in Context: Connecting Observation and Understanding,* edited by Deborah Tannen, pp. 89–113. Norwood, N.J.: Ablex.

———. 1989. *Talking Voices: Repetition, Dialogue and Imagery in Conversational Discourse.* Cambridge: Cambridge University Press.

Voloshinov, V. N. 1986 [1930]. *Marxism and the Philosophy of Language.* Translated by L. Matejka and I. R. Titunik. Cambridge, Mass.: Harvard University Press.

Welty, Eudora. 1984. *One Writer's Beginnings.* Cambridge, Mass.: Harvard University Press.

# EIGHT

# On the Necessity of Collusion in Conversation

## R. P. McDERMOTT AND HENRY TYLBOR

### INTRODUCTION

Language . . . lies on the borderline between oneself and the other. The word in language is half someone else's.

— M. M. Bakhtin

In 1928, V. N. Voloshinov[1] complained that "all linguistic categories, per se, are applicable only on the inside territory of an utterance" and are of no value "for defining a whole linguistic entity" (1986 [1930]: 110). This essay begins with a whole linguistic entity by going beyond the utterance to the social scene in which it is embedded for a unit of analysis. Unlike some recent linguistic analyses that acknowledge that speech acts do not in themselves provide for discourse cohesion but nonetheless are restricted to speech acts for a primary focus of investigation, we start with the properties of social activities as the essential guide to analysis.

We start with some assumptions that are, by now, well informed: participation in any social scene, especially a conversation, requires some minimal consensus on what is getting done in the scene; from the least significant (strangers passing) to the culturally most well formulated scenes (a wedding or a lecture), such a consensus represents an achievement, a cumulative product of the instructions people in the scene make available to each other; and, because no consensus ever unfolds simply by predetermined means, because social scenes are always precarious, always dependent on ongoing instructions, the achievement of a consensus requires collusion.

Collusion derives from a playing together (from the Latin *com* plus *ludere*). Collusion refers to how members of any social order must constantly help each other to posit a particular state of affairs, even when such a state would be in no way at hand without everyone so proceeding. Participation in social scenes requires that members play into each other's hands, pushing and pulling each other toward a strong sense of what is probable or possible, for a sense of what can be hoped for and/or obscured. In such a world, the meaning of talk is rarely contained on the "inside territory of an utterance"; proposition and reference pale before the task of alignment, before the task of sequencing the conversation's participants into a widely spun social structure. The necessity of collusion in conversation has wide-ranging implications not only for how people use their talk in conversation but for how linguistics might profitably locate units for an analysis of conversation.

In this essay, we build a case for the importance of collusion in the organization of talk ("The Case for Collusion") and offer a brief example of how collusion operates in a conversation ("An Example: From Precarious to Treacherous"). From a transcript taken from a videotaped seven-person reading lesson in grade school, we try to give a sense for the complex contexting work people do to arrange for utterance interpretations consistent with, and not disruptive of, the situation the people are holding together for each other. With an example in hand, we attempt to highlight the dimensions of a collusional stand on conversation by contrasting it to the now dominant propositional approach and the recently popular illocutionary approach to language behavior ("Three Ways of Appreciating Language"). Each is discussed in terms of its definition of such fundamental notions as units of analysis, their function, the role of context in their organization, and the theoretical prize won by their description. The relationship between collusion and power is addressed in a final section.

## THE CASE FOR COLLUSION

> Discourses on humility give occasion for pride to the boastful, and for humility to the humble. Those on skepticism give occasion for believers to affirm. Few speak humbly of humility, chastely of chastity, few of skepticism doubtingly. We are but falsehood, duplicity and contradiction, using even to ourselves concealment and guile.
>
> — Blaise Pascal

We build on two common observations on language behavior to develop the claim that collusion is necessary for any conversation. The first observation has it that everyday language is irremediably indefinite, that every utterance indexes or builds on a wide range of knowledge about the world

that would require a potentially endless expansion for precise application. The second observation, seemingly contrary to the first, has it that
talk is so amazingly exact that participants can often talk their way to
long-term concerted activities and well-shared ideas about what they are
doing together (often far beyond any agreements immediately obvious in
a transcript of their talk).

During the past decade both observations have been secured with much
data. Under the banner of pragmatics, we have been shown how much a
person must know about the world to understand even brief utterances,
and, urged on by sociologists interested in conversational analysis, we
have been shown an amazing variety of interactional mechanisms that
conversationalists have available for directing and specifying utterance interpretations.

The collusion claim takes both observations seriously. It starts with an
appreciation of how much unspecified, and likely unspecifiable, knowledge people must have in order to understand each other. At the same
time, the collusion claim recognizes the powers of conversationalists to
use local circumstances to shape their knowledge into mutually percep-
tible and reflexively consequential chunks. This marriage of indefiniteness
and precision in utterance interpretation both requires and is made possible by conversationalists entering a state of collusion as to the nature of
the world they are talking about, acting on, and helping to create. With a
little help from each other, by defining what can (or must) be left vague
or made precise, they can shape their talk to fit the contours of the world
in which they are embedded, a world they can prolong to make possible
further interpretations of their talk.[2]

At its cleanest, conversational collusion is well tuned to people's finest
hopes about what the world can be—this often despite the facts, despite a
world that sometimes offers them little reason for harboring such hopes.
Examples include "We really love each other" or "We can all be smart."
Although making believe that such statements are true does not insure our
being loved or looking smart, it is an essential first step.

At its dirtiest, people's collusion amounts to a well-orchestrated lie that
offers a world conversationalists do not have to produce but can pretend
to live by, a world everyone knows to be, at the same time, unrealizable,
but momentarily useful as stated. Examples of collusion as treachery can
be cut from the same utterance cloth we used to illustrate collusion as
hope. "We really love each other" can still be said when both know the
statement as a cover for a relationship that offers only protection from
the imagined world beyond the relationship; we have it from marriage
counselors that under such conditions demonstrations of love can further
lock the participants off from the world and further limit the possibility of

their loving each other. Similarly, "We can all be smart" has its most frequent occasion of utterance the classroom, the very place, as we shall see, in which people organize significant moments during which smartness, and its opposite, must be alternately displayed, recognized, hidden, and held back, in which displays of smartness and stupidity must be choreographed into the relations people have with each other. Without resources for organizing conditions for making possible an experience of love or intelligence, their invocation points more to oppression than to hope.

By lies, we refer to a phenomenon far more prevalent than those in which speakers must first remind themselves what not to say on a future occasion, in which "one has to remember the truth as well as the lie in order to bring consistency to a recriminatory future" that could disprove the lie (Lang 1980: 535). We think this kind of conscious lying is rare relative to the amount of treachery in the world at large. One way of understanding social structure, in fact, is that it offers differential protection from confrontations in which pure lies must be told.[3] Institutional authorities are afforded various shelters from unpredicted accountability. It is possible to live lies without having to tell them. Our institutions secure such lives for us at every turn. Starting with the generalized gender configurations available in a culture to specific institutions built around informational entanglements (Hanunóo or Mehinaku courtship, Kpelle secret societies, Mediterranean honor codes, or a therapeutic halfway house for drug offenders in America, and so on), we can find people choreographing each other's behavior according to scores that remain ad hoc and tacit and which, if made explicit, would render the behavior that seems to service them useless. We should never allow ourselves to forget the warning of Nietzsche: "To be truthful means using the customary metaphors—in moral terms: the obligation to lie according to a fixed convention, to lie herd-like in a style obligatory for all" (1954 [1873]: 47).

The collusion stand on conversation not only unites apparently disparate facts about language behavior (indefiniteness and precision) but holds out the promise of a linguistics that could be useful to understanding the social situations in which people do their talking. Although it is a century since George Simmel told us that secrecy is at the heart of any social order and William James told us that hope is a human possibility only by spitting in the face of the odds, our social sciences have proceeded pretty much as if the conditions organizing our lives were well ordered, shared, available for common understanding, and easy to talk about.[4] The social sciences have proceeded oblivious to the basic conditions of our lives together. In the language sciences, this has translated into a focus on the sentence as if truth value or illocutionary force could be found in the utterance.

Now it appears that to account for even the simplest conversations, we have to take seriously the moment-to-moment hopes and lies that connect our utterances into coherent parts of the social order. Language analysis can lead us back to social structure. To the extent that collusion is essential to conversation, then its exploration cannot leave too far behind an account of the institutional constraints that have us colluding in the ways that we do. It will leave us in the long run wondering about the constraints we are working against that, if we are making up so much of our lives together, we manage often such impoverished versions of what is possible.[5]

Our discussion of the necessity of collusion in conversation could proceed from first principles: All action, said John Dewey, "is an invasion of the future, of the unknown. Conflict and uncertainty are ultimate truths" (1922: 12). This is no less true for speaking and listening actors than it is for acrobats and subway riders (whatever the differential in risky outcome). Without a tentative agreement about what the future is (no matter, for the moment, how fanciful or harmful it might be), how else could conversationalists achieve precise understandings from ambiguous materials without ever really saying what is going on? Clearly, conversationalists have to be working together, tripping over the same defenses, stumbling into the same understandings, and working to the same ends (if only to reach the silence at the conversation's end). How they do this work should represent an answer as to how their collusion is both made necessary and subsequently organized.

## AN EXAMPLE: FROM PRECARIOUS TO TREACHEROUS

> All lies are collusional; all truths are collusional. The nature
> of the truth is always bound by the shape of the context. . . .
> Truth and falsity are matters of agreement. . . . The conditions
> of sending the signal which arranges for deception may rest in
> a variety of places within the deception system.
>
> — Ray L. Birdwhistell

For an example of collusion in conversation, we can offer some talk between a teacher and her first-grade students filmed and analyzed in some detail by McDermott (1976). It is a reading lesson, and much of the interaction is around the issue of getting turns to read. Unlike turns to talk in most conversational clusters, turns to read are not just managed in the pursuit of other conversational goals but are often the focus of the group. It is in terms of turns to read that the group's talk is made directional, that it takes on meaning and carries social facts. The details of the taking turns to read system are constantly put up for noticing, analyzing, and interpreting, and their organization helps to curb the indefiniteness of talk, to make clear, for example, that "Me" is a call for a turn to read or that "Not me" is a request not to read while constituting simultaneously a display of an agreement to listen to another child reading. Collusion is visible in the ways the members have of instructing each other in the use of turns in organizing their interaction and is essential to their production of group order.

The case for the necessity of collusion in conversation is perhaps most arresting in the talk of one child, Rosa, who is often treated as if she had said something different than a literal interpretation of her words would indicate. That is to say, her words, imprecise on their own, are made precise by those about her in ways not well predicted by their propositional content. Literalness aside, how her words are used by the group seems much better described by the conversationalists' situation together as a particular kind of reading group within a particular kind of classroom, school, and wider educational community.

Rosa constantly calls for a turn to read by shouting "I could" or "I could read it." In addition, she complains when she is bypassed, "G ... Go around" or (long later and still without a turn) "I wanna go around." But Rosa almost never gets a turn to read; she is understood to be not very good at reading, and her status as a turn-taking reader seems to be problematic enough to be commented on at various times during the children's half-hour at the reading table with the teacher. Upon careful examination, it seems that Rosa is doing much work to arrange *not getting a turn:* everyone else is on page 5, Rosa on page 7 (as everyone can tell with a first-grade illustrated reader); as the teacher begins to call on another child, Rosa calls for a turn, just a fraction of a second behind; as the other children move up from their books to face their teacher and to call for a new turn, Rosa lowers her head into the book with her face turning away from the teacher. The ploys are numerous in kind and fast in occurrence.

Linguists have not had enough trouble with the kind of duplicitous talk just described. It has been unfortunately easy to put aside. Propositional analysis can chalk it up to the abomination of actual use in social scenes. However great the evidence to the contrary, no matter how much conversationalists seem to rely on meaning one thing by saying another, traditional linguistic analysis remains intact by claiming that the *literal* meaning of an utterance must remain the point of departure for describing how speakers understand each other.[6] The argument is that the meaning of Rosa's calls for a turn to read is quite clear; how else could they have been transformed into something systematically different from a literal reading. In addition, such a transformation in use would have been most likely signaled linguistically by some marked appeal to irony or subterfuge. However transformed by the situation, for most linguists propositions remain meaningful in their own terms.

Illocutionary analysts would take Rosa a little more seriously. They would try to extrapolate the actual conditions of the social actors so that their intentions could protrude without anyone having very literally put them into words. Again, the propositions would be understood on their own, albeit in a series. In either case, Rosa would be understood cognitively, as a strategist who was manipulating the social scene and the people in it with her words. What organized her words or their systematic interpretation would have been left undiscovered. Neither Rosa nor linguistics would have been well served.

The collusional approach to Rosa's talk forces us to take her situation much more seriously. We are not interested simply in speakers, or even speaker-hearer pairs and the ways they react to each other. Rather we are interested in ongoing social scenes into which people walk and talk their lives together. As Arthur Bentley said long ago: "Terminology has been poor in the social sciences, drawn as it has been from the language of everyday life—from the vocabularies of the manipulation of one man by another. But not the point of view of one toward another is what we seek, rather the very processing itself of the ones-with-others" (Bentley 1926: 457). We are not interested in Rosa the strategist but Rosa the participant. Rosa's words, Bakhtin reminds us, are only half hers. They must be brought to completion by the group. And all their words together, if well enough studied, belong to the conversation which is in turn a moment in a far more extensive conversation we might call American education (Varenne 1983).

A collusional approach takes it that Rosa does not act on her own; that the very machinery used to transform, reframe, or to put into a new key Rosa's talk is group-produced; that every member of the group helps to instruct Rosa to say what she says in favor of what she did not say, which, in fact, if she did say would break the conditions for the group being together in an order that they can recognize, use, and perpetuate.

The collusional stand further takes it that the work members do to construct a consensus (that we are all learning how to read) while allowing, ignoring, and hiding important exceptions (namely, that some of us are here only to not get caught not knowing how to read) is a direct product of the institutional conditions under which the teacher and children are asked to come to school. Their production and interpretation of talk must be understood as a product of their collusion in response to a complex institutional setting that requires that they talk as if they could all learn while they meanwhile arrange much of their day around catching each other at not learning (Hood, McDermott, and Cole 1980). In taking up utterances that seem to mean the opposite of what they would on their own appear to say, we have moved from collusion as a necessary solution to the precariousness of everyday life situations to collusion as a defensive tactic against the treachery of everyday life. There are reasons for "using even to ourselves concealment and guile." When further pressed, there are reasons for lying even to others, although we must remember, before hunting down liars, that "the conditions of sending the signal which arranges for deception may rest in a variety of places within the deception system."

It is not easy to describe an instance of collusion in conversation. One effort, particularly directed to linguists, is available in a paper by Dore and McDermott (1982). The dedicated reader can examine that data analysis in the light of the more radical arguments of the present account. The argument of that paper is that a particular "I could read it" by Rosa, by virtue of how it is said and its timing, is seemingly accepted as such by everyone in the group while they simultaneously act as if she had said that she could not read it and that a particular someone else had been given the turn to read. Rosa's claim for a turn appears at a time when the group is somewhat at a loss for a clear definition as to what they are doing together. By interpreting Rosa's utterance as saying something different from what it seemingly proposed, an interpretation Rosa helped them to, the members of the group used Rosa's call for a turn to establish both a turn and a reader (other than Rosa) for the turn. The point is that everyone used the primary practice of the scene, namely, the constant evaluation of every reader's skill and the avoidance of such evaluation by different members at various times, to understand Rosa's call for a turn as a suggestion that she be bypassed. The very conditions that allowed for the methods Rosa used to instigate her subterfuge were not only well recognized by the group, they were maintained and supported by every member's involvement with evaluation.

The present essay offers a different fragment of talk from Rosa's reading group (table 8–1). The scene opens with the teacher calling on child 4 (numbered in order around the table). Child 1 and child 2 have read page 4 to the group. Rosa is child 3. The teacher and the children raise their heads as child 2 finishes page 4, and the teacher turns her head toward Rosa, who has moved her head further down into the book and right, away from the teacher's advancing gaze. The teacher continues turning her head left, past Rosa, until she reaches child 4. She calls on him, "All right. Let's see you do it." He moans a complaint, "Unnh." Rosa begins to suggest that they take turns in order: "G ... go around." She is supported almost immediately by child 4: "What about Rosa [screaming] Sh .. she don't get a turn." Child 5 begins to chide Rosa, "You don't get a ... ," while child 2 also calls for a more rigorous linear order, "Yeh. Let's go around." The teacher then, after a nonvocalized false start and a nervous glance away, addresses child 4 very softly, "Jimmy. You seem very unhappy. Perhaps you should go back to your seat." Simultaneously with the teacher's attribution

Table 8-1. Transcript of Procedural Positioning, Getting a Turn 3

| | |
|---|---|
| Teacher: | All right. Let's see you do it. |
| Child 4: | Unnh |
| Rosa: | G ... go around |
| Child 4: | What about Rosa [screaming] Sh .. she don't get a turn. |
| Child 5: | [to Rosa] You don't get a ... |
| Child 2: | Yeh. Let's go around. |
| Teacher: | Jimmy [very softly]. You seem very unhappy. Perhaps you should go back to your seat. |
| Rosa: | Back to Fred, then back to me. No. Back to Fred, back to Anna, and back to Fred and Maria and back to me. |
| Teacher: | All right, Fred. Can you read page 4? |

of Jimmy's feelings, Rosa begins to lay out the order of the going around that she has called for; in none of the two or three versions she suggests is there any discernible going-around order. After Rosa has her say, the teacher calls on child 6, "All right, Fred. Can you read page 4?"

How can we understand Rosa's talk? Is she calling for a turn, seeming to call for a turn, simply showing that she knows some rules about turn-taking in rounds, or, as we suspect, arranging not to read while nonetheless appearing to be part of the group? The point of this essay is that there is no one answer to this question. Rosa's "G ... go around" may yield all the interpretations just listed. Some are more interesting than others in supplying insight to life in classrooms, and some are used more than others at various subsequent moments by group members. We should not expect Rosa to have a uniform stand serviced by her words. In the complex role that teaching-learning scenes play in the lives of young children, could we expect Rosa to be free of all the tensions of her community around the issues of relative skill, smartness, competitiveness, and the like?

As we flee from utterance complexity to a consideration of social context for a key to what Rosa might be talking about, we are offered some relief by the fact that Rosa's utterance does not stand alone. The question of meaning must be rephrased: What instructions are available in the scene for the participants to organize an interpretation of Rosa's utterance? Part of the instructions, of course, is Rosa's utterance; her talk reflexively arranges its own context and helps to organize the conditions for its own interpretation. And what does Rosa's utterance have to work with in arranging a hearing?

First of all, the group is organized posturally into a procedural focus or positioning well suited for activities such as getting a turn to read (for criteria establishing postural-kinesic events and their importance to the structure of interaction, see McDermott, Gospodinoff, and Aron 1978; and Scheflen 1973). That they are at a getting-a-turn-to-read relevant moment is everywhere available in their body alignments and attentional structure. Second, that such moments are delicate can be seen in the work members do to preserve them; for example, they all attend carefully to the beginning and endings and hold each other accountable for any disruptions of the apparent order. Third, within any positioning, alternative formulations of what might be going on between the participants are often attempted and usually abandoned; for example, while most are still calling for a turn-to-read, someone might start reading. Fourth, while working hard at keeping a focus organized and rejecting rival formulations, members of the group constantly make available for use the dimensions along which they can understand each other; for example, a child who does not follow the pattern of a procedural positioning may be considered a management problem, whereas a child who does not follow a pattern in a pedagogical positioning may be understood as a learning problem. Fifth, there appears to be a strong preference about how and when different dimensions can be applied; for example, the smart-dumb continuum is constantly applied in classrooms, and much interactional delicacy must be organized to apply the continuum only in cases when someone can be called smart. The application of the continuum to instances of "dumb" behavior does occur, but participants usually work hard to have it not noticed. Sixth, a getting-a-turn positioning does not usually attract the application of a smart-dumb contract set, and it is accordingly used as a moment safe from intelligence evaluations. By virtue of its comparative safety, it is used often as a place in which the participants prepare for some next intelligence display, including preparation for who might be subject to an upcoming evaluation. It is therefore a perfect umbrella under which to perform covert, unspoken evaluations that organize for more public contests in the next moment.

With all this going on (and the reader, for purposes of this essay, has only to agree that such events could be at work; it would take a volume to complete a description of the behavioral background), Rosa's utterance enters the world pregnant. As Bakhtin noted well: "Language is not a neutral medium that passes freely and easily into the private property of the speaker's intentions; it is populated — overpopulated — with the intentions of others. Expropriating it, forcing it to submit to one's own intentions and accounts, is a difficult and complicated process" (1981: 294).

The utterance is shaped to fit its occasion. The conditions that organize its production and interpretation are distributed throughout the system.

To the extent that "G ... go around" represents a hope, the possibility (no matter how improbable at the moment) of Rosa learning to read well enough to perform must be organized by all the participants. To the extent that it represents an institutionalized lie, a delicate way to avoid a confrontation with a smart-dumb contrast set, that too has to be organized across persons. Indeed, the lie has to be told against the background that everyone is still hoping, or at least making believe that they are hoping, that Rosa can learn to read.

Instead of asking whether Rosa is intending to get a turn—an unanswerable question anyway—if we asked about the social constraints to which Rosa's remark might be an appropriate and constitutive reaction, then we have to ask how the participants are playing into each other's hands (that is, more literally, colluding) to organize the world Rosa gets systematically instructed to avoid. If we could ask more questions about what issues our every institution has us avoiding, we would have not only a better account of social structure but a better account of the language tools people use to build social structure.

### THREE WAYS OF APPRECIATING LANGUAGE

> The salient aspect of the social fact is meaning; the central manifestation of meaning is pragmatic and meta-pragmatic speech; and the most obvious feature of pragmatic speech is reference. We are now beginning to see the error in trying to investigate the salient by projection from the obvious.
>
> —Michael Silverstein

There are a number of dimensions along which to rank different approaches to language behavior. Silverstein (1979) goes to particular pains to point out what cannot be accomplished with traditional analyses that focus on reference and what might be accomplished if we were to concentrate more immediately on the social facts produced with talk. This essay proceeds in that spirit. By starting with the collusion required of conversationalists, we move the social facts of which the people are a part to the center of analysis and their language can be understood for what it does within the social order. This approach gives us a different way of appreciating language behavior. It also requires a shift in some of the tools we have used to do language analysis.

In the following chart (table 8-2), we offer a simple scheme for contrasting a collusional approach to appreciating what people do with their talk with the more traditional propositional and illocutionary approaches that dominate contemporary linguistics. At its best, the chart should offer a snapshot of what each of the approaches is trying to accomplish and its underlying conceptual assumptions.

Table 8-2. Three Ways of Appreciating Language

| | Units of Analysis | Function of Talk | Role of Context | Analytical Accomplishment |
|---|---|---|---|---|
| Propositional analysis | Speaker's propositions | Reference | An occasionally necessary afterthought to cover possible transformations under supposed conditions of actual use. | Utterance X means $a$ or under special well-marked circumstances $b$ or $c$. |
| Illocutionary analysis | Speaker-hearer propositions and intentions | Expression and manipulation | A frequently necessary afterthought to explain how apparent social conditions regularly alter canonical propositional meanings to express speaker intentions. | Utterance X means $a$ under conditions $a$, $b$ under conditions $b$, $c$ under conditions $c$, where the conditions are defined by phenomena beyond the talk, such as statuses and roles, that transform the talk. |
| Collusional analysis | Scenes and social facts | Alignment and linkage, institutional maintenance and social change | An essential dimension of language analysis. As behavior reflexively organizes its own contexts, talk can be appreciated for how it organizes its own interpretation as a sequentially relevant element in a social scene. | Utterance X helps to preserve and organize the conditions for its own interpretation as a constitutive element of social scene. Institutional treachery and social transformation are constant possibilities around which interpretations are reflexively organized. |

The propositional approach focuses on the sentence as the unit of analysis, understands sentences in terms of their referential potential, and asks questions about their clarity and possible truth value. Propositional analyses produce statements of the type, Sentence X can mean *a*, *b*, or *c*. The variation in meanings available in the sentence is understood as contained within the sentence. Context is irrelevant and invoked only in the face of the abominations of actual use; it has no systematic bearing on utterance interpretation. Meaning is framed by the capital and the period without any reference to how, as Frake (1980) reminds us, plying frames can be dangerous or in any other way consequential for speakers.

An important, if partial, advance is made in the linguistic sciences when analysts start to look at the consequences of talk, at the effects speakers have one upon another. For a unit of analysis, speech act theorists stick closely to the sentence although they focus on what the sentence is doing in conjunction with other sentences. The utterance exchange is the purported unit of analysis, although the descriptions are deemed complete with the attribution of intentions. Talk is understood as being about the expression of intentions, and variations in utterance interpretation are chalked up to the complexities of organizing an identity in social situations; thus, hedging and mitigating can rule the discourse. The analytic product gives an appearance of being more complete than that of propositional analyses.

Dimensions of context are considered crucial to the description of the illocutionary force of speech acts. However, the use of context in the analysis is nonetheless an afterthought. There is still a reliance on a soup-in-the-bowl approach to context. According to this model, the soup has a life of its own; it is the substance which is placed in a bowl and accordingly shaped. In speech act analysis, propositional meaning is the soup (an alphabet soup, most likely, good for monologue, reference, and description) and the social statuses and roles of the speaker-hearer pairs are the contexts that organize the rewrite rules allowing the referential power of talk to be obscured enough to meet the demands of the social situation. Reference remains primary in the analysis, and the conditions of context are plied against what anyone could recognize as the canonical interpretation.

The problem with the soup-in-the-bowl approach is that it allows the assumption that the soup exists independent of the bowl, that the meaning of an utterance remains, if only for a moment, independent of conditions that organize its production and interpretation, that meaning exists "on the inside territory of an utterance." If, however, soup and bowl, behavior and its contexts, utterance and the hierarchy of scenes it serves, are all mutually constituted, then the utterance cannot stand alone; it cannot make meaning on its own any more than a fiber can make a rope, or a thread a fabric.[7] An utterance can only help to piece meanings together, and in so doing erases itself as the essential unit of analysis. Along with many other behavior sequences, an utterance becomes consequential in social facts, and it is to these facts we must turn for instructions on how to appreciate language as a social tool.

The collusion approach develops from a more reticular sense of context. It rejects the traditional notion of intention-to-mean as directly homing in on its object, but instead recognizes that the pathway of meaning of talk is by no means simple and assured. The behavioral stuff to which an utterance can make connections, and the connections the utterances make possible, are primary in the analysis. The irremediable absence of strict borders between persons and others, between acts and other acts, produces interactional puzzles that require constant alignment and collusion from participants (Plessner 1965; Wieder 1974). As we saw in some moments in Rosa's life, talk is primarily about alignments with others—alignments that run a moral order gamut from institutional manipulation to social transformation for the good of all, talk that runs the moral order gamut from hiding and lying to expressing a will to believe and consciousness-raising. An appreciation of talk as collusional raises the most basic human issues for our consideration. It is demeaning to the richness of talk and its talkers to limit its description to anything less than a consideration of the most fundamental issues facing people in social life.

## REMARKS ON COLLUSION AND POWER

The necessity of collusion in conversation raises two issues for the analysis of power in discourse. The first issue concerns how an analyst can find power in talk. Linguists have not solved this problem, nor indeed have they tried very hard. The solution will not be easy. The interactional residue apparent in even the most obvious patterns of form use, for example, the use of address terms or honorifics (French *tu* and *vous* and Japanese *keigo* forms being classic), has produced little insight into the more complex constraints operative in a social structure. The more subtle interactional dynamics underlying differences in timing, for example, in the frequency of interruptions and strategic silences (as between men and women), although important for orienting us to power issues, have not been any more helpful in supplying us with an exact calculus for locating the dynamics of power in social relations.

By its emphasis on plurality, a notion of collusion suggests that we give up the question of *who* has particular powers and move instead to questions of how social institutions offer *access* to various kinds of power and how various conversational sequences supply instructions to their participants for acting consequentially for the institution of which they are a moment. We do not need to know who is powerful; rather, we need to identify the resources supposedly powerful people have available and the instructions within the power system that keep them, by simply following their nose, knowing how to wield their powers. By focusing on the collusion between the apparently powerful and the apparently impotent, conversational analysis may alert us to the institutional constraints on communicative activities.

By its emphasis on institutional treachery, a notion of collusion goes further to raise the question of what people have to arrange *not to talk about* in order to keep their conversation properly con-sequential with the institutional pressures that invade their lives from one moment to the next. Bateson once noted that the key question to be asked of any situation is what one would have to do to tell the truth while a participant (cited in Birdwhistell 1977). This is a crucial remark, for a description of the constraints on people telling the truth, indeed of their even conceiving what a telling of the truth might be, represents a good description of the powers made available, fought over, or shied away from in a conversation (which is but a moment in the life of a more inclusive set of constraints called an institution). Institutional analysis might proceed by addressing conversational data with questions about what can be talked about while at the same time being kept quiet, handled delicately, lied about in a pinch, or confronted only under the most dire circumstances.

The second issue concerns what linguistics would look like if it were to take seriously that matters of institutional access and power are at the heart of most conversations. Gone would be a preoccupation with propositions that carry their own self-contained meaning, between sentence capital and period. The lonely speaker would give way to a community of voices, the proposition to the social fact. Gone also would be the speaker-hearer pair totally circumscribed within their own competencies, jockeying intentions back and forth in the name of felicity (although often behind her back). Speakers and hearers would instead merge in a language collective, struggling to wrestle meanings to the ground and to sequence them into the harsh realities of institutional constraints.

This essay addresses both issues by way of an example of collusion in conversation taken from some classroom talk that is impossible to understand, at least as the participants understand it, without reference to the social structural constraints in terms of which some things not easy to say nonetheless seem to dominate the conversation. That it is an American school, first-grade reading lesson conversation, as significantly different, for example, from an American family conversation, a Hanunóo or Balinese reading lesson conversation, or even an American school lunch conversation, makes a great difference in the understandings available to the participants in their interpretation and use of their own talk. In American schools, children must learn that the borders between competence and incompetence are not clearly defined, but subject to constant social rearrangement. Classroom discourse is dominated by questions of "Who can?" and, just as importantly, but far less often stated, "Who cannot?" This fact about classroom life is ubiquitous in transcripts from classrooms and the key to their interpretation (the same key the participants can be shown to be using in their orientation to both the said and the unsaid).

## NOTES

This essay was prepared in anticipation of the late Erving Goffman liking it. It is reprinted with revisions from *Text* 3 (1983): 277–97 by permission of the publisher, Mouton de Gruyter.

1. Under the guidance and likely authorship of M. M. Bakhtin (Holquist 1981).

2. Garfinkel (1963) has advanced the same point with his work on "trust" as a condition of stable concerted activities. Various other terms glossing the same phenomenon with varying degrees of consistency and success are "context," "frame," "key," and "working consensus." The term "collusion" adds to these, as Garfinkel would appreciate, a sense of institutionalization and even treachery that we believe essential (institutionalization as the arrangement of persons and commodities that have us necessarily trusting reciprocally in the ways we do; treachery as a measure of how far we will drive ourselves and others to believe in a world not well connected to our experiences).

"Collusion" has the further advantage of plurality, as is essential to any analysis of social behavior such as conversation. One cannot collude alone; it takes at least three persons (as if two to collude and one to interpret).

3. As Harvey Sacks (1975) has noted, there are numerous statements across varying occasions to which the "contrast set true-false" is not sequentially relevant. A description of the distribution of occasions for which the contrast set is relevant (and of the various statements that invite its application) might give us a revealing key to social structure. The important point is that talk seems well designed for making delicacy, avoidance, mitigation, and duplicity generally possible. Against this background, it appears that inviting a lie, lying, and catching a liar are socially structured games in which people together ignore the obfuscating powers of language to construct scapegoats and degradation ceremonies. The "outraged jeremiad is the mark of a moralistic rather than a moral society" (Shklar 1979: 24). In this view, conversational "delicacy," for example, an attempt to insure that "the fact that an answerer is not giving [some requested information does] not constitute a recognizable refusal to give it" (Jefferson 1978), represents a first attempt to escape the onslaughts of a true-false contrast set; lying is a next step for people in situations with fewer social resources for doing delicacy. An appre-

ciation of this fact can help move us from a cynicism about individual morality to a political involvement for making different kinds of morality possible; at best, the outraged jeremiad "is not without affect, because this type of antihypocrite does at least have a sense of what is wrong, rather than an urge to spread the blame" (Shklar 1979: 24).

4. The alternatives to the natural attitude have been important (Bernstein 1976). Robert Murphy has offered us a helpful guide in what he calls the first principle of Irish (at least in the sense of not British) social anthropology: "My theories do fit with the well-known Irish trait by which there is little correspondence, and indeed much contradiction, between what a person thinks, what he says, and what he does. Perhaps I can best explain the tenets of Irish Social Anthropology by reversing Durkheim's formulation of the relation between restless, shifting sensate activity and the collective world of norms. My own resolution of the problem, then, is: All things real are ephemeral; all things enduring are false" (1975: 55).

Edward Casey has directed a similar insight to our understanding of a descriptive enterprise as linguistics must be: "The surface at stake in description is a moving surface. It changes in and through time; and even if such changes are not detectable in a given time interval, their description is itself a temporal event" (1981: 199).

5. Grand theories of the world usually include an account of what has to be lied about. Timpanaro has offered a lovely account of a Marx-Freud contrast on the nature of the world that organizes collusion: "It is intriguing to imagine Freud's reaction if one of his patients—a neurotic, but a politically lucid one—in reply to the question which according to Freud was the best means of 'ensnaring' the patient: 'What would you consider was the most unlikely thing in the world in that situation: What do you think was the furthest thing in the world from your mind at the time?'—had answered: 'I consider the most unlikely thing in the world would be to see a capitalist renounce his own privileges without any use of force on the part of the workers he exploits.' At this point, there would surely have been an exchange of roles: Freud would himself have succumbed to the behavior typical of a 'patient,' he would have lost his temper or changed the subject—in short, have revealed 'resistances' so strong that he would not even have been aware of their existence" (1976: 59).

6. Owen Barfield (1962) has pointed out that the best of our talk, metaphor and poetry, thrives on saying one thing to mean another; the more one meaning lives as a modification of another, the richer the metaphor. Linguists have managed to avoid a careful look at how such talk is used in social life by giving great sway to the grammatical and referential workings of language. Nietzsche has bemoaned how deep this trend runs: "I am afraid we are not rid of God because we still have faith in grammar" (1968 [1889]: 34).

7. Bateson is essential here: "It is important to see the particular utterance or action as part of the ecological subsystem called context and not as the product or effect of what remains of the context after the piece which we want to explain has been cut out from it" (1972: 338). Birdwhistell adds an equal wisdom in an account of what a context is: "I like to think of it as a rope. The fibers that make up

the rope are discontinuous; when you twist them together, you don't make *them* continuous, you make the *thread* continuous. . . . The thread has no fibers in it, but, if you break up the thread, you can find the fibers again. So that, even though it may look in a thread as though each of those particles are going all through it, that isn't the case. That's essentially the descriptive model" (quoted in McDermott 1980: 4, 14).

## REFERENCES CITED

Bakhtin, M. M. 1981. *The Dialogic Imagination.* Translated by C. Emerson and M. Holquist. Austin: University of Texas Press.

Barfield, Owen. 1962. "Poetic Diction and Legal Fiction." In *The Importance of Language,* edited by M. Black, pp. 51–71. Englewood Cliffs: Prentice-Hall.

Bateson, Gregory. 1972. *Steps to an Ecology of Mind.* New York: Ballantine.

Bentley, Arthur. 1926. "Remarks on Method in the Study of Society." *American Journal of Sociology* 32:456–60.

Bernstein, Richard. 1976. *The Restructuring of Social and Political Theory.* Philadelphia: University of Pennsylvania Press.

Birdwhistell, Ray L. 1977. "Some Discussions of Ethnography, Theory and Method." In *About Bateson,* edited by J. Brockman, pp. 103–41. New York: Dutton.

Casey, Edward. 1981. "Phenomenological Method and Literary Description." *Yale French Studies* 61:176–201.

Dewey, John. 1922. *Human Nature and Conduct.* New York: Random House.

Dore, John, and R. P. McDermott. 1982. "Linguistic Indeterminacy and Social Context in Utterance Interpretation." *Language* 58:374–98.

Frake, Charles O. 1980. *Language and Cultural Description.* Stanford: Stanford University Press.

Garfinkel, Harold. 1963. "A Conception of, and Experiments with, 'Trust' as a Condition of Stable Concerted Activities." In *Motivation,* edited by O. J. Harvey, pp. 187–238. New York: Roland Press.

Holquist, Michael. 1981. "The Politics of Representation." In *Allegory and Representation,* edited by S. J. Greenblatt, pp. 163–83. Baltimore: Johns Hopkins University Press.

Hood, Lois, R. P. McDermott, and Michael Cole. 1980. "Let's Try to Make It a Good Day." *Discourse Processes* 3:155–68.

Jefferson, Gail. 1978. "What's in a 'Nyem'?" *Sociology* 12:135–39.

Lang, Berel. 1980. "Faces." *Yale Review* 71:533–40.

McDermott, R. P. 1976. "Kids Make Sense: An Ethnographic Account of Success and Failure in One First Grade Classroom." Ph.D. dissertation, Stanford University. Ann Arbor: University Microfilms, 1977.

———. 1980. "Profile: Ray L. Birdwhistell." *Kinesis Report* 2:1–4, 14–16.

McDermott, R. P., K. Gospodinoff, and J. Aron. 1978. "Criteria for an Ethnographically Adequate Description of Concerted Activities and Their Contexts." *Semiotica* 24:245–75.

Murphy, Robert F. 1975. "The Quest for Cultural Reality: Adventurers in Irish Social Anthropology." *Michigan Discussions in Anthropology* 1:48–64.

Nietzsche, Friedrich. 1954 [1873]. "On Truth and Lies in an Extra-Moral Sense." In *The Portable Nietzsche,* edited by F. Kaufmann, pp. 42–47. New York: Viking Press.

———. 1968 [1889]. *Twilight of the Idols.* London: Penguin.

Plessner, Helmuth. 1965. *Die Stufen des Organischen und der Mensch.* Berlin: Walter de Gruyter.

Sacks, Harvey. 1975. "Everyone Has to Lie." In *Sociocultural Dimensions of Language Use,* edited by M. Sanches and B. Blount, pp. 57–80. New York: Academic Press.

Scheflen, Albert E. 1973. *Communicational Structure.* Bloomington: Indiana University Press.

Shklar, Judith. 1979. "Let's Not Be Hypocritical." *Daedalus* 108:1–25.

Silverstein, Michael. 1979. "Language Structure and Linguistic Ideology." In *The Elements: A Parasession on Linguistic Units and Levels,* edited by R. Clyne, W. Hanks, and C. Hofbauer, pp. 193–247. Chicago: Chicago Linguistic Society.

———. 1981. "The Limits of Awareness." *Working Papers on Sociolinguistics,* no. 84. Austin: Southwest Educational Development Laboratory.

Timpanaro, Sebastiano. 1976. *The Freudian Slip.* New York: NLB.

Varenne, Hervé. 1983. *American School Language.* New York: Irvington Press.

Voloshinov, V. N. 1986 [1930]. *Marxism and the Philosophy of Language.* Translated by L. Matejka and I. R. Titunik. Cambridge, Mass.: Harvard University Press.

Wieder, D. Lawrence. 1974. *Language and Social Reality.* The Hague: Mouton.

# NINE

# Culture Troping: Languages, Codes, and Texts

## ALTON L. BECKER AND BRUCE MANNHEIM

BECKER: There is a term I find very hard to accept—the metaphor behind it, I mean. The word is *code* in all its forms—used to describe the process of *languaging*—or some important part of the act of languaging.[1] To use the *code* metaphor is subversive of a dialogic image of language. Where we customarily use "code" or "encode," I would say *shape*. To use *shape* rather than *code* involves a deictic reversal. The former constitutes a reality, the latter reflects one. In thinking about language, can we assume an objective reality outside language? Do we have an extracultural way to describe that reality? Shouldn't we bracket it from the start? I think that is the first step in building a dialogic image of language.

MANNHEIM: Just as much of our technical language does, the word *code* evokes a different set of connotations and a different set of prior texts for each user. I cannot assume in advance that the word *code* evokes the same things for you as it does for me. Ironically, then, in order to begin a dialogue about the dialogic emergence of language we need to negotiate the terms of our discussion, here, the word *code*. By doing so, we both agree to act as if we were using the word in the same way and call it into question.

The word *code* seems to have four connotations for you. Though they are wrapped together, each of them alone raises an important issue for linguistic and cultural analysis, each one having to do with the "insides" and the "outsides" of a code. These are: first, the stance of objectivity in trying to understand another language or culture; second, the idea that a code preconstitutes language, so that utterances and meanings are so to speak always already written; third, that it is a cipher in which a nonsemiotic and inert world is wrapped up into signs which we somehow impose on the world; fourth, that in order to understand language or a culture we must treat it as a collection of objects or forms that exist independently of the ways in which they are used in everyday life. Each of these senses of the word *code* has helped to shape the ways in which anthropologists and linguists have worked with the grammars and texts of other cultures.

BECKER: We need a fuzzy term to set atop our common endeavor, our dialogue. I certainly have no trouble with your deconstruction of the term *code*, but I'd rather put it aside than recount its past glories. I think we must "bracket" objectivity for the same reason Charles Sanders Peirce did, because he was interested, in his words, in "all that is any way or in any sense present to the mind, quite regardless of whether it corresponds to anything real or not" (Peirce 1958 [1878]: 130ff.). A process of coding raises the question of what is encoded: thought? propositions? One source of confusion is that computer language is a code—it rests on language and encodes language. So we need two terms: code and language. A language activity like translation encodes one language into another. What I want to put aside in bracketing objectivity is the assumption that there is a simple reality that English or Burmese or Quechua speakers encode in different ways—I don't think we can know that. It cannot provide the grounding of our dialogue. But it is such a persistent image of language that it represents the deepest and most pervasive kind of cultural troping that I can think of.

MANNHEIM: To put it another way, we cannot interpret other cultures or languages by assuming that there is a culture-free, nonsemiotic world that we can use as a ground for our interpretation. By doing so, we project the objects of our language, our semiotic world, onto another language. From the start, we erase a field of difference between the two languages. We habitually ignore the fact that different linguistic and cultural forms of expression have different objects. By doing so, we create a new field of difference in which the speakers of the other language must be using language differently: deluding themselves (intentionally or habitually) with contradictions, metaphors, symbols, and analogies while we are forthright and literal. And so we translate their language differently from our own: ours is instrumental, referentially flat and transparent, unelaborated and thin; their expressions are poetic, symbolically loaded and deep, thick with meanings, but always referring to our world of objects. A classic example can be found in Rousseau's *Essay on the Origin of Language* (Rousseau 1970 [1760]: 13ff.), in which he distinguished utilitarian languages ("languages of need"), spoken in northern Europe, from emotional languages ("languages of passion"), spoken in the Mediterranean, Africa, and the Orient. According to Rousseau, "emotional languages" were rife with "images, sentiments, and figures" (ibid.: 17). The sense that other cultures are thick with metaphor and symbols is a projection on our part, "overtroping," if I may be pardoned the neologism.

BECKER: The problem side of the code metaphor is that it usually projects a tropic depth which is but a projection on our part, but which is then "encoded" by a language. The first connotation we are disentangling is "objectivity." The second is related to it: that is the notion that language reflects the world rather than shapes it. If we bracket "objectivity," that ceases to be a question. We don't want to slip here, along the well-polished Western slide from skepticism into idealism and solipsism. A dialogic stance gets us beyond that, in that we are negotiating a ground between us, by thinking with each other's terms. And this figure applies to two people talking within a language as well as to two people talking across languages, except that there are more adjustments talking across languages. But it's the same kind of thing.

MANNHEIM: Let's consider a second metaphor, that of "text." Ethnographers use the word *text* in the familiar sense of a unit of connected, usually fixed, speech or writing, and in a less familiar sense, as a paradigm for describing social action. In the less familiar sense, some writers speak of "meaningful activity as a text" (Ricoeur 1981) or culture as an "assemblage of texts . . . which [we] read over the shoulders of those to whom they properly belong" (Geertz 1972: 26, 29). By treating social action as a text, the analyst acknowledges that it has an objective quality that removes it from the grasp of individual participants (cf. Mauss 1954: 76).[2] Once an event has taken place, its meaning has escaped the grasp of the agent of the event and becomes common currency of the participants. Later events can alter the interpretation, but they cannot erase the first event entirely. Similarly, no amount of "I meant to say . . ." allows a speaker to control the meaning of her words after they have been spoken. The deed, like the word, is half someone else's.

To treat meaningful action as a text is to avoid carrying some of the assumptions of everyday life into social analysis. Social events, including speaking, cannot be reduced to individuals because the process of interpretation is outside the grasp of individuals; for the same reason, meaning cannot be reduced to intentions. This is particularly important for cross-cultural ethnographic analysis, because once we give up the possibility of grounding cross-cultural analysis in a shared, noncultural world, we are tempted to seek a new common ground and project our own motives and interests onto others. To speak of "meaningful activity as a text" lessens that temptation: texts, after all, can be read and understood without the intentions or presence of the author. The image of "meaningful activity as a text" also forces the analyst to attend to the same evidence that participants use to interpret an event: its details. So it seems to me to be both reasonable and useful to describe social action as a "text."

But paradoxically it is the earlier, more familiar sense of "text" as fixed speech or writing that gives us problems. Texts are so familiar from every-day life that we eagerly look for and construct analogues to our texts in other cultures. We trope the textuality of narrative and myth in other cultures by editing them to conform to our prototypic texts, the flat, mono-logical, consistent, neatly bounded texts of newsmagazines and academic journals. What I'd like to suggest, rather, is that the *textuality* of myth and narrative in another culture may be so different from our own that we often don't recognize a text unless we trip over it.

Here's a case in point from my fieldwork with Southern Peruvian Quechua speakers. While working on a dialect survey, I asked South-ern Peruvian Quechua speakers for narratives (*kwentu* or *istoriya* 'story', both words borrowed from Spanish). Invariably I would hear back, "I don't know any stories." But I noticed late in the fieldwork that in the course of conversations, whole stretches of discourse were spun out that looked exactly like what Andean ethnographers and folklorists have been calling "myths," "legends," and "stories." The topics, themes, and roles were the same; the order of narrated events was often the same. But they were conversations. There was often a fragmentary quality to them. The tellers were easily distracted from the topic and would often go off on tangents. I sometimes recorded what seemed to me to be part-myths, at least compared with the canonical collections of Andean myths that ap-pear in libraries. And pieces of narrative seemed to float—in roughly the same form—from conversation to conversation. My experiences were not unique. In one of the earliest sources on Inka dynastic mythology, com-piled less than twenty years after the Europeans arrived in Peru, the writer complained that the native Peruvians wouldn't give him a complete nar-rative (Betanzos 1987 [1550]: 7). Similarly, the anthropologist Catherine Allen (1988: 96) observed that Quechua historical accounts have a frag-mentary quality, "cropping up in conversation every now and then." Nor is the elaborate co-participation structure of Quechua narrative unique ethnographically. Similar traditions of constructing narrative jointly have been observed elsewhere, ranging from true joint construction of narrative to stylized audience response (see Watson-Gegeo 1975; Burns 1980; Basso 1985: 1–36; Urban 1985; Duranti 1986; Goodwin 1986; Gnerre 1987; Price and Price 1991; Polanyi 1989: 43–107).

Here's an example. During an interview about irrigation, a woman named Cipriana began to discuss the walk back from one of the sources of a canal she uses to irrigate her fields, passing a place called "Rock Path."[3]

There's a mermaid there.[4]
One time we were going along and then
while we were going along, a HUGE woman was sitting on top of a stone!

We were going from here to irrigate our fields
So a person arrived there, on top of a stone,
It's not possible, right,
a woman sitting there at night, right
a woman as large as a WIDE LOAD was sitting.

Margarita, who was responding with surprise, anticipating every pause in the narrative with "huh" and repeating every "right" with emphasis, let out a cry of fright,

    A
      -Y
        -Y
          -Y!

Cipriana has her hooked now, and continues.

"What'll she do to us?
Perhaps she'll come out after us," we said.
"We'll try to go away as quietly as soft, spongy adobe."
So she just stayed,
and we didn't look back.

Margarita asks Cipriana whether she had a look at the mermaid.

Ah, we saw her in the moonlight,
she was carrying a load, a lady wrapped in a dark shawl, sitting on a stone.

Margarita responds and Cipriana continues,

That's right, we saw her in the moonlight,
That's right, a mermaid, sitting, right.

A small child interrupts.

The mermaid—right—sat, no? And how could she sit?

Cipriana's daughter, Lucinda, cuts in now.

She was dressed like this *señorita* [the anthropologist], right?

Margarita, who hadn't seen the mermaid herself, surmises that the mermaid was lovely and brown-complexioned. Lucinda adds that she had pretty earrings, and Margarita agrees. Lucinda mentions that the mermaid had a woolly dog with her; Margarita, surprised, repeats it and Lucinda agrees. They each agree another time. Then Cipriana prompts Lucinda by telling Margarita that *Lucinda* had run into her and saw her when she was just a child. Lucinda agrees, and the child wanders over and asks for something. Margarita asks about the mermaid. Lucinda hesitates:

> I ran into a different one, the height of that little girl,

pointing to the child. Margarita expresses surprise. Lucinda repeats herself and then describes the second mermaid sitting on the stone, dressed up in beautiful new clothes.

> She turned into my girlfriend when she appeared to me.

Surprised, Margarita stumbles over her next words.

> . . . on the side of the river, right?

And Lucinda answers:

> Yes, she was sitting right on the side of the water, on top of a stone.
> So, right, I'm approaching her saying,
> "That one must be my girlfriend" —
> um . . . there was one named Santusita —
> "This is Santusita," there she is, right,
> I was going along like this, okay,
> when I threw something at her to get her attention,
> but I couldn't get it to reach her, so I said,
> "Santusita, Santusita."
> When I threw another one,
> I couldn't get it to reach her,
> so as I got a little closer to her side,
> . . . a . . . what happens?
> she goes away, into the water!

> AYYY! And then?

> I was coming just before sunrise, so then, let's see . . .
> she goes away, into the water!
> I got scared and took off, saying,
> "Maybe she'll catch up from behind."
> I went off *really* scared.
> It was like that for me, too, *señorita,* that time.

Margarita — who hadn't actually seen the mermaid — points out that she had earrings. The older woman, Cipriana, agrees, emphatically: "exactly like this *señorita,*" pointing to the anthropologist,

> beautiful earrings, beautiful and huge, white ones.
> And her head tied with a white scarf.
> Ay!
> And also her dog was in front of her,

Again, this is Margarita, who is going on hearsay . . .

> I've heard that Rock Path is full of stuff like that.

Cipriana agrees:

Even if it didn't have a mermaid it would be fearful,[5]
since it makes the sound of drums.

Margarita just responds and Cipriana continues,

It makes the sound of drums
It makes the sound of a band.
We have our fields uphill from there. So . . .
When we're dead drunk,
when we drink somewhere
we come down the path asleep, asleep
                              drunk, drunk
we get here, right,
and it makes the sounds of drums and a band.

Margarita responds and Cipriana continues.

That's right, we hear it now when we are drunk,
but you don't even care, damn!
"Are you a person or a dog?"
saying, "damn, há,"
I go on swearing *(carajo),* cause
when you're drunk it doesn't matter to you.

Margarita suggests that the path is ugly and terrifying and all agree.

The mermaid story has all the earmarks of Southern Peruvian Quechua conversational narrative. It was constructed conversationally among three people, two of whom described personal experiences and a third who moved between giving limited (but essential) responses and adding details. The narrative was told in the first person and used two bystanders as sources for descriptive detail, a small child and the anthropologist. It came up in natural conversation, triggered by the anthropologist's questions about irrigation.

It is also typical of Southern Peruvian Quechua conversational narratives that the mermaid story was not organized around a single overall plot line leading to a denouement. Instead, the point of the story was to convey specific details, such as the appearance of the mermaids and the circumstances of the encounters, along with details that seem gratuitous, such as the sounds made by the place.

These features prevented me from recognizing that I had been recording Quechua narratives even as I was being told by speakers that they didn't know any. I expected oral performances of narratives that looked like the expository summaries I had read in modern field studies and colonial-era chronicles.[6] Instead, I found performances that challenged my stereotypes of texts and textuality. Let me explain why I insist that these performances are Quechua texts rather than spontaneous fantasies invented and shared on the spot.

The mermaid story is made up of significant units: the two encounters with the mermaids, the relationships between the participants in the encounters, the noises made by the place, and the relationship between the narrative and the setting. These units, or *modules* repeat themselves in other conversational narratives, sometimes in exactly the same form, sometimes with relationships reversed or transformed in another way, sometimes through summaries or allusions. The same modules also appear in the canonical collections of Quechua myths, beginning with the myths recorded in sixteenth- and seventeenth-century accounts of native Peru. Any single performance stitches together a series of modules, which derive their meanings—in part—from a larger discursive field made up of interlocking narrative modules.[7] The modules of the mermaid story relate it to a story about a city that was flooded by a male supernatural being as revenge for refusing hospitality.[8] This story, which is known throughout the Andes, was recorded as early as the beginning of the seventeenth century. By anyone's criteria it is a "text." Both of these stories, or better, their constituent modules, are part of a larger discursive field that established a moral alignment between irrigation, gender relations, and sociability. To put it differently, these are texts—rather than spontaneous conversations—because of their relationships to other texts (or textual modules) (cf. Derrida 1967: 227; 1979: 84).

Southern Quechua narratives seem fragmented and highly context-dependent because they are constructed within a social-cultural framework that values consistency with the context of situation more than consistency within or between discourses. It is not accidental that Cipriana and Lucinda discussed mermaids in the midst of an interview about irrigation. But the modules need not be consistent with each other. For instance, you can be told in the morning about the little people of an earlier age who live beneath the earth and in the evening that the earth is filled with water, both versions by the same person. As a result, I have a great deal of difficulty with linguistic approaches to texts that assume that the linguistic features of the text are there to assure "coherence" or global consistency.

Though the two encounters with the mermaid are described in the first person, this is not an unusual feature of Southern Peruvian Quechua narratives, nor a way to distinguish narratives from other forms of speech. On another occasion, a young man described in the first person a battle that took place during the War of the Pacific (1879–83). Just as in much of South America, narrative requires the participation of more than one person in the telling. In Quechua, the degree of participation ranges from limited responses and questions (like the responder or "what sayer" described by

Ellen Basso [1985: 15–18] for the Kalapalo of Brazil), in which the listener yields authority over the narrative events to the narrator, to an open-ended conversational format in which the talk moves seamlessly from conversation to narrative and back again, and in which no single speaker assumes such authority. Southern Peruvian Quechua narrative requires at least the limited participation of a "what sayer," but in general is highly interactive. The narrative text is an emergent property of the performance (cf. Bauman 1977: 37–45; Tedlock 1983: 16–17; Basso 1985: 1–10).

Where do the single-voiced, expository texts that appear in ethnographic monographs and folklore collections come from? In good part, they are a product of the interaction between the ethnographer and native Andeans.[9] In other words, ethnographers create the contexts within which the speech forms that we identify as texts emerge. On the one hand, ethnographers typically write themselves out of the speech events in which texts are built; at most they participate as "what sayers." On the other hand, ethnographers maintain authority over the situation in which the text is inscribed as an ethnographic datum, by tape-recording a single individual or by taking dictation of a remembered text and editing it to conform to their own canons of textuality.

BECKER: So far we've put aside two metaphors that have been very useful in the past: *code* and *text*. When we treat language as code we presuppose something it encodes, and when we treat language as text we assume something like a genre, a set of prior texts of which this one is a current instance. I've always felt that the hardest thing to get to in studying southeast Asian languages is a sense of the extent to which someone is saying something new and original or something old and stereotyped. All language is both speaking the past and speaking the present. Lingual memory is something like what Alfred L. Kroeber (1944: 215ff.) called a "philology," a set of prior texts and whatever tools we need for getting at them when they are getting too distant, like grammars and dictionaries.

One of my favorite terms from Javanese, *jarwa dhosok,* means pushing *(dhosok)* old language *(jarwa)* into the present. I used to think that they sometimes pushed too hard, as when a puppeteer pushed an old Javanese word into Sanskrit or English. Part of a long colonial experience is to be troped so much that you don't trust your own philology. The claim of Sanskrit in southeast Asia was that it was the one true language, spoken by the gods. History shows that for a time this claim was believed. Philology became hunting for the Sanskritic elements in one's own language and translating Sanskrit texts into it. In that way Sanskritic philology invaded Javanese and enriched it. (I think of Bali, still living with great richness within Sanskrit texts.) Isn't troping, from inside or outside the language, a normal and healthy way for a philology to change and grow?

MANNHEIM: It is, but we might distinguish between the troping that takes place when an old text is pushed into the present, in other words, "troping within a tradition," and the troping that takes place when the tradition itself is made the object of study. Along with being a symptom of domination, "troping within a tradition" can be a potent source of the forms and symbols by which people organize their responses to domination. When a tradition is itself made the object of study and the terms of our discourse are drawn from outside of that tradition, as it is in ethnography, troping might be unavoidable. As ethnographers, we need to maintain a critical focus on the nature and sources of culture troping itself. The point of ethnography is to get out of our own skins and into the forms and interpretive patterns of other cultures. Otherwise, the best we can do is to amuse ourselves with exoticism and the worst is to lapse into solipsism.

BECKER: Isn't this where the "dialogic" comes in—where it differs from dialectic? The problem with dialectic is that it is an antagonistic trope, oppositional, in which a synthesis comes out of opposition. But we can try to *sustain* each other, and that's the better option. If I try very hard I can let my understanding of Burmese or Javanese interact with my North American mind, without harm to Burma or Java: scholarly *ahimsa*. The process by which it's done isn't new. I learned it from the Bible translators, for whom these have long been serious issues. It's what is called back-translation: that is, starting with a translation, which was usually the ending point of traditional philology, and comparing it, bit by bit, with the original, bringing out the differences between the translation (and its context) and the original (and its context). The goal is utopian, "emic understanding," as Pike (1954: 15ff.) called it. But it is nonetheless serious and important for being utopian, like many tasks we take part in, like marriage and teaching *and* translating.

In a back-translation, the translation and the source are put side by side. Each comments on the other. In back-translation the discipline comes not from me, but from the source, the distant text and its context. A back-translation is elusive, always slightly out of reach. But it is what allows me to correct errors. There are two kinds of errors, according to Ortega y Gasset (1959: 17): those things in my translation that have no counterpart in the source, *exuberances;* and those things in the source that have no counterpart in the translation, *deficiencies.* Back-translation is a process of putting aside exuberances and filling in deficiencies. It's utopian, but necessary in order to correct the pathologies of misunderstanding across languages.[10]

Here is the merest beginning of a back-translation of the first two lines of a poem by one of Java's greatest poets, Raden Ngabehi Ranggawarsita. It was translated by Clifford Geertz (1960: 281). It is a beautiful poem and there are many more things to say about it than can be said here.[11] Geertz's translation reads:

> We have lived to see a time without order
> In which everyone is confused in his mind.

His source sounds like this — a well-known phrase to all Javanese:

> Anglakoni jaman édan
> Éwuh aya ing pambudi.[12]

Now let me just list the exuberances and deficiencies of Geertz's translation. Please understand that this is not a criticism of his translation; it may well be the best translation possible in English. It has inspired and moved many readers of *The Religion of Java*. The exuberances and deficiencies are inevitable, since there are two languages involved. Neither language has to give in to the other.

Here is a partial list of exuberances in these two lines, the things in English which have no counterparts in the Javanese original:

> we
> tense-aspect
> to
> a
> in
> which
> everyone
> is -ed
> his

These are just the grammatical exuberances. There are lexical exuberances as well, such as "live," "time," "order," "confused," and "mind." There are all the exuberances of the prior texts this English passage evokes for us, unknown in Javanese understanding. There are the exuberances of the English poetics, the rhythm and sound play, exuberances of the medium itself. When we peel away exuberances we are left with the thin, sparse landscape that we often experience in careful translations from languages that are unrelated to English. It is not only a sparse landscape but an incoherent one, since the very exuberances removed from the translation, such as *we*-pronouns, tense-aspect, articles, and number, are the grammatical devices that make English coherent.

The grammatical devices that make one's own language coherent are so powerful that speakers (including linguists) often assume that person, tense, articles, and number are "understood" even when they are not expressed. This is "grammar troping." When I have said that certain southeast Asian languages don't have tense, people have heard me saying

that southeast Asians don't know today from yesterday or something out-
rageous and insulting like that. The point is that some southeast Asian
languages don't use tense to make their texts coherent.

In the same way, we don't use elaborate deixis, classifiers, reduplication,
or zero anaphora to make our texts coherent. These grammatical devices
don't have English names: the ones used here are approximations. They
are the deficiencies, the things in the original that are not in the English.
Here is the beginning of a list:

> the verb affix system: *ang-i, a-*
> derivational morphology: *pambudi-*
>> from
>> Skt: *budi* = consciousness'
>> Jav. prefix: *pam-* '-er' > "consciousness-er"
> the parallelism of the lines
> the rhyme, evoking a genre *(sinom macapat)*

The deficiencies of English defamiliarize our world, like a good poem.
Let me further defamiliarize the second line:

> *Éwuh = a + iwuh,* is a word one might use if one were staying in a strange
> house, awkward, reluctant to act, "confused" in that sense.

> *Aya,* the second word, might describe a situation in which one was wading
> upstream, against the flow, increasingly having to make more effort,

so that one is not at home in one's own consciousness, struggling more
and more. This is the statement of a Javanese intellectual, the keeper of the
canonic Javanese philology, the *Pustaka Raja,* in the court of Surakarta,
describing the state of being colonized by the Dutch, in which one's own
consciousness is like an unfamiliar house. He's talking about what we're
talking about, being troped.

So, where does the back-translation stop? One answer is that it stops
when we get an aesthetic sense of the power of the original.

MANNHEIM: "Back-translation" never stops. It is part of identifying differences between the conditions under which texts and cultural actions are
shaped within two traditions. Translation, then, is a way of questioning all
the conditions under which texts are shaped in the other culture and in
our own.

This project is fundamentally dialogical in that we give up a certain authority over both the other culture's texts and our interpretations of them.
To put it another way, at the same time as we construct an interpretation of
another culture's texts in our own tradition, we relinquish the grounds we
take for granted: the ontological, grammatical, and pragmatic grounds of
our linguistic practices are relinquished *to the text.* We interrogate the text,

as philologists should. But it also interrogates us. When it throws our foundational assumptions into doubt in the course of analyzing it, we *begin* to avoid what James Boon (1982) has called "the exaggeration of cultures," or what we have called "culture troping." If the task of anthropology is to constitute and interpret cultural difference, we need to make certain that these differences are not simply projections of our own metaphysic.

BECKER: And so, a dialogue is not an opposition but the preservation of two logics. The problem with terms like *code* and *text* is that they don't get at this idea of interactive strengthening and the interpersonal attunement that goes with it.

MANNHEIM: In our dialogue, we questioned each other's use of the words *code* and *text* as analytical terms. We argued that these terms smuggled unwanted assumptions with them that led to overinterpreting or "troping" the other culture. And in both cases we propose to bring culture troping under control by displacing these terms, *code* and *text,* from their places in our everyday discourse. For you the *text* becomes the starting point of a dialogical philology, by which the ethnographer returns a translation to its source. For me, *code* becomes a way of talking about differences in cultural patterns. I would redefine code from its usual sense as a formal system which is constitutive of practices to one by which practices are understood within a culture, a tacit philology (see Mannheim 1987). Each in our own way seeks to undermine the authority of our interpretive metaphors.

## NOTES

"Culture Troping" was originally written as the script of an oral dialogue, which was presented at the annual meeting of the American Anthropological Association in 1984. Each turn in the dialogue was written in sequence. We used the dialogue form to express very substantial differences in the ways in which we approached language ethnographically, in order to invite our listeners and readers into the fissures between us. Of the friends and colleagues who have commented on this dialogue in preliminary form, we especially wish to thank Laura Ahearn, Lee Bolinger, John D'Arms, Kenneth Dewoskin, Piotr Micholowski, Susan U. Philips, Joseph Vining, James Boyd White, and Christine Whitman.

1. Becker follows the philosopher-biologist Humberto Maturana in using "languaging" instead of "language" in order to emphasize that it is "an historical process of continuous orientation," in which "the new state in which the system finds itself after a linguistic orientation emerges from the linguistic behavior" (Maturana and Varela 1980: 34).

2. As Ricoeur (1981: 201) puts it, "the text's career escapes the finite horizon lived by its author."

3. The mermaid story was told to Diane Hopkins during joint fieldwork with Mannheim in Andahuaylillas (Quispichanchi, Department of Cuzco, Peru) in 1978. I am grateful to Dr. Hopkins for discussing her interpretation with me. The relationship between hydraulics and gender in this and related narratives is the subject of her unpublished paper, "Symbol and Structure in Quechua Myth: *Sirenas* and Sunken Cities," which I have drawn on in this analysis. The names of the speakers are pseudonyms.

4. The Quechua word for mermaid, *sirena*, is a borrowing from Spanish. There are other water beings in the Quechua world as well, so I am not certain that the idea of a mermaid is also a borrowing. It could be nothing more than a female water being.

5. Or "mermaids." Since number is not an obligatory category in Quechua grammar, the phrase could be translated as either singular or plural.

6. It would be a mistake to pose this problem in terms of "our" conventions for texts versus "theirs" or in terms of "literate" versus "oral" traditions. Although scholarly stereotypes of "texts" are based on written genres—my own expectations were formed by the conventions for expository prose—these stereotypes fall short on both counts. They do justice to neither the complex polyphony of writing in American society nor traditions of oral performance that are similar to the Quechua. See Polanyi (1989: 43–107) for an account of North American conversational narrative.

7. See Lévi-Strauss 1971: 576ff. I discuss the modular nature of Southern Peruvian Quechua narrative in more detail in Mannheim (1991).

8. The noise made by the place inhabited by mermaids is an index of the relationship between the texts.

9. Ellen Basso (1985: 11) writes, "Published myths are factitious objects—what we call texts—that are the products of a complex process of recording, transcribing, translating, and ultimately presenting them on the printed page according to a selected plan of arrangement." See Hanks (1989) and Bauman and Briggs (1990) for broad-gauged discussions of ethnographic issues surrounding textuality.

10. These points are elaborated in Becker (1982, 1988).

11. Joseph Errington (1989) has made a fine translation of the whole work from which it comes.

12. Errington (1989: 109) bases his analysis on a different textual variant in which the couplet discussed here is

> Amenangi jaman édan
> éwuh aya ing pambudi
>
> To know oneself the troubled times
> is to know trouble in one's mind.

## REFERENCES CITED

Allen, Catherine J. 1988. *The Hold Life Has: Coca and Cultural Identity in an Andean Community.* Washington, D.C.: Smithsonian Institution Press.

Basso, Ellen B. 1985. *A Musical View of the Universe.* Philadelphia: University of Pennsylvania Press.

Bauman, Richard. 1977. *Verbal Art as Performance.* Rowley, Mass.: Newbury House.

Bauman, Richard, and Charles L. Briggs. 1990. "Poetics and Performance as Critical Perspectives on Language and Social Life." *Annual Review of Anthropology* 19:59-88.

Becker, Alton L. 1982. "The Poetics and Noetics of a Javanese Poem." In *Spoken and Written Language,* edited by Deborah Tannen, pp. 217-38. Norwood, N.J.: Ablex.

———. 1988. "Attunement: An Essay on Philology and Logophilia." In *On the Ethnography of Communication: The Legacy of Sapir,* edited by Paul Kroskrity, pp. 109-46. Los Angeles: University of California at Los Angeles Department of Anthropology.

Betanzos, Juan de. 1987 [1550]. *Suma y Narración de los Incas.* Edited by María del Carmen Martin Rubio. Madrid: Atlas.

Boon, James. 1982. *Other Tribes, Other Scribes.* Cambridge: Cambridge University Press.

Burns, Allan F. 1980. "Interactive Features in Yucatec Mayan Narratives." *Language in Society* 9:307-19.

Derrida, Jacques. 1967. *De la Grammatologie.* Paris: Minuit.

———. 1979. "Living On: Borderlines." In *Deconstruction and Criticism,* edited by Harold Bloom et al., pp. 75-176. New York: Seabury.

Duranti, Alessandro. 1986. "The Audience as Co-Author: An Introduction." *Text* 6:239-47.

Errington, J. Joseph. 1989. "To Know Oneself the Troubled Times: Ronggawarsita's *Serat Kala Tidha.*" In *Writing on the Tongue,* edited by A. L. Becker, pp. 95-138. Ann Arbor: University of Michigan Center for South and Southeast Asian Studies.

Geertz, Clifford. 1960. *The Religion of Java.* New York: Free Press.

———. 1972. "Deep Play: Notes on a Balinese Cockfight." *Daedelus* 101:1-37.

Gnerre, Maurizio. 1987. "The Decline of Dialogue: Ceremonial and Mythological Discourse among the Shuar and Achuar." In *Native South American Discourse,* edited by Joel Sherzer and Greg Urban, pp. 307-41. Berlin: Mouton de Gruyter.

Goodwin, Charles. 1986. "Audience Diversity, Participation, and Interpretation." *Text* 6:283-316.

Hanks, William F. 1989. "Texts and Textuality." *Annual Review of Anthropology* 18:95-127.

Kroeber, Alfred L. 1944. *Configurations of Cultural Growth.* Berkeley: University of California Press.

Lévi-Strauss, Claude. 1971. *L'Homme Nu.* Paris: Plon.

Mannheim, Bruce. 1987. "A Semiotic of Andean Dreams." In *Dreaming: Anthropological and Psychological Interpretations,* edited by Barbara Tedlock, pp. 132-53. Cambridge: Cambridge University Press.

———. 1991. "After *Dreaming:* Image and Interpretation in Southern Peruvian Quechua." *Etnofoor* 4, no. 2:43-79.

Maturana, Humberto R., and Francisco J. Varela. 1980. "Biology of Cognition." In

*Autopoesis and Cognition: The Realization of the Living,* pp. 1–58. Dordrecht: Reidel.

Mauss, Marcel. 1954. *The Gift.* Translated by Ian Cunnison. London: Cohen and West.

Ortega y Gasset, José. 1959. "The Difficulty of Reading." *Diogenes* 28:1–17.

Peirce, Charles Sanders. 1958 [1878]. "How to Make Our Ideas Clear." In *Values in a Universe of Chance,* edited by Philip P. Wiener, pp. 113–36. Garden City, N.Y.: Anchor.

Pike, Kenneth L. 1954. *Language in Relation to a Unified Theory of Human Behavior.* Vol. 1. Glendale, Calif.: Summer Institute of Linguistics.

Polanyi, Livia. 1989. *Telling the American Story: A Structural and Cultural Analysis of Conversational Storytelling.* Cambridge, Mass.: MIT Press.

Price, Richard, and Sally Price. 1991. *Two Evenings in Saramaka.* Chicago: University of Chicago Press.

Ricoeur, Paul. 1981. *Hermeneutics and the Human Sciences.* Cambridge: Cambridge University Press.

Rousseau, Jean-Jacques. 1970 [1760]. *Essai sur l'Origine des Langues,* edited by Charles Porset. Bordeaux: Ducros. Page citations are to the manuscript pagination.

Tedlock, Dennis. 1983. *The Spoken Word and the Work of Interpretation.* Philadelphia: University of Pennsylvania Press.

Urban, Greg. 1985. "The Semiotics of Two Speech Styles in Shokleng." In *Semiotic Mediation,* edited by Elizabeth Mertz and Richard J. Parmentier, pp. 311–29. Orlando, Fla.: Academic.

Watson-Gegeo, Karen Ann. 1975. "Transferable Communicative Routines: Strategies and Group Identities in Two Speech Events." *Language in Society* 4:53–72.

## TEN

# Interpretation, Participation, and the Role of Narrative in Dialogical Anthropology

### DENNIS TEDLOCK

Q. Hasn't anthropology always been dialogical anyway? Isn't that what fieldwork is all about in the first place, conversations between anthropologists and others?

A. Yes, but when anthropologists come home and write canonical ethnographies, they adopt the voice of a third-person omniscient narrator and reduce the voices of the others to a few untranslatable "native terms."

Q. Don't some authors of ethnographies include quotations from what their informants said in interviews, or quotations from oral performances, or both?

A. They do indeed, though there are plenty of writers of ethnographies, scores upon scores of them all the way down to the present, whose only quotations are from other anthropologists. And for that matter, even when a few native lines do appear, they seem to have been inserted for the sake of illustrating some point the writer was already trying to make, the very reverse of hermeneutics.

Q. What's wrong with trying to illustrate a point? Surely you don't expect *all* anthropologists to be *interpretive* anthropologists.

A. Ah, but that's just it. Ethnographers, *all* of them, already *are* interpretive anthropologists, in practice if not in print. In the field they engage in hermeneutical dialogues with the natives, and they shift to an internal dialogue when they puzzle over their memory of what the natives said, or else their recordings or field notes. But the only kind of dialogue they put out front in ethnographies is one in which the natives speak briefly, on cue, and in support of the views of anthropologists.

Q. Are you suggesting that anthropologists suppress native statements that contradict their own lines of argument?

A. That's a problem, yes, but there's a bigger one. Anthropologists arrive at their views, or at least some of them, on the basis of native statements in the first place. But later, when they throw in an apt quotation from a native while making an argument, the original order is reversed. The native, who may have played a decisive role in the original conversation, is now reduced, in effect, to the role of confirming opinions already held by someone else.

Q. What about classic ethnographers of the kind Clifford Geertz discusses in *Works and Lives?* Didn't Bronislaw Malinowski go beyond what you're calling "apt quotation" in *Argonauts of the Western Pacific?* That book fairly bristles with quotations from Trobriand charms and stories.

A. In some ways Malinowski is indeed an exception. Where others might set up a quotation in advance and move on to something else the moment it's over, he often makes interpretive remarks afterwards, or interweaves the quotation itself with parenthetical interpretations. And his quotes are large enough, and numerous enough, to open the way for readers to make further interpretations, or even divergent ones. At the very same time, however, he works to efface the dialogical nature of the encounters from which he extracts these quotations. With one or two exceptions, he confers anonymity on all the persons he quotes. And as for those charms you mentioned, he assures us again and again that they are fixed texts, repeated word-for-word whenever they are used by whatever person.

Q. But Malinowski also quotes remarks Trobrianders made to him in conversation. What happens then?

A. Well, let's examine one of those passages and see what happens— or better yet, let's reenact it. On page 247, he quotes both sides of an exchange. Why don't I take the part of an anonymous Trobriander, and you can be Malinowski. But instead of playing him in his role as field-worker, you'll play him as a writer recalling what was said in the field. Our topic is *mulukwausi,* or flying witches.

Q. And you're explaining to me what the saying of a charm does to flying witches.

NATIVES: It darkens the eyes of the *mulukwausi,*

MALINOWSKI: or

NATIVES: It blinds,

MALINOWSKI: the natives will say. And when asked: "What do the *mulukwausi* see, then?" they will answer:

NATIVES: They will see mist only. They do not see the places, they do not see the men, only mist.

Q. Malinowski seems to want us to believe that this exchange could take place on an indefinite number of occasions, between him and an indefinite number of natives.

A. Yes, and to perform this passage properly we would have to make a multitrack recording, constructing one part of the dialogue from several native voices speaking in unison and the other part from several superimposed recordings of Malinowski's voice.

Q. Are there any other dialogues in *Argonauts?*

A. There are other fragments from Malinowski's conversations with the natives, but we've already read the only one in which he quotes both sides. Elsewhere he puts himself at a distance by describing what he said instead of quoting it. As for what the natives say on their side, between quotation marks, he frequently assures us that he's heard the same thing many times. But there is an admitted one-time exchange on page 273. You can play Malinowski the writer again, describing what you said. I'll play a man from the Amphlett Islands.

AMPHLETT ISLANDER: The Sinaketa men tell us that we will go to jail if we sleep with girls in Sinaketa. Would the Government put us into jail, in truth?

MALINOWSKI: As usually, I simply disclaimed all knowledge of the white man's arcana in such matters.

A. So just once, in the whole book, the natives ask *him* a question, and he refuses to give a straight answer. I say just once, but here again Malinowski makes a typifying move, and he doesn't spare himself: he tells us that on this occasion, he spoke "as usually . . . in such matters." As he conceives the business of writing an ethnography, one that went to press in 1921, neither he nor the natives have any proper business saying anything that should not or could not be said by a whole category of persons on a whole category of occasions.

Q. Let's try another of the classic ethnographers discussed by Geertz in *Works and Lives,* E. E. Evans-Pritchard. I seem to recall that in his introduction to *The Nuer,* he quotes a dialogue between himself and an informant that goes on a bit longer than those examples from Malinowski.

A. Let's have a look. Here it is, on pages 12–13. He presents it by saying, "Questions about customs were blocked by a technique I can commend to natives who are inconvenienced by the curiosity of ethnologists." That sounds a bit sarcastic, but since he's British we can guess that the dialogue that follows is intended for our amusement. And he goes on to soften his sarcasm to the level of irony, calling the quote a "specimen of Nuer methods."

Q. Don't you think it was sporting of him to concede that the Nuer, and not only ethnographers, have their "methods"?

A. Maybe so, but with the choice of the word "specimen," he safely removes this passage to the proper scientific distance, not only from his Nuer interlocutor but from a particular moment in history. But let's go ahead and dramatize this. We're somewhere on the Nyanding River, and it's around 1930. You take the part of E.-P., and I'll take the part of the informant.

E.-P.: Who are you?

CUOL: A man.

E.-P.: What is your name?

CUOL: Do you want to know my *name?*

E.-P.: Yes.

CUOL: You want to know *my* name?

E.-P.: Yes, you have come to visit me in my tent and I would like to know who you are.

CUOL: All right. I am Cuol. What is your name?

E.-P.: My name is Pritchard.

CUOL: What is your father's name?

E.-P.: My father's name is also Pritchard.

CUOL: No, that cannot be true. You cannot have the same name as your father.

E.-P.: It is the name of my lineage. What is the name of your lineage?

CUOL: Do you want to know the name of my lineage?

E.-P.: Yes.

CUOL: What will you do with it if I tell it to you? Will you take it to your country?

E.-P.: I don't want to do anything with it. I just want to know it since I am living at your camp.

CUOL: Oh well, we are Lou.

E.-P.: I did not ask you the name of your tribe. I know that. I am asking you the name of your lineage.

CUOL: Why do you want to know the name of my lineage?

E.-P.: I don't want to know it.

CUOL: Then why do you ask me for it? Give me some tobacco.

A. At this point E.-P. comments, "I defy the most patient ethnologist to make headway against this kind of opposition. One is just driven crazy by it." He goes on to complain of "Nuerosis." It could not be any plainer that this example of dialogue, the only example in the entire book in which both parties are quoted directly, has been offered as a pathological specimen — typical of the Nuer, but pathological among dialogues. The implication is that if he had found it easier to dialogue with the Nuer, he wouldn't have needed any example at all. A proper field dialogue would be a transparent medium through which information passed unaltered, no more substantial than the air we all breathe.

Q. But why *are* the Nuer such difficult people?

A. Well, we don't know whether they're generally difficult people on a permanent basis, or whether it's just that they were difficult with certain outsiders during the period when E.-P. was among them. He doesn't say anything about politics when he presents his specimen of dialogue, but the pieces of a possible story are scattered here and there in his book. It seems that he was in the employ of the government of the Anglo-Egyptian Sudan, a government composed of Britons and Arabs who were worried about maintaining control over the black Nuer. Not so many years before, when a prophetic movement was running strong among the Nuer, this government had used force to stop it.

Q. So the Nuer had reason to be cautious in their dealings with E.-P. As far as that goes, there could be no such thing as a field dialogue without a political context of some sort or other.

A. But there's an even broader issue here, which is that a dialogue takes place in historical time, not in the "ethnographic present." Neither the time and place of the dialogue, nor the persons who are parties to it, can be counted upon to stay outside the dialogue itself, in the realm of "context," but will enter the very language of the dialogue. At the grammatical level, there will not only be third persons but also first and second persons, as in, "Why do *you* want to know the name of *my* lineage?" There will not only be the Anglo-Egyptian Sudan, but also highly specific locations, as in "I am living *at your camp*" and "You have come to visit me in *my tent.*" There will be local places with proper names as well, and named individuals, and references to nearby objects and recent events. Such direct reminders of the human life world may be allowed to crop up in the introduction to an ethnography, as in the case of the present specimen, or else in footnotes or appendixes. Otherwise they are blurred or covered over with generalizations.

Q. What is it that makes "apt quotation" possible in the main body of an ethnography?

A. When quotations are put into a new text they must be cut out of a prior text, and the cuts that make them suitable material for the construction of an ethnographic present are the ones that remove the traces of concrete events taking place in historical time. And the first step in this process is to cut away the words of the field-worker. In the finished product, an anonymous native makes a statement to no one in particular.

Q. But once again E.-P. seems to be a bit of an exception. Look here, in chapter 4: he's talking with the Nuer again, and it's not in a footnote.

A. And amusingly enough, it's the chapter titled "Politics." But look again: the dialogue is a small part of a long passage that's been set in smaller type than the main text. It's a specifically British practice to treat precisely detailed passages in this way, even when they aren't footnotes or appendixes. Readers know they can skip ahead—unless they're the sort who like to examine the fine print, that is.

Q. It might've been an editor who chose the smaller type.

A. But even the internal construction of this passage reduces the impact of the dialogue. E.-P. makes the same moves as Malinowski: he removes himself from the field situation by describing *what* he said rather than quoting it, and he puts these particular Nuer at a distance, even while quoting them directly, by making them anonymous. Let's try reading the exchange at the top of page 183. This time, instead of playing E.-P. in his role as a field-worker, you'll be E.-P. as the writer of an ethnography. As for me, whoever I may be, I'll still be trying to give you a case of Nuerosis.

E.-P.: On one occasion some men gave me information about their lineages. Next day these men paid me a visit and one of them asked me,

NUER: What we told you yesterday, did you believe it?

E.-P.: When I replied that I had believed it they roared with laughter and called to others to come and share the joke. Then one of them said,

NUER: Listen, what we told you yesterday was all nonsense. Now we will tell you correctly.

Q. E.-P. goes on to say, "I could relate many such stories," which makes him sound like Malinowski.

A. Yes, it's like the dialogue in his introduction: he offers it as a *type* of exchange. He doesn't want us to take it for a *momentous* exchange. And once again, it's a specimen of dialogue gone wrong, dialogue as an obstacle to getting the facts about the Nuer. As for what these particular Nuer men actually said by way of "nonsense" or a "joke" on one day, and how it contrasted with what they said when they spoke "correctly" on the following day, we aren't given a single word.

Q. Why should E.-P. have used up space with nonsense?

A. Well, if the Nuer in general, and without reference to historical time, are people who are likely to devise false answers to questions when they give any answers at all, then false answers would themselves be examples of how the Nuer produce Nuer culture.

Q. If E.-P. had gone too far in that direction, he would've come even closer than he did to that old problem that goes, "All Cretans are liars."

A. That line was stuffed in the mouth of an imaginary Cretan, an "ethnic" Greek if you will, by an Athenian. In any case it's a statement of a *logical* problem, not a problem in the larger workings of a culture. Logic does its work all at once, without any reference to time outside the sequence of its own propositions, whereas a culture emerges on many different occasions—among them, yesterday's conversation with a field-worker and today's conversation. If we want Nuer culture to make sense all at once, we're in trouble. If not, we can allow the Nuer to produce a joke on one occasion and say things "correctly" on another.

Q. But how did E.-P. know they were telling him the truth on the second day?

A. If he had explored that issue in any detail, he would've had to give a full report of longer stretches of dialogue, and from more than just these two particular days. In effect, he would've been showing how culture, as reported in ethnographies, is constructed jointly by field-worker and natives. And once that comes out in the open, then the line between fact and fiction, both of them things *made,* is not as clear as it used to be.

Q. You're beginning to sound something like Geertz, in the last chapter of *Works and Lives,* where he locates ethnographic writing precisely on the frontier between fact and fiction, while warning us not to confuse the fictional with the false. Come to think of it, didn't he include some dialogue in *The Religion of Java?*

A. He did indeed, but he had his own way of keeping it at a distance. The book is full of quoted material, all presented as extracts, which is to say indented and in fine print, and in fact there may be more extracts than in any other ethnography ever published. But every one of them is a quotation from his own field notes.

Q. That sounds like an extreme case of academic self-referentiality.

A. Not quite. The texture of the notes is quite different from that of the main text. It could even be said that the person who kept those notes in Java was not quite the same person as the one who quoted them while writing a book back home. In any case, it is within the extracts from the notes that we get some idea of what some anonymous Javanese or other said to Geertz on a particular occasion, and, less often, what Geertz said to some Javanese. I say "some idea" because he mostly paraphrases what was said. Even when he breaks into direct quotation, he usually paraphrases his own side of a dialogue, just as E.-P. did in that last example. But here, on page 75, is an exception. Let's try reading it. We're in the town of Modjokuto, around 1953.

Q. And you're a seventy-year-old Javanese male.

ELDERLY JAVANESE: When you are dead you don't want anything: you don't want an auto, you don't want money, you don't want a wife, you don't have any wants at all. Like God—God doesn't need any money, or wife, or auto, does He? Well, that's wonderful, not to want anything; and after you're dead, that's the way it is.

GEERTZ: Well, if it is so good being dead, why don't people kill themselves?

ELDERLY JAVANESE: That would be wrong because it would be from your own will. It is up to God to decide when you should die, not yourself. It is wrong to commit suicide because you are trying to take into your own hands affairs which are properly God's.

Q. Geertz notes that the old man "was properly offended" by his question. I wonder why he would single out, for direct quotation, an exchange in which he gave offense?

A. I don't know. Perhaps we'd better try another example. Here's one on page 150, though it's odd because the only direct quotation is on Geertz's side of the exchange. You can play him in his person as a writing field-worker, and I'll play him in his person as a speaking field-worker. The topic is *tadkir,* which is divine determinism.

WRITER: Then I asked him (a young modernist) about *tadkir,* and he said that he believed everything was *tadkir* and that a man's fate was totally in God's hands.

SPEAKER: Well,

WRITER: I said.

SPEAKER: Why do anything then? Why did the Indonesians bother with the revolution if everything is up to God?

WRITER: He said, very strenuously, that we are commanded in the Koran to work and strive, to better ourselves.

Q. And they continue to dispute the same point. It sounds as though the "young modernist," like the seventy-year-old, got offended, or at least became defensive. Later on, it says here, "he was somewhat perplexed."

A. Let's try another exchange, the one on page 180. You can be the field-worker and I'll be the anonymous Javanese. This time the subject is *kijajis,* religious counselors or teachers.

GEERTZ: Don't the *kijajis* sometimes disagree among themselves?

JAVANESE: Yes, this is so. Sometimes England, France, and America don't agree. Isn't that so—on small things even though basically they are united?

GEERTZ: [Agrees.]

JAVANESE: That is the way it is with *kijajis.* They often disagree over details, but on the main issues agree.

GEERTZ: Well, how does the layman know which is right?

JAVANESE: He just chooses the *kijaji* he respects and follows him.

Q. This time the Javanese tries to deflect a question back to the world Geertz comes from, but Geertz won't let go. It's beginning to look as though his idea of a dialogue is a debate.

A. But there are a few other exchanges of a different character, like the one on page 316, in the chapter titled "Mysticism." This time the topic is the soul. You'll play the writer of field notes, paraphrasing himself, and I'll play the part of a guru. The word *rasa* means "feeling."

GURU: The soul is a thing, an object, but it is invisible. Although you feel it, it has *rasa.* Your name is Cliff, and [closes his eyes] you feel Cliff. This is called feeling your name.

GEERTZ: I said that I didn't understand this.

GURU: Suppose you come here in the dark. No one can see anything and you say, "May I come in?" "Who is it?" I reply. "Me," you say. "Me who?" I say. "Me, Cliff," you say. Thus you feel "Cliff"; this is your soul. Now, that which feels Cliff, which feels the "feeling of Cliff," is *aku*, "I." *Aku* is not the feeling "Cliff" — the soul is that; but the feeling *aku* is the feeling which feels the feeling "Cliff." It is the feeling which knows. It is not the soul which knows, it is what is known; *aku* is what knows. *Aku* is an eternal object, it can never be destroyed; and some say it is God —

Q. Enough of that. It isn't so much a dialogue as a monologue on the part of the guru.

A. But in theatrical terminology a monologue *is* a dialogue, a particular kind of dialogue in which a speaker has silent or imaginary partners. In this case the imaginary partner is "Cliff," or at least Cliff on an occasion other than the present one, an occasion imagined by the guru. The present occasion is clearly marked as well, when the guru uses the words "you" and "I" outside the imagined dialogue. But what's most striking here, when we back off to the level of the encounter between anthropologist and native, is that the anthropologist has appeared within the discourse of the native, who is not simply a native speaking only about natives.

Q. But there's still the matter of the relationship between these fragments of dialogue, or the fine-print extracts that encapsulate them, and the large-print arguments that come before and after. Do the fragments merely illustrate points the author is already trying to make?

A. Again and again they supplement or support what precedes them rather than providing the occasion for what follows them. In that sense, we're still dealing with hermeneutics in reverse. On the other hand, the extracts are long enough, and numerous enough, that a reader could go on interpreting them in ways that went beyond, or even contradicted, the points being made in the main text. But they're still mostly paraphrases, and they're still extracts from a longer text, a set of field notes, to which the reader has no access.

Q. Is that what interpretive anthropology is, then? The interpretation of field notes?

A. Well, that's not all it *could* be. But when interpretive anthropology is written in such a way that the voice of the author crowds all the other possible voices into the fine print or silences them altogether, then to that same extent any *re*interpretation by readers will ultimately tend to focus on the author and on authorship.

Q. Unless the reinterpreter goes off to do fresh fieldwork.

A. But that would be in a place where conditions had meanwhile changed. The point is that when interpretation is written in disciplines other than anthropology, the reader of this interpretation isn't limited to a confrontation with its author, but can move around in the space between the voices of this author and those of a separate text — an *available* text. In anthropology, these days, we've got masses of interpretation and almost no text. We need to open a wider field for reinterpretation.

Q. What about Victor Turner's work? Are all those quotations in *The Forest of Symbols* any different from the ones we've been talking about?

A. Turner's quotations are different in several ways, beginning with the fact that the persons he quotes are not anonymous, nor are their words kept at a distance by double embedding. Further, he usually gives not only a translation but a parallel text in the original language as well, both of them in full-sized type. And finally, he does most of his interpretation after a quotation, not before. Not only that, but in many instances the quoted words must be counted as part of the main text rather than as illustrations, in the sense that a reader who skipped over them would have a hard time following the passages in which they occur. There's very little ethnographic writing that comes as close as these passages to a balance of voices.

Q. Can we count this as a first on Turner's part?

A. Not quite. In 1933 Paul Radin, in the midst of an otherwise polemical book entitled *The Method and Theory of Ethnology*, inserted a seventy-page chapter devoted to a hermeneutical dialogue between himself and texts he had previously collected in the field from John Rave, Oliver Lamere, Albert Hensley, and John Baptiste, the founders of the peyote religion among the Winnebago. Radin's discourse is in constant alternation with that of the texts, and by the end he has quoted those texts in full.

Q. Are all of Turner's dialogues between himself and the texts he collected, or are some of them quoted from face-to-face encounters?

A. There is a direct encounter on page 148 of *The Forest of Symbols*. It'll take us back to 1953 again, but this time to a village in Northern Rhodesia, near the border with Angola. Turner slips into paraphrase for part of his own contribution to this exchange, just as Geertz often does, so you'll be playing him as a writer, both quoting and paraphrasing himself as fieldworker. I'll take the part of Muchona, the best Ndembu informant you ever had. I've just arrived at your camp, "looking utterly woebegone."

TURNER: "What on earth's the matter?" I asked. He replied,

MUCHONA: This is the last time we can speak about customs together. Can't you hear the people talking angrily in the village shelter? When I passed it on my way here, they were saying loudly, so that I could hear, that I was giving away our secrets, and that I was teaching you witchcraft matters.

TURNER: I was distressed and a little hurt to hear this, for my relations with the villagers had always seemed extremely friendly. I said as much to Muchona, who went on,

MUCHONA: No, it is not the people of this village, or at least only a few of them, who are talking like this, but others who come to hear a case discussed in the village shelter. But the people of this village, especially one man—I name no names—say that I am telling you only lies. Before I came, they say, you heard only true things about our ceremonies, but now you just hear nonsense. But one thing I found wonderful. The village people call me a liar, the strangers say I am betraying secrets. Their reasons don't agree, but they agree with each other!

Q. Wherever dialogue comes to the surface, it would seem, tension and conflict will be there also. Malinowski evades the questions of the natives, the natives evade the questions of Evans-Pritchard and even lie to him, Geertz debates with his informants, and Turner is on the brink of losing Muchona!

A. And when everything goes well, the informant speaks alone, or as if in unison with other informants, or by way of a paraphrase, or not at all. But there's another dialogue in *The Forest of Symbols*, on the very next page. The topic is the *ihamba*, the front tooth of a dead hunter, which can enter the body of a living person and cause pain. We should also keep in mind that "drinking" tobacco means smoking it. I'll play Muchona again, and I've already been sitting here on a hard wooden stool for a couple of hours, talking to you in your person as field-worker. But you'll start off in your person as writer.

TURNER: Full of the zest of inquiry, I had become thoughtless and had forgotten to give him his usual cushion. Eventually he burst out,

MUCHONA: You have been asking me where an *ihamba* goes. Well, just now I have an *ihamba* in the buttocks.

TURNER: I silently passed him his cushion. However, this was not all. We used to punctuate our deliberations pleasantly enough with an occasional cigarette. Today I had forgotten to pass around the yellow pack of Belgas. So Muchona said,

MUCHONA: I have another *ihamba*.

TURNER: What's that one?

MUCHONA: The angriest *ihamba* of all, the *ihamba* of drinking tobacco.

Q. So there's a problem again, but at least the informant makes a joke of it. But why tobacco? That's what Cuol wanted from E.-P.

A. Perhaps the tobacco should be understood as part of the same exchange as the dialogue itself. It would seem to be a small token of the fact that one of the parties is going to do a good deal more talking than the other. Or that one of them is going to respond to a lot more questions, which is to say requests, than the other. E.-P. doesn't tell us whether he went ahead and gave tobacco to Cuol, and whether Cuol spoke more informatively after that, but it's a good guess.

Q. Are there any other dialogues in *The Forest of Symbols*?

A. No, not unless we count a few brief exchanges in which both sides are paraphrased. As it happens, both of the passages we read are in a chapter originally written for Joseph Casagrande, who had asked each of the contributors to an edited volume to write a first-person account of a favorite informant or interpreter.

Q. Well then, would we have better luck looking for dialogues in full-length memoirs? There are whole books in which an anthropologist tells it like it really was in the field.

A. Memoirs offer a good deal of *internal* dialogue, in which the anthropologist worries about what the others are up to. But quotations are just as rare as they are in most ethnographies, and once again there are times when they come mainly from people other than the Others. In Lévi-Strauss's *Tristes Tropiques,* the reigning classic among anthropological memoirs, not a single Brazilian Indian ever utters so much as one complete sentence, not even with the aid of an interpreter. Conversations may be summarized in books of this genre, or conclusions may be drawn from them, but they aren't often quoted.

Q. So memoirs are a lot like the very ethnographies they supposedly offer an escape from.

A. They are, except that the anthropologist whose memoir it is no longer hides in the fine print, but now talks endlessly to the reader in the main text. Some of the natives may also be glimpsed as persons, but they all share the same strange handicap.

Q. They're mute!

A. Yes. But I do know of an exception, and it's one of the earliest anthropological memoirs: *Spider Woman,* by Gladys A. Reichard, published in 1934. It's full of dialogues, several of which are longer than anything we've read so far. Let's try the longest one, on pages 183–84. We're at a place called White-Sands, on the Navajo reservation. I'll play the part of John Tallman, a Navajo judge who has been assisting the performer of a curative chant, and it will take me a while to get to the point. I have just entered your house, and you offer me a smoke as you begin to speak.

REICHARD: You look tired.

TALLMAN: I am. It's lots of work.

REICHARD: I never realized how much work a sing is. I simply cannot understand how Red-Point does it. He superintends everything by day; he never loses sight of a thing, and everything necessary is ready at the proper moment. He hardly sleeps at night. Last night it was eleven before the sing was over and this morning I heard him singing at four-thirty.

TALLMAN: Yes. I just came up for a little visit yesterday morning. I did not intend to stay this long. But they need help, and I offered to try my hand at the painting.

REICHARD: Did you ever help before?

TALLMAN: Never.

REICHARD: It looks like a nice thing to do.

TALLMAN: It is. The old man said I did better than some of the others who had done it before. [long pause] One of the boys has been hunting his horse all day and has not found it. They need some medicine for tomorrow night and now there is hardly time for him to get it even if he could catch his horse.

REICHARD: Where does he have to go for it?

TALLMAN: The nearest is Crystal.

REICHARD: Why, that is sixty miles!

TALLMAN: Yes. The old man is pretty disappointed because he wanted this done so complete. I suggested that maybe you would be willing to go for it. I said I would be glad to do it, but I do not know how to cut the medicine properly nor do I know the prayers.

REICHARD: I told him at the beginning that I should be glad to do anything of that sort I could. I knew he needed this distant medicine fresh, but I didn't know when.

TALLMAN: The roads are dry and hard now. I think if we start about sunrise tomorrow we could get it in time. He said one of the boys would go with us. I said maybe you wouldn't mind getting up so early.

REICHARD: All right, but I think I better get gas tonight. I haven't enough, and no trader will be up that early.

A. Here the dialogue is suspended until you get back with your car full of gas and I break the news that we'll have to take off for Crystal right away, even though it's late at night.

Q. So this time it's a bigger favor than a smoke that's needed to keep the exchange going. But why is there so much dialogue in this book?

A. There's a clue in her subtitle, which is *A Story of Navajo Weavers and Chanters.* Reichard set out to tell a *story,* and stories, except when they're written by natural historians, have dialogue in them. It might also help to know that she was living within the homestead of an extended Navajo family, in one of the houses they themselves had built, and that she was learning how to weave from one of the women. In other words, she had plenty of occasions for conversations that didn't depend on her questions to keep them going.

Q. What about that chant she and Tallman were talking about? Does she quote any oral performances, or is there nothing but ordinary conversation?

A. She quotes an excerpt from the chant, yes, and she also weaves in a long passage from the story that accounts for its origin. But there is one place, on page 204, where the curative language of the chant doesn't just stay in its place, apart from conversation. As the ninth day of the ceremony begins, at sunset, she has withdrawn to her car, where she sits looking out through a fine rain at a greening landscape and musing about the peaceful mood that has settled upon her hosts. Red-Point, the singer, sees her in the car and comes over to talk. You can play her part again, and I'll be the singer. Both parts have been translated from Navajo.

Q. All right. It says here that I offer you a cigarette, and you speak as you look out through the smoke.

RED-POINT: White-Sands is beautiful.

REICHARD: The fields are beautiful.

RED-POINT: The vegetation is beautiful.

REICHARD: The trees are beautiful.

RED-POINT: The houses are beautiful.

REICHARD: The women are beautiful.

RED-POINT: The men are beautiful.

REICHARD and RED-POINT: The children are beautiful.

REICHARD: The Chant is beautiful.

RED-POINT: The offerings are beautiful.

REICHARD: The prayers are beautiful.

RED-POINT: The paintings are beautiful. All has been restored in beauty.

Q. And then you walk off to get ready for the final night of the chant. I have to say that this passage makes me somewhat uncomfortable. It seems—well, a bit romantic.

A. Do you read much poetry?

Q. Not really. Why?

A. Because it could be that this passage simply sounds too poetic to you. Be that as it may, I have to say that it also sounds a bit like a language-learning exercise.

Q. How so?

A. In effect, it's a series of linguistic paradigms, with some words held constant and others substituted. Even in translation, that's quite obvious. Red-Point makes a statement, then Reichard shows that she knows how to transform it and has the vocabulary to do so, and they go on playing at grammar and poetry at the same time.

Q. But that's not something Navajos would do among themselves, is it?

A. Whether or not they ever run through an exchange exactly like this one, it's simply not the case that poetry stands in isolation from every-day speech. Sociolinguists have shown this over and over again, but it was Roman Jakobson who stated the case most boldly. I don't remember the source, but the words are these: "Poetry is the grammar of an unwritten language." And where fieldwork is concerned, there's nothing like working with native texts, as Malinowski did and as nearly all the American ethnographers of Reichard's time did, for getting a feel for the movement of shapes in speech.

Q. But ethnographers are there for the culture more than the language, aren't they? Or are you about to make the Sapir-Whorf argument?

A. There's no need to do that. We can just talk about poetics. In nearly all oral traditions and quite a few written ones, poetry is largely formed at the level of words and phrases and breath groups, all of which already have meaning, rather than at the level of phonemes or syllables, which have no meaning in themselves. In other words, a recurring pattern of sound will carry a recurring pattern of meaning, and a break in sound will carry a break in meaning.

Q. What does that mean in practical terms?

A. It means that poetry is not something apart from the culture the ethnographer attempts to extract from it. Any ethnographer who takes the pursuit of culture beyond the level of giving the natives short-answer quizzes will be hard put to keep poetry out of the conversation.

Q. Well then, there are all those volumes of native texts produced during the era of Reichard and her mentors. Is that where this discussion is leading us?

A. The problem with collections of texts is that the field-worker retreats from the main text into the fine print, trading places with the native. There's a kind of apartheid here; it's as if anthropologists would not allow the natives and themselves to be fully articulate between the same two covers. And by now this state of affairs has been replicated at the institutional level. It used to be that the same people who did ethnographies also did text collections, but now the texts are done by separate specialists who are likely to be found in separate academic departments, namely linguistics departments.

Q. But there are sociolinguists, or people who do "ethnographies of speaking." Don't they have to combine native utterances and their own utterances between the same two covers?

A. Yes, but sociolinguists, like the text collectors of the past, present instances of native discourse almost as if they themselves had never spoken a word while in the field. On top of that, they have so far limited themselves to dealing with the contexts and forms of native discourse. They don't give that much thought to what the discourse might be *about*. We have come to a strange pass. While the anthropologist feels free to write about meaning without considering texts, the linguist feels free to write about texts without considering meaning. In their respective backstage activities they reverse roles: the anthropologist necessarily peeks at texts on the way to meaning, while the linguist cannot get very far in describing form or context without taking surreptitious glances at meaning.

Q. We seem to be running out of genres in our search for dialogue, or at least face-to-face dialogue with the field-worker as one of the parties. What about all those native life histories? They would seem to be the product of inescapably personal relationships.

A. Even so, anthropologists habitually retreat to the fine print of life histories, just as they do in works that purport to document the voices of tradition rather than those of individuals. And in the margins of these life histories, again and again, they inform their readers of a decision to omit their own voices from the main text. Meanwhile, the natives themselves go right on acting out dialogues, just as they would while telling any other kind of story. Indeed, whether natives speak from personal experience or from tradition, the quotation of dialogue remains the most palpable of all the differences between their discourse and that of the writers of ethnographies and ethnographic memoirs.

Q. It would seem, then, that if field-workers ever found their way into native accounts, they would be given speaking parts.

A. There is at least one collection of native stories, dating from 1936, in which an anthropologist appears among the characters. It is perhaps no coincidence that this collection was published by a native. The title is *Truth of a Hopi*, and the Hopi in question is Edmund Nequatewa. The last story in the book accounts for an anthropologist's sudden departure from the Hopi mesas in 1898. Look here on page 122: it's a November night at Walpi and the anthropologist, Jesse Walter Fewkes, has been told to lock himself in his house lest he encounter Masauwu, the Earth God, whose gaze causes a permanent state of fright. You can play Dr. Fewkes, thank you, and I'll speak the lines of Masauwu. You've been alone, working on your notes of course, but you suddenly sense that there is someone else in the room.

FEWKES: [looks up and sees a tall man with his face in shadow] What do you want and how did you get in here?

MASAUWU: I have come to entertain you.

FEWKES: Go away, I am busy and do not wish to be entertained. [The man vanishes right before his eyes.]

MASAUWU: Turn your head a moment.

FEWKES: [looks again and sees that the man's face is bone white and spattered with blood] How did you get in?

MASAUWU: I go where I please, locked doors cannot keep me out! See, I will show you how I entered. [He shrinks to the size of a straw and vanishes through the keyhole, then reappears.]

FEWKES: What do you want?

MASAUWU: I have come to entertain you. [Fewkes gives him a cigarette, but he laughs at the offer of a match.] Keep your match, I do not need it. [He lights his cigarette by blowing fire from his mouth, and Fewkes realizes who he is.]

A. The narrator goes on to say that Masauwu next transformed you into a child and took the form of a child himself. The two of you talked and played all night, and he persuaded you to be like a Hopi and believe in him. But not long after that, you left town.

Q. It would seem that the field-worker who's at work on his notes is no longer a field-worker looking for conversation. He's busy and doesn't want to be "entertained."

A. However, it's not as though the Hopis simply turn the tables, demanding an interview instead of being asked for one. They give the job of confronting Fewkes to the most dangerous of all their gods, a god he had doubtless been asking a lot of questions about.

Q. Even so, once Fewkes gives in to being interrupted, he makes the usual offer of a cigarette.

A. But Masauwu is one informant who doesn't need a match.

Q. And the next thing we know, the anthropologist is in trouble again. It's religious trouble, but not quite the same trouble Geertz got into by debating with the natives.

A. Well, whether or not Fewkes ever debated with Hopis, what he had in common with Geertz, and with any number of other ethnographers over the past hundred years, was that he wanted to understand native religion and yet remain outside it. This Hopi story about him raises the question of the relationship between curiosity and commitment, or between observation and participation. It would seem that from the Hopi point of view, Fewkes had reached a dangerous threshold in his curiosity.

Q. So they solved the problem, at least in this story, by having Masauwu pull him across that threshold and into being like a Hopi.

A. Ah, but soon after that he left the field. The story removes the mask from anthropological participation. Confronted with a *real* opportunity to be like a native, the anthropologist turns tail.

Q. Would you argue that anthropologists shouldn't even ask questions about religion?

A. No, not at all. But a dialogical engagement with the religion of others will necessarily expose the conflict between observation and participation.

Q. So we'll get a dialogue between a curious but skeptical anthropologist and a believing native?

A. Not necessarily. Anthropologists may manage to keep their disbelief in suspension nearly all the time, and beyond that they may find some aspects of the native religion quite attractive, but their questions will still carry the marks of their status as outsiders looking in. The natives, for their part, may sometimes be skeptical, or at least have their moments of irony, and they may ask questions about the religions of anthropologists. But discourse of the kind that reveals these ambiguities doesn't lend itself to the manufacture of the third-person-plural typifications that go into the construction of a conventional ethnography.

Q. What happens in the dialogues you mentioned at the beginning? Are there strains in the exchange between J. R. Walker and Finger?

A. Here it is, on pages 154–56 of Walker's *The Sun Dance and Other Ceremonies of the Oglala Division of the Teton Dakota*. Let's read the opening part, with you taking the part of Walker. We're on the Pine Ridge Sioux reservation, about a hundred years ago. The term *wakan* refers to dangerous manifestations of spiritual power.

WALKER: I heard you exclaim when a meteorite fell and heard you address the people immediately afterwards. Then I saw you burning sweetgrass. Will you tell me why you did this?

FINGER: You are a white man's medicine man and you want to know the mysteries of the Lakota. Why do you want to know these things?

WALKER: The old Indians who know these things will soon be dead and gone and as the younger Indians do not know them they will be lost. I wish to write them so they will be preserved and your people can read them in years to come. Will you tell them to me?

FINGER: My father was a shaman and he taught me the mysteries of the shamans and I will tell them to you. What is it you want to know?

WALKER: When the meteor fell you cried in a loud voice, "*Wohpa. Wohpe-e-e-e.*" Why did you do this?

FINGER: Because that is *wakan*.

Q. We don't need to read any further to see how Walker gets around the problem of participation. He presents himself as a mere scribe, wanting to write things down for the sake of "younger Indians." That sounds tricky to me. Where did he publish this?

A. In the Anthropological Papers of the American Museum of Natural History.

Q. In other words, it wasn't particularly accessible to the Lakota.

A. But it must be said that he did encourage the Lakota to make written records of religious traditions for themselves, in their own language, which they in fact did. Copies of those writings have been circulating privately among speakers of Lakota ever since, and they're only just beginning to see broader publication.

Q. That makes Walker sound like an agent of change.

A. Maybe so, but certainly not in the usual way. He wasn't the one who introduced the writing of Lakota. That had been done by missionaries, back in the eighteenth century, and with purposes quite different from his. In effect, he was a countermissionary. As far as that goes, any field-worker who shows something other than a hostile interest in an indigenous religion has a countermissionary effect and is, therefore, an agent of change.

So here is a further sense in which dialogue, even a dialogue that is going smoothly, is something more than a transparent medium for the passage of information.

Q. Marcel Griaule seems to have gone beyond showing a positive interest. He went native, didn't he? I know that he was buried among the Dogon, with the appropriate Dogon funeral rites.

A. Well, I'm not sure just what "going native" consists of. One thing is certain: Griaule and his associates never stopped turning out books and articles on the Dogon, written in French and published in France. In the case of *Conversations with Ogotemmêli*, he managed to get into print just one year after the actual conversations.

Q. Perhaps the shortness of that interval reflects a shift away from analysis and toward participation.

A. But the book he produced is already at a considerable distance from his field experiences. Griaule the writer narrates Griaule the field-worker in the third person, variously calling himself the European, the white man, and (after the manner of the Dogon themselves) the Nazarene, which is to say the Christian. None of the direct quotations of dialogue runs even half as long as Walker's. Indeed, the greater part of what was said in the field is either paraphrased or else recast in the familiar language of comparative symbolism. Still, it must be said that both the field-worker and the natives say a great deal more here than they do in standard ethnographies, and that they both inhabit the world of the main text.

Q. But is there an observational distance in the dialogues themselves, or are they participatory?

A. Let's try out the first dialogue in the book, on pages 8–9. We're in Upper Ogol, a village in the French Sudan, in 1947. I'll play the field-worker this time, since you think he's going native anyway, and you can take the part of Gana, the seventeen-year-old son of a local religious patriarch. You've come to the caravanserai, where no fewer than four Europeans are busy conducting separate interviews with villagers. One of these Europeans is myself, and I'm the one you're going to interrupt.

GANA: A hunter wishes to see you.

GRIAULE: Is he sick?

GANA: No! He wishes to sell you an amulet.

GRIAULE: What amulet?

GANA: The amulet you ordered ten years ago in return for the bullets.

GRIAULE: I have no recollection of that. [Then he bites his lip, realizing that this could be interesting.] Good. [He sends Gana to fetch the amulet, who returns with it.] And the formula? Have you got that?

GANA: What formula?

GRIAULE: The formula for its manufacture and use. Go and get it!

Q. And it says here that I go off to get the formula.

A. But the moment you're gone, the very person I've been interviewing says he knows the formula and gives it to me.

Q. Then I come back from the hunter and recite the formula to you myself.

A. Noticing that you've left out three verses, I read them to you from the notes I just took.

Q. Whereupon my jaw, or Gana's jaw, drops. So far, Griaule sounds like a diligent gatherer of information, an observer, and he's got a whole organization to back him up. He's not sure how important this hunter is, so he sends someone else to get the amulet and the formula that goes with it, even if he has to send him twice.

A. And he's quartered at the caravanserai; he's not like Reichard, living in a native house on the same grounds with a native family. In the matter of the text of the formula he sounds like Malinowski: he assumes that an invisible fixed text lies behind an oral recitation. When Gana recites three fewer verses than he's got in his notes, he's confident enough that Gana has left something out to teach him a lesson.

Q. Which also has the effect of displaying his command of Dogon culture to the reader.

A. Yet he tips his hand: it's what he's got written in his notes that enables him to appear so smart to Gana.

Q. Who's the hunter who sent the amulet? I suppose it'll turn out to be Ogotemmêli himself.

A. Indeed. And we should try out a dialogue with him in it. Here's a relatively long exchange on pages 36–37. I'll be the field-worker again. You've been telling me about a building, the Granary of the Master of Pure Earth, constructed by the first ancestor of the Dogon. It appears to be a model of the whole world and everything in it, and I've been trying to assemble a complete description, even down to the measurements.

GRIAULE: Only some of the animals and vegetables were on the building; where were the rest?

OGOTEMMÊLI: Each of those mentioned was as it were a file-leader. All the others of his kind were behind him. The antelope on the first step of the west stairway is the *walbanu,* the red antelope. After him come the white, the black, and the *kâ* antelopes. So too on the first step of the south stairway, where the poultry stand, the guinea-fowl, the partridge and the rock-fowl are behind.

GRIAULE: How could all these beasts find room on a step one cubit deep and one cubit high?

OGOTEMMÊLI: All this had to be said in words, but everything on the steps is a symbol, symbolic antelopes, symbolic vultures, symbolic hyenas. [pause] Any number of symbols could find room on a one-cubit step.

Q. Now Griaule doesn't sound as smart as he did with Gana. He comes on like an outside observer, asking a sharp question, but gets his come-uppance. And then, to the extent that he accepts the answer he gets, he's buying into the system, and that's participation.

A. But does it mean he's taken a step in the process of becoming a Dogon? At the very least, it's debatable whether Dogon become Dogon by asking how so many beasts could fit on such a small step, along with scores of other questions that occur to them as they check over their notes from previous interviews, and by getting various comeuppances.

Q. It sounds like you're about to argue, as you did earlier, that culture, as it appears in ethnographies, is constructed jointly by field-worker and natives.

A. Only this time, with Griaule, we are witnesses to that process. With E.-P., we were only shown a couple of moments when it wasn't working.

Q. But as Griaule gets more deeply into the system, he might proceed more in accordance with the system itself.

A. Perhaps, but he's never going to leave off taking notes, checking them over, asking more questions, and eventually writing for publication. Anyway, let's try a later dialogue, with you as Ogotemmêli again. By the time we get to page 58, you've told me a story about a Nummo, or water spirit, who came down from heaven to the grave of a man named Lébé and ate his remains. When people found colored stones where Lébé's bones had once been, they took these to be the excrement of the water spirit, and ever since that time the stones have served as a sign of a covenant between water spirits and Dogon priests. Now, *why* did this Nummo have to eat Lébé, that's what I want to know, and you're about to tell me.

OGOTEMMÊLI: It was to make men believe that the aged Lébé, the oldest and most venerable of them all, and he alone, was present in the covenant-stones. It was so that men might understand all the things he had done that the Nummo came down on to the skeleton of a man.

GRIAULE: You speak of "making" people "believe." Was there then something secret, which they were not to know?

OGOTEMMÊLI: If you wanted to explain what happened to someone who knew nothing about it, to an ordinary man, you would say that a Power came down from heaven to eat the old man and change his bones into beneficent stones.

GRIAULE: But what is the truth?

OGOTEMMÊLI: If one wanted to explain it to you, a Nazarene, one would say that someone came down from heaven like a woman with a woman's dress and ornaments, and ate the old man, and that the stones are not his bones but her ornaments.

Q. This is more like the dialogue with Gana, in that Griaule comes to know more about Dogon culture than some of the Dogon know. Only now he's being shown a whole new level of knowledge, he's having a priestly secret revealed to him, and that's participation again.

A. But a rather peculiar form of participation. He's been made privy to something a priest knows and "an ordinary man" doesn't, but this knowledge doesn't make him a member of the Dogon priesthood. And ironically enough, Ogotemmêli marks him as someone other than "an ordinary man" by calling him a Nazarene.

Q. What about that scene at the end of the book, with the sacrifice of a cock? That's not a "Nazarene" practice. Didn't Griaule participate?

A. Well, let's start with the fact that this was a farewell scene, not an initiation. On the morning of the appointed day, Griaule "went over his balance-sheet" and had the thought that this year's expedition had "marked a turning-point in African studies."

Q. So it's back to the observational stance. It also sounds like the beginning of an argument for further funding. And the sacrifice?

A. That was for Ogotemmêli's brother to do while all four of the European field-workers watched. Griaule had supplied a cock in advance, but when the moment arrived it turned out that the cock had flown the coup. The sacrificer had to kill a bird belonging to Ogotemmêli's own family.

Q. Who said the prayer?

A. Ogotemmêli himself.

Q. I suppose Griaule had an appropriate prayer in his possession, but instead of saying it from memory, he would've had to read it from his notes.

A. But there was a more basic limit to his participation. In the book he sometimes reveals, in a casual way, that he didn't go to Ogotemmêli's house by himself. On the day of the first visit, for example, "the man accompanying the European pronounced the usual words of greeting." During the conversation of the fifth day, when the European wanted to see the inside of a granary, he "whispered to his assistant Koguem that he ought to see one of these constructions," and "Koguem put the point to the old man." On the eighteenth day, when Ogotemmêli was conversing with a neighbor, "Koguem and the European were sitting in their usual places listening to the two men. 'Ogotemêlli,' Koguem explained, 'says he wants to eat an ox-head.'"

Q. So Griaule used an interpreter! Talk about a limit to participation!

A. The use of an interpreter isn't all that remarkable in itself. What's more interesting is that Griaule doesn't come right out and *call* Koguem an interpreter, and that most of the time he ignores Koguem's presence altogether. It's a case of transparency again. Just as dialogue that goes smoothly has a way of disappearing in the writing of a conventional ethnography, so translation that goes smoothly has a way of disappearing in the writing of dialogue. But it has to be said for Griaule that he *did* reveal the existence of Koguem. In many ethnographies of the past, the existence of interpreters, or of bilingual informants, is hidden.

Q. So you're suggesting that some authors have chosen to evade the question as to how well they learned the native language.

A. There's more to it than that. Interpreters, or informants who do their own interpreting, are among the natives most likely to offer interpretation in the broader sense that goes beyond direct translation. The very act of translation brings to mind mismatches not only between words but between cultures as well, mismatches that call for interpretive remarks that can be immensely valuable to field-workers. Some of Koguem's remarks are quoted by Griaule. Another interpreter who gets credit for doing more than just translating words and sentences is Lhacen, in Vincent Crapanzano's *Tuhami: Portrait of a Moroccan.*

Q. I didn't even remember that Crapanzano used an interpreter.

A. Maybe that's because he only deals directly with Lhacen near the beginning of the book (page 12) and again near the end (pages 147–50). He tells us that during the interviews with Tuhami, "Lhacen made himself as unobtrusive as possible," or "had an extraordinary ability to efface himself," or "had an almost uncanny ability to efface himself." And he refers to "Lhacen's faceless presence," asserting that "he could be ignored and was ignored." But he also says, in these same passages, that "had he not been there, our relationship would have been awkward," and, "We could not go on without him."

Q. It sounds as though Crapanzano's feelings about Lhacen are rather conflicted. It's as though he's not sure he should've mentioned Lhacen at all.

A. Nevertheless, he goes so far as to say, "I am indebted to Lhacen for much of what I have to say about Tuhami."

Q. Does he quote Lhacen?

A. Only in the sense that whenever he quotes Tuhami he is actually quoting Lhacen, translating for us what Lhacen translated for him. But he represents the dialogues in the book as two-way exchanges between himself and Tuhami.

Q. But it could be that some interpreters really do approach a sort of transparency.

A. Or transparency may be an appearance produced by a particular angle of vision. Perhaps the most famous interpreter of all time is Malintzin or Malinche, the native speaker of Nahuatl who interpreted for Cortés. In his letters, Cortés mentions the existence of an interpreter only twice, and names her only once. He quotes or describes his various exchanges with Aztec officials as if he had engaged in direct conversation with them, in effect absorbing Malinche into himself.

Q. Cortés sounds like Crapanzano.

A. But in the case of Cortés we also have the account of a witness to the exchanges, Bernal Díaz. He gives Malinche a major role, portraying her not only as a translator but as an advisor as well. As for the Aztecs, they absorbed Cortés into his interpreter rather than the other way around. They went so far as to name *him* after *her,* addressing him, in effect, as "Mr. Malinche."

Q. So you would argue that Lhacen's "faceless" condition is a function of Crapanzano's authorship.

A. Well, Crapanzano really tips his hand at the very end of the book, writing of a "complicity to bracket off Lhacen" that "permitted a conventional framing of our encounter."

Q. He's saying that an interpreter can help two other people keep a conversation moving.

A. Ah, but the words "bracket off" and "conventional framing" suggest the construction of a physical object. I would suggest that the object in question is the book itself, which follows the "conventional framing" of anthropological life histories. The name of the native, Tuhami, is moved into the title, leaving the authorship vacant for the field-worker, Vincent Crapanzano. His claim to authorship, which is made in the shadow of the name in the larger print of the title, would only be further weakened by the prominent naming of a third party. So if Lhacen is to be mentioned at all, he must be confined to the margins of the text.

Q. It remains that Crapanzano does mention Lhacen, and gives some idea of his importance.

A. But the problem of translation itself remains hidden. It would seem that even when ethnographers bring dialogue out front instead of hiding it or reducing it to apt quotations, the conventions of framing are still such that the passage from one language to another may remain a hidden process, except for the retention of some native terms and proper names.

Q. What about British social anthropologists who describe their task as "the translation of cultures"?

A. They've turned the process of translation into an allegory, just as their American counterparts have turned the process of textual interpretation into an allegory. And with this allegorization has come a repression of the fact that fieldwork entails the *actual* translation and interpretation of texts.

Q. Why do you call it "repression" rather than "suppression"?

A. Because the problem can rise so very close to the surface of anthropological discourse without being acknowledged. Crapanzano's essay by the title of "Hermes' Dilemma," published in 1986, is a case in point. He starts off by allegorizing Walter Benjamin's famous essay on translation, writing that "like translation, ethnography is also a way of coming to terms with the foreignness of languages — of cultures and societies."

Q. That's clear enough. He substitutes "ethnography" for "translation" and "cultures and societies" for "languages."

A. And he goes on to say that the ethnographer "must render the foreign familiar and preserve its very foreignness at one and the same time. The translator accomplishes this through style, the ethnographer through the coupling of a presentation that asserts the foreign and an interpretation that makes it all familiar."

Q. So, for Crapanazano, translation and ethnography are two separate matters. It sounds as though he's generalizing from his own field situation, where the translator and the ethnographer were two separate people.

A. But he maintains this separation even when he compares the ethnographer to Hermes, whom he variously describes as a "messenger" and a "hermeneut," as the "tutelary god of speech and writing" and a "phallic god and a god of fertility," and as a "trickster." Somehow, he never quite manages to say straight out that Hermes was also the tutelary god of translators.

Q. Which would bring translators and ethnographers together to worship at the same shrine, so to speak. But can't we get around the translation problem by concerning ourselves with the situation in which an ethnographer and a native share a language?

A. That won't get rid of the translator who speaks within the divided mind of a person who is struggling with a second or third language, whether it be in the mind of the field-worker, the native, or (as happens often enough around the world) both of them. And it won't get rid of the external translator, either. If there is any richness and depth to the native side of a dialogue, then the record of that dialogue will raise questions that can only be solved with the aid of a native speaker. Instead of being a third party to the original dialogue, the interpreter will enter the scene later, during the process of textualization.

Q. Doesn't anyone learn the native language well enough not to have to do that?

A. Well, even professional translators of contemporary European novels —from French or German, let's say, into English—have to consult native speakers of French or German when it comes to difficult allusions, speech styles, slang, and so forth. A translator can no more become a native speaker of a language than a field-worker can be totally absorbed into a culture.

Q. But what about Geertz in Java, for example. Doesn't he say that he conducted his fieldwork mostly in Javanese?

A. Indeed he does. But let's have a look at the appendix to *The Religion of Java,* where he describes his "methods of work" in some detail. Concerning interviews, he writes, "I took notes in English, translating what I and my informant were saying as I went"; in the case of informal encounters, "I wrote notes only afterwards." In either case, as he puts it, "Much of my material is thus a paraphrase, or at least a somewhat catch-as-catch-can translation, of what the informant said rather than his exact words. When, however, quotation marks are put around an informant's statement in the notes quoted above, it is, at least more or less, a literal, or close, translation of what he actually said, for I wrote down the Javanese."

Q. So that's why those excerpts from field notes in the body of the book usually offer paraphrases of what people said rather than direct quotations.

A. Yes, and we can guess that similar practices lie behind the sparsity of quotations, or even the complete lack of them, in a great many other ethnographies. What's unusual about Geertz is that he describes his own version of the practice of sorting out paraphrases from quotations, and he even offers a defense of it: "Whatever loss of accuracy is involved in non-verbatim translation," he says, "it is more than compensated for in the increased variety and quantity of material one gets and the greater degree of naturalness and free-flow quality of the interview situation." Whatever he means by the "material one gets," its production is speeded up by the use of paraphrase.

Q. That would be the material that is independent of the language it's expressed in — the facts, the information.

A. But independence is in the eye of the field-worker. As it finally comes to us, this "material" is in fact not made in just any language but in English, made by an ethnographer who thinks in English, writes field notes mostly in English, and plans to write an English-language ethnography.

Q. Surely you're not going to argue that field-workers should avoid making a record of what a native says whenever they can't get it verbatim.

A. On the contrary, I would argue that field-workers should make an effort to re-create what they can't get verbatim.

Q. Complete with quotation marks?

A. Yes.

Q. But that would make them like fiction writers.

A. And like the speakers of any language, English included. Speakers quote, in today's dialogue, what they've heard someone else say in a prior dialogue, whether they can reproduce the exact same words, or a verbatim translation of those words, or not. Ethnographers do this when they *talk* about their fieldwork, even if they don't do it when they *write* about it. It's not these re-created quotations that demand an explanation, but the lack of similar quotations in ethnographic writing. Why does Geertz say that his way of writing "has the virtue of not presenting as verbatim what is really paraphrase," that's what I want to know. What is this "virtue"?

Q. The virtue of keeping the facts straight.

A. What you mean is, *arti*facts. A paraphrase, or what Geertz also calls "catch-as-catch-can" or "non-verbatim" translation, is one kind of artifact, and a re-created quotation is another, but I don't see that the one kind of "material" is more highly processed than the other. What I do see is a misplaced concreteness, a concreteness that has its roots in the mechanical reproduction of discourse by means of printing. In effect, ethnographers approach the quotation of spoken words as if they were citing a written source — or, better, as if they were citing a native who was citing a written source.

Q. As when Malinowski took all Trobriand charms to have fixed wording, or Griaule was certain that Gana had left three verses out of a Dogon formula.

A. Yes, but Geertz's case is a subtler one. When it comes to Javanese "writings," he is less interested in canonical texts than in productions that are closely tied to the particular situations of living "authors." But he doesn't let that free him from a conservative approach to quotation.

Q. Didn't he make any recordings in the field?

A. Well, here's what he says about that: "A tape recorder was used for TAT's and some other material, but because it is so much easier to put material on to such a recorder than to transcribe it off again, I did not use it very much in interviews as such."

Q. That makes the use of paraphrase, or "catch-as-catch-can" translation, sound like a shortcut.

A. But it must be admitted that in 1953, a tape recorder was a large and clumsy contraption — and, for the natives, an unfamiliar one. The fieldworkers of that time made decisions, just as their predecessors without recorders did, as to what was worth getting verbatim and what was not. Geertz's account of the matter goes like this: "For some sorts of material — myths, folktales, linguistics texts, etc. — verbatim transcription is of course essential, and was used here as well." But in this day of the cassette recorder, the natives are as likely as not to own their own, and to find it peculiar when a field-worker doesn't use one.

Q. So at this point in the history of ethnographic writing, the absence of native voices would be a matter of *choice*, rather than necessity.

A. Except when the choice isn't even perceived as such. Some ethnographers will continue to imitate previous ways of writing that were developed under conditions that no longer hold, paraphrasing the voices of the natives or glossing them over with third-person-plural typifications. Even those who quote the natives may be slow to quote themselves, and still slower when it comes to re-creating dialogues that didn't happen to take place with an open microphone.

Q. Well, I have a complaint about the dialogical works that already exist. *Tuhami*, like *Conversations with Ogotemmêli*, is a one-on-one affair, and so is Kevin Dwyer's *Moroccan Dialogues: Anthropology in Question.* When will we start to get works with multiple voices?

A. Actually, none of those books is limited to two speakers. Griaule quotes his interpreter, along with a few people who drop in on Ogotemmêli. Crapanzano quotes a couple of people he interviewed apart from Tuhami, a trance-dancer and a body-washer. And Dwyer quotes all sorts of people he conversed with outside of his interviews with Faqir Muhammad.

Q. Those are all minor characters, heard from only briefly.

A. But letting multiple voices be heard doesn't necessarily require interviewing more people. Griaule, Crapanzano, and Dwyer all speak in their persons as field-workers, and they all speak as writers of ethnography and as questioners of established ethnographic practices as well. Ogotemmêli speaks not only in his person as a Dogon priest instructing a Nazarene but as a participant in ordinary domestic life as well. And Tuhami and the Faqir periodically depart from a discursive mode in order to speak as narrators.

Q. But too much narrative could turn a dialogue into a monologue.

A. Spoken stories are always interwoven with the larger dialogue that surrounds them. And stories themselves, you're forgetting, are internally dialogical. Tuhami and the Faqir quote the characters in their narratives. An ethnographer who quoted the natives but refused to give space to their narratives would be monopolizing the production of multivocal discourse.

Q. The stories in all three books are rather short, though. Do you think the authors might have left some stories out, or even discouraged the telling of stories in the first place?

A. Actually, Dwyer lets the Faqir go on narrating for as much as two and a half pages at a time, which is much longer than anything in the other two books. Griaule, on the other hand, presents only disconnected fragments of myths told by Ogotemmêli, almost entirely in paraphrase. Crapanzano quotes some of the anecdotes told by Tuhami in full, but he replaces others with synopses in his own words.

Q. So there's an irony here. An ethnographer who sticks to a narrow notion of dialogue as a discursive, face-to-face exchange between two speakers may end up producing a book that is less dialogical, in the broad sense of multivocality, than an ethnographer who allows or even encourages narrative.

A. Yes, because narrative expands the world of verbal interactions far beyond the scene of the interview. And the irony works the other way around as well. An ethnographer who doesn't pursue dialogue as a thing in itself might produce a thoroughly multivocal work. A case in point is Laurel Kendall's *The Life and Hard Times of a Korean Shaman: Of Tales and the Telling of Tales,* published in 1988. Like Dwyer and Crapanzano,

Kendall speaks both in her person as a writer of ethnography and as a field-worker engaged in conversation. The shaman of her title, a woman named Yongsu's Mother, doesn't just talk about her life but tells memorable stories about it, complete with dialogues. And Kendall tells the story of how these stories were told to her.

Q. But now another problem occurs to me. On the one hand, Ogotemmêli tells nothing from his personal life, while Tuhami, the Faqir — and, from what it sounds like, Yongsu's Mother — tell nothing from tradition. So it would seem that however multivocal these works might be, they conform to the division between the personal and traditional genres of narrative.

A. You have a point there, though it must be said for Crapanzano and Kendall that they do raise the question. He opens his book by quoting a narrative that is so mythologized he doesn't know where to fit it into the rest of Tuhami's story, and she points out incidents that Yongsu's Mother has reorganized or dramatized in order to make better stories out of them. But neither of them quotes the actual performance of a third-person myth, legend, or tale.

Q. Is there a book that moves across all four of the genres we've been discussing?

A. There is at least one, published in 1989. It's Kirin Narayan's *Storytellers, Saints, and Scoundrels: Folk Narrative in Hindu Religious Teaching.* Narayan writes as an ethnographer of speaking, making observations about the role of narrative in Hindu teaching, but she also tells the story of how she acquired her knowledge, becoming one of the pupils of a guru she calls Swamiji. At the same time, although she quotes Swamiji primarily as a teller and interpreter of stories given by Hindu tradition, she also quotes him as a teller of personal anecdotes.

Q. Her name sounds Indian. Perhaps there was no language problem, no need for an interpreter.

A. Oh yes there was, but it was the *ethnographer* who served as interpreter — quite a remarkable moment in the human sciences, you might say.

Q. You mean that Narayan herself translated Swamiji's narratives for use in her book.

A. Not just that. Swamiji's other pupils included Europeans and Americans, and Narayan interpreted for them.

Q. So she started in on the business of representing Hindu ways to Westerners while she was still in the field.

A. And she meanwhile conducted her field research in the presence of witnesses, both Euroamerican and Indian, who had their own notions about what she was doing.

Q. I wonder whether we'd all be better off if ethnographers in general sought out field situations of linguistic symmetry between themselves and the others they propose to write about.

A. But Narayan has an Indian father and an American mother. She describes herself as speaking Hindi with an English accent, and her narrative includes moments when she fumbles for words. Swamiji, for his part, knows a lot of English words, but uses them in Hindi sentences. The linguistic asymmetries of this field situation may not be the usual ones, but they are still palpable.

Q. All right, but what about dialogues with real symmetry?

A. With symmetry at every moment of a dialogue, it's difficult to see how one of the parties could be defined as an ethnographer and the others as Others. There would be no place for an ethnographer, nor anything that could be called fieldwork, if all parties shared the same native language and, at the same time, occupied symmetrical sociolinguistic positions. What makes Narayan's asymmetry different is that the separateness of English and Hindi, and of the worlds of those two languages, already existed within her before she went into the field.

Q. In that case, what did going "into the field" consist of for her?

A. Returning to India from the United States and making arrangements not only to study with Swamiji but to record his words, take photographs, and keep notes, all of this with the purpose of writing a dissertation that might be publishable.

Q. Now we're getting close to something more than linguistic asymmetry. The ethnographer's audience and institutional connections lie far outside the community where fieldwork takes place, which raises the issue of power relationships. I wonder whether dialogical ethnographies, by placing discourse on a cozy interpersonal footing, might end up disguising the power relationships within which field dialogues take place.

A. A lot of people who make that kind of argument seem to think the natives know nothing about power relationships, so they take it upon themselves to reveal hidden truths to their readers, entirely in their own words. In becoming the experts on power, they unwittingly adopt the monological, authoritative mode of discourse used by those who occupy positions of power.

Q. But what worries me is that dialogical ethnographers could simply avoid discussions that touched closely on power relationships.

A. You've got this issue the wrong way around. If ethnographers were to avoid questions of power in field dialogues, or at least exclude them in publication, then dialogue would be the *object* of suppression, not the *cause* of it. But let's read a passage from Narayan's book, where Swamiji raises the question of her relationship to the world outside his community. On page 59, he's been telling his pupils that many people seem to study

Bhagavan, or divinity, for material profit. You can take his part, where he suddenly speaks to Narayan in particular.

SWAMIJI: You're taking this on tape. You'll take this and do a business. Understand? Everyone's going to ask you, "What is Bhagavan? What is Bhagavan?" You'll go there and do a business. In your university you'll say, "I saw this, I saw that. This is what Bhagavan is." [pause] That's why you learn this; not to understand it.

NARAYAN: I'm also trying to understand your words.

SWAMIJI: Some people, I say. Not just you.

Q. Swamiji reminds me of Cuol, who asked Evans-Pritchard, "What will you do with it if I tell it to you? Will you take it to your country?"

A. I would argue that such exchanges necessarily arise in the course of fieldwork, whether they find their way into print or not. Narayan presents a further example on page 61, one that gives us a glimpse of the complexity of power relationships. She explains that as a young unmarried woman, she felt a lack of authority in her field situation. She tried to compensate for this by telling Swamiji she was doing research for her professors at Berkeley, rather than calling attention to her own research project. As a result, Swamiji again confronted her in the presence of his other pupils. In this exchange we need to know that a *sādhu* is an ascetic, and that *hān* signals assent.

SWAMIJI: What are your professors going to do with this?

NARAYAN: [Mumbles something about documenting Indian culture.]

SWAMIJI: But what will your *professors* do with it?

NARAYAN: They won't do anything with it. It's for me. [Takes a deep breath as he looks at her.] If it's the Goddess's wish I'll write a book. One can write a Ph.D. dissertation on anything, and I've chosen this. Many *sādhus* tell stories and you tell these stories, too. Your stories contain your teachings; your stories and your teachings are the same thing.

SWAMIJI: *Hān hān hān* [spits tobacco]. Do you know why the elephant has a trunk? There are so many stories in India that you must have heard. You must have heard the story of Ganga, you must have heard the story of the Pandavas. Haven't you heard Chandrahasa's story? No? What are you saying? You haven't heard about Chandrahasa?! There was a King in the past. You're taping this, aren't you? You can tape this one, it's very good.

Q. Of course there remains a sense in which Narayan is indeed doing this for her professors — and, more broadly, for anthropology and the academy and so on.

A. But it's for her as well, and she admits that. And when she acknowledges that Swamiji's stories are teachings and not simply objects of study, he gives her a warm and generous assent.

Q. Then this isn't a book about storytelling, but a book of stories?

A. It's both. It's an ethnography of "folk narrative in Hindu religious teaching," but the narratives are there, too. And there remain spaces, or silences, between Narayan's voices and the voices of Swamiji, openings for other interpretations. But you still seem to be anxious.

Q. I'm not satisfied in the matter of power relationships. What about the big ones, at the national and international levels?

A. There's nothing about face-to-face dialogue, in and of itself, that prohibits the discussion of even the grandest issues, but publication is another matter. Let's take the example of Dwyer and the Faqir. For political reasons, the Faqir asked Dwyer not to publish any of their direct discussions of politics, and Dwyer complied with his wishes. But it was oppression that covered up this aspect of their dialogue, not the other way around.

Q. But someone other than Dwyer might not have even raised the subject of politics in the first place.

A. There you go again. How do you know it was Dwyer who raised that subject? I'd be willing to wager that natives in general raise it at least as often as field-workers do. A case in point is the work of Allan Burns, published in 1983 under the title *An Epoch of Miracles: Oral Literature of the Yucatec Maya*. He went into the field to study oral tradition, and he got lectures on Mayan separatist politics into the bargain, complete with a plea for military aid addressed to then-president Nixon.

Q. Could it be that while ethnographers go on pursuing traditions, the natives would rather be talking about contemporary politics?

A. Why do you see a conflict between those two concerns? Take a look at *I, Rigoberta Menchú*, the 1984 autobiography of a Guatemalan Mayan political activist. The anthropologist who recorded it, Elisabeth Burgos-Debray, expected to get an account of a valiant struggle carried on in the face of government-sponsored terrorism, and she succeeded. But Menchú also insisted on giving her a thorough account of the customs of her native town, with the thought that this, too, should be in the book. She thought of herself and her people as something more than just victims.

Q. Well, we've been at this discussion for some time now, and I'm wondering how we're going to end.

A. Dialogue doesn't so much end as reach a moment of adjournment.

Q. You mean it has no goal?

A. Dialogue, in and of itself, has no goal.

Q. What if the parties to a dialogue reached complete agreement?

A. That's certainly not going to happen between us. And if we did reach agreement, we would no longer be in dialogue, but rather speaking in unison. But there can be no permanent agreement, because there is always the possibility of further interpretation.

Q. Well, we can at least agree to stop talking to one another.

A. But that's not unlike the small agreements that take place within any lengthy dialogue, whereby we leave some matter to one side so we can move on. Or we might walk into a blind alley that will stop us unless we back our way out. Here, let's read Dwyer and the Faqir, on page 219 of *Moroccan Dialogues.* You go first.

DWYER: And what do you think that I think about you? What might I say to myself about you?

FAQIR MUHAMMAD: You're the one who understands that. Why, am I going to enter into your head?

## NOTE

Earlier general discussions of dialogue in anthropology and anthropology as dialogue include those of Dwyer (1977, 1982), Tedlock (1979; 1983: part 4; 1987a), Clifford (1983), and Tyler (1987a: 65–66, 99–100, 197; 1987b). The representation of discourse within spoken discourse, especially in storytelling, is discussed in Tedlock (1983: 3, 10, 47, 59–61, 326; 1987a: 331–34; 1987b). Bakhtin (1981) completely ignores ordinary storytelling and credits the development of multivocalic discourse to novelists. Radin's call for direct dialogue is in Radin (1957: xxx-xxxi); his hermeneutical dialogue is in Radin (1933: chap. 7). The dialogue between Walker and Finger was first published in Walker (1917: 154–56). For a thorough exposition of the ways in which anthropological writing denies the historical contemporaneity of field-worker and native, assigning the latter either to an evolutionary "past" or to the ethnographic "present," see Fabian (1983). Turner's account of Muchona originally appeared as chapter 11 of Casagrande's *In the Company of Man* (1960). For more on the relationship between poetics and meaning in oral traditions, see Hymes (1981) and Tedlock (1983: part 2). Accounts of the Spanish conquest of Mexico in which Malinche appears include Cortés (1971 [1519–27]) and Díaz del Castillo (1956 [1517–21]). On the British concept of "cultural translation," see Asad (1986). Benjamin's essay on translation is in Benjamin (1969: 69–82). The radical nature of the conflict between dialogue and oppression is clearly laid out by Freire (1989: chaps. 3, 4). For an account of the ethnographic dimension of *I, Rigoberta Mechú,* see Burgos-Debray (1984).

## REFERENCES CITED

Asad, Talal. 1986. "The Concept of Cultural Translation in British Social Anthropology." In *Writing Culture: The Poetics and Politics of Ethnography,* edited by James Clifford and George E. Marcus, pp. 141–64. Berkeley and Los Angeles: University of California Press.

Bakhtin, M. M. 1981. *The Dialogic Imagination.* Translated by C. Emerson and M. Holquist. Austin: University of Texas Press.

Benjamin, Walter. 1969. *Illuminations.* Edited by Hannah Arendt. Translated by Harry Zohn. New York: Schocken.

Burgos-Debray, Elisabeth. 1984. "Introduction." In *I, Rigoberta Menchú: An Indian Woman in Guatemala,* by Rigoberta Menchú, pp. xi–xxi. London: Verso.

Burns, Allan F. 1983. *An Epoch of Miracles: Oral Literature of the Yucatec Maya.* Austin: University of Texas Press.

Casagrande, Joseph. B. 1960. *In the Company of Man: Portraits of Twenty Anthropological Informants.* New York: Harper and Row.

Clifford, James. 1983. "On Ethnographic Authority." *Representations* 1, no. 2:118–46.

Cortés, Hernán. 1971 [1519–27]. *Letters from Mexico.* Translated by A. R. Pagden. New York: Grossman.

Crapanzano, Vincent. 1980. *Tuhami: Portrait of a Moroccan.* Chicago: University of Chicago Press.

———. 1986. "Hermes' Dilemma: The Masking of Subversion in Ethnographic Description." In *Writing Culture: The Poetics and Politics of Ethnography,* edited by James Clifford and George E. Marcus, pp. 51–76. Berkeley and Los Angeles: University of California Press.

Díaz del Castillo, Bernal. 1956 [1517–21]. *The Conquest of New Spain.* Translated by J. M. Cohen. Baltimore: Penguin.

Dwyer, Kevin. 1977. "On the Dialogic of Field Work." *Dialectical Anthropology* 2:143–51.

———. 1982. *Moroccan Dialogues: Anthropology in Question.* Baltimore: Johns Hopkins University Press.

Evans-Pritchard, E. E. 1940. *The Nuer: A Description of the Modes of Livelihood and Political Institutions of a Nilotic People.* Oxford: Oxford University Press.

Fabian, Johannes. 1983. *Time and the Other: How Anthropology Makes Its Object.* New York: Columbia University Press.

Freire, Paulo. 1989. *Pedagogy of the Oppressed.* Translated by Myra Bergman Ramos. New York: Continuum.

Geertz, Clifford. 1960. *The Religion of Java.* New York: Free Press.

———. 1987. *Works and Lives: The Anthropologist as Author.* Stanford: Stanford University Press.

Griaule, Marcel. 1965. *Conversations with Ogotemmêli.* London: Oxford University Press.

Hymes, Dell. 1981. *"In Vain I Tried to Tell You": Essays in Native American Ethnopoetics.* Philadelphia: University of Pennsylvania Press.

Kendall, Laurel. 1988. *The Life and Hard Times of a Korean Shaman: Of Tales and the Telling of Tales.* Honolulu: University of Hawaii Press.

Lévi-Strauss, Claude. 1963. *Tristes Tropiques.* Translated by John Russell. New York: Atheneum.

Malinowski, Bronislaw. 1922. *Argonauts of the Western Pacific: An Account of Native Enterprise and Adventure in the Archipelagoes of Melanesian New Guinea.* New York: E. P. Dutton.

Menchú, Rigoberta. 1984. *I, Rigoberta Menchú: An Indian Woman in Guatemala.* Edited by E. Burgos-Debray. Translated by A. Wright. London: Verso.

Narayan, Kirin. 1989. *Storytellers, Saints, and Scoundrels: Folk Narrative in Hindu Religious Teaching.* Philadelphia: University of Pennsylvania Press.

Nequatewa, Edmund. 1967. *Truth of a Hopi: Stories Relating to the Origin, Myths and Clan Histories of the Hopi.* Flagstaff: Museum of Northern Arizona.

Radin, Paul. 1933. *The Method and Theory of Ethnology: An Essay in Criticism.* New York: McGraw-Hill.

———. 1957. *Primitive Man as Philosopher.* Revised edition. New York: Dover.

Reichard, Gladys A. 1934. *Spider Woman: A Story of Navajo Weavers and Chanters.* New York: Macmillan.

Tedlock, Dennis. 1979. "The Analogical Tradition and the Emergence of a Dialogical Anthropology." *Journal of Anthropological Research* 35:387–400.

———. 1983. *The Spoken Word and the Work of Interpretation.* Philadelphia: University of Pennsylvania Press.

———. 1987a. "Questions concerning Dialogical Anthropology." *Journal of Anthropological Research* 43:325–37.

———. 1987b. "On the Representation of Discourse in Discourse." *Journal of Anthropological Research* 43:343–44.

Turner, Victor. 1967. *The Forest of Symbols: Aspects of Ndembu Ritual.* Ithaca: Cornell University Press.

Tyler, Stephen A. 1987a. *The Unspeakable: Discourse, Dialogue, and Rhetoric in the Postmodern World.* Madison: University of Wisconsin Press.

———. 1987b. "On 'Writing-Up/Off' as 'Speaking-For.'" *Journal of Anthropological Research* 43:338–42.

Walker, J. R. 1917. *The Sun Dance and Other Ceremonies of the Oglala Division of the Teton Dakota.* Anthropological Papers of the American Museum of Natural History 16. New York.

# Contributors

JOHN J. ATTINASI is Professor of Education and Director of Bilingual Teacher Education at California State University at Long Beach. He received his M.A. in social sciences and Ph.D. in linguistic anthropology from the University of Chicago. The topics of his writings include bilingual education, Latino demographics and educational issues, community health, language attitudes, and Chol Mayan language and culture.

A. L. BECKER is Professor Emeritus of Linguistics and Anthropology, University of Michigan. He is author of *Beyond Translation: Essays toward a Modern Philology*, a collection of essays on southeast Asian languages and literatures.

RUTH BEHAR is the author of *Translated Woman: Crossing the Border with Esperanza's Story* and *The Presence of the Past in a Spanish Village: Santa María del Monte*. Her self-reflexive essays have appeared in *Michigan Quarterly Review, Cultural Anthropology,* and *Poetics Today*. She is Professor of Anthropology at the University of Michigan, where she is also affiliated with the programs in Women's Studies and Latina/Latino Studies.

ALLAN BURNS is Professor of Anthropology and Linguistics at the University of Florida, and has been a visiting professor at the Universidad Complutense in Madrid and a Fulbright professor at the University of Copenhagen. His publications include *An Epoch of Miracles: Oral Literature of the Yucatec Maya,* and he has produced documentaries on subjects such as cultural resistance in Micronesia, Guatemalan refugees in the United States, and immigrant women's health.

JEAN DEBERNARDI is a member of the Department of Anthropology at the University of Alberta, where she teaches and publishes in the areas of symbolic and linguistic anthropology. Her work has focused on Malaysian

Chinese popular religion, on the social history of Chinese immigrants to the Straits Settlements, and on Taiwanese linguistic nationalism. Currently she is conducting comparative research on the management of multicultural societies in mainland southeast Asia, and writing a monograph entitled *Empire over Imagination: Chinese Popular Religion in Colonial and Post-colonial Malaysia*.

PAUL FRIEDRICH, Professor of Anthropology, Linguistics, and Social Thought at the University of Chicago, was born and raised in New England, and educated at Williams College, Harvard, and Yale. He has done fieldwork with the Tarascans of Mexico (three years), the Nayars in south India, and Russian dissidents. His publications include *The Meaning of Aphrodite, Agrarian Revolt in a Mexican Village,* and *The Language Parallax;* he is currently finishing a book on Russian poetry and starting one on the *Odyssey*.

JANE H. HILL is Professor of Anthropology and Linguistics at the University of Arizona. Her interests include Native American languages (especially Uto-Aztecan languages), and she has conducted fieldwork on Cupeño, Nahuatl, and Tohono O'odham. Among her publications are *Mulu'wetam: The First People: Cupeño Oral History and Language* (with Rosinda Nolasquez), and *Speaking Mexicano: Dynamics of Syncretic Language in Central Mexico* (with Kenneth C. Hill). Her interests extend beyond linguistics to cultural critique, ranging from the study of representations in Mexican popular media to the development of regional formations of meaning in the Southwest.

BILLIE JEAN ISBELL is past director of the Latin American Studies Program and Associate Professor of Anthropology at Cornell University. Among her publications are *To Defend Ourselves* and *Making Culture: Texts and Practices in the Andes.* Her most recent research has focused on the anthropology of violence, and she has completed a drama entitled "Secrets from Peru," on the continuing war in that country.

BRUCE MANNHEIM is Associate Professor of Anthropology at the University of Michigan, where he coordinates their program in linguistic anthropology. He is the author of *The Language of the Inka since the European Invasion* and numerous articles on Andean language, culture, and history.

RAYMOND P. McDERMOTT teaches at Stanford University. His articles have been published in *Text, The Kinesis Report,* and *Semiotica.*

DEBORAH TANNEN is University Professor in the Linguistics Department at Georgetown University. Her books include *Talking from 9 to 5: How Women's and Men's Conversational Styles Affect Who Gets Heard, Who Gets Credit, and What Gets Done at Work; Gender and Discourse; You Just Don't Understand: Women and Men in Conversation; Talking Voices: Repetition, Dialogue, and Imagery in Conversational Discourse; That's Not What I Meant!: How Conversational Style Makes or Breaks Your Relations with Others;* and *Conversational Style: Analyzing Talk among Friends.*

DENNIS TEDLOCK is McNulty Professor of English and Research Professor of Anthropology at the State University of New York at Buffalo. He has done field studies among the Koasati of Louisiana, the Zuni of New Mexico, and the Maya of Guatemala and Belize. His books include *Finding the Center: Narrative Poetry of the Zuni Indians; The Spoken Word and the Work of Interpretation; Popol Vuh: The Mayan Book of the Dawn of Life; Days from a Dream Almanac;* and *Breath on the Mirror: Mythic Voices and Visions of the Living Maya.*

HENRY TYLBOR, a native of Warsaw, received his education in Europe and America and did graduate work in linguistics and semiotics at the University of Paris. He is interested in the intersection of neuropsychology and linguistics, specifically body image, and has lectured extensively on the history and phenomenology of the Holocaust.

# Index